ATHLETIC TRAINING AND PHYSICAL FITNESS:

Physiological Principles and Practices of the Conditioning Process

JACK H. WILMORE, Ph.D.

Professor and Head
Department of Physical Education and Athletics
University of Arizona

Allyn and Bacon, Inc.
Boston · London · Sydney

*This book is dedicated to those who have made the
greatest impact on my life: to Dottie, my lovely
wife, and our three beautiful daughters, Wendy, Kristy,
and Melissa, for their patience and love; to Mom
and Dad, for their love, direction, and encouragement;
and to my Lord, Jesus Christ, who is always there
providing for every one of my needs.*

Library of Congress Cataloging in Publication Data

Wilmore, Jack H   1938–
    Athletic training and physical fitness.

    Includes bibliographies and index.
    1. Physical education and training.   I.   Title.
GV341.W577   613.7′1   76-50449

ISBN 0-205-05630-X

Contents

Preface

This book was designed to provide the sport practitioner—the coach, the athlete, the team trainer, and the team physician—with a basic understanding of the physiological principles underlying the physical conditioning process that is so important to athletic performance and physical fitness.

Over the years, research in the sport sciences has provided the sport practitioner with relatively little information, of practical value, that could contribute to the development of better athletes. In addition, the information that has been provided has been poorly utilized. Unfortunately, there is a large chasm between the researcher in his laboratory and the practitioner in the gym, beside the pool, or on the field. They live in two different worlds, neither completely understanding the language, complexity of the situation, or problems of the other. On the positive side, however, during the past few years research has taken a turn toward problems of a more practical nature and a wealth of information either is, or soon will be, available to the practitioner. To achieve maximum utilization of this information, one must have or acquire a basic understanding of the foundations of physical training.

While written primarily for the coach and athlete, whose laboratory is the playing field, pool, gym, or court, this book should also provide the undergraduate major in physical education with the basic fundamental principles of exercise physiology as applied to sport and physical activity. Additionally, sections of this book were written with the intent of educating the athletic trainer and team physician in specific areas of interest that have been traditionally ignored.

Writing this book was a challenge. It had its moments of fun and levity, but there were also those moments of discouragement and despair. Such an undertaking, however, is never the result of the efforts of just one person, even though this book lists only a single author. Appreciation and much credit must be given to the following people: Mrs. Wilean Ruff, who typed the entire manuscript with remarkable speed and accuracy and with tremendous dedication; Miss Linda Hirsh, for the many hours she spent in preparing the illustrative material; Paul and Jennifer Vodak, for assisting in the final preparation of the manuscript and for serving as models for the photographs in the Appendix; Dr. Richard Parr, for his critical review of the manuscript; and finally, my wife Dottie, for the hours spent preparing the final manuscript and proofreading the final printed version. Without the help of these people, this book would still be an idea instead of a reality.

JACK H. WILMORE
Los Angeles, California
January, 1976

SECTION A

Physiological Foundations
of Physical Training

The present book was designed to provide the reader with a fundamental understanding of the physiological principles underlying the physical training and conditioning process. While psychological, kinesiological, and biomechanical principles are important in developing the "total" athlete, the thrust of physical training is primarily within the physiological realm; thus, this book will concentrate on the physiological aspects of physical training, and will bring in those other aspects where they are appropriate.

This section deals first with a brief review of those areas in anatomy and physiology that are relevant to the process of physical training. The emphasis then shifts to an explanation of the physiological alterations that result from an acute or single bout of exercise. Lastly, those changes that typically result from chronic exercise, i.e., a long-term program of physical training, will be discussed. This section should give readers the basic language that they will need to more fully understand the subsequent sections of this book.

1

Basic Anatomical and Physiological Considerations

INTRODUCTION

Man is a remarkable animal. He can sprint 100 yards in 9.1 seconds, run a sub-four-minute mile, and complete a 26.2-mile marathon at an average rate of less than 5 minutes per mile. He can swim for both distance and speed, jump over 29 feet horizontally, over 7 feet vertically, and perform many other tasks requiring high levels of skill and dexterity.*

Man is able to accomplish the above feats only through a series of complex interactions within the body involving nearly all of the body's systems. While the muscles perform the work, the heart and blood vessels deliver the nutrients and, with the help of the lungs, provide oxygen to the tissues and remove carbon dioxide. The nervous and endocrine systems integrate all of this activity into a meaningful performance. Practically no tissue or organ escapes involvement in even the most simple movement. At the cellular level, numerous *enzymes* are activated and energy is generated to enable muscles to contract. The skin becomes a critical part of the body's heating and cooling system as activity is prolonged. The kidneys assist in maintaining fluid balance. While textbooks could be, and literally have been, written on

each of the involved systems, this chapter focuses briefly on the major or most significant anatomical and physiological aspects of human performance.

THE MUSCULAR SYSTEM

There are three major classes of muscular tissue in the human body. Each class differs in structure, location, function, and manner of activation. *Smooth muscle* is found in the walls of internal or visceral organs, e.g., blood vessels and intestines, and is not under direct voluntary control. *Cardiac muscle* is restricted to the heart, has characteristics similar to skeletal muscle, but, like smooth muscle, is not under direct voluntary control. *Skeletal muscle* is usually attached to bone and is under almost complete voluntary control. The remainder of this section will be devoted entirely to a discussion of the characteristics of skeletal muscle.

Skeletal muscle, in combination with an intricate system of bones and joints, is responsible for all human movement. Obviously, any single muscle does not work by itself, contracting at will, independently of the other muscles in the body. All skeletal muscles are coordinated simultaneously by a master network of nerve cells, both within and outside the brain. The neural control of movement will be discussed in the following section, Neuromuscular Control.

---

* J. H. Wilmore and A. C. Norton, *The Heart and Lungs at Work* (Schiller Park, Ill.: Beckman Instruments, 1974).

3

Skeletal muscle is composed of many *muscle fibers* (Figure 1–1). The muscle fiber is the structural unit of muscle, and is, in itself, a single cell with multiple nuclei. The number of muscle fibers per muscle will vary considerably, depending on the size and function of the muscle. It does appear, however, that the number of muscle fibers per muscle becomes fixed once an embryo reaches four to five months of age, and that the potential for muscularity is established genetically at the moment of conception.

The muscle fiber is composed of numerous smaller elements referred to as *myofibrils*, and can be compared to a telephone cable (fiber) that consists of numerous individual wires (myofibrils). The myofibrils are surrounded by a semifluid substance known as *sarcoplasm*, the protoplasm of the muscle cell or fiber. The cell nuclei and *mitochondria* lie beside the myofibrils within the sarcoplasm. As can be seen in Figure 1–1, the myofibrils have markings that run perpendicular to their long axes. These markings are referred to as cross-striations. The striation patterns in adjacent myofibrils are aligned so that the striations appear in register as a continuous band across the entire muscle fiber. The striations form a repetitive pattern across the length of the myofibril in alternating light and dark bands. The functional unit of muscle, the *sarcomere*, is defined by these light and dark patterns. In Figure 1–1(E), the sarcomere is bound on both ends by "Z-lines." Between the Z-lines are, in sequence, a light or isotropic zone referred to as the I-band; a dark or anisotropic zone referred to as the A-band, which is broken up by an H-zone of slightly lighter contrast; and a second I-band. Numerous sarcomeres are joined end-to-end to form each myofibril.

The postulated explanation for these different bands and zones is illustrated in Figure 1–1(F). The myofibril is composed of even smaller units referred to as *filaments*. The thin filaments have been identified as the protein *actin* and the thick filaments as the protein *myosin*. The I-band represents that region occupied only by the thin actin filaments; the A-band represents that region occupied by both

FIGURE 1–1

Structure of human skeletal or striated muscle, including the whole muscle (A), muscle fibers (B), single fiber (C), myofibril (D), sarcomere (E), and actin and myosin filaments (F). (From "The Contraction of the Muscle" by H. E. Huxley. Copyright © Nov. 1958 by Scientific American, Inc., p. 68. All rights reserved)

the thick myosin and thin actin filaments; and the H-zone is that central portion of the A-band occupied only by the thick myosin filaments.

How does the muscle contract? It is necessary to look at the microstructure of the muscle to understand how it might achieve what appears to be a simple process of contraction. This requires the use of an electron microscope since the myosin filaments are only 160 angstroms in diameter and the actin filaments are only 50–70 angstroms in diameter. There are 10,000 angstroms in a micron, 1,000 microns in a *millimeter* (mm), and 25.4 mm in an inch, or a total of 254,000,000 or 2.54×10^8 angstroms in an inch; thus, the need for the electron microscope. The schematic illustration in Figure 1–2 depicts the hypothesized mode of contraction involving a shortening of the sarcomere by the sliding of the thin filaments past the thick. Projections, referred to as *cross-bridges*, have been identified on the thick myosin filaments. It is hypothesized that these cross-bridges are attached to the thin actin filaments and through a ratchet-like process cause the thin filaments to slide by the thick filaments, shortening the length of the sarcomere. While this explanation is considered to

be only a theory at the present time, and while many of the essential details are missing, evidence is rapidly accumulating in support of this hypothesis, referred to as the "sliding filament" theory.

Within the past few years, a great deal of interest has centered on the characteristics of individual muscle fibers. Recent technological advances have made it possible to take a sample of human muscle tissue, i.e., muscle biopsy, for the purpose of extensive analysis of the characteristics of the tissue. While some researchers have insisted on classifying muscle fibers into one of three types, others feel that there are basically only two types: fast-twitch fibers, which do not depend on oxygen for their energy supply, and slow-twitch fibers, which do depend on oxygen for continued contraction. The third type is an intermediate fiber that supposedly has characteristics of both the slow- and fast-twitch fibers, i.e., fast contracting but dependent to a great extent on oxygen. Fast-

FIGURE 1–2

Postulated mechanisms of muscular contraction. (From "The Mechanism of Muscular Contraction" by H. E. Huxley. Copyright © Dec. 1965 by Scientific American, Inc., p. 19. All rights reserved.)

twitch fibers can be thought of as being responsible for speed or power activities such as those performed by the sprinter or weight lifter. Slow-twitch fibers are associated with endurance activities such as marathon running or cross-country skiing. This important concept will be discussed in greater detail in subsequent chapters.

NEUROMUSCULAR CONTROL

Individuals may have highly developed muscles, but without proper neuromuscular control they will not be able to coordinate their movement patterns. It is not uncommon for a coach to spot a remarkable "physical specimen" in a physical education class and entice him into a particular sport, only to be bitterly disappointed when he finds that the boy has difficulty with even the most simple motor tasks, such as tying his shoe laces! Coordination of movement is the responsibility of the nervous system. The brain, spinal cord, and the peripheral nerves function as an intricate computer controlling every movement of the body. While coordination is impossible to define relative to the precise physiological interactions involved, it certainly depends on efficient interaction between sensory stimuli, e.g., touch, pain, and vision, nervous integration of all incoming and outgoing stimuli, and proper muscle response to neural stimulation.

The nervous system is divided into several classifications as outlined in Table 1–1.

Within the brain are several areas of critical importance to the control of movement. A primary and supplementary *motor area* exist in the *cerebral cortex*. They control all voluntary movement of the body. By stimulating the various regions within the motor cortex of an exposed brain, it is possible to map out the cortex and define those areas that control specific segments of the body (Figure 1–3). The *cerebellum*, located at the back and lower region of the brain (Figure 1–4), is responsible for body equilibrium, postural reflexes, and the coordination of all muscular activity. The

TABLE 1–1. Subdivisions of the Nervous System

Anatomical Divisions
  Central Nervous System
  A. Brain
  B. Spinal Cord
  Peripheral Nervous System

Functional Divisions
  Somatic Nervous System
  A. Cranial Nerves
  B. Spinal Nerves

  Autonomic Nervous System
  A. Sympathetic Nerves
  B. Parasympathetic Nerves

cerebellum provides for a synchronous and orderly activity of the various groups of muscles.

The *peripheral nervous system* is critical to body movement and consists of the *somatic* and *autonomic nervous systems*. The somatic nerves are basically under voluntary control and are responsible for conducting nerve im-

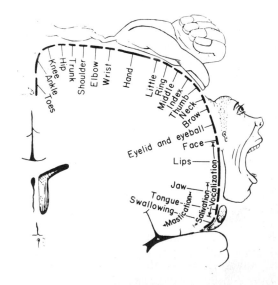

FIGURE 1–3

Representation of the different body muscles in the motor cortex of the cerebrum. (From W. Penfield and T. Rasmussen, The Cerebral Cortex of Man. *New York: The Macmillan Company, 1950. Reproduced by permission of the publisher.)*

FIGURE 1–4

The brain. (From Tuttle, W. W., and Schottelius, Byron, A.: Textbook of Physiology, *ed. 15, St. Louis, 1965, The C. V. Mosby Co.; after Quain. Reproduced by permission of the publisher.)*

pulses both to and from the skeletal muscles. The autonomic nerves are not under voluntary control and are responsible for controlling the visceral organs, the blood vessels, and glands. This section will focus on the somatic nervous system.

The basic structural unit of the nervous system is the *neuron*, which is a single nerve cell responsible for conducting nerve impulses to and from various parts of the body (Figure 1–5). The *dendrites* of the neuron receive nerve impulses from the many adjacent neurons. These impulses are transmitted along the *axon* to the dendrites of other neurons or to end organs, such as muscles. The gap between the axon of one neuron and the dendrites of another is referred to as a *synapse*. Neurons

that conduct impulses from sensory organs, e.g., eyes, ears, and pain receptors, to the central nervous system are referred to as *sensory* or *afferent neurons*. Those neurons that conduct impulses from the *central nervous system* to muscles or other effector organs are referred to as *motor* or *efferent neurons*. The afferent nerves signal to the body what is going on in the outside world, and the efferent nerves transmit the body's instructions to the muscles and other organs so that the appropriate response can be made. *Motoneurons* are those efferent neurons that terminate directly within the muscle to innervate, or supply, specific muscle fibers.

The motor unit consists of a single motoneuron and the specific muscle fibers that it

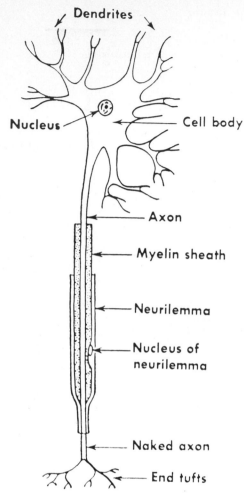

Dendrites

Nucleus

Cell body

Axon

Myelin sheath

Neurilemma

Nucleus of neurilemma

Naked axon

End tufts

FIGURE 1–5

The neuron. (From Tuttle, W. W., and Schottelius, Byron A.: Textbook of Physiology, *ed. 15, St. Louis, 1965, The C. V. Mosby Co. Reproduced by permission of the publisher.)*

innervates. The number of muscle fibers innervated by a motoneuron depends solely on the function of the innervated muscle. In the ocular muscles of the eye, a motoneuron may innervate only five or six muscle fibers, while in the large gluteus maximus muscle of the buttocks, the single motoneuron may innervate up to 2,000 fibers. Generally, the more refined the movement of the muscle, the fewer muscle

fibers/motoneuron (referred to as the *innervation ratio*), which results in better control over fine and delicate movements.

Motoneurons are subjected to the influence of two different types of neurons, those that transmit excitatory impulses and those that block or inhibit nerve-impulse transmission. If a motoneuron is simultaneously under the influence of both an excitatory and an inhibitory neuron, impulses traveling down both neurons may cancel each other out; thus, the motoneuron does not react to the stimulation (Figure 1–6). The significance of this may not be totally clear. One theory for explaining how man increases his strength, as in weight training, is that there are fewer inhibitory impulses going to the different motoneurons, allowing more motor units to be activated at any one time. This will be discussed in greater detail in Chapter 2, Acute Responses to Exercise, and in Chapter 3, Chronic Adaptations to Exercise.

Most neural control of skeletal muscles is reflex in nature. A minimum of two neurons are found in simple reflexes (Figure 1–7). An

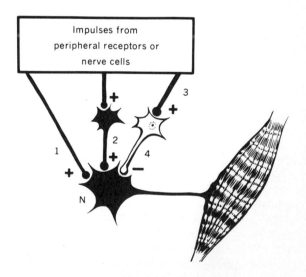

Impulses from peripheral receptors or nerve cells

FIGURE 1–6

Excitatory and inhibitory neurons. (From P. O. Åstrand and K. Rodahl, Textbook of Work Physiology. *New York: McGraw-Hill Book Co., 1970. Reproduced by permission of the publisher.)*

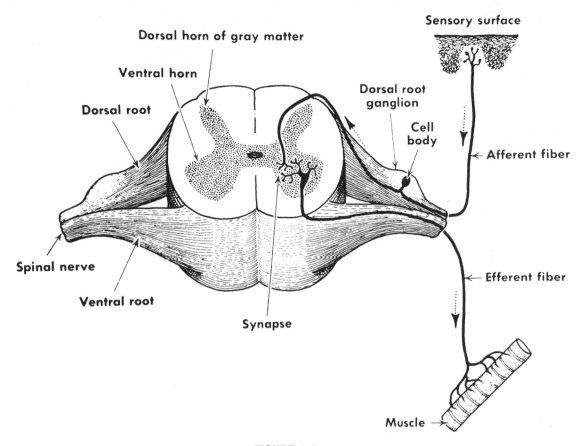

FIGURE 1–7

Simple reflex arc. (From Tuttle, W. W., and Schottelius, Byron A.: Textbook of Physiology, ed. 15, St. Louis, 1965, The C. V. Mosby Co. Reproduced by permission of the publisher.)

afferent fiber transmits the sensory impulse (e.g., the muscle is stretched by an unexpected weight) to the spinal cord where it forms a synapse with an efferent fiber; the impulse is then transmitted to the involved muscle group where it causes the stretched muscle to contract. As the movement patterns become more complex, the higher levels of the spinal cord and brain become involved.

Muscle spindles are located within the muscle and are sensitive to forces which stretch the muscle. When the muscle is stretched, the stretch receptors send impulses via afferent neurons to the spinal cord. If an extensor muscle is stretched, the impulse will travel to the

motoneuron of that extensor muscle causing it to contract. At the same time, the flexor muscle of the same segment will receive an inhibitory stimulus, causing it to relax (Figure 1–8). This is referred to as *reciprocal inhibition*. If both flexors and extensors were to receive excitatory impulses, no movement would result.

Sensory information is essential to the performance of a coordinated movement. This is provided through hearing, vision, and various *proprioceptors*. Proprioceptors are special sensory organs that provide the body with continuous feedback about the body's position in space. Some of the more important proprio-

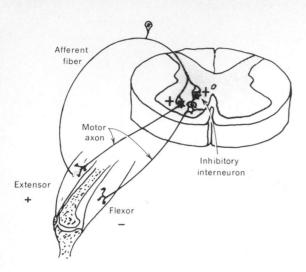

FIGURE 1–8

Reciprocal inhibition. (From P. O. Åstrand and K. Rodahl, Textbook of Work Physiology. *New York: McGraw-Hill Book Co., 1970. Reproduced by permission of the publisher.)*

Movement itself results from efferent stimuli that impinge upon the motoneuron, causing it to activate those muscle fibers that are a part of that specific motor unit. Coordination of all of these activities occurs in the central nervous system.

CIRCULATION

While the muscle depends on the nervous system to initiate and sustain contraction, it also depends on the circulation of blood to deliver energy for contraction and to remove the waste products of metabolism. Any system of circulation must have three primary components: a pump; a system of channels or vessels; and a fluid medium. The heart, blood vessels, and blood are the primary components in the body's circulatory system. Each of these three components will be discussed separately.

ceptors include the *vestibular receptors* in the ear, which are important for balance and spatial orientation; the muscle spindle; the *Golgi tendon organ*; the *Pacinian corpuscle*; *Ruffini receptors*; and free nerve endings. Golgi tendon organs are located in series with the muscle tendons and are sensitive to passive stretching as well as to active contraction. Unlike the muscle spindle, which facilitates contraction of the muscle in which it resides, the tendon organ is inhibitory in nature, protecting the muscle from being overstretched or overcontracted. The Pacinian corpuscles are located in muscle and tendon sheaths and around joints and are sensitive to pressure. Ruffini receptors are located in the joint capsule and are sensitive to joint movement and position. Free nerve endings are found throughout muscles, tendons, joints, and ligaments. Their exact function is not clearly understood.

From the above, it is apparent that movement may occur either voluntarily or involuntarily. Sensory processes provide the body with the appropriate information so that movement can be properly controlled and coordinated.

Heart

The heart, a muscle, consists of four separate chambers, two *atria* and two *ventricles* (Figure 1–9). Blood is returned to the right atrium by the inferior and superior vena cava, the two large veins that return the blood from those regions below and above the level of the heart, respectively. The blood is rhythmically pumped from the right atrium to the right ventricle, and then through the pulmonary artery to the lungs. After the blood passes through the lungs, it returns through the pulmonary vein to the left atrium of the heart. The circulation from the right ventricle through the lungs to the left atrium is referred to as the lesser or pulmonary circulation. From the left atrium, the blood is pumped to the left ventricle, and from the left ventricle to the aorta, from which it is then distributed throughout the body. Circulation from the left ventricle through the blood vessels and back to the right atrium is referred to as the systemic circulation.

Cardiac muscle has a unique feature which distinguishes it from skeletal or smooth muscle.

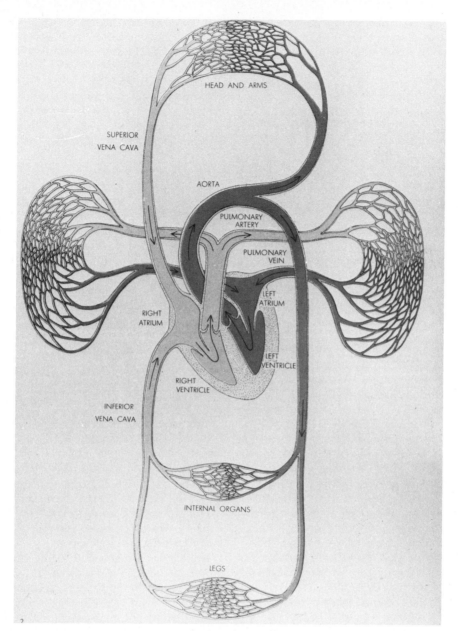

FIGURE 1–9

Schematic illustration of the vascular system. (From "The Heart" by Carl J. Wiggers. Copyright © May 1957 by Scientific American Inc., p. 74. All rights reserved.)

It can contract rhythmically on its own, without nervous stimulation from outside the heart. This is referred to as autorhythmicity. It can and does, however, receive both excitatory and inhibitory stimuli from the autonomic nervous system. The heart at rest will normally contract at rates ranging from 60–90 beats/min, depending on age and physical condition. Highly conditioned athletes can decrease their resting heart rate through physical training to values as low as or lower than 30 beats/min. Sedentary, deconditioned adults may have resting heart rates in excess of 100 beats/min.

The electrical activity of the heart can be recorded by placing electrodes on different parts of the body to create an *electrocardiogram* (*ECG*), which is extremely valuable for diagnosing potential abnormalities of the heart.

Each time the heart beats, a certain volume of blood is ejected from the left ventricle into the aorta for systemic circulation. This is defined as the *stroke volume* (SV) of the heart, i.e., the volume of blood pumped per stroke. The *cardiac output* ($\dot{Q}$) is the total volume of blood pumped per minute or the product of the *heart rate* and stroke volume ($\dot{Q} = \text{HR} \times \text{SV}$). Stroke volume at rest in the erect or upright position will vary between 70 and 100 *milliliters* (ml) in normal, healthy adults. At a resting heart rate of 60 beats/min, the resulting cardiac output would vary between 4.2 and 6 liters of blood/min (1,000 ml = 1 liter).

That period during which the ventricle or atrium is actively contracting is referred to as the *systole*. The *diastolic* period occurs during the noncontracting phase of the cardiac cycle, during which time the ventricle or atrium fills with blood. At a heart rate of 74 beats/min, diastole accounts for 0.50 *second* (*sec*) and systole for 0.31 sec of the entire cardiac cycle, which totals 0.81 sec. As the heart rate increases, these absolute time intervals are proportionally shortened.

The heart, as a muscle, must also have its own supply of blood. This is provided by the coronary vessels. The *coronary arteries* arise from the base of the aorta at the point where it joins the heart. The three major coronary arteries are the *anterior descending artery*, the *left circumflex artery* (both of which branch off of the short, left coronary artery), and the *right coronary artery* (Figure 1–10). With age, many individuals develop coronary atherosclerosis, which is the disease process whereby a lesion develops in the large- and medium-sized coronary arteries with the formation of fat-containing deposits or plaques, which reduce the interior diameter or *lumen* of the vessel (Figure 1–11). As these plaques build up, the lumen becomes smaller until there is an actual restriction of blood flow to the heart either during exercise, when the oxygen demands of the heart are high, or at rest, if the disease is fully progressed. This results in a lack of blood to certain areas of the heart (*ischemia*), which in turn, frequently leads to severe chest pain, *angina pectoris*. Those individuals who have the same pathology (ischemia), but no chest pain are classified as having silent heart disease, i.e., they have no outward signs or symptoms of having a compromised coronary circulation.

Vascular System

The *vascular system* is composed of a series of vessels that transport the blood from the heart to the tissues and back to the heart. As was mentioned above, when the left ventricle contracts, the blood is pumped through the aorta and the various arteries to the smaller *arterioles*. The blood goes from the arterioles to the *capillaries*, where the blood interacts with the tissue in that area, i.e., releases oxygen and nutrients and picks up carbon dioxide and waste products. From the capillaries, the blood goes to the *venules*, from the venules to the veins, and from the veins to the inferior and superior vena cava where the blood is finally returned to the right atrium.

Within the veins are a series of valves that allow the blood to flow in only one direction, preventing any backflow. The muscles of the extremities act as secondary pumps, as they contract, to facilitate the return of blood to the heart. When the muscles contract, the blood is actually squeezed out of the veins, and

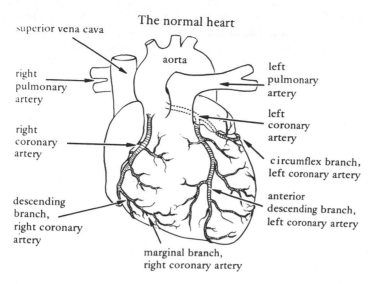

FIGURE 1–10

Blood supply to the heart, illustrating the coronary arteries. (From Cardiovascular Disease: A Matter of Prevention *by Kenneth L. Briney. © 1970 by Wadsworth Publishing Company, Inc,. Belmont, California 94002. Reprinted by permission of the publisher.)*

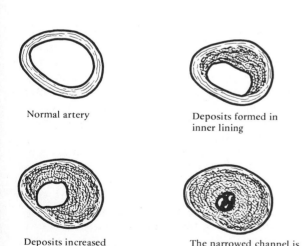

FIGURE 1–11

Progressive narrowing of a coronary artery. (From Cardiovascular Disease: A Matter of Prevention *by Kenneth L. Briney. © 1970 by Wadsworth Publishing Company, Inc., Belmont, California 94002. Reprinted by permission of the publisher.)*

because of the valves in the veins, this flow can only go in one direction—back to the heart. Changes in intraabdominal and intrathoracic pressure also assist in pumping blood back to the heart.

The vascular system has the ability to divert blood from one section of the body to another through neural control. In fact, a relatively small percentage of the capillaries are open and functioning at any one time. The capillary bed actually consists of two components: the thoroughfare channel (into which the blood from the arteriole flows) and the true capillaries. *Precapillary sphincters*, small bands of muscle-like tissue, can selectively open and close to restrict or allow blood to flow through the true capillaries. This is an essential feature of the vascular system in exercise when blood must be shunted from areas with low metabolic activity to those with high levels. The ability of the blood vessels to dilate and constrict also contributes to the redirection, or shunting of blood mentioned above. Arteries, arterioles, venules and veins have surrounding layers of muscle which give them the ability to increase or decrease the internal diameter or lumen of the vessel. Again, this is essential, for if the vessels were all relaxed and dilated, there would be no blood left for circulation. This is essentially what happens in shock, i.e., a generalized vasodilation of the blood vessels.

Blood pressure refers to the force or pressure exerted by the blood on the vessels. It is determined by or is the result of two factors, the volume of blood forced into the aorta (cardiac output) and the resistance encountered by the blood as it passes through the vessels. The degree of vessel dilation or constriction will control the amount of resistance and, thus, can cause the blood pressure to either drop or rise. Blood pressure is expressed by two values, the *systolic* and *diastolic pressures*, which reflect the highest and lowest pressures, respectively, encountered by the vessels. The systolic pressure reflects the pressure in the arteries during the systole of the heart, when the heart's contraction forces a large volume of blood into the arteries. This creates a high pressure, forcing the walls of the artery to expand. Following the systole, the arteries recoil, and the pressure drops considerably during the filling phase of the heart (diastole). Thus, the lowest pressure reached following the recoil of the artery is referred to as the diastolic pressure. Arterial systolic pressures normally vary between 110 and 140 mmHg, while diastolic pressures vary between 60 and 80 mmHg. At rest, a systolic pressure in excess of 140 mmHg or a diastolic pressure in excess of 90 mmHg is considered to be abnormally elevated and is referred to as *hypertension* or *high blood pressure*. The difference between systolic and diastolic pressures is referred to as the *pulse pressure* (pulse pressure = systolic pressure − diastolic pressure). Pulse pressure creates a pulse wave, e.g., the radial pulse at the wrist or carotid pulse at the neck, which is easily detected at various locations in the body.

Blood

Any system of circulation must have a circulating medium. This is the function of blood in the body's circulatory system. Blood and lymph are responsible for transporting various materials between the different cells or tissues. While lymph is extremely important for many body functions, it will not be discussed in this section, since its role in exercise and physical training is not well understood. Blood, however, serves many essential purposes in the body's adaptation to both acute and chronic exercise. These can be generalized into four primary functions: (a) transportation, (b) temperature regulation, (c) acid–base balance, and (d) immunologic reactions. Blood transports nutrients from the gastrointestinal area, *adipose tissue*, and liver to the cells; oxygen from the lungs to the cells; carbon dioxide, *lactate*, and other waste products from the cells to the lungs, liver, and kidneys; and hormones from their glandular or storage source to the target organ, i.e., that tissue that has a specific reaction to a particular hormone. Through its transportation role, blood is also an important medium by which the body temperature is controlled or regulated. Blood distributes the heat from the more active parts of the body to the total body, under normal conditions, and to the periphery or skin when the body is overheated. With regard to the acid–base balance, the blood is able to buffer, or neutralize, the acids produced as a result of anaerobic metabolism. The immunologic reactions of the blood are essential for continued health but will not be discussed in detail since they have little relationship to the major purposes of this book.

Blood is composed of the blood plasma and the blood cells, which constitute approximately 55 and 45 percent, respectively, of the total blood volume. The relative amount of blood plasma or blood cells is referred to as the *hematocrit*. A more complete breakdown of the blood's composition is illustrated in Table 1–2.

Total blood volume will vary considerably according to a person's age, size, and level of conditioning. Volumes of 5–6 liters in men and 4–4.5 liters in women are within the normal range of values.

The red blood cell is critical to the basic

TABLE 1–2. Composition of Whole Blood

Fraction	Constituent	Approximate Percentage of Fraction	Total Blood Volume
Blood Plasma		100.0	55.0
	Water	90.0	49.5
	Blood proteins	7.0	3.9
	serum albumin	4.5	2.5
	serum globulin	2.0	1.1
	fibrinogen	0.5	0.3
	Cellular nutrients, salts, enzymes, hormones, antibodies and wastes	3.0	1.7
Blood Cells		100.0	45.0
	Red blood cells		
	White blood cells		
	Platelets		

life-giving function of the circulatory system. Each red blood cell contains *hemoglobin*, which is composed of a protein (globin) and a pigment (hematin). The pigment portion contains iron, which binds with oxygen to provide the oxygen-carrying capability of the blood. Hemoglobin also has a high affinity for carbon monoxide. Its attraction to carbon monoxide is nearly 250 times stronger than its attraction to oxygen; thus, breathing high levels of carbon monoxide will tie up the hemoglobin molecules that are normally used to transport oxygen. This greatly reduces the oxygen-carrying capacity of the blood, and will result in death if the carbon-monoxide levels are high enough.

Red cells are continuously undergoing production and destruction. The normal life span of a red cell is four months. The rate of production of red cells in the red marrow of bones is approximately equal to their rate of destruction. *Anemia* refers to a condition where there is a marked deficiency in either or both the red cells or hemoglobin in the total blood volume. This deficiency limits the amount of oxygen that can be delivered to the muscles and other body tissues, and results in general weakness and chronic fatigue. Normal individuals have 12–18 *grams* (gm) of hemoglobin/100 ml of blood; females usually have approximately 10 percent less hemoglobin than males. In anemia, this value drops to 10 gm/100 ml of blood or lower. Anemia can result from excessive blood loss, red cell destruction, or a decrease in the rate of red cell production. Individuals who donate a unit of blood (approximately 1 pint or 500 ml) at their local blood banks, will have, approximately, a 10 percent reduction in the level of their circulating red blood cells. It will take from one to several weeks to regenerate the lost red blood cells, while the plasma volume will return to normal within 24–48 hours.

One last factor of importance with regard to blood is its viscosity. *Viscosity* refers to that property of a fluid that resists internal flow. The more viscous a circulating medium, the more resistant that medium is to flow. Blood has a viscosity that is approximately twice that of water. The higher the hematocrit (ratio of blood cells to total blood volume multiplied by 100), the more viscous the blood. While an increase in the number of red blood cells would seem desirable to facilitate the transportation of oxygen, the increased viscosity that would result from this increase would slow down the flow of blood. In polycythemia, where there is an abnormally elevated number of red cells, the viscosity can increase to such a point as to hinder the normal transport functions of blood.

RESPIRATION

The supplying of oxygen to the metabolizing cell and the subsequent removal of carbon dioxide is a process vital to life. Cells can live only a few minutes in the absence of oxygen. It is important to recognize, however, that oxygen is not the fuel from which the cell derives its energy, but that it is required for the utilization or metabolism of those substances that do provide the fuel for the cell. As oxygen is utilized in this process, carbon dioxide is produced; thus, to replenish the cell, it is necessary to remove the carbon dioxide and also to deliver new oxygen. While blood is the medium through which this occurs, the process is referred to as *respiration* and involves another of the body's complex systems (Figure 1–12).

Respiration can be separated into two different processes, *external* and *internal respiration.* External respiration refers to the process of bringing air into the lungs and the resulting exchange of gases that takes place between the *alveoli* of the lung and the blood in the capillaries that supply the lung. Internal or tissue respiration refers to the exchange of gases between the blood and the tissues to replenish oxygen and remove carbon dioxide.

The anatomy of the respiratory system is illustrated in Figure 1–13. Air is taken into the lungs (inspiration) through either or both the mouth and nose, the pharynx, larynx, trachea, *bronchi, bronchioles,* and is finally delivered to the smallest units, the *alveoli.* It is at the level of the alveoli where the capillaries form a network around the alveolar sacs and where gas exchange takes place between the blood and the lung. Inspiration is an active process which involves the primary muscle of respiration, the diaphragm, as well as the secondary muscles of respiration, i.e., those that enlarge the thoracic or chest cavity. As the diaphragm contracts, moving away from the lungs toward the abdominal cavity, the pressure within the thoracic cavity, outside the lungs, is decreased, creating a reduced pressure or vacuum within the lungs. This causes air to flow into the lung. Expiration, during which the air flows back out of the lung, is normally a passive process involving a relaxation of the diaphragm. During labored breathing, the secondary muscles of respiration play a larger role, contracting to elevate and expand the thoracic cavity during inspiration and relaxing to reduce the size of the cavity during expiration. The abdominal muscles can contract in forced expiration, assisting what is normally a

MIXED VENOUS BLOOD

ARTERIAL BLOOD

FIGURE 1–12

Respiratory gas exchange. (From Comroe, J. H.: Physiology of Respiration, 2d edition, Copyright © 1974 by Year Book Medical Publishers, Inc., Chicago. Used by permission.)

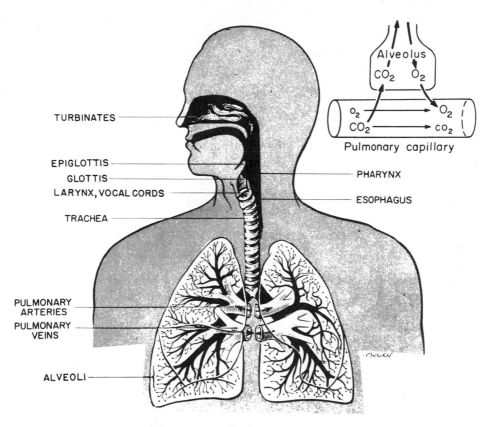

FIGURE 1–13

Anatomy of the respiratory system. (From A. C. Guyton, Function of the Human Body, *2nd ed. Philadelphia: W. B. Saunders Co., 1964. Reproduced by permission of the publisher.)*

passive process. Their contraction increases intra-abdominal and intrathoracic pressure, in addition to reducing the size of the thoracic cavity, by pulling the rib cage down and inward.

The lungs can be divided into several anatomical and functional fractions. These are illustrated in Figure 1–14. *Tidal volume* refers to the volume of air inspired or expired with each breath and can range from approximately 0.5 liters at rest to 2.5 liters or more during heavy exercise. The actual value will depend entirely on the total lung volume available to the individual. *Vital capacity* is the greatest volume of air that can be expired from the lungs immediately following the greatest possible inspiration. *Residual volume* is that vol-

ume of air that is left in the lungs following a maximal expiration (it is impossible to completely deflate the lungs voluntarily). The sum of the vital capacity and the residual volume is the total lung capacity. Thus, the total lung capacity is composed of the greatest volume of air that can be expired from the lungs in a single breath (vital capacity) and the volume of air remaining in the lung at that time (residual volume). The dead space of the lung refers to the space in those segments of the respiratory system in which gas exchange does not take place, e.g., mouth, nose, pharynx, larynx, and trachea. This space amounts to approximately 150 to 200 ml of volume.

Pulmonary ventilation ($\dot{V}_E$) refers to the volume of air breathed per minute. At a tidal

17

VENTILATION

FIGURE 1–14

Fractional lung volumes. (From J. B. West, Respiratory Physiology: The Essentials. *Baltimore: Williams and Wilkins Co., 1974. Reproduced by permission of the publisher.)*

volume of 0.5 liters/breath and a respiratory frequency of 15 breaths/min, $\dot{V}_E$ would be 7.5 liters/min. $\dot{V}_E$ is controlled through variations both in tidal volume and in respiratory frequency. This control is mediated through respiratory centers in the medulla oblongata and pons of the brainstem and is sensitive to: carbon dioxide and oxygen levels, pH changes (reflecting changes in the acid–base balance), proprioceptor impulses from muscles and joints, stretch receptors in the lungs, temperature, and cerebral or higher-brain influences.

Gas exchange at the lung level involves the removal of carbon dioxide from the venous blood (which is coming back to the lungs from the actively metabolizing tissue) and the replenishment of oxygen which was removed from the arterial blood at the level of the tissues. Since the alveoli of the lungs are in close contact with the blood, their concentrations of oxygen and carbon dioxide remain very stable from breath to breath, unlike the concentrations of these gases at the mouth, which vary considerably from the start to the finish of each

breath. This stability of alveolar-gas composition is critical to the efficient exchange of gases in the lungs. The barrier between the air in the alveoli and the blood in the pulmonary capillaries is very thin (about 0.00016 inch) and is composed of the epithelial cells of the alveoli and the endothelial cells of the capillaries. Since the red cells travel through the pulmonary capillaries in single file, each red cell is exposed to the surrounding lung tissue.

The process of gas exchange is a function of pressure gradients between the lung and the blood. At sea level, man exists in an environment with an atmospheric pressure of approximately 760 mmHg. At higher elevations, air pressure decreases in direct proportion to the altitude. Normal air is primarily composed of three major gases of importance to body metabolism: oxygen, carbon dioxide, and nitrogen. An analysis of the composition of air indicates that oxygen accounts for 20.93 percent, carbon dioxide for 0.04 percent, and nitrogen and other inert gases for 79.03 percent of the total gas volume. From the law of partial pressures, it is known that a gas exerts a partial pressure in direct proportion to its concentration. Also, the sum of the partial pressures equals the total pressure. At a total pressure of 760 mmHg, the oxygen in the air would exert a partial pressure of 159 mmHg (760 mmHg × .2093). At higher altitudes, the partial pressure of each gas will decrease in direct proportion to the increase in altitude. At 10,000 *feet* (*ft*), the total air pressure is only 523 mmHg, which reduces the partial pressure of oxygen to 109 mmHg (523 mmHg × .2093), even though the total percentage of oxygen in the air is exactly the same as it was at sea level. Henry's Law states that a gas will dissolve in a liquid in direct proportion to its partial pressure, assuming that the temperature remains constant. Thus, the gases and their movement from one part of the body to another are controlled by their partial pressure. With this in mind, the exchange of gases is influenced most by the pressure gradient between two areas or tissues. This is illustrated in Table 1–3.

As an example, the partial pressure of oxygen in dry air is 159 mmHg. At the level of the alveoli, however, it has dropped to a value of 100 mmHg and remains relatively constant at this level. The blood coming back from the venous side of the systemic circulation normally has an oxygen partial pressure of 40 mmHg; thus, the mixed venous blood in the pulmonary capillaries has a partial pressure some 60 mmHg lower than that of the air in the alveoli. This pressure gradient, or diffusion gradient, is responsible for driving oxygen from the alveoli into the pulmonary capillaries. Thus, as the blood leaves the lungs, its partial pressure will have equilibrated with that in the alveoli and it will have an oxygen partial pressure of 100 mmHg, identical to that of the alveoli. The greater the pressure or diffusion gradient, the more rapidly the gases will cross the diffusion membrane, e.g., the cellular structure between the blood and the air spaces in the alveoli. These same principles apply to the release of oxygen from the blood to the tissue, e.g., to the muscle. Diffusion gradients are not as important for carbon dioxide, since it diffuses across the diffusion membrane about twenty times more rapidly than oxygen.

The importance of the above becomes clearer when discussing the body's adaptation to altitude. At a 10,000-ft altitude, the partial pressure of oxygen in air is reduced to 109 mmHg and in the alveoli to 69 mmHg. If the partial pressure of oxygen in the mixed venous blood remains at 40 mmHg, the diffusion gradient drops from 60 (sea level value) to 29 mmHg, or more than a fifty-percent reduction. While this has relatively little influence on the degree of saturation of the blood with oxygen at the

TABLE 1–3. Composition of Atmospheric Air and the Consequent Partial Pressures of Respiratory Gases

Gas	Percent in Dry Atmosphere	Partial Pressure in Dry Atmosphere	Partial Pressure in Alveolar Air	Partial Pressure in Mixed Venous Blood	Diffusion Gradient
Total	100	760	760	705	
H_2O	0	0	47	47	
O_2	20.93	159	100	40	60
CO_2	0.03	0.2	40	45	5
N_2	79.04	600.8	573	573	

From H. A. de Vries, *Physiology of Exercise for Physical Education and Athletics*, 2nd ed. (Dubuque, Iowa: William C. Brown Co., Publishers, 1974), p. 172. Reproduced by permission of the publisher.

level of the lung, it will limit the amount of oxygen that will be released at the muscle or tissue level. Due to the characteristics of blood, with particular reference to the red blood cell, the partial pressure of oxygen must drop below 70 mmHg before the percentage of red blood cells saturated with oxygen drops below ninety–ninety-five percent. Thus, at a 10,000-ft altitude, the blood leaving the lungs will be almost totally saturated with oxygen, but at the level of the tissues, e.g., muscles, the ability to release oxygen will be reduced due to the lower pressure gradient.

METABOLISM

The primary purpose of *metabolism* is to provide energy for the body's cells. Metabolism is composed of two basic processes, *anabolism* and *catabolism*. Anabolism refers to the synthesis of cellular materials for growth, maintenance, and repair of body tissues. Catabolism is the process of breaking down cellular materials into smaller units either for energy production or excretion. Both processes occur simultaneously within the body throughout life.

The energy resulting from metabolism must ultimately come from the food taken into the body. In a normal diet this would include carbohydrates, fats, proteins, vitamins, minerals, and water. While carbohydrates, fats, and proteins provide the energy, vitamins, minerals and water are an essential part of the total metabolic process. Carbohydrates, fats, and proteins are converted in the body to glucose, fatty acids, and amino acids, respectively, prior to reaching the cell. Within the cell, the mitochondria are responsible for transforming these basic nutrients into energy that is stored within the cell. Energy is stored in the form of two high-energy compounds, adenosine triphosphate (ATP) and *creatine phosphate* (CP). Whenever ATP or CP are broken down within the cell, high levels of energy are released providing energy for the normal functions of the cell, e.g., muscle cell undergoing contraction. The basic biochemical steps involved in the synthesis of these high-energy compounds are complex and beyond the scope of this book.

A simplified schematic illustration of the major steps is shown in Figure 1–15.

Muscle contraction results from the energy released when ATP is broken down to *adenosine diphosphate* (ADP) and inorganic phosphate. Creatine phosphate breaks down to creatine and inorganic phosphate, providing the energy for the resynthesis of ATP. Oxidation, or *aerobic metabolism*, provides the energy to resynthesize creatine phosphate. Those pathways up to the Krebs cycle can function in the total absence of oxygen. This is referred to as *anaerobic metabolism*. Anaerobic metabolism results in the accumulation of lactic acid. This process can continue for only a short period of time, since there is a finite limit to the total amount of lactic acid that can accumulate. Thus, it is possible to survive for relatively short periods of time in the absence of breathing, i.e., breath-holding. Comparatively few molecules of ATP are produced through anaerobic metabolism compared with the quantity produced during aerobic metabolism; thus, anaerobic metabolism is an inefficient source of energy. It is an important pathway, however, for the body's adaptation to short, intensive bouts of exercise, e.g., sprinting.

When oxygen is available, metabolism can proceed through the aerobic stages in which oxygen is combined with hydrogen ions to form water and carbon dioxide. Without oxygen, the hydrogen ions and hydrogen atoms accumulate and effectively block the aerobic cycle, causing the body to rely on anaerobic metabolism. During exercise, at high work loads the body is not able to provide all of the oxygen necessary to regenerate sufficient ATP; thus aerobic metabolism is assisted by anaerobic metabolism and lactic acid begins to accumulate.

From Figure 1–15, it can be seen that both protein and fat are important energy sources, in addition to carbohydrate. Carbohydrate is broken down into *glucose* for transport in the blood, but glucose is converted to *glycogen* when it is stored in the muscle or liver, the major storage depots for glycogen. Glycogen is the only energy source available for anaero-

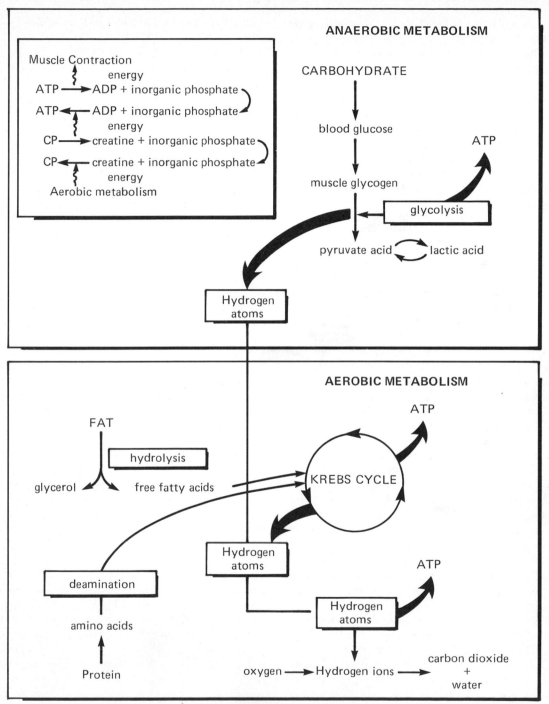

FIGURE 1–15

Simplified schematic drawing of anaerobic and aerobic metabolism, with ATP energy forma-tion, in a single muscle cell.

bic metabolism, since fat and protein enter the metabolic pathway at the Krebs cycle as energy sources for aerobic metabolism. Fat is stored as *triglycerides*, i.e., three fatty-acid molecules and a glycerol molecule. Fatty acids are released through hydrolysis of triglycerides and enter the Krebs cycle as a major energy source. Proteins are broken down into amino acids, deaminated (the amino group removed), and enter the Krebs cycle. Proteins, however, are not a common source of energy and serve far more important functions elsewhere within the body.

From the above discussion, it is obvious that food intake is an important part of the total metabolic, energy-producing process. It is also obvious that carbohydrates and fats are the major sources of energy and must therefore be a part of the daily diet. A normal mixed diet should contain approximately 15 percent protein, 35 percent fat, and 50 percent carbohydrate. While protein is not a major energy source, it is a critical part of the diet, since the amino acids derived from protein are necessary for the growth, restoration, and repair of body tissues.

The amount of food taken into the body is usually expressed in terms of the total caloric content of the food. The standard unit of energy used in nutrition is the kilogram calorie or Kcalorie. One Kcalorie is the amount of energy in the form of heat necessary to raise the temperature of 1 *kilogram* (kg) of water 1° *centigrade* (C) from 15 to 16° C. A *calorimeter* is used to measure the heat produced from burning different food materials; the results

can then be converted to the Kcalorie values for those foods. When samples of pure protein, carbohydrate, and fat are burned, they yield a net energy value of 4.35, 4.10, and 9.45 Kcalories/gm of material burned. Most foods are composed of two or more constituents. As an example, the calorie content of one egg (net weight of 50 gm) would depend on the egg's composition. Table 1–4 illustrates the manner in which this would be calculated by using the approximate caloric values of 4, 4, and 9 Kcalories per gram of protein, carbohydrate, and fat, respectively.

These Kcalorie values can also be used to calculate the number of calories necessary to lose a pound of fat. Since fat yields about 9 Kcalories/gm, a fat loss of 1 kg (1,000 gm) would require a 9,000 Kcalorie deficit. There are 2.2 lb in a kilogram, so it would take approximately a 4,000 Kcalorie deficit to lose 1 lb of fat (9,000 Kcalories/kg ÷ 2.2 lb/kg), although 3,500 Kcalories may be a more realistic value.

The amount of energy expended by the body can also be quantified in terms of kilocalories (1 kilocalorie = 1,000 calories). This can be done by placing the individual in a calorimeter and observing the changes in temperature within the calorimeter as the individual carries out his daily activities. The calorimeter, which requires expensive construction and instrumentation, must be extremely sensitive to small changes in temperature.

Fortunately, there are indirect ways of estimating energy production that are considerably more versatile than direct measurements of

TABLE 1–4. Calculation of the Caloric Value for One 50-Gm Egg

Composition	Percent of Total Weight	Weight in grams	Kcalories per gram	Total Kcalories
Water	73.7	36.8	0	0
Protein	12.9	6.5	4	26.0
Fat	11.5	5.8	9	52.2
Carbohydrate	0.9	0.4	4	1.6
Other	1.0	0.5	0	0
Total	100.0	50.0	—	79.8

energy changes and which are relatively inexpensive. The most accurate and widely used method of indirect calorimetry involves assessing the amount of oxygen consumed by the individual. When using only carbohydrates, one liter of oxygen consumed is the equivalent of 5.0 Kcalories. For fats, this value is 4.7 Kcalories, and for proteins, 4.5 Kcalories. On a normal mixed diet, the yield for an average man will be 4.8 Kcalories per liter of oxygen. Upon the assumption that the same average man uses 0.3 liters/min or 18 liters/hour (0.3 liters/min × 60 min), which will total 432 liters of oxygen/day (18 liters/hour × 24 hours), he will expend the equivalent of approximately 2,074 Kcalories/day (432 liters/day × 4.8 Kcalories/liter). This value is close to the average resting metabolic rate of a normal 154-pound or 70-kilogram man.

The *basal metabolic rate* (BMR) refers to the metabolic rate of the individual under conditions of total quiet and supine rest. For adults, the average BMR will range between 1,500 and 1,800 Kcalories/day. As the individual moves around throughout the day, the metabolic rate will increase in direct proportion to the levels of activity engaged in. This can vary from 2,000 Kcalories in relatively sedentary men to over 10,000 Kcalories in professional football players during preseason training where practice is held two or three times a day in the hot summer and fall.

ENDOCRINE FUNCTION

The *endocrine glands* have functions similar to those of the nervous system, i.e., they both coordinate the physiological functioning of the organism. The nervous system functions quickly and its stimuli are short-lived and localized. The endocrine system functions slowly, since the *hormones* are transported by the blood to their target organs, but the effect is long-lasting and more generalized. The endocrine glands are specialized glands that empty directly into the blood stream. Each endocrine gland secretes hormones that are specific to that gland and have a specific receptor organ or tissue in the body. As an example, the *thyroid-stimulating hormone* (TSH) is a hormone released by the pituitary gland that acts directly on the thyroid gland, causing an increase in the production of *thyroxin*. Hormones are extremely potent, i.e., extremely low doses can have a marked physiological effect, and are also critical to the integrated functioning of the body.

The major endocrine glands to be discussed are the *pituitary, thyroid, adrenal, pancreas,* and *gonads* or sex glands (Figure 1–16). The pituitary gland is housed in a well-protected area at the base of the brain. It was, at one time, considered to be the "master gland" of the body. Since that time, researchers have discovered that the *hypothalamus,* an adjacent area in the brain, probably plays the major role in the release and control of the many pituitary hormones. The pituitary hormones of importance to this review include the thyroid-stimulating hormone (TSH), *somatotrophic* (STH) or *growth hormone* (GH), *adrenocorticotrophic hormone* (ACTH), *vasopressin* and *antidiuretic hormone* (ADH). TSH functions to maintain thyroxin at predetermined levels. When the thyroid glands reduce thyroxin production and thyroxin falls below the desired level, TSH is released, and thyroxin production increases. STH has a general influence on the entire body. It is primarily responsible for growth; thus, its alternate name "growth hormone." Its major influence is on bone, muscle, the kidneys, adipose tissue, and the liver. ACTH is important in controlling metabolism through its influence on the *glucocorticoid output* of the *adrenal cortex.* Vasopressin has a stimulating action on almost all smooth muscles, but its major effect is generalized vasoconstriction of the blood vessels. ADH is important in regulating the body's fluid balance. Its primary function is to promote water retention at the level of the kidneys.

The thyroid gland is located just above the base of the neck, one lobe is on each side of the upper part of the trachea. Its major hormone, thyroxin, helps to regulate fat, protein, and carbohydrate metabolism, as well as influencing growth, development, and differenti-

FIGURE 1–16

Location of the primary endocrine glands important in the control of body functions during exercise. (From C. D. Turner and J. T. Bagnara, General Endocrinology, *5th ed. Philadelphia: W. B. Saunders Co., 1971. Reproduced by permission of the publisher)* ation of tissues. Release of thyroxin results in an increased metabolic rate.

The adrenal glands are situated above and in close proximity to the kidneys. They are composed of two parts, the *medulla* and the *cortex*. The medulla secretes the *catecholamines*, *epinephrine*, and *norepinephrine* (*adrenalin* and *noradrenaline*), which have marked effects on the cardiovascular system, the nervous system, smooth and skeletal muscle, and on metabolism. The adrenal cortex secretes numerous hormones that generally fall into one of two major categories, glucocorticoids and mineralocorticoids. Corticoids are concerned with maintaining the body's homeostasis through their effect on organic metabolism and water–mineral balance. The cortex can also produce both *androgens* and *estrogens*, which control the development and functioning of the sex organs.

The pancreas secretes two major hormones, *insulin* and *glucagon*. Insulin is necessary for the transportation of glucose from the blood into the cell. The high blood-sugar levels in diabetics are due to the inability of the pancreas to produce sufficient insulin; thus, the glucose is not transported into the cell. Glucagon has an effect on carbohydrate metabolism that is just the opposite to that of insulin. It produces *glycogenolysis* (breakdown of glycogen) and *hyperglycemia* (elevated blood-sugar levels).

The gonads consist of the testes in males and the ovaries in females. The testes produce the male, androgen hormones of which *testosterone* is the most significant. Testosterone stimulates development of the male sexual characteristics, influences muscle growth through a protein anabolic effect, and determines to a large extent the degree of masculinity in the male. The ovaries secrete the estrogen hormones. The estrogens promote development of the female sexual characteristics and also promote the accumulation of body fat.

GENERAL SUMMARY

The human body is one of the most complex and remarkable entities known to man. Each

day, science provides additional insight into the varied mechanisms controlling the numerous body functions, but our information is far from complete. The apparently simple process of muscle contraction, even today, eludes a satisfactory, detailed explanation. Sufficient knowledge is available, however, to provide insight into the unique problems of the athlete, with the hope of using science to help produce more efficient and better trained athletes.

In this chapter, each of the major systems of the body was reviewed to provide a basic foundation of anatomy and physiology on which the later chapters will build. Emphasis was placed on those areas that were of particular importance for the coach and athlete. Since the coverage of this chapter was rather broad in scope, a detailed summary will not be attempted.

REFERENCES

ÅSTRAND, P. O. and RODAHL, K. *Textbook of Work Physiology.* New York: McGraw-Hill Book Co., 1970.

BROBECK, J. R. ed. *Best and Taylor's Physiological Basis of Medical Practice.* 9th ed. Baltimore: Williams and Wilkins Co., 1973.

BURTON, A. C. *Physiology and Biophysics of the Circulation.* Chicago: Year Book Medical Publishers, 1965.

COMROE, J. H. *Physiology of Respiration.* 2nd ed. Chicago: Year Book Medical Publishers, 1974.

DE VRIES, H. A. *Physiology of Exercise for Physical Education and Athletics.* 2nd ed. Dubuque, Iowa: William C. Brown Co., 1974.

GANONG, W. F. *Review of Medical Physiology.* 2nd ed. Los Altos, CA: Lange Medical Publications, 1965.

GUYTON, A. C. *Textbook of Medical Physiology.* 3rd ed. Philadelphia: W. B. Saunders Co., 1966.

TURNER, C. D. and BAGNARA, J. T. *General Endocrinology.* 5th ed. Philadelphia: W. B. Saunders Co., 1971.

TUTTLE, W. W. and SCHOTTELIUS, B. A. *Textbook of Physiology.* 15th ed. St. Louis: C. V. Mosby Co., 1965.

WEST, J. B. *Respiratory Physiology: The Essentials.* Baltimore: Williams and Wilkins Co., 1974.

2
Acute Responses to Exercise

INTRODUCTION

It was not until the early twentieth century that concerted efforts were made to gain insight into man's ability to functionally adapt to the stress of exercise. With the establishment of the Harvard Fatigue Laboratory in 1927 and the work of A. V. Hill in England in the 1920's, a group of dedicated scientists began a concerted effort to push back the frontiers in the area of exercise and sport physiology. While specific aspects of man's physical performance had been investigated by isolated research laboratories and in individual research experiments as early as the mid-to-late 1800's, the efforts in the 1920's marked the start of a new era in which scientists dedicated themselves to unlocking the mysteries of man's successful adaptation to the unique environment of exercise. Since this time considerable knowledge has been accumulated about man's ability to adapt to exercise. However, with the discovery of new knowledge, we realize that there is even more to be learned than was originally anticipated. The surface has been scratched, but this area of investigation is still in its infancy. With the availability of new techniques and bright young researchers, the period of rapid growth is quickly approaching.

ASSESSING MAN'S RESPONSE TO EXERCISE

How does one go about determining the various physiological responses to exercise? The athlete in his natural sport or athletic environment does not present the researcher with the most desirable situation from which to gather this basic information. With the development of radiotelemetry, limited information can be obtained during actual competitive experiences. A small transmitter, less than two inches on each side, can be attached to the body of the athlete and, with the appropriate attachments, data relative to heart rate, body temperature, and additional physiological parameters can be transmitted to a receiver stationed alongside the field, court, or pool. While this information is of considerable interest and importance, it provides a very limited amount of insight into the body's total response to exercise.

The limitations of field testing have forced the researcher and athlete into the research laboratory. In the laboratory, the athlete can be studied in much greater depth and detail within a controlled environment. While the situation is artificial, relative to a true performance situation, a great deal of insight can be gained that leads to a better understanding of the athlete in his natural environment. How is this accomplished?

One of the goals of studying exercise in the laboratory is to be able to produce a level of exercise which can be quantified and which is reproducible. In order to determine the functional relationship between exercise as a stimulus and the resulting adaptations of the body's different systems, one must be able to measure both the exercise and the response to exercise. There are a number of ways in which the athlete can be exercised within the confines of the laboratory. The simplest form of exercise is bench stepping, in which the athlete steps up and down on a bench of standard height (which usually varies between 12 and 18 inches) at a fixed rate of stepping established by a metronome, e.g., 24 ascensions/min. This is the least expensive and most portable of the various testing devices, but it has several disadvantages. First, the total amount of work that is performed in a set period of time is totally dependent on the athlete's body weight, i.e., the heavier individual must lift more weight on each step. Second, the athlete's movements during a stepping test make it difficult to obtain certain physiological measurements.

A second device that is used for producing an exercise response in the laboratory is the

FIGURE 2–2
Supine bicycling on a bicycle ergometer.

FIGURE 2–1
Upright bicycling on a bicycle ergometer.

bicycle *ergometer*. This can be used in either the normal, upright (Figure 2–1) or supine position (Figure 2–2). In addition, the bicycle ergometer can be used for arm cycling. Ergometers work on the basis of one of two principles, mechanical friction or electromagnetic resistance. With the mechanical friction devices, a belt surrounding the flywheel of the bicycle can be tightened or loosened to adjust the resistance against which the athlete pedals. The pedal rate must be kept constant to provide a constant level of work. With electromagnetic resistance, the flywheel moves through an electromagnetic field, and the strength of the field determines the resistance to pedalling. These electromagnetic devices are designed to provide a constant level of work independent of the pedalling rate, by using a feedback loop that increases the resistance when the rate slows and decreases the resistance as the rate picks up. There are many advantages to using the bicycle ergometer. It is relatively inexpensive, portable, the work level or power output can be accurately defined, and the task is weight-independent, i.e., the work level can be set independently of the individual's body weight. The bicycle ergometer does have the disadvantage, however, of causing the athlete to become more fatigued from local, leg-muscle fatigue than from general, overall cardiovascular, respiratory, and metabolic fatigue. In addition, and closely related to the problem of local fatigue, the peak or

maximum physiological parameters obtained on the bicycle ergometer are frequently lower than the peak parameters obtained during other forms of laboratory exercise.

Probably the most widely used laboratory exercise device is the motor-driven treadmill (Figure 2–3). The treadmill is a motorized device that drives a wide belt in one direction, while the athlete walks, jogs, or runs in the opposite direction in an attempt to keep himself in the same relative position. The speed and elevation of the treadmill can be varied from a pace for very slow, level walking to the superhuman task of running up a 20 percent slope at a speed of 20–25 mi/hour. This device appears to provide the highest maximum physiological responses to exercise and

FIGURE 2–3
Walking on a motor-driven treadmill.

maintains a constant work rate (the subject either keeps up with the rate of work or he is thrown off of the back of the treadmill). The treadmill is an expensive device, however, and lacks portability. In addition, it can be somewhat dangerous if the individual loses his balance.

Two unique laboratory work devices have been recently developed, the rowing ergometer and the swimming flume. The rowing ergometer (Figure 2–4) was devised to test competitive oarsmen in an activity that more closely approximated their competitive task. The swimming flume (Figure 2–5) was developed for the same purpose. Valuable research data had been obtained by instrumenting swimmers in a swimming pool. The problems of turns and of not having a stationary swimmer led to the use of teathered swimming. The

athlete was placed in a harness that was connected to a rope and series of pulleys with attached weights. In this manner, the athlete would swim in a stationary position against different resistances. While the initial attempts provided useful data, they did not accurately duplicate the true environment of the swimmer. The swimming flume, while very expensive, has resolved this problem and has created many new opportunities to investigate almost all aspects of swimming.

Each of these laboratory modes of exercise makes it possible to exercise the athlete from low to exhaustive levels, while maintaining his body in a relatively stable position. This allows the athlete to be instrumented to measure a variety of physiological parameters. Expired air can be collected for the determination of the volume and rate of respiration as well as

FIGURE 2–4

Rowing ergometer. (From F. C. Hagerman and W. D. Lee, "Measurement of Oxygen Consumption, Heart Rate, and Work Output During Rowing." Medicine and Science in Sports, 3 (1971). Reproduced by permission of the publisher.)

FIGURE 2–5

Swimming Flume. (From P. O. Åstrand, "Do We Need Physical Conditioning?" J. Phy. Ed., March–April 1972. Reproduced by permission of the publisher.)

the amount of oxygen or energy used during exercise; electrodes placed on the chest allow the monitoring of the electrocardiogram to determine the normality and rate of the heart; blood pressure can be monitored either directly (arterial catheter) or indirectly (*sphygmoma-nometer*); arterial- and venous-blood samples can be drawn and analyzed for various components; body and skin temperature can be monitored; and many other specific parameters can either be recorded or observed. Advances in technology have made it possible to define man's response to exercise quite explicitly, but even with these advances, there are still many areas that cannot be accurately assessed or described. Only as technology pushes ahead will the total picture start to come more clearly into focus.

PHYSIOLOGICAL ADAPTATIONS TO ACUTE EXERCISE

Physiological adaptations to exercise fall into two major categories: acute and chronic. Acute

adaptations are those that occur during a single bout of work. Chronic adaptations are those that result after a period of physical training, i.e., changes that result from conditioning. Chronic adaptations will be discussed in the following chapter, Chronic Adaptations to Exercise. It should be recognized that the various acute responses and their degree of change will depend on the duration and intensity of the exercise bout.

Neuromuscular Adaptations

When the athlete is ready to spring into action, his nervous system, through either reflex action or conscious control, initiates the movement by sending impulses to the appropriate motor units. It appears that the motor units within any given muscle contract asynchronously, i.e., at different times rather than all at the same time. It is also possible that the athlete is effectively using only a small fraction of the total number of motor units that are available to him, even in a maximal contraction. Support for this theory comes from the many anecdotes of superhuman feats of strength by individuals who are under extreme emotional conditions, e.g., the slightly built woman who lifts an automobile off her son who was trapped underneath. Also, studies have shown that greater maximal force can be generated when the muscle's nerve is stimulated electrically than when the individual attempts a voluntary maximal contraction.

Study of the muscle's activity through electromyography, the process whereby the electrical activity of the muscle can be monitored and recorded, has provided essential knowledge in the area of neuromuscular coordination, recruitment of motor units, and motor unit integration. New techniques allow the observation of isolated, single motor units. By using biofeedback techniques, individuals can be taught to selectively recruit specific motor units and to have these motor units contract in defined rhythms, e.g., drum rolls. Further development in this area, hopefully, will allow a better understanding of how motor units are recruited for activity and which factors are responsible for limiting the number of motor units and the total number of muscle fibers that can contract at the same time. Only then can we begin to understand what factors limit or modify the expression of strength.

Closely related to the areas of motor-unit recruitment and strength is the area of muscular fatigue. Unfortunately, not too much more is known about muscular fatigue than is known about the expression of strength. "Muscular fatigue" is a term reserved strictly for that fatigue experienced in the local muscle or muscle group, as opposed to "overall fatigue," which is probably cardiovascular in origin, or to mental fatigue, which is thought to be associated with boredom. These other types of fatigue will be discussed in later sections.

Studies by Merton in the 1950's found that when a person reached a state of extreme fatigue and was unable to move a certain muscle, electrical stimulation of that muscle did not elicit a response, and the action potentials (electrical impulses) received by the muscle were not diminished. He also found that if the blood supply to the active muscle was occluded, recovery from fatigue did not occur until the circulation to the muscle was restored. He felt that this indicated that muscular fatigue was not due to a failure of the central nervous system but was due to peripheral circulatory factors, such as the build up of waste products which could not escape the muscle, or the lack of nutrients and oxygen. With maximal static or isometric contractions, the arterial blood flow through the contracting muscle will be either partly or totally restricted, and the venous return will be totally restricted. Thus, the fatigue can be due to a lack of oxygen or nutrients from the arterial side or to an accumulation of lactic acid, hydrogen ions, or heat. Some have suggested that the site of fatigue is at the level of the *myoneural junction*, i.e., that point where the neuron and muscle fiber connect. This would be in contradiction, however, to the studies cited above.

Cardiovascular Adaptations

The major function of the cardiovascular system during exercise is to deliver blood to the active tissues, which includes the delivery of oxygen and nutrients and the removal of the metabolic waste products. If the exercise bout is prolonged, the cardiovascular system also assists in maintaining body temperature, so that the athlete does not overheat. A series of complex interactions allow these cardiovascular adaptations to occur in an integrated manner.

Heart Rate.   The heart rate is the simplest and one of the most informative of the cardiovascular parameters that can be measured. At rest, the heart beats at a rate of 60 to 80 beats/min. This is easily determined by locating the radial (thumb-side of the wrist) or the carotid (junction of the head and neck) artery pulses, counting for 15 secs, and multiplying the result by 4 [HR = (beats/15 sec) × 4]. In very sedentary, deconditioned individuals, the resting heart rate can exceed 100 beats/min, and in highly conditioned, endurance athletes, resting heart rates have been reported in the 28-40 beats/min range.

The lowest heart rate is found at rest in the supine position. It will be elevated slightly upon sitting and increase even further with standing. This is the result of the influence of gravity, which reduces the amount of blood returning to the heart when one shifts from a supine to an upright posture, thus reducing the stroke volume. For cardiac output to remain the same, the heart rate must increase, since $\dot{Q} = HR \times SV$. Resting heart rate is also influenced by age and the environment. It usually decreases with age and increases with extremes in temperature and altitude. Prior to starting the exercise bout, the pre-exercise heart rate may be increased well above normal resting values. This is referred to as an anticipatory response and is

cretion from the adrenal medulla. Reliable estimates of actual resting heart rates should be made under conditions that are conducive to the subject's total relaxation.

When the athlete begins to exercise, the heart rate increases almost immediately. At constant, low levels of exercise, the heart rate increases and plateaus in a relatively short one- to two-minute period. As the intensity of exercise increases, it takes somewhat longer for the heart rate to reach this plateau or steady-state level. Each time the level of work is increased, the heart rate increases in direct proportion. This is illustrated in Figure 2–6. The better conditioned individual will perform the same level of work at a lower heart rate. The older individual of comparable fitness will also perform the same level of work at a lower

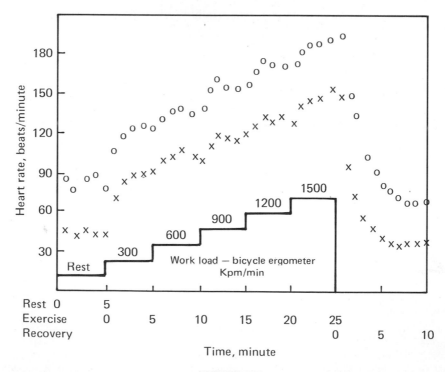

FIGURE 2–6

Relationship of heart rate to work intensity. (From J. H. Wilmore and A. C. Norton., The Heart and Lungs at Work. Schiller Park, Ill.: Beckman Instruments. Reproduced by permission of the publisher.)

heart rate. This is misleading, however, since the older individual will also have a lower maximum heart rate. On the basis of the relative intensity, submaximal, steady-state rate/maximum rate, the older and younger individuals will be similar.

As the work load is increased to progressively higher levels, eventually, a level will be reached at which even individuals who are the most fit will become exhausted. Prior to this, however, the heart rate should reach its peak or maximum value and plateau at that level, even though the work load increases further. The point at which the heart rate plateaus with increasing work is referred to as the *maximum heart rate* or HRmax. Each individual has a definable HRmax, which is highly reproducible from one test to the next. HRmax is quite variable between individuals and appears to be more closely related to the individual's age rather than to his level of fitness. Figure 2–7 illustrates the relationship between HRmax

and age. This illustrates approximately a 1 beat/min drop per year in HRmax. Some have interpreted this curve to suggest that HRmax can be predicted from age. The equation HRmax = 220 − age provides only an approximation of the normal value for any one age. It can be off considerably for any one individual, however, since the variation for any one age is very high (standard deviation approximately ± 10 beats/min).

Stroke Volume. Stroke volume during exercise is influenced by four factors: (a) return of venous blood to the heart; (b) ventricular distensibility; (c) ventricular contractility; and (d) aortic or pulmonary artery pressure. The first two factors influence the filling capacity of the ventricle, i.e., how much blood is available for filling the ventricle and the ease with which the ventricle is filled at the available hydrostatic pressure. The last two factors influence the ability of the ventricle to empty,

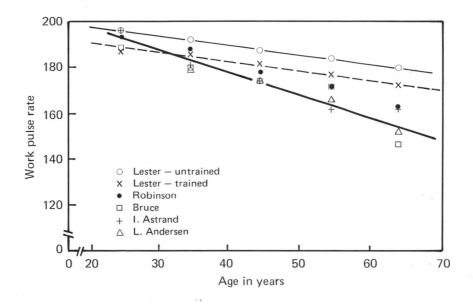

FIGURE 2–7

Decline in maximum heart rate with age in healthy men. (From H. L. Taylor, W. Haskell, S. M. Fox, III, and H. Blackburn, "Exercise tests: A summary of procedures and concepts of stress testing for cardiovascular diagnosis and function evaluation," in Measurement in Exercise Electrocardiography, *edited by H. Blackburn. Springfield, Ill. Charles C. Thomas, Publisher, 1969. Reproduced by permission of the publisher.)*

i.e., the force with which the blood is ejected and the pressure against which it must flow in the arteries.

The stroke volume response to exercise is largely dependent on the position of the individual during exercise. As was noted above with regard to resting heart rate determinations, the stroke volume decreases as the body shifts from the supine to an upright position due to a slight pooling of blood in the extremities. This is the result of the first factor listed above, reduced return of the venous blood to the heart. Gravity creates what is referred to as a hydrostatic pressure effect, in which the vascular system can be thought of as a column of blood. The pressure at the bottom of the column is considerably greater than that at the top due to the weight of the column. Thus, at the lower levels of the body, the blood is returned against a very high pressure. In the supine position, this is not a problem, since the blood flows back to the heart much more easily without having to overcome the force of gravity.

It appears that during exercise in the upright position, stroke volume increases linearly up to about 40–60 percent of the individual's capacity, at which point it reaches its maximum value and plateaus. With supine exercise, the individual is close to his maximum stroke volume at rest and only a slight increase in stroke volume is experienced with exercise. This supine resting value is also nearly identical to the maximum value obtained during upright exercise; thus, the increase from rest to maximum exercise in the upright posture is sufficient to overcome the effect of venous pooling in the lower extremities.

Stroke volume at rest in the upright position will vary between 70 and 100 ml in the average, adult male. Maximum values can reach 200 ml or higher in large, highly trained athletes. It has been suggested that stroke volume may even start to decrease at the higher intensities of exercise, those greater than 85 percent of maximal capacity, due to a shortened, diastolic filling time at the higher heart rates. At a heart rate of 180 beats/min, one complete heart cycle takes only 0.3 sec; the period of diastole would be only a fraction of this value. While this decrease in stroke volume at high intensities appears to be logically valid, it lacks experimental support.

Cardiac Output. The cardiac output, the product of the stroke volume and heart rate, increases linearly with increased levels of work up to the point of exhaustion. At exercise levels up to 40–60 percent of maximal capacity, this increase is the result of increases in both heart rate and stroke volume. Beyond this point, the increases are strictly a function of the increasing heart rate.

At rest, cardiac output varies between 4 and 6 liters/min in healthy adult males. Maximum values depend on many factors, of which body size and the extent of endurance training are the most important. A small, deconditioned man may have a maximum cardiac output of less than 20 liters/min, while the output of a large, highly conditioned athlete may exceed 40 liters/min.

Blood Flow. The flow of blood from the heart varies considerably according to the needs of the different body tissues. Figure 2–8 illustrates the differences in blood flow patterns between resting and maximum exercise conditions. The ability to control the degree of dilatation or constriction of the vessels allows blood to be shunted from areas of little need to those areas of muscular activity. The absolute amount of blood flowing to the brain remains constant; the amount to the heart increases with the increase in heart rate; and the amount to the kidneys, stomach and intestines appears to decrease with increases in exercise intensity. The amount of blood going to the active muscles increases substantially, and the blood flow to the skin also increases as the need to lose body heat increases. The volume of blood available to supply the exercising muscles is referred to as the *effective blood volume.* With prolonged exercise, this can be reduced due to blood plasma volume losses from sweating, tissue edema (fluid forced into the muscles and joints), and to the need for a greater

Heavy work
Cardiac output, 25 liters/min

100%   3-5%   4-5%   2-3%   0.5-1%   4-6%   80-85%

Left pump

Right pump

100%   25-30%   4-5%   20-25%   3-5%   15%   5%   15-20%

Rest
Cardiac output, 5 liters/min

FIGURE 2–8

Schematic illustration of blood flow distribution differences between rest and exercise. (From P. O. Åstrand and K. Rodahl, Textbook of Work Physiology. *New York: McGraw-Hill Book Co., 1970. Reproduced by permission of the publisher.)*

volume of blood at the periphery to promote heat loss.

The increased blood flow to the active muscles is the result of neural-vasodilator activity and increased metabolism. Increased metabolism causes a decrease in the pH, or an increase in the acidity, at the local-tissue level, which causes additional capillaries and arterioles to open. This is an important controlling mechanism, since it assures the availability of blood in those areas where it is needed.

Blood Pressure. The systolic and diastolic blood pressures respond differently to exercise.

Systolic pressure increases linearly with exercise, increasing from a resting value of 120 mmHg to values in excess of 200 mmHg as the individual reaches his exercise capacity. Diastolic pressure undergoes relatively little change with exercise, usually not increasing or decreasing more than 10 mmHg throughout the full range of exercise intensity. Pulse pressure, i.e., systolic — diastolic pressure, will change in direct proportion to the changes in systolic pressure. In the pulmonary circulation, systolic pressure can double from 20 to 40 mmHg, while diastolic pressure remains unchanged.

The increase in systolic blood pressure is the direct result of the increased cardiac output. The blood vessels in the working muscles are generally in a state of vasodilation, allowing more blood to flow to the active tissue. This results in a lowered peripheral resistance, which would normally lower the systolic blood pressure. The four or five fold increase in cardiac output, however, is more than sufficient to counter the effects of the peripheral vasodilation and the lowered peripheral resistance. The result is a net increase in systolic blood pressure.

Arterial–Venous Oxygen Difference.   The arterial–venous oxygen difference (a–$\bar{v}O_2$ diff) simply reflects the difference in oxygen content between the oxygen-rich arterial blood and the venous blood. This is expressed as a concentration difference, i.e., the ml of oxygen per 100 ml of blood. As an example, if there were 19 ml of oxygen in 100 ml of arterial blood and 14 ml of oxygen in 100 ml of mixed venous blood, the a–$\bar{v}O_2$ diff would be 5 ml of oxygen/100 ml of blood. These values are typical of those found at rest. With exercise, the active muscles use more oxygen. This can result from either a greater delivery of blood to these muscles or a greater extraction of oxygen from the available blood, or both. Generally, both greater flow and greater extraction occur during all stages of exercise.

As the athlete reaches exhaustion, the a–$\bar{v}O_2$ diff widens to nearly three times the resting level. Arterial oxygen content remains about the same, but venous oxygen content can drop to 2 ml/100 ml of blood or lower, thus, widening the a–$\bar{v}O_2$ diff from 5 to 17 ml/100 ml of blood. This difference is probably even higher at the tissue level, as the venous content approaches zero.

Hematological and Blood Volume Adaptations. The composition of blood changes as the individual goes from a resting to an exercising state. The red blood cell may actually undergo a decrease in size as the body is exposed to prolonged exercise that involves a substantial fluid loss. Proteins may also be lost from the plasma volume, although the results of studies at the present time are conflicting.

With substantial fluid loss in prolonged exercise due to sweating, there is a reduction in plasma volume, which results in a *hemoconcentration* of red blood cells and plasma proteins (i.e., since the fluid portion is reduced, the cellular and protein portion of the blood volume represents a larger fraction of the total blood volume). This hemoconcentration results in a substantial rise in the red blood cell count, a rise of 20–25 percent. At one time, it was thought that red blood cells were added to the circulation to facilitate oxygen transport. It is now recognized that the blood plasma is reduced with fluid loss and this causes an increase in the relative number of red blood cells, not in the absolute number. Plasma volume loss results from a shift of fluid from the plasma to the interstitial fluid (fluid between the cells).

At rest, the blood pH remains constant at a value slightly below 7.4. A pH of 7.0 is considered neutral, greater than 7.0, alkaline or basic, and less than 7.0, acidic. Thus, normal blood at rest is slightly alkaline. There is little change in blood pH up to about 50 percent intensity of exercise. As the intensity of exercise increases above 50 percent, the pH will start to drop, the blood becoming more acidic. This drop will be gradual at first, but it will become more rapid as the individual approaches exhaustion. Values of 7.0 or lower have been reported following maximal exercise. Tissue pH reaches levels even lower than 7.0. The lowering of the blood pH is primarily the result of an increased anaerobic metabolism and corresponds to the increase observed in blood lactate. Blood lactate levels range from an average of 10 mg/100 ml of blood (1.1 millimoles/liter of blood) at rest to 200 mg/100 ml (22 millimoles/liter of blood) within five minutes following exercise. Lactate values reach their maximum in the blood during the initial five minutes of recovery from exhaustive exercise. Large concentrations of blood lactate do not appear in the blood until the work load reaches or exceeds 50 percent of the individual's capacity.

Respiratory Adaptations

The pulmonary ventilation, or minute volume, increases from a resting value of approximately 6 liters/min to values above 100 liters/min during the end stages of exhaustive exercise in adult males and can reach values in excess of 200 liters/min in large, well-conditioned male athletes (Figure 2–9). This is accomplished by an increase in both the tidal volume and in the respiratory frequency. Tidal volume may increase from a resting average of 0.5 liters/min to 2.5–3.0 liters/min during maximal exercise. This would correspond to an increase in the fraction of the vital capacity from 10 percent at rest to 50 percent during exercise. The respiratory frequency can increase from 12–16 breaths/min at rest to 40–50 breaths/min during maximal exercise. There is a direct, linear relationship between the increase in pulmonary ventilation and the increase in work level up to about 80–90 percent of the individual's

FIGURE 2–9

Pulmonary ventilation with exercise up to exhaustion for normals, as well as highly conditioned endurance athletes. (From P. O. Åstrand and K. Rodahl, Textbook of Work Physiology. *New York: McGraw-Hill Book Co., 1970. Reproduced by permission of the publisher.)*

capacity. From this point through the end of maximal exercise, the ventilation increases at a much faster rate. At the present time, it is not understood why the ventilation increases disproportionately during the later stages of maximal exercise.

The movement of these large volumes of air during heavy exercise requires considerable work from the respiratory muscles. It also requires an additional expenditure of energy above that needed for the exercising muscles. At rest, the energy cost for ventilation is approximately 1 ml of oxygen for each liter of air breathed. For 6 liters of air/min, this would amount to 6 ml of oxygen/min for ventilation, which is approximately 2 percent of the total oxygen consumed at rest. During the later stages of maximal exercise, the cost of breathing may increase to 10 percent of the total amount of oxygen consumed.

The fractional lung volumes also change with the transition from rest to maximal exercise. These changes are illustrated in Figure 2–10. The increase in tidal volume comes primarily from the inspiratory reserve volume. Residual volume increases slightly, vital capacity decreases slightly, and total lung capacity remains the same. As the ventilation increases, there is also a better distribution of the ventilation in the lungs, i.e., the incoming air is more evenly distributed among the alveoli. Also, the increase in the pulmonary arterial pressure provides a better distribution of the blood (perfusion) throughout the lung. Again, due to gravity and the hydrostatic pressure effect, the perfusion of blood to the upper regions of the lung is poor while at rest; however, as exercise progresses and the pulmonary arterial pressure increases, the upper regions of the lungs receive proportionally more blood, which increases their efficiency.

Lung diffusion refers to the rate at which

Pulmonary function at rest and during maximum exercise*

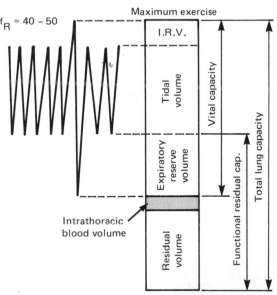

*Redrawn from Margaria & Cerretelli (1968), copyright Academic Press.

FIGURE 2–10

Fractional lung volume changes with exercise. (From K. L. Andersen, et al., Fundamentals of Exercise Testing, *p. 15. Geneva: World Health Organization, 1971.)*

gases diffuse from the alveoli to the blood in the pulmonary capillaries. It is expressed in ml of the gas per minute per partial pressure difference between alveolar gas and the capillaries. Diffusion capacity for oxygen can increase threefold from a resting value of 25 ml/min/mmHg to a maximal value of 75 ml/min/mmHg.

Two practical respiratory phenomena exist in the real athletic world that are poorly understood and almost impossible to duplicate in the research laboratory. These are the phenomena of "second wind" and "stitch-in-the-side," both brought on by running. The stitch-in-the-side is usually felt as a sharp, severe pain in the lower-thoracic or upper-abdominal area. Many theories exist to explain this phenomenon, but, to date, none have any conclusive scientific support. The two most logical explanations are: (a) ischemia, or lack of blood flow to the diaphragm; and (b) gastrointestinal gas, or ischemia of the large intestine. Whatever the

cause, there is no simple remedy that works equally well for all people. Some can continue to run with their pain, while others find it necessary to slow down or stop. Specific dietary modifications have been suggested as a preventive measure, but sufficient evidence is not available to demonstrate their effectiveness.

Second wind is an equally confusing phenomenon. During a workout at a constant pace, the effort seems labored or the athlete is not "in the groove." Suddenly, the athlete feels a sense of freedom; the distress of labored breathing is gone; he has experienced second wind. The feeling of second wind does relate to a more comfortable pattern of breathing, but this is the result of a more basic physiological alteration, which has yet to be defined. It is possibly a result of more efficient circulation to the active tissues or of a more efficient metabolic process. The answer will have to await a much better understanding of how respiration is controlled during exercise.

FIGURE 2–11

Oxygen consumption in relation to work intensity. The peak oxygen consumption would be the $\dot{V}O_2$ max. (From J. H. Wilmore and A. C. Norton, The Heart and Lungs at Work. Schiller Park, Ill. Beckman Instruments, 1974. Reproduced by permission of the publisher.)

Metabolism

As the body shifts from rest to exercise, there is an increase in the total body metabolism. While this has been documented through direct calorimetry, much more data is available using indirect calorimetry, primarily through the assessment of oxygen consumption levels.

$\dot{V}O_2$ *max.*   The increase in metabolism is in direct proportion to the increase in the level of work. As the index of metabolic activity, *oxygen consumption* ($\dot{V}O_2$) increases up to the last stage of exercise. At this point, the $\dot{V}O_2$ plateaus, even though the work level continues to increase (Figure 2–11). The value at which the $\dot{V}O_2$ plateaus is referred to as the *maximal oxygen consumption* ($\dot{V}O_2$ max). This value is a well-defined and reproducible physiological endpoint. $\dot{V}O_2$ max is regarded as the best criterion of cardiorespiratory endurance capacity or "physical fitness."

$\dot{V}O_2$ max values are influenced greatly by size, age, and level of fitness. To account for individual differences in size, $\dot{V}O_2$ max is frequently expressed relative to body weight (ml of oxygen/kg of body weight × min) or to lean body weight. This allows a more equitable comparison between individuals of different sizes. $\dot{V}O_2$ max decreases with age beyond fifteen to twenty years (Figure 2–12). This is probably due to a combination of true biological aging and a sedentary life style. In addition, females beyond ten to twenty years have $\dot{V}O_2$ max values considerably below those of males of similar ages (Figure 2–12). It is questionable whether these represent true differences between the sexes, or whether the female is a victim of her culture, which imposes a sedentary life style once she reaches menarche.

$\dot{V}O_2$ max varies from values as high as 80–84 ml/kg × min in long-distance runners and cross-country skiers to values in the mid-

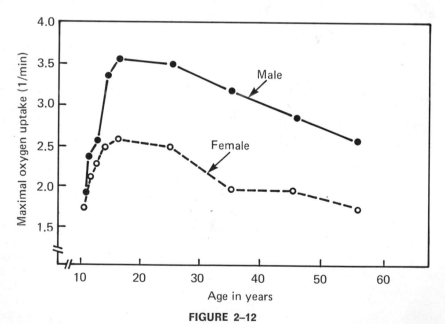

FIGURE 2–12

Variation in $\dot{V}O_2$ max with sex and age. (From L. Hermansen, "Individual Differences," Fitness, Health and Work Capacity: International Standards for Assessment. *Edited by L. A. Larson. New York: Macmillan Publishing Co., 1974. Reproduced by permission of the publisher.) Note: Refer to Figure 11–1 for a similar comparison with $\dot{V}O_2$ max expressed relative to body weight.*

TABLE 2–1. Range of Maximal Oxygen Consumption
Values for Athletes in Various Sports

Sport	Maximal Oxygen Consumption $ml/kg \times min$
Males	
Cross-Country Skiing	70–94
Long-Distance Running	65–85
Rowing	58–75
Bicycling	55–70
Long-Distance Swimming	48–68
Gymnastics	48–64
Speed Skating	50–75
Ice Hockey	50–60
Football	45–64
Baseball	45–55
Tennis	42–56
Females	
Cross-Country Skiing	56–74
Long-Distance Running	55–72
Rowing	41–58
Distance Swimming	45–60
Speed Skating	40–52
Sprinting	38–52
Basketball	35–45

20's, or lower, for poorly conditioned, sedentary adults. The highest value recorded was 94 ml/kg × min for a champion Norwegian cross-country skier. The highest value recorded for a female was 74 ml/kg × min for a Russian cross-country skier. Values for athletes in various sports are illustrated in Table 2–1.

Oxygen Debt. Oxygen debt refers to the volume of oxygen consumed during the recovery period following exercise that is in excess of the volume that is normally consumed while at rest. A quick run down the block to catch the departing bus or a fast climb up several flights of stairs leaves one with a rapid pulse and an "out-of-breath" feeling. After several minutes of recovery, the breathing and pulse appear to return to normal. Most work or bouts of exercise are performed at levels well below one's endurance capacity ($\dot{V}O_2$ max). However, it is possible to perform work that requires

considerably more energy/min than can be supplied by the body. This is accomplished through anaerobic metabolism, as discussed in Chapter 1 and illustrated in Figure 1–15. Pyruvic acid is unable to go through the Krebs cycle due to an accumulation of hydrogen ions and atoms and because of a lack of oxygen. Pyruvic acid is then converted to lactic acid, which allows glycolysis to continue until it results in the production of ATP. In addition, stored ATP and CP can be used to provide energy during this period of oxygen deficiency.

There is an oxygen debt associated with even low levels of exercise. This is due to the fact that oxygen consumption requires several minutes to reach the required or steady-state level (Figure 2–13), even though the requirement to perform the exercise is constant from the very start of the exercise. This initial period, where the oxygen consumption is below the steady-state or required level, is referred to as the period of oxygen deficit. The deficit is calculated simply as the difference between the amount of oxygen that is required and that which is actually consumed.

Energy Substrate. The *respiratory exchange ratio* (R) is the ratio between the amount of carbon dioxide produced and the amount of oxygen consumed, i.e., R = CO_2 produced/O_2 consumed. The R value will vary with the foodstuff or substrate that is being metabolized to provide the energy for work. When only fats are metabolized, the R = 0.71; for proteins, R = 0.82; and for carbohydrates, R = 1.00. By observing the R value at various stages of steady-state exercise, it is possible to estimate the type of substrate that is being metabolized to provide the necessary energy. As an example, if during 1 min of moderate exercise, the athlete consumed 2.0 liters of oxygen and produced 1.8 liters of carbon dioxide, the R value would be 0.90 (R = 1.8/2.0 = 0.9). It has been demonstrated that the oxidation of 1 gm of glycogen uses 0.828 liters of oxygen and produces 0.828 liters of carbon dioxide. Also, the oxidation of 1 gm of fat uses 1.989 liters of oxygen and produces 1.419 liters of carbon dioxide. Two equations can then be written,

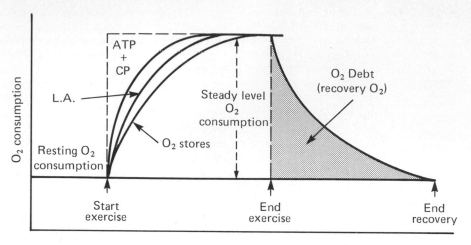

FIGURE 2–13

Oxygen debt resulting from a submaximal, steady-state exercise. (From H. A. de Vries, Physiology of Exercise for Physical Education and Athletics, 2nd ed. Dubuque, Iowa: William C. Brown Co., 1974. Reproduced by permission of the publisher.)

where x = gm of glycogen used, y = gm of fat used, and the assumption is made that no protein has been used.

$$\text{2.0 liters of oxygen}$$
$$= 1.989y + 0.828x$$
$$(-) \quad \text{1.8 liters of carbon dioxide}$$
$$= 1.419y + 0.828x$$

or
$$0.2 = 0.570y \quad (x \text{ cancels out})$$
$$y = 0.2/.570$$
$$y = 0.35 \text{ gm of fat}$$

and substituting for y in either of the above equations,

$$x = 1.57 \text{ gm of carbohydrate}$$

Thus, the energy for 1 min of moderate exercise was supplied by 0.35 gm of fat and 1.57 gm of carbohydrate.

The R value will usually vary from 0.75 to 0.81 at rest and will increase with exercise to reach values in excess of 1.0, as the athlete reaches exhaustion. During recovery, R can be elevated to values of 1.5, or higher; this peak value tends to correspond to the peak appearance of lactate in the blood. When R values exceed 1.0, the body is relying, at least par-

tially, on anaerobic metabolism, and the R value no longer provides an accurate estimate of the substrate being metabolized.

The major source of energy, or the fuel for muscular work, was previously thought to be carbohydrates, with fats serving only in a reserve, or secondary, role. It is now evident that fat is a major energy source during exercise. It appears that in aerobic work, where the intensity is below the athlete's endurance capacity, from 50–70 percent of the energy used is provided by fats; the longer the duration, the higher the contribution of fat. With high levels of work, particularly in anaerobic work, the primary source of energy is from carbohydrates. The composition of the diet can have a rather remarkable influence on athletic performance, and this will be discussed in great detail in Chapter 10, Ergogenic Aids.

Anaerobic Threshold. While $\dot{V}O_2$ max is regarded as the best physiological criterion of endurance capacity, it does have certain limitations. With a group of endurance athletes, it is not possible to predict the order of finish in an endurance race by using only the $\dot{V}O_2$ max values. Likewise, correlations between endurance-running performance tests, e.g., Cooper's 12-min run, the Balke 1.5-mi run, the 2-mi run, and $\dot{V}O_2$ max are only moderately high (r = 0.40 to 0.89), indicating that there is more to a good performance than just $\dot{V}O_2$ max. It is also well documented that $\dot{V}O_2$ max will increase with physical training for only twelve to eighteen months, at which time it plateaus, even with continued, higher-intensity training. The individual can still improve his running times for the various distances after the point at which the $\dot{V}O_2$ max stops increasing. Thus, performance can improve even though $\dot{V}O_2$ max has reached its peak.

Figure 2–14 illustrates one possible explanation for this apparent inconsistency. The athlete is able to improve his performance even after he reaches an upper limit or ceiling for his $\dot{V}O_2$ max by developing the ability to work at a higher percentage of his capacity for prolonged periods of time. Costill has found that most marathon runners complete the 26.2 mi with an average pace that corresponds to 65–80 percent of their $\dot{V}O_2$ max. Derek Clayton, holder of the best time in the world for the marathon (2 hr, 8 min, 33 sec), had a measured $\dot{V}O_2$ max below that which would normally be expected on the basis of his world-record performance (69.7 ml/kg × min). Costill, however, found that Clayton was able to work at 86 percent of his $\dot{V}O_2$ max when running on the treadmill at his racing pace, a value considerably higher than the average world-class marathoner, and a value that probably accounts for his world-record running ability. It would appear that both $\dot{V}O_2$ max and the percentage of $\dot{V}O_2$ max that the athlete can maintain for a prolonged period of time are the determining factors in performance. This could explain the lower-than-expected correlations between $\dot{V}O_2$ max and endurance performance tests, and the ability of the athlete to improve performance while $\dot{V}O_2$ max plateaus.

Recently, investigators have introduced a new parameter that may be closely related to the percentage of the capacity that one can maintain for a prolonged period of time. Wasserman has termed this parameter, the

FIGURE 2–14

Influence of physical training on maximal oxygen consumption (maximal aerobic power), as well as on the fraction of maximal oxygen consumption that one can maintain during prolonged work. (From P. O. Åstrand and K. Rodahl, Textbook of Work Physiology. *New York: McGraw-Hill Book Co., 1970. Reproduced by permission of the publisher.)*

anaerobic threshold. It is defined as that point in an exercise of increasing intensity at which the body starts increasing anaerobic metabolism above resting levels and at which blood lactate concentration starts to increase. With the proper instrumentation, this threshold can be assessed very accurately by observing the ventilation, carbon dioxide production, and respiratory exchange ratio responses to exercise. All three processes increase linearly with increases in the level of work up to the point of the anaerobic threshold, at which time their rate of change increases. This increase in rate of change results in greater nonlinear increases in ventilation, carbon dioxide production, and respiratory exchange ratio while the increases in the level of work remain linear (Figure 2–15). The anaerobic threshold can be expressed in terms of the percentage of $\dot{V}O_2$ max at which it occurs. An anaerobic threshold of 60 percent of $\dot{V}O_2$ max would indicate, theoretically, a greater performance potential for the same $\dot{V}O_2$ max than an anaerobic threshold of 45 percent of $\dot{V}O_2$ max. The higher percentage indicates that the individual can work at relatively higher levels of metabolism before having to rely on the inefficient, limiting process of anaerobic metabolism. The concept is an intriguing one and will be the topic of considerable research in the near future.

Energy Cost of Various Activities.   The amount of energy expended for different activities will vary considerably, depending on the intensity of the exercise, if factors such as duration and environmental conditions are kept constant. Many activities have been evaluated to determine the associated metabolic cost. This is usually accomplished by monitoring the oxygen consumption during exercise to determine an average oxygen cost per unit of time, which can then be converted to an energy expenditure in Kcalories/min. These values typically ignore the anaerobic aspects of exercise, since the oxygen debt is seldom used in these calculations. This is an important point, for an activity that costs a total of 300 Kcalories to perform may result in an additional 100 Kcalories expenditure above resting, during the recovery

FIGURE 2–15

Illustration of the anaerobic threshold. [From James A. Davis, "Validity, Reproducibility and Effect of Endurance Training on the Anaerobic Threshold in College-Age Males." (Unpublished doctoral dissertation, University of California, Davis, 1975) Reproduced by permission of the author.]

period; thus, the total cost of the activity would be 400, not 300, Kcalories.

The body requires 0.2 to 0.35 liters of

oxygen/min just to satisfy its resting energy requirements. This would amount to 1–1.8 Kcalories/min, 60–108 Kcalories/hour, or 1,440–2,600 Kcalories/day. Obviously, any increased activity above resting levels will add to the projected daily expenditure. Sedentary adult men and women of average weight will have an average caloric expenditure of 2,700 and 1,850 Kcalories/day, respectively. Football linemen, during preseason conditioning sessions, where two or three practice sessions are held per day, have been found to consume more than 10,000 calories/day. The range of values for total daily caloric expenditure are, thus, quite varied and will depend on factors such as sex, age, weight, environment, and activity levels.

Sport activities differ with respect to their energy cost. Some require levels of energy expenditure that are only slightly greater than those at rest. Others have levels that are so high that they can be maintained for only short periods of time, e.g., sprinting. With regard to total energy expenditure, the total duration of the activity must be considered, in addition to the level of energy expenditure. While approximately 29 Kcalories/min are expended while sprinting at a speed of 15.5 *miles per hour* (mph), this level of activity can be endured for only brief periods of time. Jogging at a 7 mph pace (approximately 8½ min/mi) will result in an expenditure of only 14.5 calories/min, or only half of that expended in running at 15.5 mph, but jogging can be maintained for a considerably longer period of time, resulting in a greater total expenditure of energy. This is an important consideration for anyone contemplating the use of exercise to reduce weight. Table 2–2 provides an estimate of energy expenditure for various activities on the basis of the average mature male with an approximate body weight of 154 lb. Since most activities involve moving the body mass, these figures will vary considerably with the weight, age, and sex of the athlete. The relative relationships of energy cost per activity, however, can be accurately evaluated.

TABLE 2–2. Typical Energy Expenditure for Various Physical Activities, Calculated on the Basis of A 154-Pound Man*

Activity	Kcalories/ min	Kcalories/ hour
Sleeping	1.2	70
Sitting	1.7	100
Standing	1.8	110
Walking		
2.0 mph	3.2	192
3.5 mph	5.0	300
4.0 mph	5.8	348
Jogging–Running		
7.0 mph	14.5	870
9.0 mph	16.8	1,008
12.0 mph	21.7	1,300
15.5 mph	28.8	1,728
Bicycling		
7 mph	5.0	300
10 mph	7.5	450
13 mph	11.1	666
Horseshoes	4.0	240
Baseball (except pitcher)	4.7	282
pitcher	6.5	390
Calisthenics	4.7	282
Dancing		
moderate	4.2	252
vigorous	7.0	420
Archery	5.0	300
Golf	5.0	300
Swimming		
Breast stroke, 1 mph	6.8	410
Crawl stroke, 1 mph	7.0	420
Back Stroke, 1 mph	8.3	500
Tennis	7.1	425
Weight Training	8.2	492
Basketball	8.6	516
Mountain Climbing	10.0	600
Football (American)	10.2	612
Squash	10.2	612
Fencing	10.5	630
Handball	11.0	660
Rowing, 3.5 mph	11.0	660
Gymnastics	11.5	690
Wrestling	13.1	790

* Adapted from L. E. Morehouse and A. T. Miller, Jr. *Physiology of Exercise.* 6th ed. St. Louis: C. V. Mosby Co., 1971.

Body Fluids and Temperature Regulation

As the length of the exercise period is increased, body fluid changes and temperature regulation become important to the efficient performance of the athlete. In activities that require several minutes or less, body-fluid changes and temperature regulation are of little or no practical importance. For the football player or the marathon runner, however, these processes are critically important, even to the point of being necessary for survival. Deaths have occurred during or as a result of various sport activities due to problems of dehydration (water deficiency) and hyperthermia (overheating).

Body Fluids. The body is divided into two major fluid compartments, the intracellular and extracellular compartments. The intracellular-fluid compartment includes the fluid that exists within all of the cells in the body. The extracellular fluid compartment includes the plasma volume of the blood and the interstitial fluid, or that fluid that lies outside of and bathes the cells. The fluid volume is slightly larger than the water volume since fluid volume includes the water volume and those substances that are suspended or dissolved in the water.

With exercise, there is a loss of nonprotein fluid almost immediately from the plasma volume to the interstitial and intracellular fluid spaces, which is probably the result of increased hydrostatic pressure within the vascular system. The increase in blood pressure forces water from the vascular compartment to the nonvascular compartment. Up to a 10–20 percent or greater reduction in plasma volume can occur with prolonged work. If the exercise intensity or the environmental conditions are such that the individual starts to sweat, additional fluid loss can be expected from the plasma volume, although the major source of fluid for sweating is from the interstitial and intracellular spaces. This reduction in plasma volume with exercise results in an increased concentration of red blood cells, serum proteins, and hemoglobin. However, this is a relative, not an absolute, increase, as was mentioned earlier in this chapter.

The reduction in plasma volume is likely to be detrimental to performance. For long-duration activities, where heat loss is a problem, the total flow of blood to the active tissues must be such that an increasingly higher percentage of blood can be diverted to the skin to reduce body heat. If the plasma volume is already reduced by the hydrostatic pressure increase, the reduction will have a negative influence on the performance of that activity. Also, the reduced plasma volume will result in more concentrated red blood cells, thus, increasing the viscosity of the blood. Recent evidence suggests that an increased blood viscosity can limit the oxygen-transporting ability of the blood.

As sweating continues, there will be a loss of interstitial and intracellular fluid. This will create an increased osmotic pressure (higher concentration of solids) in the interstitial fluid, which will cause even more fluid from the plasma volume to diffuse into the interstitial fluid. While intracellular fluid volume is impossible to measure directly and accurately, research suggests that there is also a fluid loss from the intracellular fluid and even from the red blood cells, which may shrink.

Temperature Regulation. As the body starts to exercise, the rate of metabolism increases in direct proportion to the intensity of the exercise. The body, like a machine, is not 100 percent efficient, since it uses more energy than is actually needed for the exercise. The mechanical efficiency of the human body varies from ten percent or less for activities such as swimming to over thirty percent for some other types of activities. The remaining energy that is not used in the process of muscular contraction is lost in the form of heat. This creates a considerable heat load within the body, which necessitates physiological adjustments to reduce body temperature. Exercise in a hot climate, particularly in one with elevated humidity, places additional heat stress on the body, and further temperature adjustments must be made.

The major physiological adjustment that promotes heat loss from the body is the shunting of blood to the periphery, as is evidenced by the red skin of an overheated athlete. When blood is brought to the body's surface, heat is lost more efficiently by convection and radiation. Convection is the process by which heat is lost or transferred from a body to a moving liquid or gas, e.g., cool air passing over the warm body. Radiation is the process through which heat is lost through electromagnetic waves. Two other forms of heat loss are important in the total attempt to regulate body temperature: conduction and evaporation. Conduction is the process in which heat is lost by direct contact with a cooler object or medium. Evaporation is a major form of heat loss at high body temperatures in a relatively dry environment. When water evaporates, 580 Kcalories of heat are lost for every liter of water that is evaporated. As one sweats, the sweat evaporates and cools the surrounding skin.

Body temperature is controlled in the brain by the hypothalamus and the adjacent preoptic area. At rest, even under considerably varying environmental conditions, body temperature is maintained at a relatively constant value of approximately 98.6° F. Temperature receptors in the skin assist the hypothalamus in maintaining this temperature constant. With exercise, body temperature increases in proportion to the intensity and duration of activity. Moderate exercise can raise the body temperature to over 100° F, and in severe exercise, temperatures can exceed 106° F.

Problems of temperature regulation become critical when the surrounding temperature equals or exceeds the skin temperature (approximately 92–93° F). Convection and radiation are ineffective avenues of heat loss and actually become avenues of heat gain when the surrounding temperature exceeds the skin temperature. The body must then rely on evaporative heat loss. This works well as long as the air immediately surrounding the body is dry, i.e., of low humidity. However, when it becomes saturated with water, the last major avenue of heat loss is closed and exercise must stop. Frequently, the micro-environment created by clothing, e.g., the football uniform or a rubberized sweat suit, can result in surrounding temperatures that are above the skin temperature and in air that is fully saturated with water vapor, creating a potentially dangerous situation. Problems of temperature regulation will be discussed in detail in Chapter 9, Environmental Factors and Athletic Performance.

Exercise in the cold presents certain problems, but these are not nearly as severe or frequent as those that occur in the heat. In the cold, one can always wear additional clothing so that heat that is normally lost in the body's metabolism is used to maintain body temperature. In addition, the blood vessels to and near the surface of the skin constrict, shunting blood away from the periphery and back to the center of the body to conserve the body's internal heat. Thus, body temperature during exercise in the cold is usually controlled effectively and efficiently.

Fluid Replacement. In addition to the need for adequate body fluid to maintain the sweating mechanisms necessary for temperature regulation in warm or hot climates as discussed above, it is apparent that fluid should be replaced during exercise. Costill has suggested that 200–300 ml of fluid be ingested every fifteen minutes during prolonged bouts of exercise. This fluid should be relatively low in sugar and electrolyte content, since high levels decrease the absorption of fluid from the stomach and intestine. While glucose and electrolyte replacement are important, the replacement of the lost fluid appears to be of much greater importance for the purposes of fluid balance and temperature regulation. The quantity of fluid ingested should be approximately equal to the quantity of fluid lost. The body can lose up to 1–2 liters/hour under extreme conditions of exercise and environment, thus, replacement of the fluid during the activity is extremely important.

GENERAL SUMMARY

The field of exercise and sport physiology has advanced considerably since pioneering efforts began in the 1920's, although there is still considerably more knowledge to be gained than is presently available. The human body has demonstrated a remarkable physiological adaptability to the stress of exercise. Due to the limitations of field testing, these physiological adaptations are normally measured in the laboratory while the individual exercises on a stationary piece of equipment, such as a treadmill or bicycle ergometer.

The nervous system calls the body into action, either through conscious, central nervous system control or through sensory reflex action. Nerve impulses pass from the central nervous system to the motor neurons to activate the appropriate motor units. While strength is a function of the number of motor units activated simultaneously, endurance depends on adequate circulation to these active units. The cardiovascular system is, therefore, involved in supplying the working muscles with the necessary oxygen and nutrients and in removing metabolic waste products, in addition to serving as the body's cooling system in the regulation of body temperature. As the intensity of the exercise increases, the heart rate and stroke volume increase, although stroke volume tends to reach its peak and plateau at approximately 40–60 percent of the individual's capacity. The changes in the heart rate and stroke volume result in a large increase in cardiac output, allowing an increased blood flow to the active tissues. The increase in cardiac output is of much greater magnitude than the decrease in vascular resistance due to the dilation of the vessels in the active tissue. The net result is an increase in the systolic blood pressure with little or no change in the diastolic pressure. All of these changes are in direct proportion to the increase in exercise intensity.

The arterial–venous oxygen difference widens with increasing exercise intensity, indicating a greater extraction of oxygen at the tissue level. Plasma volume is reduced and the blood becomes hemoconcentrated. Blood pH decreases after exercise exceeds fifty percent of the individual's capacity, a change that is related to the appearance of lactate in the blood. Ventilation volume is increased to help meet the demands for increased oxygen consumption and carbon dioxide elimination. This is accomplished by an increase in both tidal volume and respiration rate, the increases again being directly related to the intensity of the exercise. Lung-diffusion capacity increases to facilitate oxygen loading, and the ventilation–perfusion ratio becomes optimized as the upper regions of the lung are better ventilated and better perfused with blood.

Metabolism also increases in direct proportion to the intensity of exercise, as reflected by the level of oxygen consumed. The peak or maximal level of oxygen consumed at or prior to reaching the point of exhaustion is referred to as the maximal oxygen consumption ($\dot{V}O_2$ max) and reflects the body's overall endurance capacity or cardiorespiratory fitness. Oxygen debt reflects anaerobic metabolism. The anaerobic threshold may play an important role in determining the individual's endurance performance potential when used in conjunction with his $\dot{V}O_2$ max value.

Last, fluid volume and temperature regulation are important aspects of prolonged exercise. Plasma volume may decrease by 20 percent or more as sweating reduces both plasma volume and interstitial fluid. The body relies on convection, radiation, conduction, and evaporation for heat loss to maintain body temperature. Evaporation appears to be the most critical avenue of heat loss in intense, prolonged exercise or in exercise in hot environments. Adequate fluid replacement during the activity is essential for both fluid balance and temperature regulation.

REFERENCES

ANDERSON, K. L.; SHEPHERD, R. J.; DENOLIN, H.; VARNAUSKAS, E.; and MASIRONI, R. *Fundamentals of Exercise Testing.* Geneva: World Health Organization, 1971.

ÅSTRAND, P. O., and RODAHL, K. *Textbook of Work Physiology.* New York: McGraw-Hill Book Co., 1970.

COSTILL, D. L. "Physiology of Marathon Running." *J. Amer. Med. Assoc.* 221 (1972): 1024–29.

COSTILL, D. L. "Muscular Exhaustion During Distance Running." *Physician and Sportsmedicine.* 2 (1974): 36–41.

DE VRIES, H. A. *Physiology of Exercise for Physical Education and Athletics.* 2nd ed. Dubuque, Iowa: William C. Brown Co. 1974.

FALLS, H. B., ed. *Exercise Physiology.* New York: Academic Press, 1968.

JOHNSON, W. R., and BUSKIRK, E. R., eds. *Science and Medicine of Exercise and Sport.* 2nd ed. New York: Harper and Row, 1974.

KARPOVICH, P. V., and SINNING, W. E. *Physiology of Muscular Activity.* 7th ed. Philadelphia: W. B. Saunders Co., 1971.

MERTON, P. A. "Voluntary Strength and Fatigue." *J. Physiol.* 123 (1954): 553–64.

MOREHOUSE, L. E., and MILLER, A. T. *Physiology of Exercise.* 6th ed. St. Louis: C. V. Mosby Co., 1971.

SHEPHERD, R. J. *Endurance Fitness.* Toronto: University of Toronto Press, 1969.

WASSERMAN, K., and McILROY, M. B. "Detecting the Threshold of Anaerobic Metabolism in Cardiac Patients During Exercise." *Am. J. Cardiol.* 14 (1964): 844–52.

WILMORE, J. H., and NORTON, A. C. *The Heart and Lungs at Work.* Schiller Park, Illinois: Beckman Instruments, 1974.

3
Chronic Adaptations to Exercise

INTRODUCTION

The preceding chapter focused on the physiological adaptability of man to an acute bout of exercise. The present chapter looks at those changes that result from chronic exercise, i.e., physical training. These are changes that develop slowly after repeated bouts of exercise and that result in lasting physiological adaptations.

FACTORS INFLUENCING THE CHRONIC RESPONSE TO EXERCISE

Alterations resulting from chronic exercise will depend in magnitude on six basic factors.

· Type of training activity
· Frequency of participation
· Duration of each training session
· Intensity of performance
· Duration of the total program
· Initial level of fitness of the subjects

Each of these factors is of considerable importance and will be discussed independently.

There are many ways in which physical exercise can be performed, e.g., bowling, golf, calisthenics, tennis, weight training, bicycling, and jogging. These are just a few of many forms. All activities, however, basically fall into one or a combination of several major categories: (a) flexibility or joint loosening; (b) strength and power; (c) speed and agility;

(d) endurance; and (e) relaxation. The types of activities or exercises that are selected will depend to a large extent on the purpose of training. The forty-five-year-old who wants to "get back into shape" will emphasize endurance activities because of their ability to improve function of the cardiovascular and respiratory systems, both systems being susceptible to chronic, disabling and death-causing diseases. The young shot putter, however, would stress strength and power activities, with some attention to activities that would also develop his speed and agility. Thus, the outcome of the conditioning program will be determined largely by the type of activity or activities that are selected.

The frequency of participation influences the magnitude of change or improvement. However, the change is highly dependent on the interaction between frequency, duration, and intensity. The forty-five-year-old "fitness seeker" can improve considerably with a training frequency of three days per week. Training programs of two days per week produce desirable changes, but they are substantially less than the changes that are produced by training programs of three-or-more days per week. Training more than four days per week will result in further gains, but, generally, they will not be worth the additional time invested, i.e., the degree of improvement decreases to a point where a great deal of time must be invested to achieve small, additional gains. Thus, for the "fitness seeker," three to four days per week appear to be optimal. For the competitive athlete, the small gain attained by working out an additional two or three days (a total of six or seven days per week) may be necessary, since it could mean the difference between first and second place.

The duration of each training session will depend largely on the purpose of the training program, i.e., for competition or for health and fitness, and on the type of activity. A minimum investment of twenty to thirty min per day is adequate to accomplish a good training response for general fitness. For the athlete, one to two hr on the track or field or five hr in the water might be necessary to prepare for the higher levels of competition. Similar to frequency, the magnitude of the change is dependent on the total time spent in training; the more time in training, the greater the degree of change.

The intensity at which the activity is performed is probably the most critical of the various factors that dictate the magnitude of change. Cardiovascular endurance changes begin to occur once the individual starts exercising at fifty percent of his capacity or above. This appears to be a threshold below which changes will not occur. Again, the higher the intensity, the greater the change. With strength training, the muscle apparently must be taken to fatigue or near fatigue for significant strength changes to occur. Unlike cardiovascular endurance, training at 50–70 percent intensity will not result in any major gains in strength, although gains in muscular endurance might be found at these submaximal levels. The level of intensity needed to maximize gains in cardiovascular endurance has not been clearly established. Good improvement is possible both with interval training, where the intensity is close to maximum and rest or recovery periods are interspersed, and with long, slow distance (LSD) training, where an intensity of 75–90 percent of maximum is maintained for long periods of time. At the present time, neither of these two extremes appears to provide a distinct advantage over the other, although additional research in this area is certainly necessary.

The duration of the total program will obviously make a difference as to how much change one might expect from a specific training regimen. From Figure 2–14 in Chapter 2, it can be clearly seen that the duration of training will substantially influence the improvement in VO_2 max. Assuming that each individual has an innate, finite limit, or ceiling, that he can reach but not exceed, it seems reasonable to postulate that the closer the individual comes to attaining that limit, the more difficult it will be to elicit change, i.e., the rate of improvement will not be as great. As an example of this limitation, to train a 13.0 sec/100-yd-dash sprinter to lower his time to 11.5 sec may take only three to six months, but to take a 9.4 sec/100-yd-dash sprinter and lower his time to 9.2 sec may require a lifetime, or it may never occur. For every type of training program, the time needed to reach the peak or level of best performance will vary, according to which of the particular fitness components are being trained. $\dot{V}O_2$ max (endurance) may reach the individual's highest maximum, or peak, within six months to a year. With the anaerobic threshold (speed and endurance), it may take several years to reach the ultimate value. For strength and power, it may take many years to achieve the individual's best efforts. Unfortunately, little research has been conducted in this area. The present views are based largely on observations of how long it takes successful athletes to reach their peak performance.

Just as the time that is required to reach the level of peak performance varies, the subject's initial level of fitness also appears to have a marked influence on his potential for change. It has been postulated that the closer one is to his ultimate performance, the more difficult it is to make substantial improvements. This is illustrated in Figure 3–1. Unfortunately, even though this postulate is sound, it is difficult to prove, since everyone has a unique, genetically determined, upper limit that he can reach. To assess this value would be extremely difficult. Using endurance capacity for illustrative purposes, it is clear that an individual with a $\dot{V}O_2$ max of 30 ml/kg $\times$ min should have both a greater absolute and a greater rela-

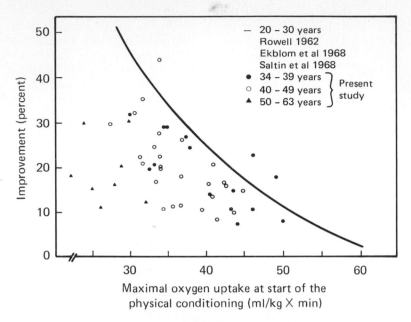

FIGURE 3–1

Percentage improvement in $\dot{V}O_2$ max relative to the initial level of fitness. (From B. Saltin et al., Scand. J. Clin. Lab. Invest. 24, 323–34. Oslo: Universitetsforlaget, 1969. Reproduced by permission of the publisher.)

tive improvement in $\dot{V}O_2$ max than an individual of the same age who has an initial $\dot{V}O_2$ max of 50 ml/kg × min, providing that the two individuals are given the same duration, frequency, and relative intensity of training. Training at 75 percent capacity, three days/week, 30 min/day, for 20 weeks may improve the first individual from 30 to 40 ml/kg × min (10 ml/kg × min or 33.3 percent improvement), while the latter individual may improve from 50 to 55 ml/kg × min (5 ml/kg × min or 10 percent improvement). However, a third individual trained in the same manner could vidual's ultimate potential or even his basic make it extremely difficult to predict an individual's potential for improvement. While these illustrations are limited to endurance capacity, similar principles apply to each of the other areas, while the individual who improved from 50 to 65 may have had an ultimate ceiling of 85 ml/kg × min. Thus, individual differences improved from 50 to 55 may have had an ultimate increase his $\dot{V}O_2$ max from an initial level of

50 to a final level of 65 (15 ml/kg × min or 30 percent improvement). The individual that mate ceiling or capacity of 58 ml/kg × min, e.g., strength, power, and speed.

BONE, CONNECTIVE TISSUE, AND NEUROMUSCULAR CHANGES WITH TRAINING

It appears that chronic exercise is necessary to maintain normal bone strength and function. Studies in which subjects are placed in bed for prolonged periods of time show a substantial loss of calcium and phosphorus from the bone. Lack of exercise or activity is associated with a bone structure that is deficient in mineral content, a condition that results in weak and brittle bones. It is not at all clear whether physical training will make bones any stronger or larger than bones that undergo only normal levels of activity, e.g., walking and lifting. Some evidence suggests that high levels of activity, particularly those that involve carrying or lifting heavy objects, may increase the breadth or width of bones with little or no effect on their length. Even during periods of bone growth, chronic exercise has not been found to facilitate long-bone growth or to increase height.

Chronic exercise does have a facilitative effect on cartilages, tendons, and ligaments. Cartilages appear to increase in thickness with additional exercise. This provides a better cushion, or shock absorber, for jarring types of activities, e.g., running or jumping, and results in a better, more-functional joint through better articulation of the bones that form the joint. Ligaments and tendons become stronger and larger with chronic exercise, thus, providing a greater degree of protection to the joints. While stronger ligaments and tendons will not give absolute protection against injury, the incidence and severity of injury should be greatly reduced.

Changes in muscular strength with chronic, weight training exercises have been well documented. Different weight training methods and protocols have quite different results. This aspect of chronic exercise will be discussed in extensive detail in Chapter 4, Strength, Power and Muscular Endurance. It is possible to achieve sixty to ninety percent, or even greater, gains in strength from chronic weight training over a three to six month period. This increase may, or may not, be associated with gains in muscle size (*hypertrophy*). It is well documented that extended periods of inactivity or limited usage will result in a loss of muscle size or mass (*atrophy*). This is best illustrated by the shrinkage of muscle that occurs when a broken limb is placed in a cast to immobilize it and facilitate healing. When the limb is healed and the cast removed, exercise is necessary for the atrophied limb to regain muscle mass. Weight training in normal limbs, however, does not necessarily involve extensive muscle hypertrophy. For example, studies show that women who weight train increase their strength substantially but have very limited muscle hypertrophy. Hypertrophy is probably a by-product, but not a necessary consequence,

of these strength gains, i.e., strength gains can occur in the absence of hypertrophy. Thus, hypertrophy cannot be the cause of gains in muscular strength. This leads to the discussion of two separate, and possibly unrelated, aspects of chronic, weight-training exercises: hypertrophy and the mechanisms responsible for strength increases.

Hypertrophy, as mentioned above, is not a necessary consequence of weight training and does not always accompany gains in strength. Since weight training of males, but not of females, is usually associated with hypertrophy, it has been suggested that the predominantly male hormone, testosterone, determines the degree of muscular hypertrophy that will occur. Individuals with higher natural levels of testosterone should experience considerably more hypertrophy than those with low levels. Females generally have very low levels of testosterone; thus, they are less inclined to gain muscle bulk. It has been observed that the size of muscles in some females tends to increase with weight training. It is felt that this is probably due to the presence of higher, naturally occurring levels of testosterone. New methods of measuring testosterone levels in the blood will soon make it possible to confirm this theory.

Hypertrophy must result from basic changes in the structure of the muscle. Transient hypertrophy ("pumping up the muscle") is that increase in muscle bulk or size that occurs with an acute or single bout of exercise. This is largely the result of fluid accumulation, or edema, in the muscle, a condition that is probably caused by fluid being forced from the vascular to the interstitial spaces. Chronic hypertrophy, however, is a totally different phenomenon. It is the result of changes in the structural components of muscle. It can be explained as either an increase in the number of muscle fibers (*hyperplasia*) or an increase in the size of the muscle fibers. Studies conducted on both animals and humans suggest that hypertrophy is the result of an increase in the size of the individual fibers rather than an increase in the number of fibers. The number of fibers appears to be established at birth and probably does not change from that time to full maturity. Although several recent studies have indicated that under extreme conditions, in certain animals, muscle fibers may split and increase in actual number, the implications of these findings for humans are not clear at this time.

Hypertrophy appears to be largely, if not totally, the result of increases in the size of the individual fibers. It has been shown that there is an increase in both the length and diameter of the individual fibers, due to an increase in the number of sarcomeres and myofibrils, respectively. This is apparently the result of either or both an increase in the actin and myosin content of the enlarged fiber. While most research on animals and humans supports the increased fiber size theory of muscular hypertrophy, recent evidence of possible fiber splitting and increase in fiber number makes it impossible to discount the possibility of hyperplasia, or increased fiber number.

If an increase in muscle size does not explain gains in strength, what explanation can be given? In Chapter 2, it was suggested that strength may be more a function of the central nervous system than of the muscle itself. Man apparently does not have the ability to recruit all motor units within a given muscle simultaneously. One possible explanation is that each motor unit is controlled by a number of different neurons or interneurons that produce both excitatory and inhibitory impulses. The final decision to contract or to remain in a relaxed state depends on the summation of these many impulses. If the inhibitory impulses equal or exceed the excitatory impulses, no contraction will occur. If the excitatory impulses exceed the inhibitory impulses, contraction will occur. Gains in strength may result from the blocking or reduction of the number or frequency of inhibitory impulses, which allows more motor units to contract simultaneously. This theory, while unproven, is one of the few ways in which superhuman feats of strength that occur instantaneously, without prior practice or training, can be accounted for.

The ability to change one muscle fiber type to another with physical conditioning is a topic of current interest. Based on the simple classification system of slow-twitch and fast-twitch fibers (See Chapter 1), it appears that neither heavy strength and power (anaerobic) training nor endurance (aerobic) training will alter the basic fiber types. As an example, an individual who possesses 75 percent slow-twitch fibers and 25 percent fast-twitch fibers will have these same proportions even after intensive anaerobic training, which, theoretically, would promote fast-twitch fibers, if fibers could change characteristics. The fibers will, however, begin to take on certain characteristics of the opposite fiber type if the training is of the opposite kind, though actual conversion from one fiber type to the other appears to be impossible. This has led researchers to postulate that if fiber types are established genetically, it might be possible to perform muscle biopsies on young children to determine their relative fiber types. In this way, children could be placed in activities in which the muscular demands were matched to their relative fiber types. While this idea is intriguing from the scientific viewpoint, it is not practical and would tend to destroy the fun and enjoyment of sport.

CARDIOVASCULAR CHANGES WITH TRAINING

Training causes a number of changes that improve the transportation function of the cardiovascular system during exercise. These changes, which occur following endurance conditioning programs, will be discussed under several major categories.

Heart Rate

The heart rate at rest will decrease markedly as a result of endurance conditioning. For a sedentary adult with an initial resting heart rate of 80 beats/min, the resting heart rate will decrease by approximately one beat/min for each week of training during the first few weeks. Following ten weeks of modest endur-

FIGURE 3–2

Response of submaximal heart rate to a constant level of work, following a period of bed rest and a subsequent period of retraining. (From B. Saltin et al., Response to Exercise after Bed Rest and after Training, *American Heart Association Monograph, No. 23 (1968):* 20. Reproduced by permission of the American Heart Association, Inc.)

ance training, the resting rate should drop to 70 beats/min. Highly conditioned endurance athletes, typically, have resting heart rates of 40 beats/min or lower, and, occasionally, values lower than 30 beats/minute.

During exercise, the heart rate will be less for the same level of work as the individual becomes more highly conditioned. Figure 3–2 illustrates changes in heart rates for a constant level of work in five men who underwent twenty days of deconditioning (total bedrest) followed by sixty days of retraining. The submaximal heart rate for that constant level of work provides an excellent insight into the functional status of the cardiovascular system for each of these five subjects, who were studied longitudinally. Unfortunately, the heart rate from a single submaximal test on any one individual provides relatively little insight into the status of the cardiovascular system of that individual in comparison with others, since people of identical cardiovascular fitness will respond with substantially different heart rates to the same level of work. Compar-

ing the individual with himself at varying points in time, however, provides valuable information about any changes that might be taking place within that individual as a result of changes in activity patterns. It is not unusual to observe a 20 to 40 beat/min decrease in submaximal heart rate at a standardized work load following a six-month training program of moderate intensity. Since the work performed by the heart has a high correlation with the resting and exercise heart rates, the reduced submaximal heart rate indicates that the heart is working more efficiently, i.e., doing less work.

At maximal levels of exercise, the maximal heart rate will remain approximately the same following endurance training. Several studies have suggested that there is a slight reduction in HRmax in those individuals who have HRmax values in excess of 180 beats/min. There is also a tendency for highly conditioned endurance athletes to have HRmax values lower than untrained individuals of the same age.

55

The heart rate recovers from exercise at a much faster rate following endurance conditioning. This is true following exercise such as standardized, submaximal work bouts as well as maximal bouts of work. Under both submaximal and maximal conditions, there is a faster return of the heart rate to the pre-exercise level. The faster heart-rate recovery following endurance training has led to the use of the pulse rate recovery as an index of cardiovascular fitness, i.e., the more fit individual will recover faster from a standardized level of work. As was mentioned above in the case of the submaximal heart rate during standardized bouts of exercise, the heart rate recovery curve is an excellent way to quantify changes in cardiovascular conditioning of an individual at varying points in time, but it is not a very accurate means of comparing one individual with another. Too many factors other than cardiovascular fitness are involved when absolute heart rate recovery values are compared among different people.

Stroke Volume, Cardiac Output, and Heart Volume

Changes in stroke volume are closely related to the changes in heart rate that result from training. At rest, the stroke volume is substantially higher following an endurance training program. Similarly, stroke volume is higher at submaximal, standardized levels of work and also at maximal levels of work. This increase is probably due to a more complete filling of the heart during the period of diastole, which results in a greater ventricular blood volume. In addition, the walls of the left ventricle tend to hypertrophy, which indicates a greater ventricular muscle mass, and the power of contraction (contractility) is increased, i.e., the ventricle contracts more forcefully, reducing the volume of the residual blood that remains following the contraction. Thus, a stronger heart and the availability of a greater blood volume appear to account for these increases in resting, submaximal, and maximal stroke volumes. In turn, it appears that the increased stroke volume allows the heart to beat at a slower rate, both at rest and during submaximal levels of exercise. Resting stroke volumes can range from 70 ml for the untrained to 90 ml for the trained and up to 130 ml for the highly trained, endurance athlete. Likewise, maximal stroke volumes will vary from 125 ml to 150 ml and up to 220 ml for individuals in the same three classifications of training status.

Cardiac output is not greatly changed either at rest or for standardized levels of submaximal work following training. For the same metabolic workload, e.g., 1.5 liters of oxygen/min, there may even be a slight decrease in the cardiac output, due to a more efficient extraction of oxygen, i.e., larger $a-\bar{v}O_2$ diff or to better mechanical or metabolic efficiency. At maximal levels of work, however, the cardiac output is increased considerably. This is the result of an improved maximal stroke volume, since HRmax changes very little, if at all. Maximal cardiac output ranges from 14–16 liters/min in sedentary to 20–25 liters for trained and up to values in excess of 40 liters/min in highly conditioned, large, endurance athletes.

The weight of the heart and the heart volume are both increased as a result of training. Figure 3–3 illustrates the changes in heart volume with inactivity (bedrest) and with activity (retraining). Cardiac muscle, like skeletal muscle, appears to undergo hypertrophy as a result of chronic endurance training. Once, there was great concern over the possible pathological consequences of cardiac hypertrophy induced by exercise, or "athlete's heart," as it was called. It is now recognized that this is a normal adaptation to chronic endurance training. The left ventricle, which does most of the work, is the chamber that is most affected.

Blood Flow, Blood Pressure, and Peripheral Vasculature

Blood flow through the muscles appears to be enhanced by endurance training. This could be due to an increased number of capillaries in the muscle, but recent evidence suggests

FIGURE 3–3

Changes in heart volume, following bed rest and a subsequent retraining program. (From B. Saltin et al., Response to Exercise after Bed Rest and after Training, *American Heart Association Monograph, No. 23 (1968): 16. Reproduced by permission of the American Heart Association, Inc.)*

that there is little or no change in the number of capillaries with training. However, since the muscle fibers tend to increase in size during training, the muscle fibers and capillaries are closer together, which results in a more favorable capillary-to-fiber ratio. It is also possible that the increased blood flow is the result of the existing capillaries in the muscle opening up wider to provide better perfusion of the muscle. Since endurance training also increases the blood volume, this latter adaptation can occur without severely compromising the venous return.

Arterial blood pressure is altered very little during standardized, submaximal levels of work as a result of chronic exercise. Likewise, maximal systolic and diastolic blood pressure are not substantially altered with training. Resting blood pressure, however, is reduced

with training in those individuals who are hypertensive or who have abnormally high resting blood pressures prior to training. Resting blood pressure appears to remain stable in those who are considered normal prior to training. Unfortunately, few studies have actually measured blood pressure directly before and after training. Most studies have used indirect measurement techniques which are difficult to interpret during exercise.

Blood Volume and Composition

Blood volume increases with endurance training. This is accomplished through an increase in both plasma volume and in red blood cell volume. However, the increase in plasma volume is so much greater than that of the red blood cell volume that the hematocrit (ratio of cell volume to total blood volume) actually decreases. It can decrease to the point where the trained athlete appears to be anemic on the basis of the relative concentration of red cells and hemoglobin. In fact, the total amount of hemoglobin and the total number of red blood cells (their absolute values) are typically above normal in the trained athlete, even though the relative values are below normal. This condition leads to a reduction in the viscosity of the blood, which facilitates its movement through the blood vessels. Recent research has pointed to the importance of a low blood viscosity for enhancing the delivery of oxygen to the active muscles.

The oxygen content of the arterial blood changes very little with training. Even though total hemoglobin is increased in absolute terms, the amount of hemoglobin per unit of blood is the same, or even slightly reduced. The a–$\bar{v}O_2$ diff, is changed, however, with training. This may, or may not be evident at rest or during submaximal levels of exercise, but the a–$\bar{v}O_2$ diff is widened or increased at maximal exercise, although the change is not of a very great magnitude. Since the arterial blood oxygen concentration is unaltered, this increase in a–$\bar{v}O_2$ diff implies a greater extraction of the available oxygen, which results in a lower oxygen content of the mixed venous blood.

Blood lactate levels are lower for each level of submaximal exercise following training but they increase to higher levels at the point of exhaustion. This suggests a greater tolerance to the pain associated with anaerobic metabolism. Unfortunately, changes in the anaerobic threshold that occur with training have yet to be evaluated. It is suspected that these, too, would increase, because of the lowered blood lactate levels at standardized submaximal levels of exercise.

RESPIRATORY ADAPTATIONS TO TRAINING

The static lung volumes change very little with training. There is a tendency for vital capacity to increase slightly and for residual volume to decrease by approximately the same amount.

Thus, the total lung capacity remains unchanged.

Pulmonary ventilation is unchanged at rest but is slightly reduced at standardized submaximal levels of work, indicating a greater efficiency of the respiratory system. Maximum pulmonary ventilation is increased substantially with training, typically increasing from 100 to 125 liters/min. Large, endurance athletes can exceed 240 liters/min. Tidal volume is unchanged at rest and during submaximal exercise but appears to increase at maximal levels of exercise. Respiratory rate is usually lowered at rest and during submaximal exercise, although the change is small. During maximal work, this rate is substantially increased.

Pulmonary blood flow appears to be increased following training, particularly the flow to the upper regions of the lung when the individual is sitting or standing. This results in increased perfusion of the lung. Lung diffusion is unaltered at rest and during submaximal exercise but is increased during maximal exercise. This increase is probably due to both the enhanced perfusion and ventilation of the lung, which provides a larger and more efficient area for gas exchange.

METABOLIC ADAPTATIONS TO TRAINING

Oxygen consumption at rest is either slightly decreased or unaltered following endurance training. At submaximal levels of exercise, $\dot{V}O_2$ is either unchanged or slightly reduced. A decrease in $\dot{V}O_2$ either at rest or during submaximal exercise, or at both times, would suggest an increase in metabolic efficiency or in mechanical efficiency. While this might be a postulated change, conclusions from studies are divided as to whether this change does, in fact, occur. It is possible that researchers in those studies that demonstrated a reduced $\dot{V}O_2$ for the same level of submaximal work following training may have observed a practice effect on their testing devices. If the subject is not allowed prior practice on the bicycle ergometer, treadmill, or other appropriate testing device, he may perform at a lower energy cost ($\dot{V}O_2$) the second time he performs on the same device simply because he is more relaxed, accustomed to performing on the device, and knows what is expected of him. Thus, the observed change may not be due to training.

$\dot{V}O_2$ max is increased substantially with endurance training. Increases of from 4–93 percent have been reported in the literature. An increase of 16–20 percent is more typical for the average individual who was sedentary prior to training and trained at 75 percent of his capacity, 3 times/week, 30 min/day, for 6 months. The $\dot{V}O_2$ max of a sedentary individual might increase from an initial value of 35 ml/kg × min to 42 ml/kg × min as a result of such a program. This is far below the values for world-class, endurance athletes, whose values generally range from 75–94 ml/kg × min.

The factors responsible for this change have been identified, but there is, at present, extensive controversy as to their relative importance. On the one hand, logical arguments have been raised and supported with documented research that suggest that a substantial portion of the increased $\dot{V}O_2$ max is the result of increases in the size and number of mitochondria, as well as an increase in the quantity of enzymes available in the mitochondria. On the other hand, it has been traditionally stated, with good supporting evidence, that the predominant factor in the $\dot{V}O_2$ max increase is the delivery of more oxygen to the active tissue through an increase in both maximal cardiac output and in local perfusion. The latter theory states that it is an inadequate oxygen supply or delivery that limits maximal performance; the former contends that, for the most part, the oxygen supply is adequate, but that the number, size, and content of the mitochondria are insufficient to utilize the available oxygen. Since both theories are supported by impressive research, it is probably a combination of the two that accounts for the total change. At the present time, it is impossible to determine which of the two is of greatest importance.

As was mentioned earlier in this chapter, and also in Chapter 2, Acute Responses to Exercise, the $\dot{V}O_2$ max will reach its peak value within six months to two years following the start of an endurance training program, even though the intensity of the training program and the individual workouts continue to increase. Yet, the athlete will still note improvements in his endurance performance after his $\dot{V}O_2$ max has leveled off and can no longer increase. Few athletes are able to run at a level of work that requires their $\dot{V}O_2$ max for more than a minute or two; thus, athletes who run for distances that require more time than this are competing at a level that is less than or below their $\dot{V}O_2$ max. As was mentioned in Chapter 2, marathon runners typically run for periods of time in excess of two hours and are able to maintain their pace at approximately 75–80 percent of their $\dot{V}O_2$ max. It is theorized that once the peak $\dot{V}O_2$ max is attained, further performance improvements are made by being able to compete at a higher percentage of the $\dot{V}O_2$ max. Some athletes are able to work for prolonged periods of time at levels approaching 90 percent of $\dot{V}O_2$ max.

As an example, a young runner who starts training with an initial $\dot{V}O_2$ max of 52.0 ml/kg × min reaches his genetically determined peak $\dot{V}O_2$ max of 71 ml/kg × min two years later and is unable to increase it to a higher level, even with more intensive workouts. At this point, the young runner is able to run at 75 percent of his $\dot{V}O_2$ max ($0.75 \times 71.0 = 53.3$ ml/kg × min) in a 6-mi race. Following an additional two years of intensive training, his $\dot{V}O_2$ max is exactly the same, but he is now able to compete at 88 percent of his capacity ($0.88 \times 71.0 = 62.5$ ml/kg × min). Obviously, by being able to sustain an oxygen consumption of 62.5 ml/kg × min, the runner will be able to run at a much faster pace than when he was able to sustain only 53.3 ml/kg × min. The mechanisms of this increased fractional utilization of the $\dot{V}O_2$ max can not be explained at the present time, but they undoubtedly concern increased metabolic efficiency and, possibly, are related to shifts in the blood lactate and anaerobic threshold responses. It is also known that oxygen-debt capacity increases with training, a change that could also be associated with this phenomenon.

BODY COMPOSITION ADAPTATIONS WITH TRAINING

For purposes of simplicity and the convenience of discussion, the total body weight will be divided into two components: the lean body weight and the fat weight. When working with body composition data, the following relationships are important.

total body weight =
        lean body weight + fat weight
relative lean weight (percent) =
    (lean body weight/total body weight) × 100
relative fat weight (percent) =
    (fat weight/total body weight) × 100

Lean body weight refers to that part of the total body weight that remains after all of the body fat is removed. It is composed of muscle, skin, bone, organs, and all other nonfat tissue. It can be assessed in a number of ways, but the most common is through densitometry, using the underwater weighing technique. The individual is weighed while totally submerged under water (Figure 3–4). The weight is measured when the individual has blown all of the air out of his lungs and only the residual volume remains. The residual volume is also assessed and is used to correct the underwater weight. In this way, the increased buoyancy afforded by the trapped residual volume is taken into account, also.

Archimedes determined, several thousand years ago, that a body immersed in a fluid experiences a loss in weight equal to the weight of the displaced fluid. In water, the weight of the displaced fluid can easily be converted to the volume of water that has been displaced; thus, the loss of weight in water is directly proportional to the volume of the water that is displaced or to the volume of the body that displaces that water. Since density is equal to the ratio of mass to volume, or

$$D_{body} = \frac{\text{mass or weight}_{body}}{\text{volume}_{body}},$$

it is relatively simple to calculate the density of an individual's body. The density of fat is known, and the density of the lean tissue of the body has been calculated to be a relatively

stable constant. By knowing the density of the body, of fat, and of the lean tissue, it is a simple calculation to determine the relative fat weight and relative lean weight of the body.

With this in mind, the average college-age male and female will be approximately 15 and 25 percent fat, respectively. With increased age and sedentary living, the relative percentages of fat increase. The endurance athlete will have considerably lower values for relative body fat, while the large, football lineman or the shot putter usually will have values greater than the average for their ages.

With training, there are marked alterations in body composition. Strength training through weights or progressive resistance exercises decreases body fat and increases lean body weight, the latter due to increases in muscle mass. With endurance training, similar changes can occur. If a 175-lb man were to jog 3½ mi in 30 min, he would expend approximately 500 Kcalories/session. If this routine were car-

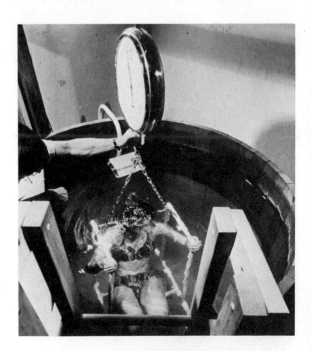

FIGURE 3–4

Underwater weighing technique for determining body density. Body density is used to estimate the lean and fat body weights.

ried out an average of 3½ days/week, the weekly caloric expenditure would be 1,750 Kcalories, which is approximately equivalent to losing ½ lb of body fat/week. Studies have confirmed the fact that endurance programs reduce stores of body fat and increase the lean body weight, presumably due to hypertrophy of the active muscle mass. In a six-month training program of previously sedentary adult men, it is typical to observe a decrease of 6–8 lb of fat and an increase of 2–3 lb of lean weight when they jog an average of 3 mi in 24 min for 2½ days/week.

SPECIFICITY OF PHYSICAL TRAINING

Research into the value of various training programs and techniques has gradually led to the realization that training, to be most efficient, must be specific to the sport. The long-distance runner must run to maximize the conditioning process for his sport. Two hours of hard swim training each day will do little to improve running ability. Likewise, the golfer will gain little, if any, help for his golf game by shooting free throws on the basketball court. While these are obvious examples, there is a point at which both the coach and researcher are uncertain as to how valuable certain related activities are for various sports. For example, can the baseball player improve aspects of his game through strength training? Another question of considerable importance that relates to strength training is how valuable is strength training at slow speeds for activities that require a quick application of strength? Does bench pressing 350 lb by a football lineman in a very slow and labored movement improve the explosive power needed in a game situation, where he has to apply his strength in a fast movement to catch his opponent off balance?

Unfortunately, research into the various aspects of specificity of training is limited, but what has been done underlines the need for further research. Clarke (1973), in his extensive review of the literature on adaptive changes in strength and muscular endurance with training, cites several examples where specificity of training was a major factor in interpreting the results of studies on various aspects of strength and endurance training. As one example, when comparing isometric and isotonic strength training, those subjects who train isometrically, typically show the greatest improvement when they are tested isometrically, while the isotonic group shows the greatest improvement when tested isotonically. Additionally, isometric training appears to be specific to the joint angle at which training occurs. If the subject trains at 90 degrees in the arm curl, the strength gained will be isolated to within a few degrees of that joint angle, and there will be little strength gain in the same movement at joint angles less than 60 degrees and greater than 120 degrees. Other studies have shown low or poor correlations between limb strength and the speed of movement or the muscular endurance of the limb.

Specificity of training has also been demonstrated in the area of cardiovascular endurance training. In one study, both an experimental and a control group were given maximal tests on a treadmill and also in a swimming pool, prior to participation by the experimental group in a swim-training program (Magel et al., 1975). On repeat testing at the conclusion of the twelve-week training program, the experimental group had a significantly higher swimming $\dot{V}O_2$ max compared with their pre-training values and with the post-training values for the control group. No improvement was found, however, in the treadmill $\dot{V}O_2$ max, which demonstrates the highly specific nature of the training program.

Another study (Holmér and Åstrand, 1972) illustrates the principle of specificity in an entirely different manner. A pair of identical twins were given a series of maximal tests under varying conditions: treadmill, swimming, arm work in the water, arm cycle work, etc. While both girls had been outstanding swimmers, one had stopped competitive swim training three years prior to this study. She had remained active in intramural-type sports while her sister continued with her competitive-

TABLE 3–1. Hypothetical Physiological and Body Composition Changes in a Sedentary, Normal Individual Resulting from an Endurance Training Program*, Compared to the Values of a World-Class Endurance Runner of the Same Age

Variables	Sedentary Normal Pre-training	Sedentary Normal Post-training	World-Class Endurance Runner
Cardiovascular			
HR_{rest}, beats/min	71	59	36
HR_{max}, beats/min	185	183	174
SV_{rest}, ml**	65	80	125
SV_{max}, ml**	120	140	200
$\dot{Q}_{rest}$, liters/min	4.6	4.7	4.5
$\dot{Q}_{max}$, liters/min	22.2	25.6	34.8
Heart volume, ml	750	820	1,200
Blood volume, liters	4.7	5.1	6.0
Systolic BP_{rest}, mmHg	135	130	120
Systolic BP_{max}, mmHg	210	205	210
Diastolic BP_{rest}, mmHg	78	76	65
Diastolic BP_{max}, mmHg	82	80	65
Respiratory			
$\dot{V}_E$ rest, liters/min (BTPS)	7	6	6
$\dot{V}_E$ max, liters/min (BTPS)	110	135	195
f_{rest}, breaths/min	14	12	12
f_{max}, breaths/min	40	45	55
TV_{rest}, liters	0.5	0.5	0.5
TV_{max}, liters	2.75	3.0	3.5
VC, liters	5.8	6.0	6.2
RV, liters	1.4	1.2	1.2
Metabolic			
$a–\bar{v}O_2$ $diff_{rest}$, ml/100 ml	6.0	6.0	6.0
$a–\bar{v}O_2$ $diff_{max}$, ml/100 ml	14.5	15.0	16.0
$\dot{V}O_2$ rest, ml/kg × min	3.5	3.7	4.0
$\dot{V}O_2$ max, ml/kg × min	40.5	49.8	76.7
Blood $lactate_{rest}$, mg/100 ml	10	10	10
Blood $lactate_{max}$, mg/100 ml	110	125	185
Body Composition			
Weight, lbs	175	170	150
Fat Weight, lbs	28	21.3	11.3
Lean Weight, lbs	147	148.7	138.7
Relative Fat, %	16.0	12.5	7.5

* Six-month training program, jogging three–four times/week, thirty min/day, at seventy-five percent of his $\dot{V}O_2$ max.
** Upright position.
(From J. H. Wilmore and A. C. Norton, *The Heart and Lungs at Work.* Schiller Park, Ill. Beckman Instruments, 1974. Reproduced by permission of the publisher.)

level swim training. The peak $\dot{V}O_2$ max values attained in the maximal swim-type tests were considerably higher for the swim-trained sister, while the values on the treadmill were identical for the two girls. For the two cycling tasks (arm cycling and arm plus leg cycling), the differences between the sisters were only moderate, favoring the swim-trained sister.

Studies have demonstrated that specificity of training also exists at the histochemical and biochemical levels. Endurance training programs develop the slow-twitch muscle fibers and those enzymes associated with aerobic metabolism. Likewise, anaerobic training develops the fast-twitch muscle fibers and those enzymes associated with anaerobic metabolism.

From these studies, it is apparent that the body adapts to the specific type of stress under which it trains, and the adaptation is specific to the training activity. Thus, to maximize the training effect, one must train specifically for that sport or activity. Undoubtedly, there are certain general factors that contribute to success in a given sport or activity, but these appear to be secondary in importance to the theory of specificity.

GENERAL SUMMARY

Physical conditioning or training results in a number of changes within the body, all of which will depend to a great extent on the purpose of the training program. Weight training produces increases in muscular strength and endurance but has relatively little influence on the respiratory and cardiovascular systems. Likewise, endurance exercise produces great changes in the cardiovascular and respiratory systems but has relatively little effect on muscle strength. Training changes are specific to the activity being pursued and are also dependent on the frequency, duration, and intensity of participation.

Table 3–1 lists typical values before and after an endurance training program for a number of physiological and body composition parameters. In addition, the values for a world-class runner are listed for comparative purposes. This will illustrate the tremendous adaptability of man, as well as demonstrate the great genetic differences between normally trained and highly trained and skilled athletes. It appears that athletes are born, and that training can take an individual only to the limit of his genetic potential.

REFERENCES

ÅSTRAND, P. O., and RODAHL, K. *Textbook of Work Physiology.* New York: McGraw-Hill Book Co., 1970.

BOOTH, F. W., and GOULD, E. W. "Effects of Training and Disuse on Connective Tissue." In *Exercise and Sport Sciences Reviews*, vol. 3, edited by J. H. Wilmore. New York: Academic Press, 1975.

CLARKE, D. L. "Adaptations in Strength and Muscular Endurance Resulting from Exercise." In *Exercise and Sport Sciences Reviews*, vol. 1, edited by J. H. Wilmore. New York: Academic Press, 1973.

DE VRIES, H. A. *Physiology of Exercise for Physical Education and Athletics.* 2nd ed. Dubuque, Iowa: William C. Brown Co. 1974.

FALL, H. B., ed. *Exercise Physiology.* New York: Academic Press, 1968.

HOLMÉR, I., and ÅSTRAND, P. O. "Swimming Training and Maximal Oxygen Uptake," *J. Appl. Physiol.* 33 (1972): 510–13.

JOHNSON, W. R., and BUSKIRK, E. R., eds. *Science and Medicine of Exercise and Sport.* 2nd ed. New York: Harper and Row, 1974.

KARPOVICH, P. V., and SINNING, W. E. *Physiology of Muscular Activity.* 7th ed. Philadelphia: W. B. Saunders Co., 1971.

MAGEL, J. R.; FOGLIA, G. F.; McARDLE, W. D.; GUTIN, B.; PECHAR, G. S.; and KATCH, F. I. "Specificity of Swim Training on Maximum Oxygen Uptake." *J. Appl. Physiol.* 38 (1975): 151–55.

MOREHOUSE, L. E., and MILLER, A. T. *Physiology of Exercise.* 6th ed. St. Louis: C. V. Mosby Co., 1971.

POLLOCK, M. L. "Quantification of Endurance Training Programs." In *Exercise and Sport Sciences Reviews*, vol. 1, edited by J. H. Wilmore. New York: Academic Press, 1973.

SHEPHERD, R. J. *Endurance Fitness.* Toronto: University of Toronto Press, 1969.

WILMORE, J. H., and NORTON, A. C. *The Heart and Lungs at Work.* Schiller Park, Illinois: Beckman Instruments, 1974.

SECTION B

Fundamentals of Physical Training

The skilled performance of an athlete is the final result of many long hours of physical training. This final result does not happen by chance but requires an intense dedication on the part of the athlete and exceptional insight by both the coach and athlete as to what the best training program may be for the athlete in that particular sport or event. Just as each sport is different and requires its own unique training program, each athlete is also unique and requires his own individualized training program to maximize his potential.

To individualize training programs requires a basic knowledge of those components that constitute the foundation of physical training. This section is devoted to a discussion of each of these individual components. Each component will be defined, an explanation will be given as to how it is measured or assessed, and finally, there will be a discussion of the importance of that component for various sports. The last chapter in this section will focus on the problems of deconditioning and the importance of off-season conditioning programs.

This section is intended to apply to all sports and activities. Unfortunately, however, much of the research has been conducted on a limited number of sports. As a result, the individual chapters may appear to be biased toward one or two specific sports or activities. Hopefully, the basic principles will be presented in such a way that readers will be able to apply them to their own sports.

4
Strength, Power, and Muscular Endurance

INTRODUCTION

As the shot putter crouches low at the back of the circle in preparation for his next put, it is obvious that great muscular strength and power will be necessary for a successful performance. Likewise, as the wrestler assumes the referee's position, it is apparent that strength and muscular endurance will be critical if he is to beat his opponent. What about the basketball player, golfer, or long-distance runner? Are strength, power, and muscular endurance of major importance to them? The answer, here, is not so obvious, but it is indeed, yes! Training for strength, power, and muscular endurance gains was, at one time, considered taboo for all athletes other than those in competitive weight lifting, weight events in track and field, and, on a limited basis, for football players, wrestlers, and boxers. It is now recognized that strength, power, and muscular endurance are important to successful performance by almost all athletes. Consequently, strength, power, and muscular endurance training is an integral part of the training programs for almost all sports and activities. This change in attitude or philosophy has been largely the result of innovations in training procedures that have taken place over the last few years.

What is the exact meaning of the terms strength, power, and muscular endurance? Are these terms synonymous, and can they be used interchangeably? The answer to this last question is no. Although the terms are interrelated,

each has its own meaning. Strength can be defined as the ability to apply or to resist force. The individual who can press 200 lb of weights over his head has twice the strength of the individual who can only press 100 lb. Power is simply the product of strength and speed. If two individuals can each bench press 250 lb, but one is able to do it in one half of the time of the other, the faster individual would have twice the power of the slower individual. While absolute strength is an important component of performance, power is probably even more important for most activities. Muscular endurance refers to the ability of a group of muscles to sustain repeated contractions, such as in the performance of sit-ups or push-ups, or to sustain a fixed or static contraction for an extended period of time, such as in hanging from a bar, or holding a heavy weight horizontally to the side. While strength appears to be a pure component, independent of power and muscular endurance, both muscular endurance and power are dependent on the individual's level of strength.

ASSESSMENT OF STRENGTH, POWER, AND MUSCULAR ENDURANCE

A better understanding of the concepts of strength, power, and muscular endurance can be gained through a knowledge of how each is assessed or measured. This information is also valuable in helping the coach and athlete design tests or programs of evaluation that will provide accurate estimates of the athlete's progress in each of these areas.

Strength

Strength is exhibited in various ways, which must be taken into consideration in evaluative techniques. The area of strength can be subdivided as follows:

· Static strength
  isometric
    concentric
    eccentric
· Dynamic strength
  isotonic
    concentric
    eccentric
  isokinetic
    concentric
    eccentric

Static or *isometric* strength is that strength that is applied against a fixed, nonmoving resistance. An attempt to move or push over a building would be an example of an isometric contraction. The building represents a fixed or immovable resistance, and no matter how much strength one applies, the building will not move. Thus, the muscle or muscle group may contract to its maximal potential without the resistance, the muscles and joints, moving (Figure 4–1).

Dynamic strength involves actual movement, both of the involved muscles and joints and the resistance. Dynamic strength can be applied and assessed either *isotonically* or *isokinetically*. In isotonic movements, the resistance is constant throughout the full range of movement. As an example, when the athlete curls 130 lb, the constant resistance is 130 lb. To accomplish the lift, the elbow flexors must apply a constant force greater than 130 lb. Due to the mechanics of the elbow joint, however, the force of 130 lb represents different fractions of the maximal potential at each angle in the range of motion. Strength is the result of the contractile force and the angle of

pull, as is illustrated in Figure 4–2. Thus, in the above example, the 130 lb in the biceps curl may represent maximal strength at the angles of 30 degrees and 150 degrees, but only 75 percent of maximal strength at 90 degrees, where the contractile force and angle of pull are optimal. In isotonic movements, therefore, the muscle is not contracting at its capacity or at a constant percentage of its capacity throughout the entire range of motion.

Isokinetic movements can be defined as the maximal contraction of the muscle group at a constant speed throughout the full range of movement, by varying or accommodating the

A. Head flexion

B. Arm curl

C. Knee extension

FIGURE 4–1

Isometric contractions. (From J. DiGennaro, Individualized Exercise and Optimal Fitness: A Review Workbook for Men and Women. *Philadelphia: Lea and Febiger, 1974. Reproduced by permission of the publisher.)*

FIGURE 4–2

Variation in strength relative to the angle of contraction, with 100 percent representing the angle where strength is maximal. (From C. R. Jensen and A. G. Fisher, Scientific Basis of Athletic Conditioning. *Philadelphia: Lea & Febiger, 1972. Reproduced by permission of the publisher.)*

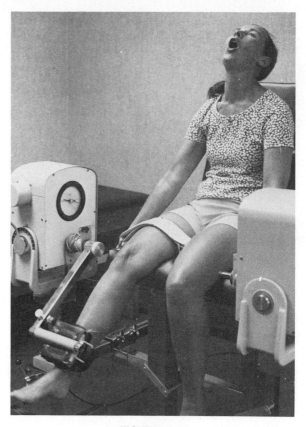

FIGURE 4–3

Isokinetic testing device. (Lumex, Inc., Bayshore, New York.)

resistance. This is a new concept that has tremendous potential in the area of muscular strength, power, and endurance development. The resistance is controlled at a fixed speed, and no matter how much strength is applied, the resistance will not move any faster. An isokinetic testing device is illustrated in Figure 4–3.

With either dynamic or static movement, there can be both *concentric* and *eccentric contractions.* Concentric contractions refer to muscle shortening, while eccentric contractions involve muscle lengthening. With the biceps curl, lifting the weight from the arms fully extended position to a position of complete

flexion at the elbow would be an example of muscle shortening, or a concentric contraction. Lowering the weight from the fully flexed to the fully extended position involves muscle lengthening, or an eccentric contraction. With static or isometric contractions, where there is no perceptible movement, a concentric contraction would be illustrated by a push or pull on an immoveable object or resistance, while eccentric contraction would be illustrated by an attempt to hold a heavy weight in a fixed position, i.e., the resistance is only immobile due to the force applied in the isometric contraction.

Strength can be assessed in a number of different ways. Static strength is usually meas-

FIGURE 4–4

Grip strength measured with a handgrip dynamometer.

ured by either a *dynamometer* or a cable tensiometer. The angle of the joint is fixed in a constant position and the individual exerts a maximal isometric contraction. The use of dynamometers has been primarily restricted to measuring grip strength and strength of the back and legs (Figure 4–4). The cable tensiometer has been adapted to measure the strength of just about any muscle group or joint movement in the body (Figure 4–5). With both the dynamometer and the cable tensiometer, the magnitude of tension developed in the isometric contraction is sensed by the testing device and displayed on a meter. Strength can be measured very accurately with either of these devices but only for the particular joint angle tested. On the basis of the data from Figure 4–2, it is obvious that the

strength measured at 90 degrees flexion will be quite different from that measured at 30 degrees or 150 degrees flexion. This is a basic limitation of static strength testing.

Dynamic strength can also be assessed in several different ways. The most popular way is to determine how much weight the individual can lift just one time. This is referred to as a *one-repetition maximum* (1-RM). As an example, to test elbow flexion strength, the individual would attempt to determine how much weight he could lift just one time. He might start at 75 lb and find that it is too light, go to 90 lb and find that it is too heavy, and back off to 85 lb, which he would be able to lift just once. His 1-RM for the curl would then be 85 lb. Like the static strength tests, this test is accurate, but it only gives an indication of the individual's strength at the weakest point in his range of motion, i.e., he will not be able to lift any more than the weight that he can just lift through the weakest point in his range of motion.

A relatively new testing device, which is available commercially, utilizes the concept of isokinetics and allows the muscle to apply full force at each point in the range of motion and records the resulting strength curve. This allows an accurate quantification of the strength at each point in the range of motion and also allows the peak strength in the full range to be identified. A typical strength curve is shown in Figure 4–6 using a testing device similar to the one illustrated in Figure 4–3.

There appears to be a high degree of specificity for strength. A single strength test of an isolated muscle group does not appear to be representative of total muscle strength. Several studies have shown that testing three or four selected sites provides an adequate estimation of total body strength.

Power

Power is a much more difficult component to measure. Several field tests of power have been devised, including the vertical jump, standing long jump, and softball throw for distance

FIGURE 4–5

Cable-tension, leg-strength test. (From T. A. Baumgartner and A. S. Jackson, Measurement for Evaluation in Physical Education. *Boston: Houghton Mifflin Co., 1975. Reproduced by permission of the publisher.)*

tests. While these tests are repeatable and reliable, their validity is questionable, i.e., do they really measure power? Margaria et al. devised a power test in 1966. In this test, the individual runs up a flight of steps as rapidly as possible. Once he reaches full speed, he is timed over a set distance that represents a certain vertical distance climbed. The vertical distance covered in a specific time, related to the weight of the individual, gives an absolute measure of power (See Appendix C, Field Tests for Assessing Physical Fitness). As an example, let us assume that the individual, who weighed 200 pounds, covered a vertical

distance of 4 ft in 1 sec. He then performed 800 ft-lb (4 ft × 200 lb) of work in 1 sec, or 48,000 ft-lb of work/min. This would be the equivalent of 1.45 *horsepower* (hp) of work (1 hp = 33,000 ft-lb/min). This test, however, would reflect only the power of the legs, primarily the hip and knee extensors, and not of any other parts of the body.

The isokinetic testing device allows for an estimate of power from almost any muscle group or joint motion. By varying the speed at which the resistance moves, it is possible to quantify explosive power as well as general power. Explosive power can be defined as that

FIGURE 4–6

Strength curve, using the isokinetic testing device illustrated in Figure 4–3.

Muscular Endurance

Muscular endurance can be measured by a number of field tests, including maximum number of pull-ups, push-ups and sit-ups. In the laboratory, muscular endurance can be measured by several different devices. The *ergograph* is a device developed in the early 1900's, which provides a means for continuously lifting and lowering a constant weight through a fixed distance at a constant rate. The subject continues lifting the fixed weight at the established cadence until he is no longer able to lift the weight, i.e., until the point of exhaustion.

The same principle can be applied using fixed weights in standard weight-training movements. As an example, a 100-lb weight could be used in the bench press and the total number of lifts or repetitions counted. This method has several drawbacks, however. Variations in arm length will influence the distance that the weight is lifted. Secondly, this technique does not allow for partial lifts.

The isokinetic testing device illustrated in Figure 4–3 gives a very accurate estimate of muscular endurance. The subject applies maximum force throughout the full range of motion and continues this as long as he can, until no further movement is possible. After the initial three or four contractions, there is a decrease in the peak strength attained. A summation of the peak strengths for each contraction or a

initial burst of power that initiates limb movement (a ballistic movement) and can be estimated from the slope of the initial part of the strength curve, i.e., the steeper the slope, the greater the explosive power. General power can be estimated from the total area directly beneath the strength curve, since this represents the product of strength and time. Figure 4–7 illustrates both of these forms of power.

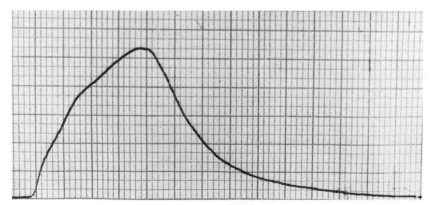

FIGURE 4–7

Power curve, using the isokinetic testing device illustrated in Figure 4–3.

FIGURE 4–8

Assessing muscular endurance, using the isokinetic testing device illustrated in Figure 4–3.

summation of the areas under each contraction curve provide an accurate assessment of muscular endurance (Figure 4–8).

MUSCLE TRAINING PROCEDURES

Alterations in strength, power, and muscular endurance will result from muscle training programs. There are three basic types of muscle training: isometric, isotonic, and isokinetic. All three result in substantial increases in strength and power, but only isotonic and isokinetic procedures increase muscular endurance.

Isometric Procedures

Isometric training procedures follow the theory that strength can be efficiently gained by training the muscle or muscle group against a fixed, immovable resistance. The concept evolved in the early twentieth century, but gained great popularity and support in the mid-1950's as a result of the work of Hettinger and Müller (1953) in Germany. Their initial studies indicated that tremendous gains in strength would result from isometric training procedures, and, in fact, that these gains would exceed those resulting from the more traditional isotonic

procedures. This caused a considerable change in the training patterns during this era; most athletes switched exclusively to isometric training or combined isometric training with isotonic training. Hettinger and Müller claimed increases of 5 percent of the original strength value per week as a result of one 6 sec contraction per day at only 67 percent of maximum contraction strength. Supposedly, little difference in improvement resulted when the tension was increased to 100 percent of maximum contraction strength or when repeated exercises totalling 45 sec were given.

Subsequent research has been unable to confirm the original work by Hettinger and Müller. Most of the later studies demonstrated sizeable strength increases with isometric exercises but not increases of the magnitude of 5 percent/week found in the original studies. However, it is difficult to use the percentage improvement as an objective evaluation of the value of any program. This is due to the widely accepted belief that the closer one is to his theoretical maximum strength, the more difficult it is to show a high percentage improvement in strength. The farther one is from his theoretical maximum, the easier it is to demonstrate substantial improvement. Thus, the same procedure or program may result in a 5 percent increase in a group of highly trained athletes and a 20 percent increase in a group of sedentary, deconditioned individuals.

Those studies that have followed the original work by Hettinger and Müller appear to support their contention that it does not require a contraction of 100 percent of maximum contraction strength or more than one, 6-sec contraction to attain significant gains in strength. One study compared two groups, one exercising at 67 percent of maximum contraction strength one 6-sec contraction per day and the other at 80 percent of maximum contraction strength with five, 6-sec contractions per day. Both groups made significant gains in strength, but there were no differences between the groups in their increases in strength. However, recent studies by Müller and Rohmert suggest that, while the 67 percent contraction held for 6 sec once per day will increase strength, the more demanding routine of 6-sec contractions at 100 percent of maximum contraction strength, repeated five to ten times, gives substantially greater strength gains. Obviously, additional work in this area will be necessary to gain an understanding as to which is the best routine for maximizing strength gains.

Thus, in the area of isometric training, it appears that the best results can be obtained by using maximum contractions, held for a period of 6 sec, repeated five to ten times per day. In addition, the muscle group should be trained at more than one angle in the range of motion. Several studies have indicated that the strength gains are specific to the joint angle trained. As an example, performing isometric training at a 90 degree angle in the biceps curl will lead to substantial strength gains at that angle but will result in only small increases at 45 degrees and 135 degrees, in that same range of motion. To optimize training, it seems justified to suggest that the athlete perform his series of five to ten, 6-sec maximal contractions at each of three angles in the full range of motion. Otherwise, strength gains will be limited to a rather small portion of the total range of motion. Specific isometric exercises will not be reviewed in this book, since they can be easily designed to fit the specific needs of the athlete. Also, since there are no equipment needs, simple props, such as chairs and doorways, can be improvised to provide suitable resistance. An isometric power rack can be constructed inexpensively and used for a wide variety of exercises (Figure 4–9). All that is needed are two 4 x 4-in. posts with holes drilled every 2–3 in. and several bars to insert into the holes to provide the static resistance to the exercise.

A new concept in the area of isometrics that was introduced in the early 1960's is referred to as functional isometric training. O'Shea has devoted an entire chapter to this concept in his book, *Scientific Principles and Methods of Strength Fitness.* The athlete applies maximum strength in one explosive movement and then sustains this effort in a fixed position for a short duration. A power rack is used. The barbell is placed on the bars of the power rack and additional bars, or pins, are placed 2–4 in. above the bars supporting the barbell. The athlete gets into the starting position, executes a fast isotonic movement through the 2–4 in. and then holds the barbell isometrically against the upper bars or pins for 3–5 sec (Figure 4–10). Thus, functional isometric training is a combination of both isometrics and a short explosive period of isotonics. In performing this system of training, it is important to isolate that muscle group that is to be trained. As an example, it is better to perform an overhead press in a sitting position to isolate the upper-body muscles and to eliminate unwanted assistance from the legs.

FIGURE 4–9

Isometric Power Rack. (From J. P. O'Shea, Scientific Principles and Methods of Strength Fitness. *Reading, Mass.: Addison-Wesley Publishing Co., 1974. Reproduced by permission of the publisher.)*

FIGURE 4–10

Illustration of functional isometric training. (From J. P. O'Shea, Scientific Principles and Methods of Strength Fitness. *Reading, Mass.: Addison-Wesley Publishing Co., 1974. Reproduced by permission of the publisher.)*

To date, little, if any, research has been conducted on the advantages of functional isometric training over the more traditional procedures.

Isotonic Procedures

Traditionally, isotonic training has involved the use of weights in the form of barbells, dumbbells, and pulleys. Weight training procedures using the isotonic concept date back as far as recorded history and are even mentioned in Greek mythology. According to mythology, Milo of Crotona desired to become the strongest man in the world. When he was a young boy, he began lifting a young bull once a day and continued lifting it daily until the bull was fully grown. Milo eventually developed enough strength to lift the full-grown bull and to carry it around on his shoulders.

This story, although mythical, does illustrate two important, basic concepts in isotonic muscle training: the concept of overload and the concept of progressive resistance exercises. The concept of overload refers to the fact that to gain strength through muscle-training procedures, it is necessary to load the muscles beyond that point to which they are normally loaded. Consider the example of a worker on an assembly line who must remove a 75-lb object from a conveyor belt and place it into a packing carton. For his first few days on the job, this is a considerable stress and taxes his muscles nearly to capacity. As a result, his muscles increase in strength to the point where he can handle this task with ease, a process that may take several months. At this point, however, his muscle strength levels off and does not continue to increase. If the factory suddenly shifted to 90-lb objects, this would constitute an overload, and he would then continue to gain in strength. Thus, the muscles must be taxed beyond so-called "normal" levels of work in order for significant increases in strength to occur.

The concept of progressive resistance exercise was illustrated by Milo in the above example, i.e., as the muscles become stronger they must work against a proportionately greater resistance to increase strength further. In essence, this is the systematic application of the overload principle. As an example, an individual who can perform only ten repetitions of a bench press using 150 lb of weight, will, as he weight trains and gets stronger, be able to increase his repetitions for the same weight to fourteen or fifteen within a week or two. If he then adds 5 lb of weight to the bar, giving him a total of 155 lb, his repetitions will drop to eight to ten. As he continues to train, the repetitions continue to increase and within another week or two, he is ready to add an additional 5 lb of weight. Thus, there is a progressive increase in the amount of weight or resistance lifted.

DeLorme (1945) and later DeLorme and Watkins (1948), are credited with the initial efforts to systematize isotonic training procedures. Their initial interests were in the areas of physical medicine and rehabilitation. The DeLorme and Watkins system emphasized the use of heavy resistance and low repetitions to develop strength, power, and volume of muscles, as opposed to light resistance and high repetitions to develop muscular endurance. Initially, it was suggested that the subject do 70 to 100 repetitions divided into seven to ten sets of ten repetitions per set. Later, this was modified to the traditional DeLorme system in which three sets of ten repetitions are performed. The *ten-repetition maximum* (10-RM) is first determined. This represents the greatest resistance that can be lifted ten, but no more than ten, consecutive times. The first set is then performed at a resistance equal to 50 percent of the 10-RM, the second at 75 percent of the 10-RM, and the third at 100 percent of the 10-RM. The amount of weight used is adjusted, periodically, as strength increases. This is determined by the individual's success in his third set, when he is lifting his 10-RM. If he can lift this fourteen to fifteen times, it no longer represents his 10-RM, and a new, heavier weight or resistance must be used.

Zinovieff (1951) proposed an alternate technique, since he felt the DeLorme technique had inherent weaknesses. He felt that it was difficult to maintain the quality of contraction in the last set at a full resistance of 10-RM, because of the impaired range of motion and painful joints with maximal contraction. He proposed the Oxford technique, which consisted of a total of 100 contractions, divided into ten sets of ten repetitions each, the first being performed at 10-RM. Subsequent sets were performed at a lowered resistance to match the decrease in strength that accompanies fatigue. Theoretically, this allowed the individual to do all ten sets at 10-RM, since the decrease in resistance (theoretically) matched the decrease in strength.

Subsequent research has attempted to identify the best possible combination of sets, repetitions, and resistance to maximize strength gains. Clarke, in the January 1974 issue of the *Physical Fitness Research Digest*, summarized the many experiments of Berger in this area. The results include the following.

1. Training with loads as low as 67 percent of maximal strength, two times per week, combined with maximal loads one time a week, results in as much strength improvement as training maximally for three times per week. Training solely at 67 percent of maximal strength, three times per week did not increase strength.

2. The resistance was between 3-RM and 4-RM for training to provide optimum improvement in strength, when training three times per week.

3. Training with 2-RM for six sets, three times per week was as effective in increasing strength as training with 6-RM for three sets, three times per week.

4. Training with 6-RM for three sets, three times per week resulted in greater strength gains than training at either 2-RM or 10-RM for three sets, three times per week.

5. Training with 10-RM for three sets, two times per week was as effective in gaining strength as training the same way three times per week.

6. Training with three sets per day improves strength more than the same training with only one or two sets per day.

Another study by Withers in 1970, compared three sets of 7-RM, four sets of 5-RM, and five sets of 3-RM. He found substantial strength gains in all three groups, following a nine-week training program with exercises two days per week. He failed to find any differences between the groups.

From the above findings, it would appear that weight training should be performed at 5 to 7-RM, with three sets being executed per training session, in order to maximize the strength gains. Training frequency should be three times per week, although this can be increased to five times per week if the muscles have been preconditioned to take this stress. Jensen and Fisher (1972) have suggested additional factors which should be considered by the athlete when establishing a weight-training program. These would include the following:

1. Analyze the athlete's basic movements and identify those muscles or muscle groups that should be isolated for strength training.
2. Select exercises that train the identified muscles.
3. Perform at least three sets of each exercise, resting several minutes between sets.
4. Work out on alternate days.
5. Increase the resistance as rapidly as possible.

The length of the total work out will be determined by the number of exercises selected and can vary from 10–15 min up to 90 min. It has been determined from experience that with longer work outs, the specific exercises should be varied to alternate between upper-limb, trunk, and lower-limb exercises. To perform three consecutive upper-arm exercises only reduces the quality of the last two exercises. Selected isotonic exercises are illustrated in Appendix A, Strength Exercises.

Isokinetic Procedures

Isokinetic muscle training procedures are relatively new in concept and in practice. The concept, which was introduced by Perrine in 1968, was briefly explained in an earlier section of this chapter. First, in an isometric contraction, the contraction can always be performed at 100 percent of maximum contraction strength, but the strength gains are localized to that specific joint angle which is trained. In isotonic exercise, the resistance is constant, and since the maximum strength will vary according to the angle of pull and the length of the muscle throughout the entire range of motion, the contraction must be defined as submaximal through most of the range of motion, even if the resistance can be lifted only once. The lift would be maximal only at the weakest points in the range of motion. Isokinetic exercise attempts to utilize the advantages and eliminate the disadvantages of isometric and isotonic exercise.

In true isokinetic exercise, the resistance is accommodating, i.e., it adjusts so that it is exactly matched to the force applied by the muscles. Thus, if the individual is able to motivate himself to apply maximum force throughout the entire range of the lift, the resistance will vary directly with the force to allow a maximum performance throughout the same range. This is accomplished by having the individual exert his force against a resistance that has a fixed speed of movement. No matter how much force is applied, the resistance will only move at a set speed and no faster. As an example of this behavior, if a car were placed on a hoist in a service station and raised to the chest level of a standing man, no matter how hard that man pushed on the hoist, the car would not move upward. If, however, the hoist were moved farther upward at a slow speed by its normal hydraulic operation, the man could then push upward with maximal force. The car and hoist would move upward but no faster than the hoist was set to go. Isokinetic training equipment works on the same principle.

Figure 4–11 illustrates an isokinetic bench-press device that employs a hydraulic cylinder to regulate the speed of contraction. With the cylinder totally closed, it is impossible to move the bars; the result being an isometric contraction. As the cylinder is altered to allow progressively more hydraulic fluid to flow through it, the speed of contraction is progressively increased in direct porportion to the changes. The ability to vary the speed of contraction is another interesting aspect of the isokinetic concept. Traditionally, strength training has been performed either at zero velocity (isometric contraction) or at very low velocities (traditional isokinetic 6-RM to 10-RM sets). Athletic performances, however, are typically performed at very high velocities. The question must then be raised, Would muscle training at high velocities have a more favorable influence on the athlete's performance than the traditional, slow training pro-

cedures of isometric and isokinetic exercise? It would appear that high-velocity strength training would develop substantial muscle power. Unfortunately, since this concept is relatively new, only a few studies have been conducted on various aspects of isokinetic exercise.

Several studies have investigated the ability of isokinetic exercise to facilitate increases in muscle strength. Unfortunately, however, most of the limited work completed has been of a clinical nature. A recent study by Pipes and

FIGURE 4–11
Isokinetic bench-press training device. (Photo courtesy of Lumex, Inc.)

Wilmore (1975) considered both slow- and fast-speed, isokinetic muscle training and found that both speeds increased strength substantially over an eight-week period of training. Average relative improvements varied from 16–44 percent tested with static strength, 12–21 percent tested by the 1-RM, and 4–79 percent when tested isokinetically, for a variety of exercise movements, including the bench press, biceps curl, triceps extension, bent rowing, and leg press or extension. The isokinetic, fast-speed group exhibited greater increases in strength for nearly all of the movements, when compared with the slow-speed group. This would tend to suggest that athletes need to train at relatively high speeds of limb movement in order to achieve the greatest strength increases.

Comparison of Isometric, Isotonic, and Isokinetic Procedures

From the results described in the above sections, it is obvious that substantial strength gains can be obtained from each of the three, different, muscle-training procedures. Does any one of the three offer a distinct advantage over the other two? Do all three provide equal gains in strength, power, and muscular endurance for an equal quantity of time and effort invested? These are questions that should be asked by both the coach and the athlete, since they are both interested in obtaining the greatest benefit in the shortest time possible.

The majority of research that has been conducted to date in evaluating these three types of muscle training, has dealt only with isometric and isotonic training. This is to be expected, however, since isokinetic training is a relatively new concept and has not been explored more than superficially from a research standpoint. As was discussed in an earlier section, the potential of the isokinetic concept is particularly impressive; thus, the concept probably will be extensively tested by researchers in the very near future.

A number of studies have compared isometric with isotonic training procedures. The problem in making this comparison, however, is in equalizing the intensity of training by equating isometric and isotonic work loads. Because of the principle of isometrics, i.e., static contraction, to accurately equate work loads is nearly impossible. Irrespective of this problem, many studies have attempted to equate the two, for purposes of accurate comparison, with reasonable success. These studies can be summarized as follows.*

1. Both isometric and isotonic procedures produce substantial gains in muscular strength. While most studies indicate little or no difference between the two procedures, several studies have suggested that isotonic exercise provides greater gains.
2. Muscular endurance is more effectively developed through isotonic procedures, and recovery from muscular fatigue is faster in muscles that have been trained isotonically. These results would be expected on the basis of the static nature of isometric exercise, and the fact that it is not a rhythmical, repetitive type of exercise.
3. Isometric procedures appear to develop strength in only a limited portion of the total range of motion; therefore, isotonic procedures will produce a more uniform development of strength.
4. Isometric procedures can be used during a period of convalescence from injury. Normally, the athlete with a joint or bone injury is completely immobilized, and the lack of exercise will result in a reduction in both muscle size (atrophy) and strength. Isometric contractions involve no joint movement and can be safely and effectively used during the period of recovery from injury, to prevent substantial loss of muscle function.
5. Isotonic procedures appear to cause a greater degree of muscle hypertrophy. This may or may not be a desired outcome of the muscle training program.

* Adapted from H. H. Clarke, "Development of Muscular Strength and Endurance," *Physical Fitness Research Digest*. President's Council on Physical Fitness and Sports. Washington, D.C.: U.S. Government Printing Office, January 1971.

In addition to the above research findings, there are several practical considerations. Isometric exercises can be performed with little or no supportive equipment, eliminating the need for expensive equipment. They also can be performed anywhere, at anytime, and the time requirement for completing a work out is considerably less than that for isotonic exercises. This would allow the coach the freedom to assign strength-conditioning exercises for his athletes to perform at home, both in-season and during the off-season. On the negative side, isometric exercises present motivational problems. Unless the exercise is performed with elaborate testing equipment, it is impossible to quantify the amount of strength that is applied during the contraction. Furthermore, with training, it is difficult to demonstrate improvement. This lack of positive feedback has led many athletes to abandon their isometric program. Lastly, isometric exercises are potentially dangerous for older individuals and individuals who have diagnosed cardiovascular disease, such as coronary artery disease (heart disease), hypertension, or stroke. When performing isometric exercises, the individual, typically, closes his glottis, creating a very high pressure within the thoracic, or chest, cavity. This is similar to taking in a full breath of air and then trying to exhale it as forcefully as possible with the mouth closed. The resulting high pressure in the thoracic cavity makes it difficult, if not impossible, for the blood to be returned from the lower extremities, since the intrathoracic pressure will exceed the pressure in the inferior vena cava. This results in an increased blood pressure and a reduced availability of blood to the heart and brain.

As was mentioned earlier, little research has been conducted in the area of isokinetic procedures. Of the few studies that have been conducted, two have shown the isokinetic procedure to be as effective as both isometric and isotonic procedures. A recent study by Pipes and Wilmore (1975) found substantial differences between isokinetic and isotonic training procedures. Two groups training with isokinetic procedures, one at a slow- and one at a fast-limb speeds, and a third group training with isotonic

procedures, trained three days a week for a total of eight weeks. All three groups were matched relative to their work load per training session. Both isokinetic groups exhibited greater gains in strength when tested isometrically and isokinetically and equivalent gains when tested isotonically (1-RM). In addition, the isokinetic groups demonstrated substantial improvements in the forty-yd dash, softball throw for distance, and vertical jump, while the isotonic group did not improve in their performances of any of these tasks.

One additional advantage of isokinetic exercises over either isometric or isotonic exercises is related to the problem of muscle soreness. While extreme soreness is present a day or two following muscle training with isometric and isotonic exercises, little or no soreness has been noted with isokinetic exercises. The possible reason for this is discussed in one of the following sections.

MECHANISMS OF STRENGTH, POWER, AND MUSCULAR ENDURANCE GAINS

The mechanisms that are responsible for gains in strength, power, and muscular endurance that result from muscle-training programs are not at all clear. It was mentioned in several of the earlier chapters that the ability to improve strength may be more of a neurological phenomenon than an actual change in the properties or quality of the muscle. Steinhaus (1968) believes that inhibitory mechanisms in the neuromuscular system are necessary to keep an individual from literally tearing himself apart, i.e., breaking bones and pulling muscle tendons out of their bony attachments. Autogenic inhibition is a reflex inhibition of the lower, motor-neuron discharge to a specific muscle when the tension on that muscle's tendons and internal, connective tissue structures exceeds the threshold of the imbedded, Golgi tendon organs. At higher levels in the nervous system, the reticular formation in the brain stem and the cerebral cortex both have the ability to initiate and propagate inhibitory impulses. It is quite possible that these inhibitory impulses are gradually overcome or counteracted, which then allows the expression of higher levels of strength which typically occur following a muscle training program. This theory certainly deserves considerable scientific investigation.

The early work of Hettinger and Müller (1953) pointed to the possibility that strength gains resulted from lack of oxygen in the exercising muscle. This was referred to as the *hypoxia* theory of strength gains. This theory has subsequently been tested on several occasions and found to have no validity. Other attempts to identify the mechanism for strength gains at the level of the muscle fiber have likewise not been fruitful. It appears that strength is probably mediated or controlled by the nervous system, but changes in the muscle tissue itself cannot be ruled out at this time.

Power is simply the product of strength and speed; thus, any increase in power must be the result of improvements in either strength or speed, or both. Since muscle training substantially increases muscle strength and can also increase speed of movement (to be covered later in this chapter), the increase in power with muscle training is also substantial. Unlike strength, the mechanisms responsible for these increases in power are obvious.

It is generally accepted that muscular endurance is best increased through muscle training that emphasizes high repetitions and relatively low resistance. Yet, there is also a high correlation between strength and absolute muscular endurance. This would tend to suggest that even programs designed to produce optimal gains in strength, i.e., low repetitions and high resistance, will provide some improvement in muscular endurance. It appears, therefore, that strength is one of the major determinants of muscle endurance. What are some of the others? Local patterns of circulation appear to be important. Since muscular endurance is a repeated or prolonged contraction of a muscle or a muscle group, substrate for metabolism becomes a factor as does the removal of waste products. The more efficient the circulation and the greater the development of circulatory capacity within that local area, the greater the potential for muscular endurance. Research has indicated that muscle training at 20- to 30-RM is the most efficient way to increase muscular endurance. This routine will have little effect on muscle strength and bulk. Thus, factors other than strength are important to the development of endurance. The ability to tolerate higher levels of pain or an increase in anaerobic threshold are two additional factors that might explain increases in muscular endurance independent of changes in strength.

MUSCLE SORENESS

Muscle soreness may be present either during the latter stages of an exercise and immediate recovery or between twelve and forty-eight hours after a strenuous bout of exercise or at both times. Pain that is felt during and immediately after exercise is probably due to the accumulation of the end products of exercise and tissue edema caused by the high hydrostatic pressures that force fluid to shift from the blood plasma into the tissues. This is the "pumped-up" feeling that the athlete is conscious of following heavy endurance or strength training. This pain and soreness is usually of short duration, disappearing within an hour following the cessation of exercise.

The muscle soreness that is felt a day or two following a heavy bout of exercise is the result of factors yet to be defined. There are several theories that have been presented to explain this form of muscle soreness, but they do not have universal support or agreement. One theory states that soreness is the result of small tears in muscle or connective tissue. While actual structural damage is a possible outcome of certain types of explosive or violent exercise, it is suspected that this would account for only a limited percentage of cases of muscle soreness. deVries (1974) has suggested a theory for muscle soreness, which he labels the "spasm theory." According to this theory, exercise brings about localized muscle ischemia (deficiency of blood), the ischemia causes pain, the pain generates increased reflex motor activity, greater motor activity creates even greater local muscle tension, which results in even greater degrees of ischemia. His research supports this theory, and he has found, additionally, that static stretching procedures help to prevent soreness, as well as to relieve soreness when it is present.

This is an attractive theory and probably is closely related to the basic cause. The theory fails, however, to explain two phenomenon. First, muscle soreness will usually haunt the athlete only during the initial stages of training, i.e., the first week or two. Following this initial period, the athlete has relatively little trouble with soreness, even though he may be working at substantially higher absolute and relative work loads. The spasm theory does not seem to explain this phenomenon.

Secondly, isokinetic strength training has produced an interesting and an unexpected outcome. Little or no muscle soreness has been found following exhaustive bouts of isokinetic exercise. Talag (1973) investigated the relationship of muscle soreness to eccentric, concentric, and isometric contractions, and she found that a group trained solely with eccentric contractions experienced extreme muscle soreness, while the isometric- and concentric-contraction groups experienced little soreness with their training. The fact that isokinetic procedures use only concentric contractions with a passive recovery, combined with the results from the preceding study, suggests that muscle soreness is unique to those activities that have a component of eccentric contractions. Again, this does not seem to support the spasm theory.

The actual cause of muscle soreness, however, must still be considered as unknown, at this time. The recent clue that soreness appears to be related solely to eccentric contraction should help researchers determine the basic cause of this perplexing and aggravating problem.

SEX DIFFERENCES

There are considerable differences in strength, power, and muscular endurance between males and females, once they reach puberty. Prior to this time, they are nearly identical to each other in these characteristics at each age. The superiority of the boys, once they are past puberty, can be traced to several factors, both cultural and genetic. As a result of genetic factors, the young boy starts producing increasingly greater amounts of testosterone once he reaches puberty. This produces large increases in muscle bulk and an associated increase in strength. For cultural reasons, at the onset of puberty in the female, it becomes "unlady-like" for her to be involved in large-muscle activities. Without the stimulus of exercise, the muscles will not continue to gain in strength or in size, except for the increases that accompany the normal growth curve. This topic will be covered in much greater depth and detail in Chapter 11, The Female Athlete.

MUSCULAR TRAINING AND ATHLETIC PERFORMANCE

Gaining strength, power, or muscular endurance simply for the sake of being stronger, more powerful, or possessing greater muscular endurance is of relatively little importance to athletes, unless it will also result in improvements in their athletic performance. The application of muscular training to field-event athletes in track and to competitive weight lifters, intuitively makes a greater deal of sense. What about the gymnast, distance runner, baseball player, high jumper, or ballerina? Will muscular training assist them in the preparation for their events, activities, or sport? Since training is costly in terms of time, athletes can not afford to waste time on activities that will not result in better athletic performances. What do research findings indicate? Clarke (1974b) has recently summarized all of the research in this area.

With regard to specific sports, muscular training appears to be a highly desirable supplement to the general training program for almost any athlete. In three studies of baseball, muscle training as a supplement to regular baseball practice resulted in significant improvements in throwing speed and in the speed to sprint 90 ft. In a single study of softball, underhand throwing ability for distance was improved with functional, isometric exercises, as well as the endurance to maintain maximum distance for 80 underhand throws. In all of these studies, the improvements noted were significantly greater than those in other groups which did not supplement their practice with muscular training.

Several studies have used isotonic or isometric weight training to supplement swim-training programs. Those groups which supplemented their swim training with muscle training, with one exception, exhibited greater improvement at distances of 25 and 50 yd. Dr. James Counsilman, swimming coach at the University of Indiana and recognized developer of many Olympic and world-record-holding swimmers, is a strong advocate of supplementing swimming work outs with strength training. He recently has developed a series of isokinetic exercises that he believes will substantially influence swim-training procedures in the near future.

In football, the influence of both isometric and isotonic strength training on the speed and force of the offensive football charge was investigated in a single study. The isometric group and the isotonic group improved significantly in both speed and the force of the offensive charge, while the control group did not improve on either test.

A number of studies have observed the influence of muscular training on the speed of movement. At one time, it was felt that muscle training would result in a muscle-bound, inflexible athlete and that speed would actually be decreased. Most studies, subsequently, have shown that speed can be improved with muscular training, although there are several studies with conflicting results. A recent study using isokinetic exercises found a substantial improvement in 40-yd dash speed, from 5.3 to 5.1 sec, following eight weeks of training.

Many studies have investigated the influence of muscular training on the performance of general motor tasks. Most studies have found that isotonic training substantially improves vertical jumping ability, while isometric training does not. The standing long jump has also been found to improve with isotonic training. Campbell (1952) observed the effects of systematic isotonic exercise on the motor fitness of college football, basketball, and track and field squads during their competitive seasons. Motor fitness was assessed from a composite score consisting of performances for right grip, vertical jump, squat thrusts, pull-ups, sit-ups, 300-yd shuttle run, and 50-yd dash. Each team was divided into two groups: one group trained the first half of the season with isotonic exercises to supplement their normal training, while the other group used only normal training procedures. At the mid-point of the season, the groups switched procedures. Isotonic training resulted in large gains in motor fitness, but the group that stopped weight training at mid-season had actually decreased in motor fitness when tested at the end of the season.

From the above findings, muscle training does appear to have a great deal to offer to athletes who wish to improve their performances. A word of caution must be inserted, however. Only a handful of activities or sports have been studied. It is possible, but not too likely on the basis of the information presently available, that muscle training will not be beneficial for every athlete, event, activity, or sport. At this time, the best advice appears to be to proceed with caution, and if the results prove beneficial, a more aggressive approach can be taken. Refer to Table 4–1 for suggested exercise movements for selected sports.

GENERAL SUMMARY

The athlete's performance can be separated into a number of individual components. The components of strength, power, and muscular endurance appear to be extremely important for most athletic performances. Strength is defined as the ability to apply or to resist force. Power is the functional application of both strength and speed. Muscular endurance refers

TABLE 4–1. Strength Training Activities for Various Sports or Events.*

Sport, Activity, or Event

Movement	Baseball	Basketball	Golf	Gymnastics	Football	Soccer	Rowing	Tennis	Wrestling	Skiing	Hockey	Swimming Backstroke	Breaststroke	Butterfly	Freestyle	Track and Field Sprinting	Hurdling	Javelin	Long jump	Distance running	Pole vault	High jump	Discus and Shot Put
Neck flexion and extension				X	X				X		X												
Shoulder shrug					X				X	X	X								X			X	
Military or overhead press				X	X				X	X						X			X				X
Behind the neck press												X		X									
Upright rowing	X	X	X	X			X	X			X	X	X	X		X					X	X	
Bent rowing					X				X							X	X						
Lat machine		X		X	X		X		X	X	X	X	X	X		X							
Triceps extension	X		X					X	X	X		X	X	X					X	X	X		X
Lateral arm raise		X		X				X				X										X	
Bent-arm pull-over	X	X			X	X						X	X	X					X	X		X	X
Biceps curl			X		X																		X
Dumbbell curl	X	X	X	X	X	X	X	X	X					X					X	X	X		
Bench press		X			X		X		X			X	X	X	X				X	X		X	X
Incline press	X		X	X		X		X		X	X	X				X	X	X			X	X	X
Parallel bar dip		X	X		X	X			X	X	X		X										
Back hyperextension		X	X		X			X			X		X	X					X				
Trunk extension	X							X		X	X	X				X							X
Weighted sit-ups	X	X	X		X	X	X	X	X	X	X	X						X	X		X	X	X
Hip flexion												X	X	X	X		X						
Stiff leg dead lift				X		X	X		X						X				X				
Knee flexion													X	X	X	X	X						
Knee extension		X		X	X				X	X	X	X				X	X	X	X			X	X
Squat	X	X	X		X	X	X		X														X
Hack squat			X	X		X	X				X	X	X	X	X	X	X	X	X	X	X	X	X
Toe raise	X									X						X	X	X			X	X	

* Adapted from J. P. O'Shea, *Scientific Principles and Methods of Strength Fitness*. Reading, Mass.: Addison-Wesley Publishing Co., 1969. Reproduced by permission of the publisher.

to the ability of a group of muscles to sustain either repeated or static contractions for an extended period of time.

Strength can be expressed either statically (isometric contraction) or dynamically (isotonic or isokinetic contraction), and muscular contractions can either be concentric (shortening) or eccentric (lengthening). With muscle training programs, there are generally increases in strength, power, and muscular endurance. Isometric and isotonic training procedures result in similar gains in strength, but isotonic training appears to produce substantially greater gains in muscular endurance. Isokinetic training may have the greatest potential of the three types of muscle training for gaining strength, power, and muscular endurance, but this will have to await confirmation following additional research.

Maximum gains in isometric strength appear to come from five to ten, 6-sec isometric contractions at 100 percent of maximal strength, repeated at three different points in the full range of motion. Isotonic training apparently is maximized by performing three sets per day of each exercise at 5 to 7 RM. Research is too limited at this point to make recommendations relative to an optimal training procedure for isokinetic exercise. High-speed contraction does appear to be important, but again, it is too early to tell at this time. Training three to five days per week appears to be optimal for all three training procedures.

Strength gains probably result from changes occurring within the central nervous system. While it is impossible to rule out changes in the muscle itself at this time, it does appear that the central nervous system plays the major role. Power is increased by gains in either or both strength and speed. Muscular endurance is increased through gains in muscular strength and probably through changes in local circulatory patterns, also.

Muscle soreness is a phenomenon that is poorly understood. One theory attempts to explain soreness on the basis of small tears in the muscle or its connective tissue. A second theory attributes soreness to localized muscle spasms. Neither theory appears to hold under all conditions. The recent finding that soreness results predominantly from eccentric contraction types of exercises, or from activities that use eccentric contractions, should direct the efforts of future research in this area into more productive avenues.

Finally, muscle training has been shown to have a significant influence on the performance of several sports and on a number of motor activities. It seems obvious at this time that almost all athletes, no matter what their sports, can gain substantial benefits from muscle training. For most sports, however, the specific programs have yet to be established, so the athlete should proceed with caution.

REFERENCES

CAMPBELL, R. L. "Effects of Supplemental Weight Training on the Physical Fitness of Athletic Squads." *Res. Quart.* 33 (1962): 343–348.

CLARKE, D. H. "Adaptations in Strength and Muscular Endurance Resulting from Exercise." In *Exercise and Sport Sciences Reviews*, vol. 1, edited by J. H. Wilmore. New York: Academic Press, 1973.

CLARKE, H. H. "Development of Muscular Strength and Endurance." *Physical Fitness Research Digest*, President's Council on Physical Fitness and Sports. Washington, D.C.: U.S. Government Printing Office, January 1974a.

CLARKE, H. H. "Strength Development and Motor-Sports Improvement." *Physical Fitness Research Digest*, President's Council on Physical Fitness and Sports. Washington, D.C.: U.S. Government Printing Office, October 1974b.

DeLORME, T. L. "Restoration of Muscle Power by Heavy Resistance Exercise." *J. Bone Joint Surg.* 27 (1945): 645–67.

DeLORME, T. L., and WATKINS, A. L. "Technics of Progressive Resistance Exercise." *Arch. Phys. Med.* 29 (1948): 263–73.

DeVRIES, H. A. *Physiology of Exercise for Physical Education and Athletics.* 2nd ed. Dubuque, Iowa: William C. Brown, 1974.

HETTINGER, T. *Physiology of Strength.* Springfield, Ill.: Charles C. Thomas, 1961.

HETTINGER, T., and MÜLLER, E. A. "Muskel-leistung and Muskel Training." *Arbeitsphysiol.* 15 (1953): 111–26.

JENSEN, C. R., and FISHER, A. G. *Scientific Basis of Athletic Conditioning.* Philadelphia: Lea and Febiger, 1972.

MARGARIA, R.; AGHEMO, P.; and ROVELLI, E. "Measurement of Muscular Power (anaerobic) in Man." *J. Appl. Physiol.* 21 (1966): 1662–64.

MÜLLER, E. A., and ROHMERT, W. "Die geschwindigkeit der muskelkraft zunahme bei isometrischen training." *Internationale Zeitschrift Angewandte Physiol.* 19 (1963): 403–419.

O'SHEA, J. P. *Scientific Principles and Methods of Strength Fitness.* Reading, Mass.: Addison-Wesley Pub. Co., 1969.

PERRINE, J. J. "Isokinetic Exercise and the Mechanical Energy Potentials of Muscle." *J. Health Phys. Ed. and Rec.* 39 No. 5 (1968): 40–44.

PIPES, T., and WILMORE, J. H. "Isokinetic vs. Isotonic Strength Training in Adult Men." *Med Sci Sport.* 7 (1975): 262–74.

STEINHAUS, A. H. "Inhibitory Mechanisms Operative in the Expression of Human Strength." Paper presented at the Annual Meeting, American College of Sports Medicine, Pennsylvania State University, May 1968.

TALAG, T. S. "Residual Muscular Soreness as Influenced by Concentric, Eccentric and Static Contractions." *Res. Quart.* 44 (1973): 458–69.

WITHERS, R. T. "Effect of Varied Weight-Training Loads on the Strength of University Freshman." *Res. Quart.* 41 (1970): 110–14.

ZINOVIEFF, A. N. "Heavy Resistance Exercises: The Oxford Technique." *Brit. J. Phys. Med.* 14 (1951): 129–32.

5
Speed, Agility, Neuromuscular Coordination, and Flexibility

INTRODUCTION

The average spectator who observes various athletic events would conclude that to be successful the sprinter running the 100-yd dash must rely on speed, the soccer player must depend on *agility* and neuromuscular coordination and skill, and that the gymnast performing free-exercise must have exceptional flexibility. Are these qualities or components important to athletes in other sports, activities, or events? The answer to this question must be, yes! For example, the football player, regardless of his position, must be concerned with each of these components. Since he is dependent on high levels of power for successful execution of his assignment, speed is essential to his performance, because speed and strength, by definition, constitute power. Agility and neuromuscular coordination are particularly important to those players who handle the ball, i.e., to backs and receivers, but they are also of concern to the big linemen, who must maneuver, pursue, and elude. Lastly, flexibility is important, not only for proper execution, but also for injury prevention, an area that will be discussed in detail later in this chapter. While this example illustrates the requirements for only one sport, equally impressive cases can be developed for practically all sports. The information in this chapter will, therefore, be applicable to all athletes.

Speed is easily defined as the rate of motion or the velocity of the body, or any one of its parts. For the sprinter, his time for a set distance, e.g., 9.6 sec for 100 yd, represents an average velocity, e.g., 100 yd/9.6 sec = 10.4 yd/sec. The average velocity, however, is the result of two independent factors, acceleration and maximal velocity. Thus, the sprinter with good acceleration, but only average maximal velocity, will excel in the short sprints of 40 to 100 yd, but will appear to fade with distances over 100 yd. This is an important point, for some sports rely on the accelerative component of speed, while others are concerned only with maximal velocity. The running back in football must have good acceleration, or quickness, to break through the line, but maximal velocity would also become important once he broke into the open 20–30 yd from the line of scrimmage.

Agility and neuromuscular coordination are terms which are much more difficult to define. Agility refers to the maneuverability of the individual, i.e., the ability to shift the direction of movement rapidly, without loss of balance or sense of position. It is, therefore, a combination of speed, strength, quick reactions, balance, and coordination, and can refer to the total body or to a specific part, such as the hands or feet. Neuromuscular coordination reflects the ability of athletes to perform their sports, activities, or events with a smooth, balanced, and fluid motion. This component is exemplified by the diver who performs a complex series of twists, bends, and somersaults, and concludes with a poised entry into the water, or by the gymnast who performs a complex routine on the balance beam.

Flexibility refers to the range of motion, i.e., looseness or suppleness of the body or specific joints, and involves the interrelationships between muscles, tendons, ligaments, and the joint itself. Limited flexibility is usually the result of muscles and tendons that are too tight, restricting the range of motion. A good example of this occurs in the hip and knee joint. The hamstring muscles, which are the flexor muscles of the knee and the extensor muscles of the hip, cross both the hip and knee joints. A tightness of the hamstrings and the associated muscle tendons seriously limits flexibility at the knee and hip joints. This can be simply illustrated by having the athlete sit on the floor with his legs extended in front of him. He then leans forward, grabs his ankles, and bends slowly as he attempts to touch his head to his knee. Few athletes can do this. Most can bend no further than 45° forward from the vertical position. Tightness and pain can be felt in the backs of the knees and thighs and in the lower back. Extremely large muscles and excessive quantities of fat also tend to limit joint flexibility, but these are not as frequent a cause of limited flexibility as muscle and tendon tightness.

ASSESSMENT OF SPEED, AGILITY, NEUROMUSCULAR COORDINATION, AND FLEXIBILITY

Speed can be assessed in a number of ways, varying from simple timing procedures to procedures that require elaborate and expensive equipment. The assessment can be restricted to a body segment, such as measuring the velocity of the arm in a particular movement; it can focus on the total body, as in timing an individual's speed in the 100-yd dash; or it can be applied to external objects propelled by the body, as in measuring the speed of a thrown ball or the speed of the head of a golf club. In addition, the assessment of speed can also be separated into the two components acceleration and maximal velocity.

The speed of individual body segments can be assessed in several ways. Two of the more widely used techniques involve elaborate timing devices or *cinematography*. With a timing device, the body segment, e.g., foot, is placed on, or pressed against, a microswitch. The instant the foot moves to initiate the movement, the microswitch is triggered and starts a timer. The foot travels a fixed distance and either contacts a target or crosses the path of a light beam, either of which stops the timer. Since the distance that the foot moves is fixed, the result of dividing this distance by the time to complete the task provides an estimate of the movement time of the segment for that task. Reaction time, another component of speed, can be assessed in a similar manner. Reaction time is defined as the length of time that it takes to respond to a stimulus, i.e., the time elapsed between the presentation of the stimulus and the actual start of the movement. In the above example, using an additional timer, the subject can be instructed to react as quickly to a stimulus, e.g., switching on a light, as he can and then to move his foot as quickly as possible from the microswitch to the target. Switching on the light would start the second timer, and the initial movement of the foot would stop it, thus measuring the length of time it took the subject to react to the stimulus. A variety of visual, verbal, or tactile stimuli can be used. The timers must be extremely accurate, as the times are frequently recorded to the hundredth or thousandth of a second.

With cinematography, movements can be more natural, since they are actually measured during competition. A special high-speed movie camera is used to record movements. The camera is set at a fixed distance from the subject, with objects of known size included in the field of vision, so that accurate distance estimates can be made. The camera is calibrated to use film at a fixed speed, so that segment speed can be estimated from a knowledge of the distance moved per frame and the number of frames taken per second. This is a very useful way to look at not only speed but also at acceleration. Camera location, with regard to planes of movement, is extremely important. Frequently, several cameras will be used to provide a three-dimensional analysis of the movement.

Speed of the total body is usually assessed by timing the athlete as he runs as fast as possible for a given distance. Traditionally, football players are timed over a distance of 40 yd, and baseball players over a distance of 90 ft, or for a full trip around the bases. The objective is to select a distance that has some relationship to the sport in which the athlete is competing. As was mentioned earlier, speed is the result of both acceleration and maximal velocity. For certain sports or events, it is advantageous to be able to differentiate between the two. Since maximal velocity is usually obtained within the first 30 to 50 yd of a sprint, maximal velocity can be measured by having the athlete run an all-out, 100-yd dash and timing him between the 50-yd and 100-yd markers. This provides a 50-yd-dash time, which, theoretically, is run at maximal running velocity. To assess acceleration, a crude estimate could be made by measuring the time to complete the 40-yd dash. A better method of evaluation, however, would be to have the athlete run all-out for 50 yd, starting from either a standing or crouched start, with timers stationed at 10, 20, 30, 40 and 50 yd. It would then be possible to determine true acceleration from one 10-yd segment to the next, since acceleration is defined as the rate of change in speed.

$$\text{acceleration} = \frac{(\text{final velocity} - \text{initial velocity})}{\text{time required to change velocity}}$$

As an example, if a sprinter went from a crouched start (defined as zero velocity) to the first 10-yd marker in 2.1 sec, he would have an average velocity of 4.8 yd/sec. This is the arithmetical average between a starting velocity of 0 and an unknown velocity at the 10-yd marker. Since the average and initial velocities are known, the final velocity at 10 yd can be calculated, i.e., average velocity = (final velocity + initial velocity)/2, or in the above example,

$$4.8 \text{ yd/sec} = (x + 0)/2$$
$$x/2 = 4.8 \text{ yd/sec}$$
$$x = 9.6 \text{ yd/sec}$$

The acceleration for the initial 10-yd segment would then be,

$$\text{acceleration} = (9.6 \text{ yd/sec} - 0 \text{ yd/sec})/2.1 \text{ sec}$$
$$= (9.6 \text{ yd/sec})/2.1 \text{ sec}$$
$$= 4.6 \text{ yd/sec}^2$$

To continue with this example, if the athlete crossed the 20-yd marker in 3.05 sec, the 30-yd marker in 3.90 sec, the 40-yd marker in 4.73 sec, and the 50-yd marker in 5.56 sec, he would have attained the following accelerations.

10–20 yd

Calculate average velocity ($\bar{v}$):

$$\bar{v} = 10 \text{ yd in } 0.95 \text{ sec } (3.05 - 2.1)$$
$$= 10.53 \text{ yd/sec}$$

Calculate final velocity (v_f):

$$10.53 \text{ yd/sec} = (v_f + 9.6 \text{ yd/sec})/2$$
$$21.06 \text{ yd/sec} = v_f + 9.6 \text{ yd/sec}$$
$$v_f = 11.45 \text{ yd/sec}$$

Calculate acceleration (a):

$$a = (11.45 \text{ yd/sec} - 9.6 \text{ yd/sec})/0.95 \text{ sec}$$
$$= (1.85 \text{ yd/sec})/0.95 \text{ sec}$$
$$= 1.95 \text{ yd/sec}^2$$

20–30 yd

Calculate average velocity ($\bar{v}$):

$$\bar{v} = 10 \text{ yd in } 0.85 \text{ sec } (3.90 - 3.05)$$
$$= 11.76 \text{ yd/sec}$$

Calculate final velocity (v_f):

$$11.76 \text{ yd/sec} = (v_f + 11.45 \text{ yd/sec})/2$$
$$23.52 \text{ yd/sec} = v_f + 11.45 \text{ yd/sec}$$
$$v_f = 12.08 \text{ yd/sec}$$

FIGURE 5–1. Illustration of Running Speed, Maximal Velocity, and Acceleration

Acceleration, yd/sec²	4.6	1.95	0.74
Average velocity, yd/sec	4.8	10.53	11.76
Time/segment, sec	2.1	0.95	0.85
Distance/segment, yd	10	10	10

Cummulative distance, yd	0	10	20	30
Cummulative time, sec	0	2.1	3.05	3.90
Velocity, yd/sec	0	9.60	11.45	12.08

Calculate acceleration (a):

$$a = (12.08 \text{ yd/sec} - 11.45 \text{ yd/sec})/0.85 \text{ sec}$$
$$= (0.63 \text{ yd/sec})/0.85 \text{ sec}$$
$$= 0.74 \text{ yd/sec}^2$$

30–40 yd

Calculate average velocity ($\bar{v}$):

$$\bar{v} = 10 \text{ yd in } 0.83 \text{ sec } (4.73 - 3.90)$$
$$= 12.05 \text{ yd/sec}$$

Calculate final velocity (v_f):

$$12.05 \text{ yd/sec} = v_f + 12.08 \text{ yd/sec})/2$$
$$24.10 \text{ yd/sec} = v_f + 12.08 \text{ yd/sec}$$
$$v_f = 12.02 \text{ yd/sec}$$

Calculate acceleration (a):

$$a = (12.02 \text{ yd/sec} - 12.08 \text{ yd/sec})/0.83 \text{ sec}$$
$$= (-0.06 \text{ yd/sec})/0.83 \text{ sec}$$
$$= -0.07 \text{ yd/sec}^2$$

40–50 yd

Calculate average velocity ($\bar{v}$):

$$\bar{v} = 10 \text{ yd in } 0.83 \text{ sec } (5.56 - 4.73)$$
$$= 12.05 \text{ yd/sec}$$

Calculate final velocity (v_f):

$$12.05 \text{ yd/sec} = (v_f + 12.02 \text{ yd/sec})/2$$
$$24.10 \text{ yd/sec} = v_f + 12.02 \text{ yd/sec}$$
$$v_f = 12.08 \text{ yd/sec}$$

Calculate acceleration (a):

$$a = (12.08 \text{ yd/sec} - 12.02 \text{ yd/sec})/0.83 \text{ sec}$$
$$= (0.06 \text{ yd/sec})/0.83 \text{ sec}$$
$$= 0.07 \text{ yd/sec}^2$$

These calculations are summarized in Figure 5–1. From these results, it is obvious that this athlete had finished accelerating after 30 yd, reached his peak acceleration during the first 10 yd, and maintained his maximal running velocity from the 30-yd marker to the 50-yd marker, i.e., approximately 12.05 yd/sec. Had he been able to maintain his maximal running speed for the full 100 yd, he would have completed the 100 yd in 9.7 sec, i.e., 5.56 sec for the first 50 yd and 0.83 sec/10 yd for each of the final 10-yd segments. A detailed analysis, such as this, enables the coach and athlete to analyze the performance to determine in which segments the athlete's running speed can be improved.

Lastly, the speed of movement of external objects that are propelled by the body can also be assessed. The techniques that are used are identical to those described for measuring the speed of limb movement with cinematography or for measuring maximal velocity and acceleration with precision measuring devices. These techniques have been used to measure the speed at which a baseball or football can be thrown, the maximal speed and acceleration of a baseball bat or the head of a golf club, and the acceleration of the discus or javelin. These measurements can be of tremendous assistance to the coach or athlete who is attempting to improve performance. As a practical example of their utility, suppose a baseball coach is faced with the problem that three of his best pitchers want to change from a full wind up preparatory to the pitch to a no wind up position. Will this change alter their pitching effectiveness? One of the factors that must be considered is whether the pitchers will sacrifice or gain maximal velocity by making this change. With the ability to measure pitching velocity, the coach will be able to determine the influence of this change in style. Consider another example in a similar situation. A coach or athlete may want to determine whether an isokinetic weight-training program that is designed for baseball pitchers will effectively increase maximal pitching velocity. With the ability to determine pitching speed accurately, this information can be easily attained.

While not a measure of speed, as such, the anaerobic capacity or power of the athlete is closely related to speed and burst-type activity. The sprinter trains to develop anaerobic power, as well as acceleration and maximal velocity, the components of speed. It is not yet clear as to how anaerobic power specifically influences performances that are of a speed or burst-type nature. However, it is suspected that a highly developed anaerobic power, or capacity, is related to the ability to maintain the maximal running velocity or to perform repeated runs up and down the court or field, without substantially decreasing the quality or speed of the runs. Thus, some appropriate measure of anaerobic power would be an important assessment to have for any athlete who depends on speed. The Margaria Power Test was designed specifically to assess anaerobic power or capacity. This test was described in Chapter 4, Strength, Power, and Muscular Endurance. This particular test is restricted to the legs and appears to be heavily dependent on body weight in order to attain a high score. As was mentioned in the first section of this book, the entire subject of anaerobic metabolism is just beginning to be explored in depth. With addi-

tional research, hopefully, additional tests of anaerobic power will be developed, which will provide more realistic estimates of the factors associated with anaerobic metabolism.

Agility and neuromuscular coordination are much more difficult to assess objectively. This is due, primarily, to the lack of adequate definitions for both agility and neuromuscular coordination. The definitions for these terms are likely to vary somewhat from one sport or activity to another. Neuromuscular coordination to the ballerina implies balance and sense of position, while the basketball player thinks of hand-eye coordination and the ability to control his body in the air. As a result, test batteries have been devised to provide two or more specific tests, which, when combined into a single score, provide an estimate of either one or both of these two components. These tests have fallen into the general category of motor-fitness or motor-ability tests. Test batteries include the shuttle run, squat thrust, dodge run, obstacle race, balancing tasks, and specific sports-skill tasks. Two of the more comprehensive test batteries developed, so far, are the Iowa-Brace Test and the Fleishman Test. Opinion at present, questions the usefulness of tests of "general" motor fitness or ability and favors the concept that skill or ability is specific to the individual task.

Flexibility is somewhat easier to measure than agility and neuromuscular coordination, but it is difficult to quantify it objectively. In the past, simple tests such as the sit-and-reach test provided a fair estimate of general flexibility. In the sit-and-reach test, the athlete sits on the floor with his feet extended forward in front of him (Figure 5–2) pressed flat against

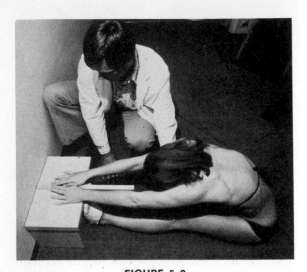

FIGURE 5–2

The sit-and-reach test to determine flexibility at the hip joint.

FIGURE 5–3

Electrogoniometer (ELGON). (From P. V. Karpovich and W. E. Sinning, Physiology of Muscular Activity, *7th ed. Philadelphia: W. B. Saunders Co., 1971. Reproduced by permission of the publisher.)*

a box that supports the measuring device. With the back of his knees pressed flat against the floor, the athlete leans forward and extends his finger tips as far as he can reach. The distance that he reaches is recorded and serves as an approximation of his flexibility at the hips. Several tests of this nature have been developed for assessing the flexibility of different parts of the body.

While tests such as these are adequate for mass screening, they do have inherent limitations. Most importantly, they do not allow for differences in limb length or proportional differences between the legs and arms. The individual with long arms and short legs will attain a good score on the sit-and-reach test, even if he has limited or poor flexibility. Likewise, the individual with short arms and long legs will be penalized and find it difficult to attain an acceptable score.

More accurate estimates of flexibility can be made with the Leighton flexometer or the ELGON, two devices that are available commercially. Both of the devices assess the degrees of rotation through the full range of motion.

The Leighton flexometer has a weighted, 360 degree dial and a weighted pointer mounted in a case. The dial and pointer move independently and are both controlled by gravity. Both can be locked in position independently of each other. The segment is usually positioned at one extreme in the range of motion, the dial locked in position, and then the segment moved through the full range of motion. The pointer follows the movement of the segment, thus indicating the extent of joint movement in degrees. Since the length of limbs or segment does not influence this assessment, the device provides a more accurate estimate of joint flexibility than cruder instruments or tests.

An electrogoniometer or ELGON is illustrated in Figure 5–3. A goniometer is a protractor-like device, which is used to measure the joint angle at both extremes in the total range of movement. With the ELGON, the protractor has been replaced by a potentiometer that can provide an electrical signal proportional to the angle of the joint. This device can give continuous recordings during a variety of activities. Assessments of movement have been made during jumping, running, basketball shooting, and general sports movements. The versatility of this unit allows a much more accurate and realistic assessment of functional flexibility, i.e., the degree of flexibility exhibited during an actual physical activity, as opposed to the more conventional measures of static flexibility, as described above.

TRAINING PROCEDURES FOR DEVELOPING SPEED, AGILITY, NEUROMUSCULAR COORDINATION, AND FLEXIBILITY

Speed

The development of speed is not an easy task. While strength and endurance can be developed by 20 to 50 percent or more, it is unusual for speed to be increased more than 10 percent, even after years of specialized training. A fully mature boy, who can run the 100-yd dash in 10.9 sec prior to extensive training or coaching, would be extremely fortunate to lower his time to 10.0 sec, a time that would represent an improvement in speed of slightly more than 8 percent. Speed appears to be, primarily, the result of a proper genetic combination, i.e., good sprinters are more than likely born rather than developed into good sprinters. An internationally famous college track-and-field coach once told a story of how a student from Africa, who attended his university as a freshman, had wanted to run the sprints on the track team, although he had never competed or been coached previously. On his first time trial in the 100-yd dash, he coasted to a 9.9-sec clocking, exhibiting the poorest possible form. Immediately, this coach knew that with proper coaching and training, he would be a world-record-setting sprinter. After four years of intensive training and diligent coaching, the

athlete was able to sprint the 100 yd with outstanding form, great stamina, and a 10.1 sec clocking!

On the other hand, the Russian sprinter Borzov, who was outstandingly successful during the early 1970's, including winning gold medals in the 1972 Olympic Games, was developed by Russian sport scientists at one of the several Russian institutes for research in the sport sciences. The scientists, following an exhaustive analysis, established a comprehensive anthopometric, biomechanical, physiological, and performance profile of the characteristics that were necessary for an individual to become a world-class sprinter. A careful search and screening of athletes in Russia led to the discovery of Borzov, who was then a long jumper, and others. Following months of scientifically designed training within the confines of the Physical Education Institute at Kiev, Borzov was unveiled and immediately became one of the top sprinters in the world. Obviously, genetics were important in the initial selection process, but the important point to be made is that Borzov was developed through specialized training into a world-class athlete. The science of sport is just beginning to develop to the point where athletes can be preselected for their best sport or event on the basis of rigid scientific criteria and then placed on training programs that are individually designed to take advantage of their strengths and to develop those areas in which they are weak.

Training programs to develop speed must concentrate on the type of speed to be developed, i.e., total body, limb, acceleration, or maximal velocity. Speed is specific to the area being developed. The 9.3 sec/100-yd-dash sprinter will not necessarily be able to fire a fastball into a catcher's mitt at 95 mph or throw a left jab into the face of his opponent with "lightning-like" speed.

The training program must be carefully selected to concentrate on those areas that are important to the athlete. deVries (1974) has stated that speed is the result of both positive and negative forces. Muscular contractions are positive forces, while air or water resistance, gravity, friction, and inertia are some examples of negative forces. Increases in speed can result from decreasing the influence of the negative forces or increasing the influence of the positive forces, or both. Thus, a swimmer might shave his body free of hair to reduce friction and water resistance, and strength train his upper body to increase the force of the muscular contractions. The track sprinter might select a better pair of shoes, alter his forward lean to reduce friction and air resistance, and strength train his lower body to increase the force of muscular contractions. This illustrates the importance of individualizing training on the basis of the sport or event. Each sport, event, and position must be analyzed in the closest detail to determine how each positive and negative factor can be altered to maximize the performance potential of the individual.

While speed is highly specific to the movement, there are general factors that influence speed, which should be considered when designing a training program. These include strength, reaction time, and flexibility. As was discussed in Chapter 4, Strength, Power, and Muscular Endurance, strength training does result in increases in speed, both specific speed of isolated limbs or body segments, as well as general body speed. One study cited an improvement from 5.3 to 5.1 sec for the time to sprint 40 yd, which could be considered a substantial improvement. Strength training has also been shown to decrease reflex time, which should facilitate overall speed. Reaction time can be improved by repeated practice of that specific movement. Lastly, flexibility can be greatly increased within a very short period of time, i.e., within several weeks. This could assist in the development of speed, although the value of increased flexibility is based more on logic than on objective, experimental evidence.

Biomechanical factors probably play the largest role in determining speed and the ability to increase speed. Stride length and stride frequency are two factors that are extremely critical. Research tends to point to stride length as the more critical of the two since stride frequency potential is much higher than is ever used in competition. However, it must be realized that it is important to increase stride frequency and stride length when running, up to a certain speed. At a critical point, it will be necessary to increase either one or the other, since the resulting speed is too fast for both frequency and length of stride to be increased. In fact, increasing one of these factors may even lead to a decrease in the other, e.g., if the stride length becomes too long, it will take too much time to initiate the next stride, decreasing the stride frequency. Factors such as foot position relative to the center of gravity, knee lift, angle of the back leg at push off, and positioning of the various body segments are just some of many biomechanical factors that influence speed. Therefore, a detailed biomechanical analysis of each athlete would be necessary to determine individual strengths and weaknesses.

Increasing total body neuromuscular coordination is also an important goal of training for speed improvement. Running as rapidly as possible is an extremely complex task and requires intense concentration and coordination of all of the body movements. The movement patterns of the highly skilled sprinter appear to flow and are not at all forced. This is the result of perfectly integrated movement patterns. While this trait must be inherent, it is possible to improve the coordination of the movement patterns through repeated practice and intelligent coaching.

Recently, track and cross-country coaches have started using hill running to improve speed. This was one of the most important training concepts used by the Russians in training Borzov. A hill with a gradual 5–10 percent grade is used. The athlete runs up one side of the hill, a distance of 400 to 800 yd and down the other side, as rapidly as possible. Running up the hill helps develop dynamic strength and power, while the downhill run helps develop rapid leg-movement patterns. While no formal research has been conducted on the advantages of this type of training compared to traditional sprint training, many coaches feel that it has been of tremendous value in training their runners for speed.

Several methods of speed training have been employed on the track, with varying degrees of success. Interval training is a form of training that alternates fast with slow periods of exercise. Using running as an example, for interval training, the variables that must be considered are the distance of the fast runs, the interval of recovery between the fast runs, the number of repetitions of fast runs, the duration of the fast runs, and the type of recovery activity (walking or jogging). An example of a typical, interval-training program would be ten repetitions of 110 yd, each completed in 14 sec, and 110 yd of jogging during the recovery, after each repetition. The athlete would sprint 110 yd in 14 sec, jog 110 yd slowly, sprint a second 110 yd in 14 sec, jog 110 yd slowly, etc., until he had completed the full ten repetitions. Either slow or fast interval training can be effectively employed, the two differing only in the pace that is used in the sprint part of the interval program.

Repetition running is similar to interval training but involves repetitions of comparatively longer distances, with nearly complete periods of recovery. In comparison, the distances are shorter and the recovery is not complete in true interval training. In repetition running, the distances are normally 880 yd to 2 mi, with recovery being determined by a reduction in heart rate well below 120 beats/min.

Interval sprinting involves alternating sprints of 50 yd and jogs of 60 yd for distances up to 3 miles. The recovery period is quite short and the athlete fatigues quite rapidly. Acceleration sprinting is a gradual acceleration from jogging to striding and then to sprinting. As an example, the athlete would jog 50 yd, stride 50 yd, sprint 50 yd, walk 50 yd and then repeat the entire sequence for a set number of repetitions.

The majority of the information in this section is geared toward improving running speed, primarily because this is the area in which most of the research has been conducted, to date. However, many of the principles covered can also be used to train the swimmer, bicyclist, or athlete in any other sport where speed, other than running speed, is important. To improve basic speed, the development of

strength, reaction time, neuromuscular coordination, and flexibility would be equally important. It is somewhat ironic that, not too many years ago, weight training was not allowed in training programs for most athletes because it was felt that the gains in strength and muscle hypertrophy would limit flexibility and reduce speed. Fortunately, formal research and informal experimentation by the athletes have proven that strength training has just the opposite effect, i.e., increased strength and flexibility, in almost all sports. The importance of the different biomechanical factors vary with each sport and have to be carefully analyzed. Swimming, for example, is performed in water, a medium which involves a totally unique set of biomechanical factors and principles for successful performance. Several recent textbooks in biomechanics and review articles on specific activities or sports are listed in the reference section of this chapter for a detailed analysis of each sport, activity, or event.

Most of the specific training areas that have been discussed require the individual to use the activity that he is training for as the vehicle or mode of training. The track sprinter must run, the sprint swimmer must swim, and the sprint cyclist must ride his bicycle. They must all perform repetitious training in their specific activity. This has usually been accomplished through interval training. Interval training is used for both speed and endurance training and will be covered in greater detail in Chapter 6, Cardiovascular Endurance. Circuit training, another form of training that can influence the development of speed, will be covered in depth toward the end of this chapter.

Agility and Neuromuscular Coordination

Agility and neuromuscular coordination in a particular sport can be improved by developing a training program that works on those specific components of agility and neuromuscular coordination that are unique to that sport or activity. The soccer player must work on eye-foot coordination and balance. The tennis player is more concerned about developing hand-eye coordination and a sense of position relative to his opponent. Strength, power, reaction time, flexibility, mental alertness, and the ability to concentrate and focus on the task at hand, all contribute to agility and neuromuscular skill. Each of these components can be trained separately, or they can be integrated and practiced as a whole. As an example, a basketball player can practice his fade-away jump shot as an integrated movement pattern, and he can also work on each of the specific components. He can weight train his hip and leg extensor muscles to develop strength and power, enabling him to jump higher and quicker. He can practice his reflexes to varying situations, attempting to improve his reaction time. He can perform hamstring flexibility exercises to increase the flexibility of his hamstring muscle group. Mental alertness and concentrative powers can be greatly increased through optometherapy, an exciting new area that is presently being developed. Again, however, because of the specificity of training, the majority of the training must be specific to the sport or activity in which the athlete is participating.

Optometherapy is an area with great promise for "fine-tuning" the athlete's neuromuscular coordination. Emphasis is placed on the visual system and its interaction with other body components and systems. Reilly, Harrison, and Lee (1973) summarized the results of their work in this area with professional athletes as follows:

- Increased concentration and span of attention
- Ability to cope with the negative influence of crowd noise, movements, visual stimuli, or other stresses during performance
- Ability to generate visual pictures and to use these in the acquisition and perfection of new skills, including preprogramming performance and anticipating plays and situations
- Relaxation before and during performance
- Development and maintenance of rhythm and timing
- More rapid and easier learning
- More efficient performance

- Improved balance and body control
- Ability to critically analyze performance
- More accurate perception of time, space, and direction

The development of conditioned reflexes appears to be an important part of this training. The skilled athlete is one who can immediately recruit a coordinated movement pattern without having to think it through. As the athlete develops in any skill, the recruitment of movement patterns changes from conscious control to conditioned reflexes. The more the activity is conditioned into a natural reflex action, the greater the athlete's degree of skill. This frees the mind to concentrate on more detailed aspects of the activity. Repetitious practice is the primary way in which motor patterns become conditioned reflexes. The athlete repeats the movement so often that the neural pathways become fixed and the movement becomes automatic. Once a skill is learned, it can be recalled with ease in a movement pattern that is coordinated and exact. A word of caution must be included at this point. Poor movement patterns or bad habits can be learned just as easily as good movement patterns. Therefore, the athlete must be observed closely at first, to make certain that he is performing the movement correctly. Constant repetition of an incorrectly learned pattern is extremely difficult to correct. This is the reason many tennis instructors dislike working with individuals who have attempted to learn tennis on their own. Frequently, they have already developed many bad habits, which are difficult to correct. It is easier to start fresh with a novice who has never held a tennis racquet in his hand prior to his first lesson.

As the basic skills are learned and become conditioned reflexes, the athlete can start to embellish his basic performance. Once the fast ball can be thrown accurately to the catcher, the pitcher can start working on the curve ball or slider. As the tennis player masters the backhand and forehand drives, he can start concentrating on how to vary the speed and the spin on the ball. The more movements the athlete can commit to conditioned reflexes, the more versatile will be his performance and the greater his potential for success.

Flexibility

A great deal can be done to increase the athlete's flexibility. Flexibility training is not difficult, requires little time and effort, and can be a pleasant experience. Most flexibility training can be accomplished during either the warm-up or cool-down phases of the daily work out.

deVries (1974) pioneered much of the work in the area of flexibility and athletics. He defines two types of flexibility, static and dynamic. Static flexibility refers to the range of motion of a particular joint. Dynamic flexibility refers to the flexibility of motion, i.e., the ease with which a joint moves through its range of motion during dynamic activity. If a muscle contracts quickly or in a jerky motion, it will stretch the antagonist muscles causing them to contract, thus limiting the range of dynamic motion. A firm, static stretch involves the inverse myotatic reflex, which results in an inhibition of the antagonist group of muscles, allowing them to relax, which enhances or increases the range of motion.

Methods of improving flexibility range from those involving rapid or ballistic types of movement, i.e., bobbing or jerking, to those that require slow positioning and static stretching. An example of each type can be illustrated using the hip flexion movement from the front sitting position. In the ballistic approach, the individual bends forward and attempts to touch his toes with his fingers and his knees with his head by using five or six, rapid, jerking or bouncing motions. In the static approach, the individual grabs his ankles with his hands and slowly stretches forward attempting to place his head on the knees. Although research has shown both methods to be equally effective, the static stretching method might be preferred, since there is less danger of injury and soreness and the antagonistic muscles are fully relaxed.

Since the early 1970's, coaches, trainers, and athletes have become more interested in flexibility training programs. Paul Uram, a high school physical education teacher and coach in Butler, Pennsylvania has developed ideas about flexibility exercises since the early 1960's. His program, which has been adopted by a number of professional, college, and high-school teams, is fairly simple, requiring 10 to 15 min before each game or practice. The program is employed on a year-round basis, and all of the major muscle groups and joints are included in the workout. An example of a flexibility workout routine is illustrated in Appendix B, Warm-Up and Flexibility Exercises.

Circuit Training

Circuit training, a new and innovative type of conditioning program, was developed by R. E. Morgan and G. T. Adamson in 1953 at the University of Leeds, England. This type of conditioning incorporates almost all of the training factors that have been described into a single routine. Circuit training can be designed to develop strength, power, muscular endurance, speed, agility and neuromuscular coordination, flexibility, and cardiovascular endurance. The concept has a built-in versatility, which allows the program to be varied to meet the needs of the group. Logically, circuit training should be one of the most popular of the many training programs. Unfortunately, it has not been rapidly accepted in the United States, probably because those individuals who develop and operate conditioning programs lack information about it.

Circuit training is a formal type of training in which an athlete goes through a series of selected exercises or activities that are performed in sequence or in a circuit. Circuits can be set up inside gymnasiums, exercise rooms, hallways, or outside on courts and fields or on tops of roofs. There are usually six to ten stations in a circuit. The athlete performs a specific exercise at each station and then proceeds to the next station. The idea is to progress through the circuit as rapidly as possible, attempting to improve either by decreasing the total time it takes to complete the circuit or by increasing the amount of work accomplished at each station, or both. The stations are distributed throughout the area assigned to circuit training. The greater the distance between stations, the greater the degree of cardiovascular conditioning as the individual runs from one station to the next. An example of a circuit-training program is illustrated in Table 5–1.

Various levels are established, depending on the skill level and ability of the group. A group of highly skilled and well-conditioned athletes would have higher levels of accomplishment than a group of sedentary college students who were attempting to get into condition. The individual would start at the lowest level, i.e., level Red–1 for the example in Table 5–1. He would go through the circuit a total of three times without stopping. The total time it took him to complete three repetitions of level Red–1 is recorded. If he is able to finish under the target time of 23 min, he can move to the next level, Red–2.

Circuit training offers a number of unique advantages. It combines a number of different components of training, thus total fitness is emphasized. It provides an interesting training environment for the athlete, and there are established times and levels to motivate the athlete to continue improving. The circuit can be modified to fit the needs of any one group or individual, it can be adapted within the time constraints of the individual, and it can accommodate large groups of individuals at a relatively low expense. Lastly, progression in all activities is assured.

In designing a circuit, first establish the training needs of the athletes who will be using the circuit. Adapt the circuit to fit the specific needs of the individuals, if possible. Identify an area that can be used for the circuit. An area where permanent stations can be established is most desirable. Next, determine the number of stations that can be accommodated in the space allotted. Arrange the stations in such an order that exercises for similar body areas do not follow one another sequentially. Alternate with an upper-body strength exercise, flexibility exercise, muscular-endurance, lower-body strength exercise and cardiovascular endurance exercise, in sequence. Place the station number and the specific instructions at each station. This information should also include a list of the various levels and the required weights and repetitions.

As mentioned, the trainer or coach who has

TABLE 5–1. Example of a Circuit Training Circuit*

Station Number	Exercise	Weight, lbs	Red Circuit Repetitions 1	2	3	Weight, lbs	Blue Circuit Repetitions 1	2	3
		Target Times	*Red—23 minutes*			*Blue—25 minutes*			
1	Bench press	60	8	10	12	80	8	10	12
2	Squat thrust		10	13	16		19	22	25
3	Chins		1	3	5		7	9	10
4	Stair climb		4	6	8		10	12	14
5	Two-arm curl	45	8	10	12	55	8	10	12
6	Half-squat	75	9	12	15	100	12	14	16
7	Sit-ups		10	14	18		20	25	30
8	Running lap		1	1	2		2	3	3

* Adapted from R. P. Sorani, *Circuit Training.* Dubuque, Iowa: William C. Brown Co., 1966. Reproduced by permission of the publisher.

a basic knowledge of the principles behind circuit training will find that it is one of the easiest training programs to implement. Once established, it requires little or no supervision and can be an excellent adjunct to any regular training program, or it can function as a complete off-season training program in itself.

MECHANISMS OF GAINS

The way in which speed is increased is not clearly understood, primarily because those factors that determine an individual's speed have not been clearly defined or established. Speed increases are probably the result of changes in the central nervous system, which facilitate recruitment of motor units, allow a more rapid response to external stimuli, and provide a better, overall coordination of movement patterns. Improvements in strength and flexibility also play a major role. Athletes have stated that they feel that they can throw harder and faster with increased muscle and joint flexibility. This is attributed to the fact that they can get their arms back farther in the preparatory action, which results in a greater "whip-like" action on the ball.

Agility and neuromuscular coordination improvements also come from changes within the central nervous system, although the proprioceptors are important in any functional adaptations that result from training. Repetition of basic movement patterns appears to be the major consideration in improving these characteristics. Establishing learned patterns of movement that can be recalled quickly and integrated into the ongoing activity is the desired goal. The specific changes that occur within the nervous system are not clear at the present time.

Flexibility is gained through either passive, static-types of stretching or through ballistic-types of movement. The muscles, tendons, and ligaments appear to be the site of any changes in flexibility, whether increased or decreased. The mechanism of change appears to be a simple stretching of the involved tissue.

RELATIONSHIP OF SPEED, AGILITY AND NEUROMUSCULAR COORDINATION, AND FLEXIBILITY TO ATHLETIC PERFORMANCE

Throughout this chapter, many examples have been given as to the importance of the factors of speed, agility and neuromuscular coordination, and flexibility to athletic performance. It is obvious that the track sprinter and the football running back rely on speed for success in their various sports. What about the other less obvious sports? Speed is a component found in just about every sport, with the possible exception of bowling. While baseball is a relatively slow sport, the sprint to first base to beat out a drag bunt or the attempt to break home on a hit-and-run play require bursts of speed. Fencing is an art of finesse and agility, but the weapon is moved with great speed in both offensive and defensive mancuvers, as well as in making quick advances and retreats. Speed, therefore, is an essential component that must be emphasized in every conditioning program.

Agility and neuromuscular coordination are critical to the success of any athlete. This area, more than any other, must receive priority attention when training programs are designed. It is important to use the activity itself in most phases of the training program, since this will help reinforce the movement patterns. Even with strength training, it is helpful and probably more beneficial if the type of training activity can be performed in a way that imitates the actual sport activity. The swimmer should duplicate his swimming motion, the pitcher his throwing motion, and the place-kicker his kicking motion. This will reinforce the movement patterns and should develop a more functional strength.

Lastly, flexibility is of major importance to the athlete. Research shows that the flexible athlete not only is more proficient but that he is less prone to serious injury. Flexibility in the antagonistic muscles is important in preventing muscle injuries, particularly with rapid limb movement. Muscle pulls and joint injuries occur when the muscles and joints have poor or limited flexibility. On the other hand, muscles and joints that are too loose or flexible also present a greater potential for injury. Thus, the athlete must adjust his training program to provide himself with a degree of flexibility that prevents injuries but is not so extreme that there is too much flexibility, leaving the muscles and joints in a vulnerable position.

GENERAL SUMMARY

Speed, agility and neuromuscular coordination, and flexibility are components of physical training that are extremely important for athletes in all sports and events. Speed is defined as the rate of motion or the velocity of the body or any one of its parts. While average velocity is the most frequently used measure of speed, speed can also be measured in terms of acceleration and maximal or peak velocity. Agility and neuromuscular coordination refer to the maneuverability of the individual and the ability to perform in a smooth, balanced, and fluid motion. Flexibility refers to the looseness or suppleness of the body or specific joints through their range of motion.

Speed can be assessed relative to a specific body segment, e.g., speed of the arm movement, to the total body, and to the external objects propelled by the body. Assessment can be simple, such as timing the individual through a set distance, or it can be complex, using cinematography, elaborate timing devices, or fundamental equations to calculate acceleration, sequentially, at fixed segments in the total movement.

Agility and neuromuscular coordination can be assessed by a number of different tests of general motor fitness or motor ability. These tests generally contain test items, such as the shuttle run, squat thrust, dodge run, obstacle race, balancing tasks, and specific sports skill tasks. Flexibility can be assessed by a number of simple, stretching-type tests, such as the sit-and-reach test, but it is more accurately measured with either a flexometer or an elec-

trogoniometer. While a flexometer measures static flexibility through the full range of motion, the electrogoniometer can measure continuous changes in the range of motion during a variety of activities, thus providing an assessment of dynamic flexibility.

Although speed is an inherent characteristic, determined largely through genetics, it is possible to train the sprinter to develop greater speed. The degree of improvement, however, is considerably less than would be found with either strength or endurance training. Since speed is specific to the activity, the training must be specific. In addition, since general factors such as strength, reaction time, and flexibility influence speed, training programs should include specialized development in these areas. Biomechanical factors are also extremely important in the development of speed and should be carefully analyzed to determine where the athlete should concentrate his training.

Agility and neuromuscular coordination must be developed specifically for the sport or activity, since each has its own unique demands. Considerable, repetitious practice is required to develop conditioned reflexes that respond in a smooth and integrated manner. In addition, attention should be given to developing strength, power, reaction time, flexibility, mental alertness, and the ability to concentrate on the task at hand.

Flexibility can be incorporated into the training program either through ballistic-types or static stretching-types of flexibility exercises. Both types appear to be equally effective; however, the static stretching exercises are less likely to result in injury and soreness.

Circuit training was developed in England in the 1950's and spread throughout the United States in the 1960's. This is a unique concept, since it incorporates strength, power, muscular endurance, speed, agility and neuromuscular coordination, flexibility, and cardiovascular endurance. A circuit usually consists of six to ten stations. Each station focuses on one exercise, e.g., pull-ups, so that all areas of the body are covered in a complete circuit. The athlete goes through the entire circuit as rapidly as possible, repeating the circuit three times. He is assigned a specific amount of work to accomplish at each station. As he becomes better conditioned, he is able to reduce his time through the circuit. In addition, the circuit is designed for different levels of competence so that the athlete can move up to the next highest level, as he improves. Each level requires a greater amount of work at each of the stations.

Lastly, this chapter considers the possible mechanisms of gains in strength, agility and neuromuscular coordination, and flexibility, in addition to how they are related to the athlete's actual performance. It is concluded that each of these factors is important for successful performance, no matter what the sport.

REFERENCES

ATWATER, A. E. "Cinematographic Analysis of Human Movement." In *Exercise and Sport Sciences Reviews*, vol. 1, edited by J. H. Wilmore. New York: Academic Press, 1973.

BARNEY, V. S.; HIRST, C. C.; and JENSEN, C. R. *Conditioning Exercise*. St. Louis: C. V. Mosby Co., 1965.

CRETZMEYER, F. X.; ALLEY, L. E.; and TIPTON, C. M. *Track and Field Athletics*. 8th ed. St. Louis: C. V. Mosby Co., 1974.

DEVRIES, H. A. *Physiology of Exercise for Physical Education and Athletics*. 2nd ed. Dubuque, Iowa: William C. Brown Co., 1974.

DILLMAN, C. J. "Temporal and Kinematic Analyses of Running." In *Exercise and Sport Sciences Reviews*, vol. 3, edited by J. H. Wilmore. New York: Academic Press, 1975.

DYSON, G. H. G. *The Mechanics of Athletics*. 5th ed. London: University of London Press, 1971.

GARRISON, L.; LESLIE, P.; and BLACKMORE, D. *Fitness and Figure Control: The Creation of You*. Palo Alto: Mayfield Publishing Co., 1974.

HAY, J. G. *Biomechanics of Sports Techniques*. Englewood Cliffs, N.J.: Prentice-Hall, 1973.

HAY, J. G. "Biomechanical Aspects of Jumping." In *Exercise and Sport Sciences Reviews*, vol. 3, edited by J. H. Wilmore. New York: Academic Press, 1975.

JAMES, S. L., and BRUBAKER, C. E. "Biomechanical and Neuromuscular Aspects of Running." In *Exercise and Sport Sciences Reviews*, vol. 1, edited by J. H. Wilmore. New York: Academic Press, 1973.

JENSEN, C. R., and FISHER, A. G. *Scientific Basis of Athletic Conditioning*. Philadelphia: Lea and Febiger, 1972.

MORGAN, R. E., and ADAMSON, G. T. *Circuit Training*. London: G. Bell and Sons, 1961.

REILLY, R. E.; HARRISON, W. D.; and LEE, W. C. *Introduction to Optometherapy*. Davis, Cal.: Vision Center for Sports, 1973.

SORANI, R. P. *Circuit Training*. Dubuque: William C. Brown Co., 1966.

6

Cardiovascular Endurance

INTRODUCTION

Of the various components that comprise the total physical training program, endurance is probably the most underrated. It is given relatively little attention in the training programs of most nonendurance athletes. The football player fails to understand why an endurance component is important in his total training program. He perceives football as an anaerobic activity, consisting of repeated bouts of high-intensity work of short duration. Seldom does a run exceed 40 to 60 yd, and even this is followed by a substantial rest interval. From all outward appearances, football is an anaerobic or burst-type of activity, and the need for endurance is not readily obvious. Sport scientists, however, are beginning to recognize the importance of endurance training to all activities, whether sprint-type, slow and skilled, or of an endurance nature. What the football player fails to realize is that he must repeat this burst-type of activity a number of times throughout the game. With a high level of endurance, the quality of the burst activity is maintained, and the athlete is still fresh at the start of the fourth quarter. It is now believed that those teams that fall apart in the final quarter are the teams that have ignored the endurance component in their training programs. A similar case can be made for athletes in most sports and will be presented in detail later in this chapter.

Endurance can be defined as the ability to perform prolonged bouts of work without experiencing fatigue or exhaustion. As was mentioned in Chapter 4, Strength, Power, and Muscular Endurance, endurance is comprised of two separate components, which are related but different in importance to athletic performance and in their manner of development through physical training. Muscular, or local, endurance refers to the ability of a single muscle or muscle group to sustain prolonged exercise. The exercise can be either of a rhythmical and repetitive nature, e.g., pull-ups, or of a static nature, e.g., sustained, isometric contraction. The resulting fatigue is confined to the local group of muscles that was exercised. General, or cardiovascular, endurance refers to the ability of the total body to sustain prolonged, rhythmical exercise. This type of endurance is typified by the long-distance runner who is able to run long distances at a fairly fast pace. Absolute muscular endurance is highly related to the muscular strength of the individual, while cardiovascular endurance is highly related to the development of the cardiovascular and respiratory systems. Muscular endurance was discussed in Chapter 4. Cardiovascular endurance will be the topic of the present chapter.

Although cardiovascular endurance is one of the most neglected components in the athlete's training program, exercise physiologists recognize it as probably the most important component in the athlete's physiological profile. Cardiovascular endurance has become synonymous with the term "physical fitness." A minimal level of cardiovascular endurance is essential for any sport or activity, and current opinion is that even higher levels can facilitate the athlete's performance and reduce his chances for serious injury.

ASSESSMENT OF CARDIOVASCULAR ENDURANCE

Cardiovascular endurance can be assessed in the field or in the laboratory. The maximal oxygen consumption ($\dot{V}O_2$ max) is regarded by most sport scientists as the best objective laboratory measure of endurance capacity. As described in Chapter 2, Acute Responses to Exercise, $\dot{V}O_2$ max is defined as the highest-attainable, oxygen consumption value in maximal or exhaustive exercise. Just as the athlete reaches exhaustion, the volume of oxygen consumed ceases to increase and either plateaus or decreases slightly. It is felt that the attainment of this plateau signals the end of the exercise, since the athlete has taxed his ability to deliver oxygen to the working muscles to its finite limit. This finite limit will dictate the levels of work or the pace that the athlete can tolerate. He can continue for a brief period beyond that time at which his $\dot{V}O_2$ max is attained by calling on his anaerobic reserves, but these also have a finite capacity. With endurance training, this finite limit is increased, with improvements in $\dot{V}O_2$ max of 20 percent or more following a six-month training program. This results in the athlete being able to work at higher levels of work or at a faster pace, thus improving his athletic performance potential.

In the laboratory, the endurance capacity, or $\dot{V}O_2$ max, is determined while the athlete walks, jogs, or runs on a treadmill (see Figure 2–3), rides a stationary bicycle ergometer (see Figure 2–1), rows on a rowing ergometer (see Figure 2–4), or swims in a swimming flume (see Figure 2–5). While the $\dot{V}O_2$ max may differ by 10 percent or slightly more between these different modes of laboratory exercise,

the principles of testing are similar. Using the treadmill as an example, the athlete is first instrumented for the test. This involves attaching a set of electrodes to his chest and placing a mouthpiece in his mouth with a noseclip positioned to divert all inspired and expired air through the mouthpiece. The electrodes conduct electrical signals from his heart for transmission to an electrocardiogram (ECG), which provides a recording of the heart's electrical activity. An ECG is used to determine the normality of heart function and also to provide an objective assessment of the athlete's heart rate during exercise.

The mouthpiece is attached to a two-way breathing valve, which allows inspired air, i.e., normal room air, to come in from one side and expired air to be diverted through the other side. All expired air goes through a gas meter, which measures its total volume. Periodically, samples of the expired air are analyzed for oxygen and carbon dioxide content. This information and other factors, such as barometric pressure and temperature of the expired air, are used to calculate the volume of oxygen consumed, the amount of carbon dioxide produced, the respiratory exchange ratio, and the volume of air expired.

The athlete is placed on the treadmill and allowed to relax in the sitting position. Once resting measurements have been obtained, the athlete stands to the side of the treadmill, off the belt, while the treadmill is started. The athlete then steps on the treadmill and begins walking at a moderate speed. After several minutes of adjustment to the unique situation of walking on a treadmill, the speed of the treadmill is increased to a fast walk. There are many different tests that can be performed on the treadmill, but the principles are basically the same. The ultimate purpose is to gradually bring the athlete to a state of total fatigue or exhaustion within a period of 8 to 20 minutes. This can be accomplished by either increasing the speed of the treadmill or the slope of the treadmill, or both. Changes in speed or slope usually occur every minute or two. A typical protocol for highly conditioned track athletes would be as follows

Time (min)	Speed (mph)	Grade (%)
0–1	3.5	0
1–2	3.5	2.5
2–3	3.5	5.0
3–4	6.0	5.0
4–5	6.0	7.5
5–6	6.0	10.0
6–7	9.0	10.0
7–8	9.0	12.5
8–9	9.0	15.0
9–10	9.0	17.5

If, after 10 min, the athlete has still not reached total exhaustion, the grade would be elevated another 2.5 percent each minute, until that state was reached.

Testing on the bicycle ergometer, rowing ergometer, or swim flume all use the same basic approach to reach the end point of the test, i.e., exhaustion. Throughout these tests, continuous measurements are made of the athlete's physiological responses to the exercise. In many cases, it is only the final few minutes of exercise that are important in defining the physiological determinants of endurance capacity. However, the information collected during the early stages of the exercise bout can be of significance in indicating the athlete's efficiency in performing at submaximal levels of work. In fact, several laboratories have their athletes run at a fixed speed, e.g., 200 meters/min or approximately 7.5 mph at a 0 percent slope, and determine the average oxygen consumption once the athlete reaches a steady state. The lower the average oxygen consumption/kg of body weight, the more efficient the athlete. The actual significance of these differences in efficiency is not clearly understood at the present time, but they are of obvious importance to the endurance athlete's performance.

Additional tests of cardiovascular endurance capacity include those tests that are referred to as field tests, or performance tests. Over the years, researchers have found that certain field tests have a relatively high correlation or relationship with laboratory tests of endurance capacity, i.e., $\dot{V}O_2$ max. $\dot{V}O_2$ max is regarded as synonymous with the term "aerobic power," indicating that endurance capacity is almost, or completely, dependent on the aerobic process. From Figure 6–1, it is possible to determine the relative contribution of aerobic and anaerobic metabolism on the basis of how long an individual exercises at full capacity for a particular length of time. For up to 2 min of maximal effort, the exercise is primarily of an anaerobic nature. Maximal effort that lasts between 2 and 2½ min is divided nearly equally between aerobic and anaerobic work. Maximal effort that lasts more than 2½ min is considered to be more of an aerobic work task. To predict maximal aerobic power, or $\dot{V}O_2$ max, it is necessary to have a field test that lasts substantially longer than 2–3 min. Theoretically, the higher the aerobic component of the total exercise metabolism, the better predictor that exercise test will be of $\dot{V}O_2$ max.

With this in mind, Dr. Bruno Balke developed one of the first field tests of endurance capacity ($\dot{V}O_2$ max), the 1.5-mi endurance run. In this test, the athlete attempts to run the 1.5-mi test distance as fast as possible. When

FIGURE 6–1

Relative contribution of anaerobic and aerobic metabolism to total energy expenditure in maximal work of up to sixty-minutes duration. (From P. O. Åstrand and K. Rodahl, Textbook of Work Physiology. *New York: McGraw-Hill Book, Co., 1970. Reproduced by permission of the publisher.)*

the individuals taking this test have some experience with pacing, the results correlate reasonably well with $\dot{V}O_2$ max. Dr. Kenneth Cooper, in his book, *Aerobics*, proposed a slight modification of the Balke test. He proposed that the distance an individual could run in 12 min was a good predictor of $\dot{V}O_2$ max. He reported a correlation of 0.90 between the distance covered in 12 min and $\dot{V}O_2$ max in a large group of Air Force personnel. Subsequent studies have reported substantially lower correlations, but this could be partially the result of using subjects that are unaccustomed to running and do not have any feel for the pace they should or could maintain over the 12-min interval. Instructions and scoring tables for both of these tests are presented in the last section of this book.

Other tests have been proposed to predict cardiovascular endurance capacity. The American Alliance of Health, Physical Education, and Recreation has proposed the 600-yd walk-run as a test of endurance capacity. The California State Physical Fitness Test uses a 6-min walk-jog to test for endurance capacity. Both the 600-yd walk-run and the 6-min walk-jog test have been found to have low relationships to actually measured $\dot{V}O_2$ max, which would indicate that neither test is a good predictor of endurance capacity. By referring to Figure 6–1, it is not difficult to determine why neither of these tests are successful predictors of endurance capacity. The 6-min walk-jog test relies on less than 80 percent aerobic effort, and the 600-yd walk-run test takes not more than 3–4 min to complete, which would require less than 60–65 percent aerobic effort. The running-type of field test should require a minimum of 12–15 min, which would result in greater than a 90 percent aerobic effort.

Other field tests have been proposed over the years to provide an accurate estimate of cardiovascular fitness, aerobic capacity, or $\dot{V}O_2$ max. Probably the most popular and simple tests to administer are the step tests. Several different types of step tests have been proposed, but they are all similar in principle. The athlete steps up and down on a bench of a set height (usually 12–20 in.), at a fixed rate (usually 18–36 steps/min), for a fixed time (usually between 2 and 5 min). An example of this type of test is the Harvard step test, developed at the Harvard Fatigue Laboratory in the early 1940's. The purpose of the test was to measure the ability of the body to adapt to and recover from hard physical work. The athlete would step up and down on a 20-in. bench at a cadence of 30 steps/min for a period of 5 min, or shorter, if he could not last the full 5 min. The athlete, following the exercise, would sit down and his pulse would be counted for three, 30-sec intervals during the recovery period, i.e., from 1–1.5 min, from 2–2.5 min, and from 3–3.5 min. The index of fitness was calculated as follows

$$\text{Fitness Index} = \frac{\text{Duration of exercise (sec)} \times 100}{2 \times (\text{sum of three, 30-sec pulse counts})}$$

As an example, if the athlete stepped up and down for 4 min and 25 sec and his pulse count for the first 30-sec counting period was 80 beats, 60 beats for the second counting period, and 50 beats for the third, his index would be,

$$\text{Fitness Index} = \frac{265 \text{ sec} \times 100}{2 \times (80 + 60 + 50)}$$

$$= \frac{26,500}{2 \times (190)}$$

$$= \frac{26,500}{380}$$

$$= 69.7 \text{ or } 70.0$$

This would place the athlete in the average category on the basis of standard scoring tables that have been derived for this test.

Unfortunately, the results from the Harvard step test, or any of the other modifications of the Harvard test, have not correlated very highly with endurance capacity. The principle behind the tests is good, i.e., the better-conditioned individual will have a lower pulse rate during the period of recovery. However, there is simply too much variability between and within individuals to make this a valid test of endurance capacity.

A similar criticism can be made of another form of endurance capacity test, the physical working capacity (PWC) tests. The PWC tests are usually administered on a bicycle ergometer, and the athlete is exercised at increasing work loads, usually changed every two to three minutes, until he reaches some predetermined heart rate. As an example, in the PWC_{170} test, the athlete is exercised to a heart rate of 170 beats/min. The level of work that is required to get his heart rate to this level is referred to as the PWC_{170}. The athlete who is able to perform 1,500 kilopond-meters of work per minute at a heart rate of 170 has a greater endurance, or working capacity, than the athlete who can only reach 1,350 kilopond-meters of work per minute. Again, the principle is sound, i.e., the better-conditioned athlete will have a lower pulse rate for the same level of work or will be able to do more work at the same pulse rate, but the correlations with $\dot{V}O_2$ max are relatively low.

It is unfortunate that these tests are not better predictors of $\dot{V}O_2$ max, for they are very simple to administer and do not require a maximal or exhaustive effort by the subject. The heart rate both during submaximal exercise and recovery should be lower for the same rate or volume of work in the individual with the higher endurance capacity (see Figure 2–6). The tremendous variability between subjects, however, precludes an accurate assessment of endurance capacity utilizing these relationships. But it should be mentioned that these tests can be used with fairly high validity to compare an individual with himself at different points in time. If an athlete undergoes a strenuous conditioning program, or becomes relatively sedentary or inactive, these pulse rate response tests are sensitive to the resulting changes in his cardiovascular condition. In fact, one of the last tests given to an astronaut prior to space flight and one of the first tests given immediately upon his return from space is a variation of the PWC test. This has been found to be an accurate indicator of the degree of cardiovascular deconditioning that results from extended periods of weightlessness.

TRAINING PROCEDURES FOR DEVELOPING CARDIOVASCULAR ENDURANCE

There are a number of specific endurance training programs, ranging from interval training to long, slow distance (LSD) training, all of which provide similar results and take similar factors into consideration in their designs. The factors to be considered in the development of any cardiovascular endurance program would be progressive overload, duration of each training session, frequency of the training sessions, intensity of the training sessions, the ratio of intense work to rest intervals, and the purpose of the training program. Progressive overload was discussed in Chapter 4 as it applied to the development of strength, power, and muscular endurance. Progressive overload is also important to endurance conditioning and simply implies that the work load for each training session should be greater than the load that can be comfortably performed (overload), and that this work load should be gradually increased as the athlete becomes better conditioned (progressive overload). The duration of the training session will depend on several factors, including the sport or activity that is being pursued and the intensity of the individual training sessions. The competitive swimmer may have to spend 5 hr per day in the water, while the football player using jogging as a general conditioning activity may work out for only 20 to 30 min. The frequency of the training sessions will depend on the endurance training program. For general endurance fitness, three to four days per week are sufficient, but for endurance competition, five to seven days per week are essential. The intensity of the training session will also depend on the purpose of the endurance training program, i.e., fitness or competition, as well as on the philosophy of training for each session, i.e., short-duration, high-intensity or long-duration, low-intensity training. The ratio of the work to the rest intervals also depends on the philosophy of the training program. High-intensity training will necessitate frequent rest intervals, while no rest intervals are needed with low-intensity, continuous training.

With the above factors in mind, the basic foundations of several endurance training systems will be explored in the following sections.

Interval Training

Interval training, which was briefly discussed in Chapter 5, Speed, Agility, Neuromuscular Coordination, and Flexibility, in relation to its use for the development of speed, will be discussed in much more detail in this section. The concept of interval training has existed for a number of years in one form or another. deVries (1974) credits the collaboration of a coach, Gerschler, and a physiologist, Reindell, both from Germany, with formalizing a structured system of interval training in the 1930's.

With interval training, short periods of work are alternated with short periods of rest or reduced activity. The concept has a firm foundation in physiological principles. Researchers have demonstrated that athletes can perform a considerably greater volume of work by breaking the total work into short, intense bouts with rest intervals interspersed between consecutive work bouts. The intervals of work and rest are usually equal and can vary from several seconds to five minutes or more. In addition to the work interval and the rest, or relief, interval, the vocabulary of interval training also includes the terms "set," "repetition," "training time," "training distance," and "frequency." These terms are comparable to the same terms used in previous sections of this book and will, therefore, not require definition. Interval training is frequently prescribed on the basis of the above terms, as illustrated in this example,

Set 1   6 × 440 at 75 sec (90 sec jog)
Set 2   6 × 880 at 180 sec (200 sec jog-walk)

In the above example, for the first set the athlete would run six repetitions of 440 yd each, completing the work interval in 75 sec and resting 90 sec between work intervals with slow jogging. The second set consists of running six repetitions of 880 yd each, completing the work interval in 180 sec and resting 200 sec between work intervals with slow jogging and walking.

The interval training approach can be used in almost any sport or activity but has received its greatest use in track, cross-country, and swimming. Interval procedures can be adapted to the sport or activity by selecting the form or mode of training and then manipulating the primary variables to fit the sport and athlete. Fox and Mathews (1974) have identified the following five variables that must be individually adjusted for each athlete.

· Rate and distance of the work interval
· Number of repetitions and sets during each training session
· Duration of the rest or relief interval
· Type of activity during the rest interval
· Frequency of training per week.

Several methods can be used to determine a sufficient work rate. One, which can be used for any form of physical activity, is to monitor the pulse rate. The athlete can be assigned a training pulse rate on the basis of his maximal heart rate. Since few people have access to a treadmill and electrocardiogram, this can be determined fairly accurately by having the athlete run an all-out, 440-yd run, and then monitoring his pulse rate during the first 15 sec of recovery. It can be assumed that the athlete attained his maximal heart rate during the 440-yd run, and it is known that the first 10–15 sec of recovery provide an accurate reflection of the heart rate during the last few seconds of exercise. This procedure can be accomplished quite easily by locating the carotid pulse at the juncture of the head and neck, the radial pulse on the thumb-side of the wrist, or by simply placing the hand directly over the heart. With the second hand of a watch, start by counting the first pulse beat as zero and then count the number of beats in the following 15-sec interval. This value multiplied by four will provide a reasonably accurate estimate of the maximal heart rate (HRmax) in beats per minute. A set percentage of HRmax can then be used to guide the runner's rate or intensity of work during the work interval. A high-intensity work interval would be run at 95 percent of HRmax, and a moderate-intensity work interval would be run at a rate between 85 and 95 percent of HRmax. Frequently, the duration of the rest intervals is dictated by the return of the HR to a pre-set level, e.g., 120 beats/min. When the heart rate reaches this level, the athlete starts his next work interval.

Another method for establishing the rate or intensity of the work interval is to assign a specific duration for a set distance, e.g., 30 sec for 220 yd. Wilt (1968) has derived a simple way of establishing these durations. The times for distances between 55 and 220 yd are established by adding between 1.5 and 5.0 sec, respectively, to the fastest time the athlete can run those distances from a running start. For the distance of 440 yd, 1-4 sec should be subtracted from one-quarter of the athlete's fastest mile time, e.g., for a 5-min mile, 300 sec/4 = 75 sec − 4 = 71 sec. For distances over 440 yd, each 440 yd of the distance should be run at a speed equal to the average 880-yd time in his best 3-mi run, minus 4 sec, e.g., for an 880-yd interval and a 15 min, 3-mi best time, 300 sec/4 = 75 sec/440 yd − 4 sec = 71 sec/440 yd or 142 sec (2:22) for the 880 yd.

The distance covered during the work interval can be varied from 20 to 30 yd to distances in excess of several miles. The length of the interval will depend on the athlete. Athletes who run short distances, such as sprinters, basketball players, and football players, will utilize short intervals of 30 to 220 yd, although the 220-yd sprinter will frequently run over-distances of 330 or 440 yd. The miler may run intervals as short as 220 yd, but most of his training would be at distances of 440 yd, 880 yd, 1 mi and some over-distance work. In running over-distance intervals, the athlete extends the length of the interval beyond that distance normally run in competition. Theoretically, this type of training will allow the athlete to complete his racing distance at top speed, without experiencing fatigue or exhaustion toward the end of the run. While this is a widespread practice among coaches and the

theory appears sound, no research is available to substantiate the value of its use.

The number of repetitions and sets will also be largely determined by the sport, activity, or event of the athlete. Generally, the shorter and more intense the interval, the greater the number of repetitions and sets. As the training interval is lengthened in both distance and duration, the number of repetitions and sets is correspondingly reduced. Fox and Mathews (1974) have established a series of guidelines that can be followed in the selection of the number of repetitions and sets.

The duration of the rest interval will depend on how rapidly the athlete recovers from his work interval. This period of rest can be determined individually, using the athlete's pulse rate to dictate at what time he is physiologically ready to start the next work interval. For athletes 30 yr of age and younger, it is a common practice to allow the pulse rate to drop to 130–150 beats/min before starting the next repetition and to below 120 beats/min before starting the next set. For those over 30 yr of age, since the maximum pulse rate declines with age, reduce the above pulse rate guidelines by 1 beat/min for every year over age 30. As an example, the 45-yr-old, Masters-competition athlete would use 115–135 beats/min for his recovery pulse rate between intervals and 105 beats/min for his recovery pulse rate between sets. Since absolute accuracy is not essential in determining these recovery rates, the pulse can be counted for a 6-sec period and multiplied by 10. This can result in a counting error as large as 10 beats/min, but this is acceptable for these purposes.

The type of activity performed during the rest interval can vary from slow walking to rapid walking and jogging, or the equivalent of these activities in other sports. Generally, the more intense the work interval, the lighter or less intense the work performed in the rest interval. As the athlete becomes better conditioned, he will be able to increase the intensity or decrease the duration of the rest interval, or do both.

The frequency of training will depend largely on the purpose of the interval training. The world-class sprinter or middle-distance runner will need to work out five to seven days per week. The athlete who plays team sports, where interval training is used only as a supplement to his general conditioning program, can obtain benefits from two to four days per week. For general conditioning or for off-season conditioning programs, two to four days per week appear to be adequate, although the improvement gained from two days per week programs will be minimal.

The coach or athlete who is interested in the specific details of how to organize and administer an interval training program should refer to the excellent text by Fox and Mathews (1974) cited in the reference section of this chapter. These authors have provided many excellent examples of how interval training can be utilized for various types of conditioning programs. The text by Costes (1972) also provides an excellent practical approach to interval training.

Continuous Training

Continuous training, as the name implies, involves continuous activity, without rest intervals. This has varied from high-intensity, continuous activity of moderate duration to low-intensity activity of an extended duration, i.e., long, slow distance, or "LSD," training. High-intensity, continuous activity is performed at work intensities that represent 85–95 percent of the individual's HRmax. As an example, the middle-distance runner may run a total distance of 5 mi, averaging approximately a 5 min/mi pace, with an average pulse rate of 180 beats/min (HRmax = 200 beats/min). The longer-distance runner maintains a pace that is just below his racing pace, although this will depend on the competition distance and the distance of the training runs. This has been a very effective way of training endurance athletes without requiring high levels of work that are stressful and uncomfortable for the athlete. One advantage of this type of training for the competitive runner is the constant pace at near-competition levels. Running

at an even pace during a race appears to be the most efficient way, physiologically, to attain the runner's best time. Therefore, this type of training would greatly aid the runner in preparing himself for actual competition. A word of caution should be introduced at this point, however, since the demands of this type of training program are extraordinary, particularly when extended over weeks and months. It is suggested that slower-paced variations, such as LSD or Fartlek, be introduced periodically, e.g., twice per week, to give the athlete some relief from the exhaustive, high-intensity, continuous training.

LSD training became extremely popular during the latter part of the 1960's. Dr. Ernst VanAaken, a German physician and coach, is credited with introducing and popularizing this system of training. Dr. VanAaken's work in this area started in the 1920's but received widespread support only recently. With LSD training, the athlete performs at a relatively low intensity, e.g., 60–80 percent of HRmax. Pulse rates seldom get above 160 beats/min for the young athlete and 140 beats/min for the older athlete. Distance, rather than speed, is the main objective. Endurance runners may train 15–30 mi/day using LSD techniques, with weekly distances of 100–200 mi. The pace of the run is considerably slower than the maximum pace that the individual can sustain. The individual capable of running a 5 min/mi pace will train at a 7–8 min/mi pace. While the cardiovascular and respiratory stress is considerably less and much more tolerable compared to high-intensity, continuous training, the extreme distances required can result in significant muscle and joint discomfort and actual injury.

LSD training is probably the most widely used form of endurance conditioning for the jogger who wants to stay in condition for health-related purposes, the athlete who participates in team sports and endurance-trains for general conditioning, and the athlete who wants to maintain his endurance conditioning during the off-season. For these purposes, the pace is kept at 60–80 percent of HRmax, but the distance is reduced to 3–5 mi. This appears to be an excellent approach to general endurance conditioning, since it has been shown to be effective and can be performed at a comfortable level of work. For the middle-aged, or older, individual who is attempting to attain or maintain an acceptable level of physical fitness, this is also the most judicious way to train from a medical viewpoint. Vigorous exercise in the older individual is potentially dangerous and burst-types of activity should not be encouraged.

Fartlek training, or speed play, is another form of continuous exercise that has a flavor of interval training. This form of training was developed in Sweden and is used primarily by distance runners. The athlete varies the pace from high speed to jogging speed as his will dictates. This is a free form of training where fun is the main goal and distance and time are not considered. Fartlek training is normally performed in the countryside where there are a variety of hills. Each athlete is free to run whatever course and speed he prefers, although the speed should, periodically, reach high intensity levels. Many coaches have used Fartlek training to supplement either high-intensity, continuous training or interval training, since it provides variety to the normal training routine. Fartlek runs are normally performed for durations of 45 min or longer.

Interval-Circuit Training

A relatively new concept in training has been introduced in several of the Scandinavian countries. This concept combines interval and circuit training. The circuit may be 1 to 5 mi in length, with stations every 400 yd to 1 mi. The athlete jogs or sprints the distance between stations, stops at each station to perform a strength, flexibility, or muscular endurance exercise in a manner similar to actual circuit training and continues on, jogging or running, to the next station. These courses are typically located in parks or in the country where there are many trees and hills.

Combination Programs

Dr. Per-Olof Astrand, a world-famous exercise physiologist in Sweden, has developed his own personal conditioning program which is a combination of interval and Fartlek training (Figure 6–2). It begins with a slow warm-up of 5 min of walking and slow jogging, followed by running up a hill at top speed, walking back down the hill, and then repeating the hill run approximately five times. This is followed by a run on the level at about 80 percent of top speed for 3 to 4 min, resting for several minutes, and then repeating the sequence three to

FIGURE 6–2

Illustration of a combined interval and Fartlek training program. (From P. O. Åstrand and K. Rodahl, Textbook of Work Physiology. McGraw-Hill Book Co., *1970. Reproduced by permission of the publisher.)*

four times. This is followed by a good sauna (Bastu) bath and, if the athlete chooses, a jump into a cold lake. Like pure Fartlek training, this program provides variety and fun.

Most training programs do not rely purely on any one method or system of training. Each of the training methods presented in this chapter are unique and has inherent advantages or strengths not present in the other methods. Combining methods or systems gives both the coach and athlete variety in their total training program. Boredom is a real hazard of any intense training program, and variety tends to reduce the chances of the athlete becoming bored with a particular training routine.

Wilt (1968) has developed two tables to assist the coach and athlete in designing training programs for competitive runners. Tables 6–1 and 6–2 provide estimates of the training emphasis for various racing distances and the contributions of these different training systems to the major components of run-training, i.e., speed, aerobic endurance, and anaerobic endurance. On the basis of a survey of twenty to thirty top runners in each event conducted by *Runner's World* magazine, the most efficient training patterns for each event were deter-

TABLE 6–1. Training Requirements for Various Running Distances* (Expressed Relative to the Percentage of Emphasis)

Event	Speed	Aerobic endurance	Anaerobic endurance
Marathon	5	90	5
6 mi	5	80	15
3 mi	10	70	20
2 mi	20	40	40
1 mi	20	25	55
880 yd	30	5	65
440 yd	80	5	15
220 yd	95	3	2
100 yd	95	2	3

* From F. Wilt "Training for Competitive Running," in *Exercise Physiology*, edited by H. B. Falls. (New York: Academic Press, 1968.) Reproduced by permission of the publisher.

TABLE 6–2. Components of Various Systems of Endurance and Sprint Training* (Expressed Relative to Percentage Involvement)

Type of training	Speed	Aerobic endurance	Anaerobic endurance
Repetitions of sprints	90	4	6
Continuous slow running	2	93	5
Continuous fast running	2	90	8
Slow interval	10	60	30
Fast interval	30	20	50
Repetition running	10	40	50
Speed play	20	40	40
Interval sprinting	20	70	10
Acceleration sprinting	90	5	5

* Adapted from F. Wilt "Training for Competitive Running," in *Exercise Physiology*, edited by H. B. Falls. (New York: Academic Press, 1968.) Reproduced by permission of the publisher.

mined. A summary of this survey is presented in Table 6–3.

It appears that a total program of training should include several different systems of training. This is true not only from the standpoint of variety, as mentioned above, but also from a physiological point of view. It has been recently theorized that a combination program is essential for the success of the runner, irrespective of the distance of his competitive runs. The sprinter can benefit greatly from endurance training, since it allows him to maintain the quality of his repeat sprints with interval training. Likewise, the distance runner can benefit from speed work, since he is frequently called on to give a finishing kick which is performed at a considerably faster pace than the earlier part of his run. Undoubtedly, further research in this area will bring forward even better systems of training and a better understanding of the training needs for various sports, activities, or events.

TABLE 6–3.   *Runner's World* Survey* of the Training Patterns of Top-Level Runners

Race	Ave Time	Days/ Week	Miles/ Day	Types of Running† (% each)					Training Site (% each)		
				S.D.	F.D.	Int.	Flk.	Race	Track	Road	C-country
100 yards	9.8	5.8	4.8	17	16	49	12	6	50	30	20
220 yards	21.9	5.9	5.0	35	12	39	10	4	37	37	26
440 yards	48.8	5.9	7.5	40	12	35	9	4	44	33	23
880 yards	1:52	6.4	9.0	55	17	17	7	4	28	50	22
1 mile	4:10	6.8	10.5	55	19	15	6	6	22	52	26
2 miles	9:00	6.8	11.0	58	18	11	7	6	17	60	23
3 miles	13:50	6.8	12.8	53	26	9	8	4	18	50	32
6 miles	29:00	6.9	13.0	59	21	10	4	6	18	63	19
9–15 miles	—	6.9	13.0	51	21	5	15	8	17	54	29
Marathon	2:26	6.9	13.1	51	25	5	13	6	13	63	24

* S.D. = slow distance; F.D. = fast distance; Int. = intervals; Flk. = fartlek.
† From *The Complete Runner*, Mountain View, Calif.: World Publications, 1974. Reproduced by permission of the publisher.

However, the basic components have been identified and are probably present in the various systems presently being used.

MECHANISMS FOR GAINING CARDIOVASCULAR ENDURANCE

Cardiovascular endurance can be increased dramatically with endurance training. From previous research, it is clear that an untrained individual can expect to improve his $\dot{V}O_2$ max between 15 and 25 percent following six months of moderate endurance training, i.e., 3 days/week, 30 min/day, at 60–80 percent of endurance capacity. The better the condition of the athlete, the smaller will be the relative improvement for the same program of training. In fact, it appears that in fully mature athletes, the highest attainable $\dot{V}O_2$ max is reached within twelve to eighteen months of heavy endurance training, indicating that each athlete has a finite level that can be attained. This finite level is clearly influenced by genetic factors and may also be influenced by training in early childhood. The latter observation is purely conjecture, at this point in time, and needs substantiation by experimental research.

The genetic aspects of $\dot{V}O_2$ max have been clearly demonstrated by Klissouras in a series of studies conducted in the late 1960's and early 1970's. Figure 6–3 illustrates the fact that identical, or monozygous, twins have nearly identical HRmax values, while the variability for dizygous, or fraternal, twins was much greater. Similar results have been found for $\dot{V}O_2$ max, as illustrated in Figure 6–4. Åstrand (1972) has stated that the best way to become a champion Olympic athlete is to be selective when choosing one's parents. World-class athletes who have been away from endurance training for many years have been found to have high $\dot{V}O_2$ max values in this sedentary, deconditioned state. It appears that both genetic and environmental factors can influence $\dot{V}O_2$ max values, and that the genetic factors probably establish the boundaries for the athlete, but endurance training can push the $\dot{V}O_2$ max value to the upper limit of these boundaries.

Age and sex can also influence $\dot{V}O_2$ max values, as was illustrated in Figure 2–12. However, these values may lead to an improper interpretation of true age and sex differences. Figure 6–5 illustrates the $\dot{V}O_2$ max values of a group of older sprinters and distance runners between 40 and 74 yr old. Their $\dot{V}O_2$ max

FIGURE 6–3

Comparison of HRmax between monozygous and dizygous twins. (From V. Klissouras, J. Appl. Physiol. 31 (1971): 338–44. Reproduced by permission of the publisher.)

values do decrease with age but they are considerably higher than the mean values for their particular age. Similar trends have been found in highly conditioned, female endurance athletes when compared to the normal, sedentary population of females. In both cases, the average $\dot{V}O_2$ max values for the older individual and for the female are lower than they should be due to the sedentary nature of the two populations.

When $\dot{V}O_2$ max does improve with endurance training, what physiological factors are responsible for this improvement? As was stated in Chapter 3, Chronic Adaptations to Exercise, this is an area of great controversy at present. Two theories exist at this time. The first states that endurance performance is not limited by the supply of oxygen coming into the tissue by way of arterialized blood but, rather, by the lack of oxidative enzymes in the mitochondria. Proponents of this theory provide impressive evidence that endurance

training programs increase these oxidative enzymes, allowing the active tissue to utilize more of the available oxygen, which would also result in a higher $\dot{V}O_2$ max. In addition, endurance training results in increases in muscle mitochondria. Thus, this theory argues that it is not solely a lack of oxygen coming into the active muscles that limits endurance performance, but that it must also involve an inability of the existing mitochondria to utilize the available oxygen.

The second theory proposes that central and peripheral circulatory factors limit endurance capacity, i.e., an inability to deliver a sufficient amount of oxygen to the active tissue. In this theory, improvement in $\dot{V}O_2$ max following endurance training is believed to result from increases in blood volume, cardiac output (via stroke volume), and a better perfusion of blood in the active tissue. Again, impressive research evidence provides strong support for this theory. In one study, endurance athletes

FIGURE 6–4

Comparison of V̇O₂ max between monozygous and dizygous twins. (From V. Klissouras, J. Appl. Physiol. 31 (1971): 338–44. Reproduced by permission of the publisher.)

breathed a mixture of carbon monoxide and air during exercise to exhaustion. The decrease in $\dot{V}O_2$ max was in direct proportion to the percentage of carbon monoxide breathed. The carbon monoxide molecules would have been bonded to approximately 15 percent of the total hemoglobin, exactly the same percentage as the reduction in $\dot{V}O_2$ max. In another study, approximately 15–20 percent of the total blood volume was removed, and the $\dot{V}O_2$ max decreased by approximately the same relative amount. In both of these studies, the reduction in the oxygen-carrying capacity of the blood, by either blocking hemoglobin or removing whole blood, resulted in less oxygen being delivered to the active tissues and a corresponding reduction in $\dot{V}O_2$ max. Similarly, breathing oxygen-enriched mixtures, where the partial pressure of oxygen in the inspired air is substantially increased, resulted in large increases in endurance capacity. These studies tend to indicate that it is the available oxygen supply that limits endurance performance.

It is obvious that more research is needed before the mechanisms can be identified that enable gains to be made in endurance capacity with endurance training. Both of the above theories are attractive and have good supporting evidence. Undoubtedly, both theories involve the complex mechanisms that interact to improve endurance capacity.

Although it was stated that the highest attainable endurance capacity is usually reached within eighteen months of intense endurance conditioning, endurance performance will continue to improve for many, additional years with continued training. In Chapter 3, it was theorized that this improvement in endurance performance in the absence of improvements in $\dot{V}O_2$ max might possibly be related to being able to perform at increasingly higher percentages of $\dot{V}O_2$ max for extended periods of time (see Figure 2–14 and the text in Chapter 3). The mechanisms for this improvement are probably related to greater mechanical and metabolic efficiency, improved anaerobic me-

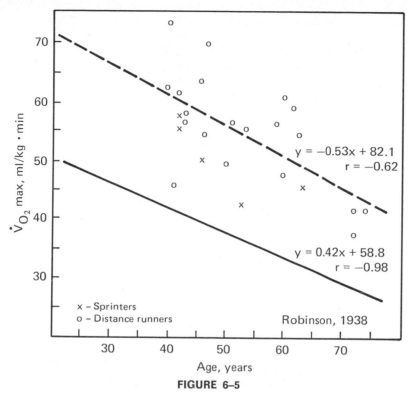

$y = -0.53x + 82.1$
$r = -0.62$

$y = 0.42x + 58.8$
$r = -0.98$

x – Sprinters
o – Distance runners

Robinson, 1938

Age, years

FIGURE 6–5

$\dot{V}O_2$ max values for a group of older sprinters and distance runners in comparison to normal values for the same age range. (Normal data from S. Robinson, "Experimental Studies of Physical Fitness in Relation to Age." Arbeitsphysiol. 10 (1938): 251–323. Reproduced by permission of the publisher.)

tabolism, and greater utilization of anaerobic metabolism. Research interest is starting to focus in this area, and a better understanding of the various factors involved should be possible in the near future.

The use of interval training methods is based on sound physiological principles, as was stated earlier in this chapter. Research has demonstrated that the total amount or volume of work accomplished in a given period of time is much greater if the work is broken into short, intense bouts of work with rest periods interspersed between them, as compared to continuous bouts of work without rest intervals. It should be pointed out, however, that the few studies that have compared interval training with continuous training have not found any differences in results between the two

systems, but have found that both systems produce substantial gains in endurance capacity. Additional research in this area is certainly necessary before any final conclusions can be drawn.

RELATIONSHIP OF CARDIOVASCULAR ENDURANCE TO ATHLETIC PERFORMANCE

Cardiovascular endurance is generally regarded as the most important component of physical fitness. Since all athletes should have above-average levels of physical fitness, endurance conditioning becomes an important part of their training program. Even the golfer, whose sport is considered relatively sedentary, will benefit from cardiovascular endurance conditioning. The gains in endurance from such conditioning will allow him to complete his round of golf with less total fatigue and his legs will be better able to withstand the long periods of walking and standing. For the sedentary, middle-aged adult, this should be the primary emphasis of the training program. This will be discussed at length in Chapter 13, Physical Activity for Health and Fitness.

For any athlete, fatigue represents a major deterrent to his best performance. Even minor or low levels of fatigue have negative influences on the athlete's total performance. Muscular strength is decreased, the reaction and movement times are prolonged, agility and neuromuscular coordination are reduced, the speed of total body movement is slowed, and the level of concentration and alertness is reduced. This latter factor is particularly important, for the athlete may become careless and more prone to serious injury, especially in contact sports. Even though this decrease in the athlete's performance may be small, it may be just enough to cause him to miss the critical free-throw in the basketball game, the 3-point field goal in football, or the 20-ft putt in golf.

The extent of endurance training that is necessary will vary considerably from one athlete to the next, depending on their existing endurance capacity and the endurance demands of the sport. It is obvious that the marathon runner will use endurance training almost exclusively, with limited attention to strength, flexibility, and speed. The baseball player, however, has very limited demands placed on his endurance capacity, so his training program will emphasize endurance conditioning to a much lesser extent. Nevertheless, the baseball player could gain substantially from endurance running, even if the periods are limited to 3 mi/day for 3 days/week at a moderate intensity. He would have little or no trouble with his legs (a frequent complaint of baseball players), and he would be able to complete a double header with little or no fatigue. Many athletes in nonendurance sports, activities, or events have never incorporated even moderate endurance training into their training programs. Those that have incorporated endurance training, generally, are well aware of their improved physical condition and its impact on their improved athletic performance.

GENERAL SUMMARY

Cardiovascular endurance, in contrast to muscular endurance, is probably the most important component of general physical fitness. As a result, it is an important area that should be developed in the training programs of all athletes. Cardiovascular endurance is defined as the ability of the total body to sustain prolonged, rhythmical exercise. The best measure of cardiovascular endurance capacity in the laboratory is the athlete's maximal oxygen consumption ($\dot{V}O_2$ max), which is assessed by having the athlete exercise to total exhaustion on a stationary work device, such as a motor-driven treadmill or a bicycle ergometer. At higher levels of work as the athlete approaches exhaustion, his oxygen consumption values will start to plateau, or even decline, indicating that he has attained $\dot{V}O_2$ max and that the end of the exercise bout is near. Field tests such as the 12-min run, the 1.5-mi run, step tests, and PWC tests have been used in the past and are presently being used to assess endurance capacity. Several of these tests provide a moderately accurate estimate of endurance capacity, but most of the submaximal tests are inaccurate for a high percentage of the population.

A number of specific training methods or systems exist for developing cardiovascular endurance. The two major classifications of training systems are interval training and continuous training. Interval training involves periods of high-intensity work with rest periods interspersed between the work bouts. In designing an interval training program, attention must be given to the rate and distance of the work interval, the number of repetitions and sets during each training session, the duration of the rest interval, the type of activity during the rest interval, and the frequency of training per week.

Continuous training involves continuous activity without rest intervals. This type of training can be of high intensity, or of moderate intensity and an extended duration (LSD). A third type of continuous activity is the Swedish Fartlek system, which consists of jogging and bursts of sprinting dictated by the will of the athlete. Interval-circuit training involves an extended circuit one to five miles long, with several stations along the circuit for exercises of a strength, flexibility, or muscular endurance nature.

Most coaches and athletes develop comprehensive training programs that combine two or more of the above systems. In this manner, the athlete can have more variety in his training, as well as gain from the strengths of the additional systems.

It is known that endurance capacity is influenced by genetic factors, sex, and age. In addition, it can be greatly influenced by physical conditioning. The mechanisms by which the $\dot{V}O_2$ max is increased with endurance training are unclear at the present time, but it is probably the result of a combination of increased mitochondria and oxidative enzymes in the active tissue, as well as an increased blood volume, increased cardiac output, and better perfusion of the active tissue.

Lastly, cardiovascular endurance conditioning is a critical aspect of any athlete's training program. Low endurance capacity leads to fatigue, even in the more sedentary sports or activities. Such a condition can only work to lower the performance potential of the athlete, since fatigue will reduce strength, speed, reaction and movement time and will have a negative influence on agility and neuromuscular coordination. In addition, the athlete becomes more prone to serious injury, due to an inability to fully concentrate on his performance, as well as to the above factors. Adequate cardiovascular conditioning must be the foundation of any athlete's general conditioning program.

REFERENCES

ÅSTRAND, P. O. *Journal of Physical Education*, March–April 1972, pp. 129–36.

ÅSTRAND, P. O., and RODAHL, K. *Textbook of Work Physiology*. New York: McGraw-Hill Book Co., 1970.

COOPER, K. H. *Aerobics*. New York: M. Evans, 1968.

COSTES, N. *Interval Training*. Mountain View, Calif.: World Publications, 1972.

DEVRIES, H. A. *Physiology of Exercise for Physical Education and Athletics*. 2nd ed. Dubuque, Iowa: William C. Brown Co., 1974.

FOX, E. L., and MATHEWS, D. K. *Interval Training Conditioning for Sports and General Fitness*. Philadelphia: W. B. Saunders Co., 1974.

KLISSOURAS, V. "Adaptability of Genetic Variation." *J. Appl. Physiol.* 31 (1971): 338–344.

JENSEN, C. R., and FISHER, A. G. *Scientific Bases of Athletic Conditioning*. Philadelphia: Lea & Febiger, 1972.

POLLOCK, M. L. "Quantification of Endurance Training Programs." In *Exercise and Sport Sciences Reviews*, vol. 1, edited by J. H. Wilmore. New York: Academic Press, 1973.

Runner's World. The Complete Runner. Mountain View, Calif.: World Publications, 1974.

WILT, F. "Training for Competitive Running." In *Exercise Physiology*, edited by H. B. Falls. New York: Academic Press, 1968.

7

Body Build and Composition

The appropriate size, shape, build and composition of the athlete's body is of major importance to success in almost all athletic endeavors. It is obvious that the 7-ft 1-in. center in basketball could never have been developed into a proficient jockey. Similarly, the 130-lb marathon runner would not be the ideal candidate for a starting assignment on the defensive line of a professional football team. As was discussed earlier in regard to other components of physical training, each athlete has a genetic profile that largely dictates limits for both his body build and composition. Muscle training will develop increased muscle mass to varying degrees, and diet and vigorous exercise, when combined, will lead to substantial losses in body fat. However, when compared to the broad range of body sizes and builds in the total world of athletics, from the small gymnast to the gigantic Sumo wrestler, the range of variability within any one individual is small and quite restricted. The athlete is then limited by what was given to him by his parents. This does not imply that athletes should dismiss this aspect of their physical profile with the feeling that nothing can be done to improve themselves. While body type or build can be altered only slightly, substantial alterations can occur in body composition that can be of major importance for the athlete's performance.

What is the difference between body build, body size, and body composition? Body build refers to the morphology, or the form and structure, of the body. *Somatotyping* is a procedure used in science to describe the morphology of the body in a quantitative manner. Most somatotyping systems utilize the concept that the body has three major components, or dimensions: muscularity, linearity, and fatness. The three components have been termed *mesomorphy* for muscularity, *ectomorphy* for linearity, and *endomorphy* for fatness. Since almost everyone has some degree of each of these components, a rating procedure was developed in which each person could be given a rating in each of these three major areas. The original system developed by Sheldon used a rating scale of from 1 to 7 to designate, on an increasing basis, the absence of the component to the preponderance of the component, respectively. As an example, a rating of 2–7–2 (endomorphy-mesomorphy-ectomorphy) would indicate an individual who would be described as having a preponderance of muscle, very little fat, and a stocky frame (lack of linearity).

Body size simply refers to the height and mass, or weight, of the individual, e.g., short and small or tall and large. The distinctions of being short or tall, large or small, heavy or light depend entirely on the sport, position within a sport, or a particular event. A height of 6 ft 3 in. would be relatively short for a professional basketball player but tall for a long-distance runner. Similarly, a weight of 230 lb would be heavy for a quarterback but light for a defensive end in football. Body size, therefore, must be considered relative to the sport, position, or event.

Body composition adds a new dimension to the athlete's understanding of himself. To know that the athlete weighs 200 lb means very little to either the athlete or his coach. To know that only 10 lb is fat and the remaining 190 lb is lean provides considerably more information that can be of use in assisting that athlete to reach his performance potential. With this distribution, the athlete knows that only 5 percent of his body weight [(10 lb/200 lb) × 100] is fat, which is about as low as any athlete should go. He would realize that his weight was not a problem, and that he should not be concerned about a weight loss. However, an athlete of the same weight, 200 lb, who had 50 lb of fat and 150 lb of lean weight would be 25 percent fat, which would constitute a serious weight problem. If the amount of fat in proportion to an individual's total weight is high, it will have a negative influence on his athletic performance, i.e., the higher the fat percentage, the poorer the performance. Thus, an accurate assessment of the athlete's body composition will provide him with valuable insight into his most efficient weight for his sport or event. As was stated in Chapter 3, Chronic Adaptations to Exercise, total weight is composed of the fat weight and the lean weight. The lean weight is merely a convenient term to account for all of the body tissue which is not fat, e.g., muscle, bone, skin, and weight of the organs. Fortunately, when working with athletes and weight gains and losses, it is primarily the fat and muscle mass that change, therefore, any changes in lean weight are generally reflective of changes in muscle mass.

ASSESSMENT OF BODY BUILD AND COMPOSITION

Somatotype

As was mentioned in the previous section, body build is usually assessed by one of the standard systems of somatotyping. Somatyp-

ing dates back to the time of Hippocrates, who used two basic body types; phthisic habitus, or a long, thin body, and apoplectic habitus, or a short, thick body. Several somatotype systems were developed in the 1800's and early 1900's. In the 1930's, Sheldon revolutionized the science of somatotyping by assigning ratings to each of the three categories, endomorphy, mesomorphy and ectomorphy. Prior to this time, somatotyping systems attempted to classify each individual into one of only two or three broad categories. Sheldon's system allowed for the extreme variability between individuals.

In Sheldon's system, endomorphy is characterized by roundness and softness, as typified by the grossly obese individual. Mesomorphy is characterized by a square body with prominent musculature, as illustrated by the middle-weight weight lifter. The ectomorph is linear and fragile with small muscles and prominent bones, as illustrated by the long-distance runner.

The Sheldon system of somatotyping is quite complex and requires the assistance of a highly skilled, trained technician. First, photographs of the athlete are taken showing the front, rear and side views. Figure 7–1 illustrates the somatotype photograph of former world-record holder and Olympic champion Peter Snell, a middle-distance runner from New Zealand. Snell, regarded by many as the best all-around track athlete of the 20th century, was rated 2–6–2, which is predominently mesomorphy, with very little endomorphy or ectomorphy. Once the photograph has been taken, a history of the athlete's height and weight is recorded with special attention to his maximal achieved weight throughout his lifetime. Two indices are calculated: the *ponderal index* (height/$\sqrt[3]{\text{weight}}$) and the trunk index. The trunk index is the ratio of the photographic area of the thoracic trunk to that of the abdominal trunk. It is a measure of the relative degree of endomorphy and mesomorphy, while the ponderal index provides an index of ectomorphy. A series of tables is then used to derive the final somatotype values for the three categories.

A somatogram is used for plotting the vari-

FIGURE 7–1

Somatotype photograph of former world-record holder and Olympic-champion, middle-distance runner Peter Snell. Somatotype was rated as a 2–6–2. (From J. M. Tanner, The Physique of the Olympic Athlete. *London: George Allen and Unwin, Ltd., 1964. Reproduced by permission of the publisher.)*

ous somatotypes of different athletes. This is illustrated in Figure 7–2. A distribution of somatotypes for 4,000 American college students is shown in Figure 7–3 and can be compared with those for Olympic track and field athletes (Figure 7–4). It is interesting to note the absence of any athletes in the endomorphic section of the somatogram.

More recently, several individuals have attempted to simplify the Sheldon system of somatotyping. Probably the most widely used system was introduced by Heath and Carter in 1967. Their technique can be effectively utilized by anyone trained in anthropometry,

i.e., the study of human body measurements, and it does not require a somatotype photograph. For the first component, endomorphy, the triceps, subscapular and suprailiac skinfolds are measured, the resulting values are added together, and the total compared with a scale of values to obtain the component rating (Figure 7–5). For the second component, mesomorphy, measurements are taken of height in inches, the width of the upper arm bone (humerus) at the elbow joint; the width of the upper leg, or thigh bone (femur), at the knee joint, the girth or circumference of the upper arm and calf, and the skinfold at the

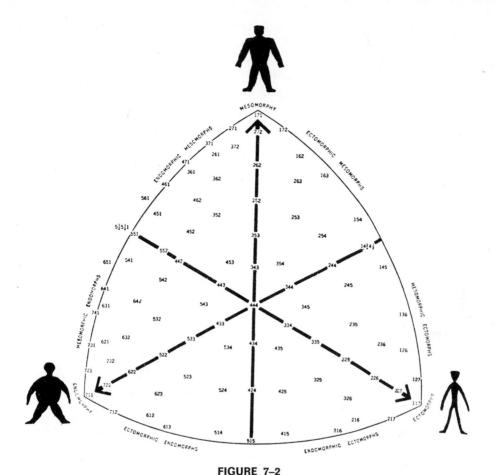

FIGURE 7–2

Illustration of a somatogram. (From J. M. Tanner, The Physique of the Olympic Athlete. London: George Allen and Unwin, Ltd., 1964. Reproduced by permission of the publisher.)

triceps and calf. Again, using a series of scales, the appropriate component rating is obtained. The third component, ectomorphy, is determined by calculating the ponderal index, i.e., height/$\sqrt[3]{\text{weight}}$, and comparing this value with a scale to obtain the rating component. The resulting somatotype is similar to a Sheldon somatotype, as the athlete is rated in all three components. However, the rating scale is open-ended, instead of varying between only 1 and 7. The scale allows an individual to have a rating that exceeds 7 for any one component, but realistically, this seldom happens. The primary advantage of the Heath-Carter system is the ease with which a somatotype can be obtained.

Body Composition

Few body composition assessments have ever been conducted directly. A direct analysis can only be performed on a dead body, or cadaver, where the different body tissues can be very carefully dissected. This requires a tremendous amount of time and effort, and cadavers are not easy to obtain. Furthermore, of what value is the assessment to the individual or cadaver who has been assessed? Because of the problems associated with direct analysis and the relatively limited use of the resulting data, a number of indirect techniques have been developed to provide an estimate of the body's

SOMATOTYPES OF ATHLETES

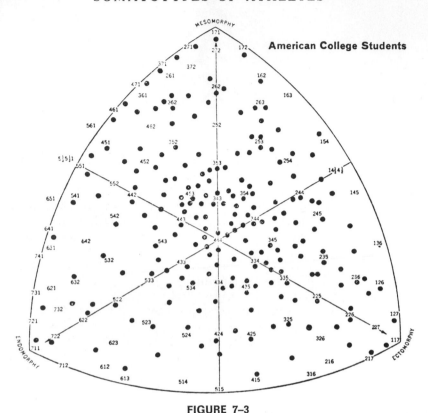

FIGURE 7–3

Somatogram, illustrating the distribution of somatotypes of 4,000 American male, college students. (From J. M. Tanner, The Physique of the Olympic Athlete. *London: George Allen and Unwin, Ltd., 1964. Reproduced by permission of the publisher.)*

composition in the living human. The majority of these techniques fractionate the body into only two components, or compartments, the lean body weight and the fat weight. These indirect techniques can be divided into either laboratory or field assessment techniques.

Laboratory Assessment. Probably the most widely used and most accurate laboratory method for assessing body composition is to determine the density of the body. As was explained in Chapter 3, Chronic Adaptations to Exercise, body density = (body weight/body volume). Body weight is easily determined. The determination of body volume presents a slight problem, but it can be determined rather

easily in the laboratory. While there are several ways of determining body volume, the easiest and least expensive way is to measure the athlete's loss of weight in water, which Archimedes discovered was equivalent to the volume of the body. The athlete is weighed while totally submerged under water (refer to Figure 3–4), and this weight subtracted from the athlete's body weight provides an estimate of his volume. A correction must be made for the volume of air trapped in the lungs. This is not difficult and can even be estimated in young athletes.

As an example of these calculations, an athlete who weighs 200 lb is found to weigh only 12 lb when totally submerged under water. The volume of air trapped in his lungs at the

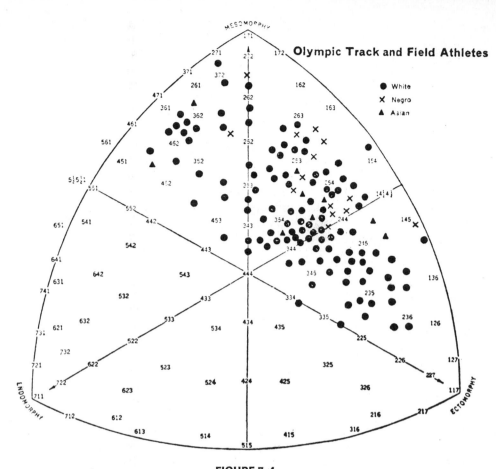

FIGURE 7–4

Somatogram, showing the distribution of the somatotypes of 137 male Olympic, track-and-field athletes. (From J. M. Tanner, The Physique of the Olympic Athlete. *London: George Allen and Unwin, Ltd., 1964. Reproduced by permission of the publisher.)*

time he was weighed under water was 1.5 liters. Since 1 liter of water weighs approximately 1 kg, it is easier to convert the above weights to metric units; thus, his weight would be 90.7 kg, and his underwater weight, 5.4 kg. Since the 1.5 liters of air trapped in his lungs gave him an increased buoyancy and caused him to weigh lighter than his actual or true weight under water, the equivalent water weight of 1.5 liters, i.e., 1.5 kg, must be added to his underwater weight. This would give the athlete a submerged weight of 6.9 kg. Since body volume is equal to the loss of weight in water, this athlete's volume would be equal to

90.7 kg − 6.9 kg, or 83.8 kg, which is the equivalent to a volume of 83.8 liters of water. His density would be,

$$\text{Density}_{body} = \text{Weight}_{body}/\text{Volume}_{body}$$
$$= 90.7\,\text{kg}/83.8\,\text{liters}$$
$$= 1.082$$

Several investigators have derived equations that allow the conversion of body density to relative, or percentage, body fat. This is possible since the density of fat is known to be approximately 0.907 and that of the lean tissue is estimated to be 1.100. According to the equation developed by Siri,

HEATH-CARTER SOMATOTYPE RATING FORM

NAME .... AGE .... SEX: M   F   NO: ....

OCCUPATION .... ETHNIC GROUP.......................... DATE ....

PROJECT: .... MEASURED BY:...........................

Skinfolds mm		TOTAL SKINFOLDS (mm)
Triceps =	Upper Limit	10.9 14.9 18.9 22.9 26.9 31.2 35.8 40.7 46.2 52.2 58.7 65.7 73.2 81.2 89.7 98.9 108.9 119.7 131.2 143.7 157.2 171.9 187.9 204.0
Subcapular =	Mid-point	9.0 13.0 17 0 21.0 25.0 29.0 33.5 38.0 43.5 49.0 55.5 62.0 69.5 77.0 85.5 94.0 104.0 114.0 125.5 137.0 150.5 164.0 180.0 196.0
Supraliac =	Lower Limit	7.0 11.0 15.0 19.0 23.0 27.0 31.3 35.9 40.8 46.3 52.3 58.8 65.8 73.3 81.3 89.8 99.0 109.0 119.8 131.3 143.8 157.3 172.0 188.0

TOTAL SKINFOLDS = [ ]
Calf =

FIRST COMPONENT	½ 1 1½ 2 2½ 3 3½ 4 4½ 5 5½ 6 6½ 7 7½ 8 8½ 9 9½ 10 10½ 11 11½ 12

Height cm [ ]	139.7 143.5 147.3 151.1 154.9 158.8 162.6 166.4 170.2 174.0 177.8 181.6 185.4 189.2 193.0 196.9 200.7 204.5 208.3 212.1 215.9 219.7 223.5 227.3
Humerus width cm [ ]	5.19 5.34 5.49 5.64 5.78 5.93 6.07 6.22 6.37 6.51 6.65 6.80 6.95 7.09 7.24 7.38 7.53 7.67 7.82 7.97 8.11 8.25 8.40 8.55
Femur width cm [ ]	7.41 7.62 7.83 8.04 8.24 8.45 8.66 8.87 9.08 9.28 9.49 9.70 9.91 10.12 10.33 10.53 10.74 10.95 11.16 11.36 11.57 11.78 11.99 12.21
Biceps girth [ ] -T* [ ]	23.7 24.4 25.0 25.7 26.3 27.0 27.7 28.3 29.0 29.7 30.3 31.0 31.6 32.2 33.0 33.6 34.3 35.0 35.6 36.3 37.0 37.6 38.3 39.0
Calf girth [ ] -C^ [ ]	27.7 28.5 29.3 30.1 30.8 31.6 32.4 33.2 33.9 34.7 35.5 36.3 37.1 37.8 38.6 39.4 40.2 41.0 41.7 42.5 43.3 44.1 44.9 45.6

SECOND COMPONENT	½ 1 1½ 2 2½ 3 3½ 4 4½ 5 5½ 6 6½ 7 7½ 8 8½ 9

Weight kg =	Upper limit
Ht. /√³ Wt. = [ ]	

	Upper limit	39.65 40.74 41.43 42.13 42.82 43.48 44.18 44.84 45.53 46.23 46.92 47.58 48.25 48.94 49.63 50.33 50.99 51.68
	Mid-point and	40.20 41.09 41.79 42.48 43.14 43.84 44.50 45.19 45.89 46.32 47.24 47.94 48.60 49.29 49.99 50.68 51.34
	Lower limit below	39.66 40.75 41.44 42.14 42.83 43.49 44.19 44.85 45.54 46.24 46.93 47.59 48.26 48.95 49.64 50.34 51.00

THIRD COMPONENT	·½ 1 1½ 2 2½ 3 3½ 4 4½ 5 5½ 6 6½ 7 7½ 8 8½ 9

	FIRST COMPONENT	SECOND COMPONENT	THIRD COMPONENT	
Anthropometric Somatotype				BY: ....
Anthropometric plus Photoscopic Somatotype				RATER: ....

*Biceps girth in cm corrected for fat by subtracting triceps skinfold value expressed in cm.
^Calf girth in cm corrected for fat by subtracting medial calf skinfold cm.

FIGURE 7–5

Heath-Carter somatotype form.

Relative fat = [(495/Density$_{body}$) − 450]

or, for our 200-lb athlete,

$$\text{Relative fat} = [(495/1.082) - 450]$$
$$= 457.3 - 450$$
$$= 7.3\%$$

Body volume can also be determined by other methods. One method determines the actual volume of water displaced by the athlete when he is totally submerged under water. This can be done by having the athlete climb into a large cylinder filled to the top with water. As he lowers himself into the water, his volume will displace an equivalent volume of water. The volume of water that spills over, or the volume of water necessary to refill the cylinder to the top once the athlete is out of the cylinder, will give approximations of the athlete's body volume when corrected for the air trapped in the lungs. Another technique uses an air-tight booth, similar in appearance to a telephone booth. A small known volume of helium is introduced into the booth where the athlete is sitting relaxed in a chair. The athlete's body volume is determined by the degree of dilution of the helium within the chamber. With a small athlete of low volume, the air space in the booth is quite large and the helium concentration is low due to the dilution by the large volume of air surrounding the athlete. With a large athlete, his body volume is large and fills most of the booth, leaving a small volume of surrounding air. Introducing the same volume of helium will result in a higher concentration of helium in the chamber, since the air volume is so small. This technique is relatively complex, requiring a rather elaborate engineering design, but it does provide a comparatively comfortable experience for the subject.

Additional methods are available for determining the composition of the body. Radiography is an excellent way to assess local areas of the body, such as the calf, thigh, or upper arm. Soft tissue X-ray differentiates between the various layers of skin, fat, bone, and muscle. An example of this technique is shown in Figure 7–6, illustrating the X-ray of a world-class shot-putter. Measurements of bone, muscle, and fat are taken at three specific sites and combined to provide an estimate of the individual's total body composition. While this technique allows a direct quantification of all three major components, it does present the problem that all areas of the body are not similarly developed. Thus, the estimation of the total body composition could be considerably in error.

Another method that is frequently used in the body composition assessment of athletes is the whole-body counter, which measures the amount of gamma radiation emitted by the body from its naturally occurring potassium-40. There is a rather constant relationship between the total amount of potassium-40 in the body and the lean body mass. Again, the technique is complex and requires expensive equipment, but the analyses are accurate and the subject discomfort is minimal.

One last method, which has been used in the past, employs ultrasound. Muscle, bone, and fat have different densities and accoustical properties, so it is possible to use high-frequency

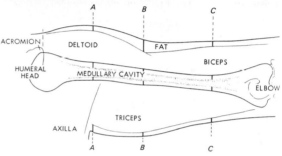

FIGURE 7–6

Radiographic analyses of body composition, using the upper arm of a world-class, male shot-putter. (From Albert R. Behnke and Jack H. Wilmore, Evaluation and Regulation of Body Build and Composition, © *1974, p. 28. Reprinted by permission of Prentice-Hall, Inc., Englewood Cliffs, New Jersey.)*

sound waves to differentiate between tissue types. A special transducer generates sound waves, which pass into the tissue. When a change in density is encountered, some of these waves are reflected, received by a pickup device, and converted to an electrical impulse. The impulse is passed to a detecting device for amplification and recording. The thickness of the fat, muscle, and bone of any one particular segment can be calculated from the recording.

Field Assessment. A number of techniques have been devised for assessing body composition outside of the laboratory. One of the most accurate is the underwater weighing technique. While this is normally a laboratory

FIGURE 7–7

Underwater weighing technique conducted outside of the laboratory.

technique, it can also be easily performed outside of the laboratory, if a swimming pool, or smaller body of water, and a hanging scale are available. Figure 7–7 illustrates a system used to assess the body compositions of an entire professional football team while at their summer, preseason training camp. The technique is simple, fast, and accurate. The air remaining in the lungs at the time the underwater weight is determined can be estimated

from normal population values for the same age, height, and sex as the athlete. A comprehensive description of how to conduct a complete assessment using this technique, is presented in Appendix C, Field Tests for Assessing Physical Fitness.

Over the years, a number of different anthropometric techniques have been derived to estimate various components of body composition. As stated earlier, anthropometry is the study of human body measurements and usually includes girths or circumferences of limbs or segments, e.g., girth of the calf, breadths or diameters of bones, e.g., width of the hips or pelvis, and skinfold estimates of the thickness of subcutaneous fat, e.g., triceps skinfold. By using girths, breadths, or skinfolds, or a combination, equations have been derived to predict body density, relative and absolute body fat, lean body weight, and ideal weight. These equations have been found, however, to be population-specific, i.e., they provide an accurate assessment only for groups or populations that are similar in age, sex, nationality, and general physical fitness. This simply implies that it is necessary to select an equation that was derived from a group of subjects as similar as possible to the group of athletes or individuals to be studied. It would not be appropriate to use an equation derived from a group of middle-aged males for the evaluation of a group of young, adolescent males.

Anthropometric techniques are simple to apply and require little in the way of equipment. Most of the equations that have been derived are reasonably accurate. However, almost all existing equations have been derived from normal, nonathletic populations. Their applicability to athletic populations, particularly to extremely lean athletes or athletes with highly developed musculature, is unknown at the present time. It has been assumed that these equations are equally accurate for all athletes, but this requires confirmation by additional research. Another area of uncertainty in using anthropometric equations is the question of their ability to accurately estimate changes in body composition. While most equations predict, with reasonable accuracy, the individual's body composition at any one point in time, there is some doubt as to how accurately these equations can predict those changes in body composition that occur with either weight gains or weight losses through diet and exercise. Again, further research will be necessary to determine the ability of these equations to estimate change. Several anthropometric techniques for estimating body composition are outlined in Appendix C, Field Tests for Assessing Physical Fitness.

ALTERATIONS IN BODY BUILD AND COMPOSITION WITH PHYSICAL TRAINING

Body build can be altered to a limited extent with physical training. However, previous research has suggested that somatotypes change very little within the individual's total life span. In fact, one study has shown that adult somatotypes can be predicted with a high degree of accuracy during the period of pre-adolescence. It is apparent that muscle mass can be both lost and gained with physical inactivity and strength training, respectively, and that body fat can be gained or lost with manipulations in both diet and exercise patterns. These changes are usually of a limited nature, resulting in little or no change in the somatotype. This inability to substantially alter somatotype is largely the result of the inherited, or genetic, nature of body type.

Body composition can undergo substantial alterations with physical training. In the past, it has been frequently stated that physical activity has only a limited influence in changing body composition. It was argued that even exercise of a vigorous nature required the expenditure of too few calories to result in substantial reductions in body fat. To illustrate, it has been estimated that a 150-lb woman would have to climb up and down a 10-ft flight of stairs approximately 1,000 times at a moderate pace in order to loose 1 lb of fat. Chopping wood for 8 hr at a moderate pace would cause the same weight loss. These examples tend to discourage the use of exercise for weight loss and weight control. Yet, exer-

cise has been found to be very effective in the past in promoting major alterations in body composition. How is this apparent conflict in results accounted for?

When estimating the energy cost of an activity, it is customary to use the steady-state, energy-expenditure value during the exercise. If, for example, it requires 7.5 Kcals/min to shovel snow, i.e., steady-state value during exercise, it would require a total of only 450 Kcals for one hour of work, or a loss of approximately 0.13 lb of fat. As was explained in Chapter 2, Acute Responses to Exercise, the metabolism remains elevated during the period immediately following exercise. This was referred to as the "period of oxygen debt." This recovery back to pre-exercise levels can require several minutes for light exercise, up to several hours for heavy exercise, and up to 12 to 24 hr for prolonged, exhaustive exercise. The elevation of the metabolism above normal levels during the recovery period from heavy to prolonged exhaustive exercise can total a substantial number of Kcals. If the oxygen consumption following exercise remains elevated by only 100 ml or 0.1 liter/min, this will amount to approximately 0.5 Kcal/min or 30 Kcal/hr. If the metabolism remains elevated for 10 hr, this would amount to an additional 300 Kcal expended that would not normally be included in the calculated total energy expenditure for that particular activity. Therefore, this major source of energy expenditure, which occurs as a result of the exercise bout, is frequently ignored in most calculations of the energy cost of various activities. If the individual in the above example exercised 5 days per week, he would have expended 1,500 Kcal, or approximately 0.4 lb, in one week just from the recovery period alone.

Among those who accept the fact that exercise can substantially alter body composition, there are many who feel that the process is too slow. The average jogger who jogs three days a week for 30 min a day at a 7-mph pace, or slightly over an 8 min 30 sec/mi, will use approximately 14.5 Kcal/min, or 435 Kcal, for the total run/day, resulting in a total expenditure per week of approximately 1,305 Kcal, or slightly over ⅓ lb of fat loss each week. Why even bother for that small amount? Individuals who are short sighted might conclude that there are better and easier ways, and that exercise is a painfully slow way to significantly reduce fat. What if the jogger described above were stubborn and stayed with his routine? In 52 weeks, providing his energy intake remained constant, he would lose a total of 17 lb, a figure that looks more impressive.

Generally, present society is time-oriented and has to have what it wants immediately, if not sooner. Consider the 25-yr-old professional athlete who finds that his weight is 15–20 lb more than it was at 21 yr. He finally decides to lose his excess poundage but wants to accomplish this by the start of the preseason training, which is less than three weeks away. Obviously, exercise is of no value to him, for he would need nine to twelve months to lose this much weight through exercise alone. He needs to lose more than 5 lb per week, so he relies on a "crash" diet, selecting whichever diet is in vogue at that time. Everyone knows that it is possible to lose 6 to 8 lb per week with these diets. What kind of success might our athlete have?

This example is not unique. Many athletes find themselves out of shape and overweight as a result of overeating and inactivity during the off-season. Also, they typically will wait until the last few weeks prior to reporting for their sport before they attempt to attack the problem. In the above example, the athlete may be able to shed 15 lb in less than three weeks as a result of his crash diet. However, much of this weight loss will be from the body's water compartment and very little from stored fat. Several studies have reported that substantial weight losses will occur with starvation and semi-starvation (500 Kcal/day or less) diets, but that of the weight lost, over 60 percent came from the body's lean weight and less than 40 percent from the fat weight. Much of the lean weight lost is in the form of water. Most of these crash diets require a very low carbohydrate intake. As a result, the carbohydrate stores of the body become depleted. With every 1 gm of carbohydrate used,

approximately 3 gm of water are lost. With a total body glycogen content of 800 gm, a depletion of the stored glycogen would result in a loss of approximately 2,400 gm of water, or slightly more than 5 lb of the weight lost. Much of this loss will occur during the first week of the diet.

It is literally impossible to lose more than 4 lb of fat per week, even if on a total starvation diet. This can be demonstrated quite easily. Assuming that it requires a 3,500 Kcal deficit to lose 1 lb of fat, the athlete in the above example could lose no more than 0.7 lb per day on a total starvation diet. His maintenance level would be approximately 2,500 Kcal/day, so he would have a 2,500 Kcal deficit per day if he abstained completely from food. However, during a starvation diet, research indicates that the total body metabolism is reduced by 20–25 percent. A 20 percent reduction in the athlete's metabolism would lower his total deficit to only 2,000 Kcal per day, or approximately 0.57 lb of fat loss per day. In one week this would result in a loss of only 4 lb of fat. And this is on a total starvation diet! Few people would be able to tolerate the discomfort associated with prolonged periods of starvation.

The sensible approach to weight reduction is to combine moderate dietary restriction with increased levels of exercise. The appetite is delicately balanced with the actual caloric needs of the body. Simply removing one buttered slice of bread from the diet each day and keeping the activity levels and diet constant will result in a weight loss of 10 lb per year (100 Kcal/day × 364 days), which is not an insignificant amount. Combined with a modest 0.25–0.30 lb weight loss per week from a 3 day per week jogging program, the total weight lost would amount to 25–30 lb in a single year. Patience is a virtue, for this form of weight loss has been found to be more permanent. The rapid weight losses experienced with crash diets are quickly regained, probably due to the fact that when a balanced diet is substituted for the low-carbohydrate diet, the water that was lost is quickly regained. In addition, research evidence suggests that combining exercise with diet reduces the proportion of the weight lost from the lean tissue to an insignificant level. Since the purpose of the weight-loss program is to lose body fat, and not lean tissue, the combination diet and exercise program is the preferred approach.

When combining diet and exercise, the exercise should be performed a minimum of 3 days per week. The greater the frequency, intensity, and duration of training, the greater will be the resulting weight loss. With respect to dietary modifications, a reduction of 200–500 Kcal/day from the athlete's normal diet will add up to a substantial weight loss over time. Weight losses of approximately 1 lb per week, which represents a more realistic goal, can be achieved with such a combination. It should be added that a balanced diet is essential to assure the necessary vitamins and minerals that the athlete needs. Vitamin sup-

plementation may or may not be essential. Results of research at this time conflict. This topic will receive additional coverage in Chapter 10, Ergogenic Aids. Lastly, the diet should be consumed over at least three meals per day. Many athletes make the mistake of eating only one or two meals per day, skipping either breakfast or lunch, or both, and then consuming a very large dinner. Research in animals has demonstrated that, given the same number of total calories, the animals that ate their daily food ration in one or two hours gained more weight than those that nibbled their ration throughout the day.

Another misconception that has been used frequently to discount the benefits of exercise in weight control is the contention that the exercise, itself, will stimulate the appetite to such an extent that voluntary food intake will be increased to account for the additional expend-

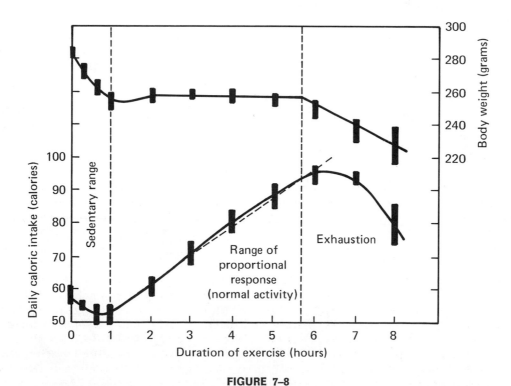

FIGURE 7–8

Food intake and body weight changes with increasing durations of exercise. (From J. Mayer, Amer. J. Physiol. 177 (1954): 544–48. Reproduced by permission of the publisher.)

iture of energy through exercise. Jean Mayer (1954), world-famous nutritionist at Harvard University, reported many years ago that animals that exercise for up to 1 hr, there is actually a decrease in appetite when compared to the appetites of sedentary animals (Figure 7–8). Similar results have been reported for humans. Exercise does appear to be a mild, appetite suppressant.

From the above discussion, it can be concluded that exercise plays an important role in weight-loss and weight-control programs. The exercise does not have to be of an extended and exhaustive nature to be effective. The athlete should select an endurance-type of activity that he can enjoy, and participate in this activity for 30–40 min/day, 4–5 days/ week, at an intensity of from 60 to 75 percent of his endurance capacity. Over time, this exercise program will produce the desired results. Table 7–1 provides an example of the caloric expenditure of running on the basis of the pace of running.

The role of exercise in spot weight reduction is a controversial area. Many individuals, including athletes, believe that by exercising a specific area the fat in that localized area will be utilized, thus reducing the locally stored fat. Several research studies have reported results that tend to support the concept of spot reduction. However, recent work suggests that spot reduction is a myth and that exercise, even when localized, draws from all of the fat stores of the body, not just from the local depots. A study by Gwinup et al. (1971) utilized outstanding tennis players to investigate this phenomenon. The researchers theorized that the tennis players would be ideal subjects for studying spot reduction since they could act as their own controls, i.e., the dominant arm exercises vigorously every day for several hours, while the nondominant arm is relatively sedentary. They postulated that if spot reduction were a reality, the nondominant (inactive) arm should have substantially more fat than the dominant (active) arm. In fact, while the arm girths were substantially greater in the dominant arm, due to exercise hypertrophy, there were absolutely no differences in the fat contents of the two arms, as assessed by subcutaneous skinfold fat thicknesses. The general impression among researchers, at the present time, is that fat is mobilized from those areas of highest concentration and not

TABLE 7–1.   Caloric Expenditure of Running and Jogging at Different Paces on the Basis of Body Weight*

| Weight | *Calories/hours Pace per mile* | | | | | | | |
	5:20	6:00	6:40	7:20	8:00	8:40	9:20	10:00
120	936	828	726	654	594	540	498	456
130	1,014	888	792	708	642	582	534	492
140	1,086	954	846	756	690	630	576	528
150	1,164	1,020	906	810	738	672	612	564
160	1,236	1,086	966	870	780	708	654	600
170	1,314	1,152	1,020	918	828	762	690	636
180	1,386	1,212	1,080	972	876	798	732	672
190	1,464	1,278	1,140	1,020	924	840	774	708
200	1,536	1,344	1,194	1,074	972	888	810	744
210	1,614	1,416	1,230	1,122	1,020	930	846	780
220	1,686	1,482	1,314	1,176	1,068	972	888	816

* Adapted from J. Henderson, "Planning High-Calorie Workouts." *Runner's World* 9 (1974): 24–25. Reproduced by permission of the publisher.

from specific localized areas, thus negating the spot reduction theory.

The effectiveness of spot reduction has been promoted by many health studios with the claim that they can take off several inches from the customer's waist in a few short weeks. Substantial reductions of the abdominal girth can result from localized exercise, e.g., bent-knee sit-ups, but this is not due to localized fat losses. A loss of 3 to 4 in in the abdominal girth can occur from sit-up exercises alone, without any loss at all in either total or localized fat. This is due to a strengthening of the abdominal muscles, which pulls the abdominal contents back into their normal position. Progressive abdominal weakness leads to a spilling-out of the abdominal contents, which results in a "pot belly" appearance. Strengthening these abdominal muscles pulls everything back into place but does little if anything to alter the fat content of that area.

Exercise can also lead to substantial weight gains. These gains, however, appear to be predominantly, if not totally, increases in lean body weight. Strength and power training programs lead to the largest gains in lean weight, as a result of their relationship with muscle hypertrophy. Even limited muscle hypertrophy will result from endurance training programs. It is somewhat ironic that in previously sedentary, middle-aged men, an endurance training program will frequently lead to little or no change in total body weight but that body composition will undergo a marked change. Typically, there is a substantial loss in body fat, but also an increase in lean tissue of about the same magnitude. This phenomenon can be deceiving, since there is no change in scale weight even after months of hard work. Although it is natural to become quite angry over the apparent inability to lose weight, individuals, when questioned, admit that their clothes do not fit as well as they once did. Usually, their clothes are tight in the arms and legs and loose in the abdominal area, which illustrates both the gain in muscle as well as the loss in fat. As was mentioned earlier, with regard to body composition, the scale weight of the individual is not an accurate indication of body composition, nor does it accurately reflect the changes that result from chronic exercise.

MECHANISMS OF CHANGE

It would appear that weight losses and weight gains are a simple matter of either energy input, energy expenditure, or both. To lose weight, one can reduce the caloric intake, increase the caloric expenditure, or combine the two. Likewise, with weight gains, one can increase the caloric intake, reduce the energy expenditure, or combine the two. Unfortunately, common observation and recent research suggest that energy balance is not that simple. Nearly everyone has known of individuals who can, literally, gorge themselves daily, yet remain lean, or conversely, of individuals who continue gaining body fat even though they eat only limited amounts, well below what would be expected to be their maintenance levels. Individuals do metabolize food differently, some being more efficient than others. Also, some individuals are more efficient in their expenditure of energy for fixed work tasks. These phenomena are not well understood at the present time, and considerably more research will be necessary to determine which factors are involved and their relative importance.

With specific reference to exercise, it would appear that the reduction in fat by exercise is solely the result of an added expenditure of calories. Yet, the body might be expected to adapt to this additional expenditure by increasing the appetite to compensate for the deficit. This is a difficult problem that defies a simple solution. Several research studies have pointed to the possible role of human growth hormone as being responsible for the increased fatty acid mobilization during exercise. Growth hormone levels do increase sharply with exercise and remain elevated for up to several hours in the recovery period. Other research has suggested that the adipose tissue is more sensitive to the sympathetic nervous system or to the levels of circulating catecholamines, which would result in increased lipid mobilization. More recent research suggests that a specific fat-mobilizing substance, which is highly responsive to elevated levels of activity, is responsible. At the present time, it is impossible to state with certainty which factors are of greatest importance in mediating this response.

It was demonstrated in the previous section that exercise tends to suppress the appetite. While this is true for male laboratory animals, it has been shown that exercise actually increases the appetites of female laboratory animals. The reason for this sex difference is not presently known. In humans, most of the research has been conducted on males, and the results indicate either no change in appetite with increased levels of exercise or slight decreases. It is possible that the decrease in appetite occurs only with intense levels of work in which the increased catecholamine levels suppress the appetite.

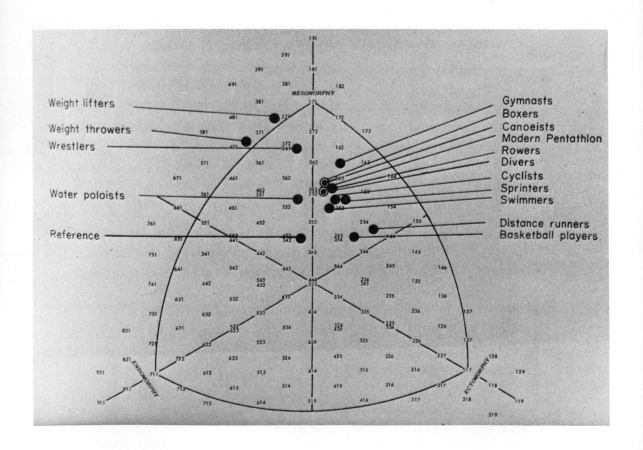

FIGURE 7–9

Somatotype distribution of mean somatotypes for male participants in various sports at the 1968 Olympic Games. (From A. L. deGaray et al., eds., Genetic and Anthropological Studies of Olympic Athletes. *New York: Academic Press, 1974. Reproduced by permission of the publisher.)*

The gains in lean weight with exercise are undoubtedly due to increases in protein anabolism, or synthesis, which leads to muscle hypertrophy. In Chapter 3, Chronic Adaptations to Exercise, the potential cause of muscle hypertrophy was explored and found to be the result of increases in muscle fiber size, possibly due to an increased number of myofibrils. The possibility of fiber splitting was also discussed. Without knowing the specific changes that occur within the muscle, it is difficult to postulate the possible mechanisms that trigger these changes. Again, since the human growth hormone has anabolic properties, its rise with exercise and its continued elevation during recovery have led several investigators to suggest that this might explain the gains in lean

tissue. Obviously, further research is needed before the actual mechanisms for these changes can be adequately defined.

RELATIONSHIP OF BODY BUILD AND COMPOSITION TO ATHLETIC PERFORMANCE

It was stated in an earlier section of this chapter that the body build of an individual is determined largely through genetics. Characteristics that are inherited from parents establish rather narrow limits of variation in an athlete's body build. Size is also largely determined genetically. With this in mind, it is important to understand that most sports require a certain body type for success. This is

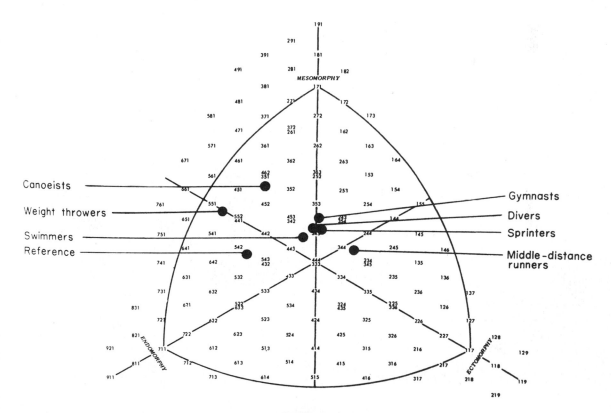

FIGURE 7–10

Somatotype distribution of mean somatotypes for female participants in various sports at the 1968 Olympic Games. (From A. L. deGaray et al., eds., Genetic and Anthropological Studies of Olympic Athletes. New York: Academic Press, 1974. Reproduced by permission of the publisher.)

illustrated in Figures 7–9 and 7–10, which present somatotype data from a large number of participants in the 1968 Olympic Games in Mexico City. While the values for females tend to be clustered around the central area of the somatogram, the values for males are quite well spread out, although they are all predominantly mesomorphic. Within any one sport, there is considerable variation, as is illustrated in Figure 7–11. From this information, it is obvious that the athlete, to be successful, should select a sport in which his somatotype will be an asset, rather than one in which he is bound to fail. Almost all sports, with few exceptions, require a moderate to high rating in mesomorphy. On the other hand, extreme endomorphs and extreme ectomorphs do very poorly in most sports.

A number of studies have related somatotype and body size to athletic performance in various sports. These have typically been associated with the Olympic Games in a particular year. Cureton (1951) studied the structural and functional capacities of 21 male members of the 1948 United States Olympic Team and 24 national- and international-caliber track

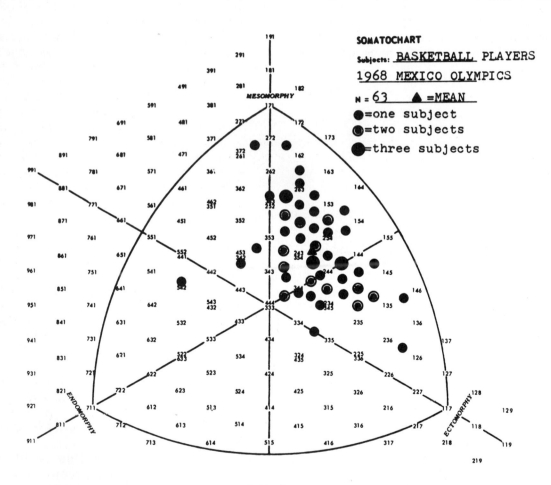

FIGURE 7–11

Somatogram, illustrating the variation in somatotype for basketball players from various countries participating in the 1968 Olympic Games. (From A. L. deGaray et al., eds., Genetic and Anthropological Studies of Olympic Athletes. *New York: Academic Press, 1974. Reproduced by permission of the publisher.)*

and field athletes. He found considerable differences between sports and between events in the same sport. Correnti and Zauli (1964) observed 166 Olympic track and field athletes and 8 swimmers at the 1960 Olympics in Rome. They observed differences in age, height, and weight for athletes in different events, but they found that the body shapes were similar within the same event.

Tanner (1964) studied 137 track and field athletes at the 1960 Olympics in Rome. He found that there were racial differences between athletes within the same event, that the somatotypes tended to cluster in specific areas, depending on the event, and that athletes can be separated by certain body dimensions according to their events. deGaray et al. (1964) conducted an exhaustive study on the athletes participating in the 1968 Olympic Games in Mexico City. A summary of their results was presented above in Figures 7–9 and 7–10. From all of these studies, it is apparent that body size and somatotype are important in determining success within any one sport, activity, or event. Since somatotype is largely genetically determined, this points to the importance of placing athletes in sports in which they can achieve, at least, a modest degree of success.

Body composition must be considered equally important to body build when attempting to maximize the athlete's performance potential. Several studies have found a high, negative relationship between performance in various activities and the relative amount of body fat (Wilmore and Haskell, 1972). The higher the percentage of body fat, the poorer the performance of the individual. This was true of all activities in which the body weight had to be moved either vertically or horizontally through space, e.g., sprinting and long jumping. Many athletes are under the impression that they must be big to be good in their sport. Size has been associated with the quality of the athlete's performance; the bigger the athlete, the better the performance. It is now recognized that this is true only if the size increase is due to an increase in the lean tissue. To add additional fat to the body just to increase the weight and

overall size is detrimental to performance, with the possible exception of the heavyweight weight lifter. Weight lifters may put on large amounts of fat weight under the pretense that the additional weight will help to lower their center of gravity and give them a greater mechanical advantage in lifting. To the best of the author's knowledge, the value of this has yet to be confirmed through research. Another notable exception to the theory that overall size is not the major determinant of athletic success is the Sumo wrestler. The larger individual does have a decided advantage, but the wrestler with the higher lean weight should have the greatest, overall success.

Rather than being concerned with overall weight, most athletes should be specifically concerned with their lean body weight. Eventually, techniques will be available that will allow a young athlete to undergo an extensive evaluation to provide an estimate of fat weight, lean weight, and a projected estimate of his potential for increasing lean body weight. In this way, the athlete could design a training program that would develop his lean tissue to this projected maximum, while maintaining his fat content at relatively low levels. While this would be a desirable approach for the athlete dependent on strength, power, and muscular endurance, it would be counterproductive for the endurance athlete, who is forced to move his total body mass horizontally for extended periods of time. Increased lean weight may prove to be a major detriment to successful performance for this athlete since it is an additional load that he must carry. The same may also be true for the high jumper, long jumper, and triple jumper, who depend on maximizing their vertical and horizontal distances. Additional weight, even though it is active lean tissue, may decrease rather than facilitate performance potential for these athletes.

An accurate assessment, or estimate, of the athlete's body composition is essential. Use of standard height-weight tables does not provide an accurate estimate of what the athlete should weigh. This fact was established in the original classic study relating body composition to athletics. Welham and Behnke studied the body compositions of twenty-five professional football players in 1942. Of these twenty-five professional athletes, seventeen were physically unqualified for military duty or first-class insurance on the basis of their weight. Of the seventeen "overweight" players, eleven were found to have very low levels of body fat, indicating that the overweight condition was the result of an excess of lean tissue and not excess fat. Wilmore and Haskell (1972) investigated the body composition of forty-four professional football players according to the positions that they played. The defensive backs were the leanest, lightest, and shortest of the five groups analyzed, while the defensive linemen were the fattest, heaviest, and nearly the tallest. The offensive backs and receivers were similar to the defensive backs, and the offensive linemen were comparable to the defensive linemen. The linebackers were unique and fell approximately between the linemen and backs relative to the observed variables. In comparison with the Welham and Behnke data for the 1942-era ball players, the linemen studied in 1969 through 1971 were taller and considerably heavier, but there were no substantial differences between the backs. The increased weight of the players studied recently was due to an increase in both the lean and fat weights of the linemen. These results, combined with additional results from 1972–76, are summarized in Tables 7–2 and 7–3.

Body composition values tend to vary with the sport. Those sports or activities that have a high endurance component will typically have

TABLE 7–2. Body Composition Characteristics of Professional Football Players Grouped by Position

Position	Num-ber	Height (in.)	Weight (lb)	(%)	Fat (lb)	Lean Weight (lb)
Defensive backs	26	71.9	187.0	9.6	18.1	168.9
Offensive backs and wide receivers	40	72.4	200.0	9.4	19.2	180.8
Linebackers	28	74.3	225.3	14.0	32.0	193.3
Offensive linemen and tight ends	38	76.0	248.3	15.6	38.7	209.0
Defensive linemen	32	75.8	258.2	18.2	47.0	211.2
Quarterbacks and kickers	16	72.8	198.7	14.4	28.7	170.0

TABLE 7–3. Comparison of the Body Composition of Professional Football Players of the Early 1940's with Those of the Late 1960's and Early 1970's

Position	Number	Height (in.)	Weight (lb)	Fat (%)	Fat (lb)	Lean Weight (lb)
Backs						
1940–41	13	71.3	189.0	7.1	13.5	175.6
Present	66	72.2	194.9	9.5	18.8	176.1
Linemen						
1940–41	12	73.1	214.1	14.0	30.0	184.1
Present	70	75.9	252.8	16.8	42.5	210.0

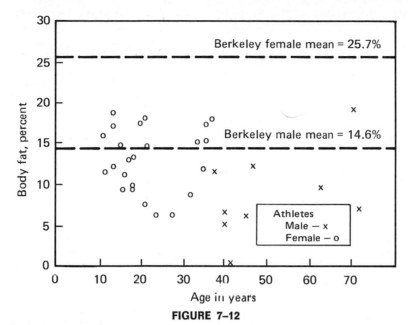

FIGURE 7–12

Relative body fat values for a group of female competitive runners compared to a group of older, male runners. (Unpublished data from J. H. Wilmore and C. H. Brown.)

athletes who have low, relative body fats. Long-distance runners generally have less than 10 percent body fat. By contrast, the male and female of college age will average 15 percent and 25 percent fat, respectively. However, even the better women endurance runners have body fat levels below 10 percent (Figure 7–12). Is this the result of natural selection of lean individuals for distance running, or is this the result of running 60 to 100 mi or more per week as a part of their training program? Information is not available to answer this question at the present time, although it undoubtedly is a combination of both.

Relative body fats for various sports are presented in Table 7–4. These are not presented as ideal values or goals that the athlete should strive for, since some of these values for both individual and team sport activities are higher than would normally be considered desirable. For almost all sports, however, low relative body fats are desirable due to the high negative relationship between performance and percentage body fat.

Lastly, of great concern to the medical and

TABLE 7–4. Range of Relative Body Fats for Various Sports

Sport	Relative Fat (%) Males	Females
Distance running	4–8	6–10
Wrestling	4–8	–
Gymnasts	6–10	8–12
Swimmers		
Sprinters	6–10	8–12
Distance	8–12	10–14
Basketball	8–12	12–16
Baseball-softball	12–16	14–18
Football		
Backs and receivers	5–10	–
Linebackers	10–16	–
Linemen	12–20	–
Tennis	12–16	15–20
Track-field events	15–23	18–35

scientific community, as well as the involved coach and athlete, is the area of "making weight." While the major concern has been with the sport of wrestling, many schools, districts, or state-level organizations have organized their athletic programs on the basis of size, including weight as the predominant factor. The athlete attempts to get down to the lowest weight possible in order to gain an advantage over his opponent. In so doing, many athletes have jeopardized their health. In a manner similar to using crash diets as mentioned earlier in this chapter, these athletes will lose large amounts of weight predominantly through dehydration. They will exercise in rubberized sweat suits, sit in steam and sauna baths, chew on towels to lose saliva, and keep their food and fluid intake minimal. Such severe water losses compromise kidney and general cardiovascular function and are potentially dangerous. Weight losses of 2 to 4 percent of the athlete's weight due to dehydration can even impair performance. Standards should be established on the basis of the athlete's lean body weight. His total body weight should consist of not less than 5 percent fat.* This would imply that 95 percent of the athlete's weight should be lean. With a knowledge of his lean weight, his competition weight should not drop below the following weight

$$\text{Minimal Competitive Weight} = \text{Lean Weight}/0.95$$

Of course, as the lean weight is increased, the minimal competitive weight will increase.

GENERAL SUMMARY

It has become increasingly more evident that the athlete's body build and composition play a major role in determining athletic success. Body build refers to the form and structure of the body and is quantified by determining the athlete's somatotype. In somatotyping, the body is rated for each of three different components, endomorphy, mesomorphy and ectomorphy, which reflect adiposity, muscularity, and linearity, respectively. Body size simply

* T. K. Tcheng and C. M. Tipton, "Iowa Wrestling Study; Anthropometric Measurements and The Prediction of a 'Minimal' Body Weight for High School Wrestlers." *Med. Sci. Sport* 5 (1973): 1–10.

refers to the height and body mass or weight of the individual. Body composition refers to the individual components that constitute the total body mass. Of primary concern to the athlete is the distinction between fat weight and lean weight, the latter refers to the fat-free weight of the body, which includes the weight of muscle, bone, skin, and organs among others. Body composition can be measured in the laboratory or estimated in the field. The underwater weighing technique is one of the more accurate and reliable techniques and can be used both inside and outside the laboratory. This technique provides an estimate of the body's volume. Body density is then calculated by the ratio of body mass or weight to body volume. From the body density, accurate estimates can be made of the body's lean and fat components. Anthropometric techniques, using girths of body segments, breadths of bones, and thicknesses of subcutaneous fat, provide fairly accurate estimates of the lean and fat components of the total body weight.

Physical training has only a modest influence on the athlete's body build. The somatotype is established early in life and is primarily determined by the genetic constitution of the individual athlete. Body composition is changed markedly with physical training. With chronic exercise, the lean body weight is increased and the fat weight is decreased. The magnitude of these changes is largely dependent on the type of exercise used in the training program, with strength training facilitating gains in lean weight and endurance training facilitating losses in fat weight. For purposes of losing body fat, the athlete should combine a moderate endurance training program with a modest reduction in total caloric intake of 200–500 Kcal/day. A goal of one pound of weight loss per week is attainable and much more desirable than more rigid goals of 3 to 4 pounds of weight loss per week.

Exercise up to one hour in duration does not markedly increase the appetite of the individual, and, in fact, may tend to suppress it. This could be the result of the increased levels of circulating catecholamines, which accompany moderate to heavy levels of exercise.

These catecholamines may also have a fat mobilizing effect on the adipose tissue, which may explain the fat loss normally experienced with chronic exercise. Human growth hormone may also play a significant role in the mobilization of fat and it may, possibly, be responsible for the increase of lean tissue with chronic exercise, due to its known anabolic action.

Spot reduction has been investigated in a number of studies and is now generally regarded as a myth. The body apparently mobilizes fat from the general body stores, calling first on those areas of highest concentration. Selective utilization of fat from isolated areas undergoing vigorous exercise has not been confirmed in recent research and is probably not possible.

Body build and composition are extremely important to the athlete. A certain body type is necessary for almost all sports, and each sport appears to require a different type. While mesomorphy is a predominant component for all athletes, few athletes are extreme endomorphs or ectomorphs. Body composition is of primary importance where the athlete must move his body vertically or horizontally through space. Many studies have found substantial negative correlations between athletic performance and relative fat; the higher the percentage of body fat, the poorer the athletic performance. While there is considerable variation between athletes in different sports with regard to relative fat values, it is generally felt that the lower the relative body fat, the greater the performance potential of the athlete, with only a few possible exceptions.

REFERENCES

BEHNKE, A. R., and WILMORE, J. H. *Evaluation and Regulation of Body Build and Composition.* Englewood Cliffs, N.J.: Prentice-Hall, 1974.

CORRENTI, V., and ZAULI, B. *Olimpionici 1960.* Rome: Marves, 1964.

CURETON, T. K., JR. *Physical Fitness of Champion Athletes.* Urbana, Ill.: University of Illinois Press, 1951.

deGARAY, A. L.; LEVINE, L.; and CARTER, J. E. L. eds. *Genetic and Anthropological Studies of Olympic Athletes.* New York: Academic Press, 1974.

deVRIES, H. A. *Physiology of Exercise for Physical Education and Athletics.* 2nd ed. Dubuque, Iowa: William C. Brown, Co., 1974.

GWINUP, G.; CHELVAM, R.; and STEINBERG, T. "Thickness of Subcutaneous Fat and Activity of Underlying Muscles." *Annals Int. Med.* 74 (1971): 408–11.

KARPOVICH, P. V., and SINNING, S. E. *Physiology of Muscular Activity.* 7th ed. Philadelphia: W. B. Saunders Co. 1971.

MAYER, J. *Overweight Causes, Cost, and Control.* Englewood Cliffs, N.J.: Prentice-Hall, 1968.

MAYER, J.; MARSHALL, H. B.; VITALE, J. J.; CHRISTENSEN, J. H.; MASHAYEKHI, M. B.; and STARE, F. J. "Exercise, Food Intake, and Body Weight in Normal Rats and Genetically Obese Adult Mice." *Amer. J. Physiol.* 177 (1954): 544–48.

OSCAI, L. B. "The Role of Exercise in Weight Control." In *Exercise and Sport Sciences Reviews*, vol. 1, edited by J. H. Wilmore. New York: Academic Press, 1973.

TANNER, J. M. *The Physique of the Olympic Athlete.* London: George Allen and Unwin, 1964.

WELHAM, W. C., and BEHNKE, A. R. "The Specific Gravity of Healthy Men." *J.A.M.A.* 118 (1942): 498–501.

WILMORE, J. H., and HASKELL, W. L. "Body Composition and Endurance Capacity of Professional Football Players." *J. Appl. Physiol.* 33 (1972): 564–67.

8

Detraining and Off-Season Training Programs

INTRODUCTION

The preceding chapters have been concerned with the actual process of physical training and the physiological adaptations that result, which allow the athlete to improve his athletic ability and performance in competitive situations. An area that is equally important but that has been given considerably less attention by both the athlete and coach and has practically been ignored by the researcher in the exercise and sport sciences is the area of detraining and off-season conditioning programs. What happens to the highly conditioned athlete, who has fine tuned his performance potential to its peak, when the competitive season comes to a sudden end and the mandatory, daily training program is no longer required? Most athletes in team sports go into physical hibernation following the completion of their competitive season. Many have been working two to five hours per day in perfecting their skills and improving their levels of physical condition and welcome the opportunity to completely relax, purposely avoiding any strenuous physical activity. How does total physical inactivity affect the highly trained and conditioned athlete? Does the body need this period of rest, or will it undergo rapid, physical deterioration? Are physical training programs necessary during the off-season to maintain the athlete's general physical condition? These and other related questions will be discussed in the first section of this chapter. The last section is devoted to a discussion of off-season, physical training programs.

PHYSICAL DETRAINING

Much of our knowledge about physical detraining comes from research by the National Aeronautics and Space Administration to improve the safety of astronauts on missions requiring extended periods of weightlessness in a relatively confined living environment. In addition to forced inactivity, the lack of gravity also imposes a number of physiological stresses on the human body. Man has successfully adapted to the earth's environment and has extreme difficulty in adapting to the weightless state. Physical detraining has been investigated through two major approaches: by observing changes following total bed rest for extended periods of time, and by observing changes in trained individuals as they cease formal physical training and become physically inactive. The results of these various studies will be discussed individually, according to the specific components of physical training.

Strength, Power, and Muscular Endurance

When an individual breaks an arm or a leg and the broken limb is placed in a rigid cast to render it completely immobile, changes immediately start taking place in both the bone and surrounding muscles. Within a period of only a few days, the cast, which was applied very tightly around the injured segment, becomes quite loose. By the end of several weeks, there is a large space between the cast and the limb. Is this the result of the cast expanding with use or of the limb decreasing in size with a lack of use? It is now clearly understood that skeletal muscles will undergo a substantial decrease in size with inactivity. Accompanying this decrease in size is a considerable loss in strength, power, and muscular endurance. While total inactivity will lead to very rapid losses in each of these areas, even periods of decreased activity will lead to gradual losses that become sizeable as the losses accumulate over long periods of time.

Research confirms that levels of strength, power and muscular endurance are reduced once the athlete stops training. However, these reductions are not very large during the first few months following the cessation of training. In one study, no loss in strength was noted 6 weeks after a 3-week training program. In another study, 45 percent of the original strength gained from a 12-week training program was lost by the time the subjects were reevaluated one year later. Similar results have been found for muscular endurance. Thus, for the trained athlete, it appears that the strength and muscular endurance gained during the training period will be fully retained for periods up to 6 weeks and approximately 50 percent of the strength gained will be retained for up to a year following the end of the training program. Also, studies have shown that it takes far less effort than originally required to regain the strength which was lost. In addition, it appears that by working out once every 10 to 14 days, the athlete will be able to maintain the strength, power, and muscular endurance that he gained through more vigorous and frequent training.

These findings tend to conflict with the observations, noted earlier, that rather sizeable losses in strength, power, and muscular endurance, in addition to losses in muscle mass (atrophy), result from periods of inactivity when a limb is totally immobilized. Apparently, the average individual gets sufficient exercise through walking, climbing stairs, pushing, pulling, and lifting to allow a substantial retention of the strength previously gained through strength training. With immobilization, there is almost no activity at all within the muscle. Evidently, it requires only a minimal stimulus to retain the strength, power, endurance, and size of a muscle or muscle group. This has extremely important implications for the injured athlete. There will be a great savings in time and effort during the period of rehabilitation if the athlete can perform even a very low level of exercise in the injured segment, starting in the first few days of the recovery period. Simple, isometric contractions have been found to be very effective in this respect, since they can be graded in intensity and do not require movement at the joint. Any program of rehabilitation, however, must be worked out in cooperation with the supervising physician.

Speed, Agility, and Flexibility

As was stated in Chapter 5, physical training can influence speed and agility, but the degree of improvement will be far less than in the areas of strength, power, muscular endurance, flexibility, and cardiovascular endurance. Consequently, the loss of speed and agility with physical inactivity is relatively small, and peak levels can be maintained with only a limited amount of training. This does not imply that the sprinter in track can get by with training only a few days a week. His success in actual competition relies on factors other than basic speed, such as timing and the finishing kick. It takes many hours of practice during the week for him to tune his performance to its optimal level, but most of this time is spent in developing aspects of his performance other than speed.

Flexibility, on the other hand, is lost rather quickly and must be worked on throughout the year. Stretching exercises, such as those outlined in Appendix B, Warm-Up and Flexibility Exercises, should be incorporated into both the in-season and off-season training programs. While flexibility can be attained in a relatively short period of time, it is in the best interests of the athlete to maintain the desired levels of flexibility on a year-round basis. Many athletes, however, tend to ignore flexibility training during the off-season, since it can be regained so rapidly. Reduced flexibility leaves the athlete more susceptible to serious injury; this could be a major factor in determining the longevity of his athletic career.

Cardiovascular Endurance

It is now well understood that periods of inactivity lead to substantial, cardiovascular deconditioning. Astronauts returning from extended periods of weightlessness have been found to have severe cardiovascular deterioration, resulting from the combination of inactivity and weightlessness. Even limited activity on earth provides considerable work for the heart, since the heart must contract forcefully enough to circulate the blood throughout the body against the forces of gravity. In the weightless state, this is no longer necessary, and the work of the heart is reduced considerably. The result is a decrease in heart function. For this reason, astronauts in the series of Space Lab flights during the early 1970's were required to perform daily bouts of exercise on a stationary bicycle ergometer or on an ingeniously designed "space treadmill." This exercise was found to be essential in preventing serious cardiovascular deterioration.

These same types of results have been observed in studies conducted on subjects undergoing long periods of total bed rest. In these

FIGURE 8–1

Reduction in maximal oxygen uptake with a 20-day period of physical inactivity (bed rest). (From B. Saltin et al., "Response to Submaximal and Maximal Exercise after Bed Rest and after Training," Circulation 38 (Suppl. 7) (1968). By permission of the American Heart Association, Inc.)

studies, the subject is not allowed to leave the bed and his physical activity while in bed is kept to an absolute minimum. Many of these studies attempted to use total bed rest to simulate weightlessness. Figure 3–2 (Chapter 3) illustrates the heart rate at a constant metabolic load before and following a 20-day period of bed rest, and at varying times during a subsequent 50-day period of physical reconditioning, in a study conducted by Saltin et al. (1968). The considerable increase in the working heart rate was indicative of the 25 percent decrease observed in the stroke volume at this level of work. In addition, at maximal levels of work, the period of bed rest resulted in a 25 percent reduction in maximal cardiac output and a 27 percent decrease in maximal oxygen uptake (Figure 8–1). This reduction in cardiac output and $\dot{V}O_2$ max was due primarily to a reduction in stroke volume, which was probably the result of a decrease in heart volume, a decrease in total blood volume and plasma volume, and a decrease in ventricular contractility.

It is interesting to note in Figure 8–1 the relatively large decrease in $\dot{V}O_2$ max in the two more highly conditioned subjects in this study, compared to lesser decreases in the remaining three subjects who were considered sedentary. Furthermore, the three relatively sedentary subjects regained their initial, or pre-bedrest level of conditioning within the first 10 days of reconditioning, while the two physically active subjects needed about 40 days to regain their initial levels. This would tend to suggest that the more highly trained individuals will not be able to afford long periods of inactivity away from endurance training activities. The athlete who goes into total hibernation at the completion of the season will experience a great deal of difficulty in getting back into physical condition when the new season begins.

Studies have also observed changes in the cardiovascular endurance capacity of trained subjects during periods of inactivity following intensive endurance conditioning. Most of these studies have shown rather marked decreases in endurance capacity with detraining or periods of

inactivity. This reduction is of considerably greater magnitude than that observed in the areas of strength, power, and muscular endurance for the same period of inactivity. Drinkwater and Horvath (1972) observed seven female track athletes at the end of the competitive season and again 3 months after the cessation of formal training. During the 3-month period following formal training, the girls participated in physical activities normal for their age group, including required physical education. They observed a 15.5 percent decrease in $\dot{V}O_2$ max over the 3-month period, and noted that the new $\dot{V}O_2$ max levels were similar to those found in nonathletic girls of the same age.

Michael et al. (1972) observed ten female runners, 15–18 years of age, during 23 weeks of inactivity following a 3–4 month training program for competitive track. They found that by the third week of detraining, the heart rate response to standardized submaximal levels of work was considerably higher than those values found at the beginning of the study when the girls were still in training. These results are nearly identical to those illustrated in Figure 3–2 for five men undergoing complete bedrest.

Brynteson and Sinning (1973) attempted to determine the amount of exercise necessary for the maintenance of those gains attained from a formal training program. The subjects exercised 5 days per week for 5 weeks to develop their initial training levels. They were then divided into four groups exercising either one, two, three, or four times per week to determine the minimal frequency that would maintain the initial training level. They found that cardiovascular fitness was maintained by exercising three times per week, and that there were significant losses in conditioning in the two groups that exercised only once or twice per week. Siegel et al. (1970) found an increase in $\dot{V}O_2$ max of 19 percent following 15 weeks of training in nine men who trained 12-min/day, 3 days per week. At the end of training, five subjects continued to train once a week for an additional 14 weeks, at which time their $\dot{V}O_2$ max had decreased to only

6 percent above their initial control level. The remaining four subjects stopped training altogether, and their $\dot{V}O_2$ max values following 14 weeks of detraining dropped below their original control values.

From the above studies, and other studies of a similar design, it is apparent that cardiovascular endurance capacity is lost very rapidly following the cessation of formal endurance training. While complete bedrest provides the most dramatic decreases, even periods of light activity or formal endurance training once or twice a week, are not sufficient to prevent the loss of cardiovascular conditioning. Thus, the athlete must consciously work on maintaining his endurance capacity during the off-season, for once it is lost, it takes a considerable period of time to regain the peak levels. For the injured athlete, the sooner he can get back into some modified form of endurance exercise, the smaller will be his loss in cardiovascular endurance capacity. While it may be impossible to return to a running or swimming type of activity, stationary or regular bicycling are excellent cardiovascular conditioning exercises that will place little stress on the joints or muscles.

Body Composition

Changes in body composition with decreased physical activity are similar to those found for increased physical activity, except that they are in the opposite direction. With inactivity, the lean body weight tends to decrease and total body fat tends to increase. This is illustrated in Figure 8–2 by changes in subcutaneous fat as measured by skinfold thicknesses in a group of female gymnasts over a period of several years, with indicated periods of total inactivity, moderate training, and intense training. A substantial variation in skinfold thickness occurs over this period of time, reflecting the influence of marked changes in activity patterns. The degree of change in lean and fat weight will depend to a large extent on the initial size and composition of the individual and on the eating and activity habits

of the athlete during the period of detraining. The athlete who has developed considerable muscle bulk from strength training activities during the season will lose a considerable amount of lean weight once he stops training. Losses of 10–20 lb or more are not uncommon. The extremely lean athlete, such as the long-distance runner who trains 100 mi or more per week, will gain a considerable amount of fat if he becomes totally inactive.

Optimal body composition levels can be maintained during the off-season with a modest level of physical training and a conscious effort to control the diet. Although most athletes who work hard during the season can eat almost anything and as much as they want to, they must watch their weight carefully during the off-season and regulate their diet, accordingly.

OFF-SEASON TRAINING PROGRAMS

From the data in the previous section, it is obvious that the athlete undergoes considerable change as a result of periods of inactivity or detraining. Is this necessarily bad? The athlete can always start the reconditioning process several weeks before he begins a new season. Maybe the athlete needs several months of total inactivity to help him pull things back together! While a definite answer to this question is not presently available, it appears that the athlete can receive great benefits from a comprehensive off-season conditioning program that is individually designed to meet his needs and interests. The highly conditioned athlete who becomes totally inactive loses a considerable amount of that conditioning. Regaining this takes a considerable amount of time and effort, which could mean that the athlete might not regain peak form or performance potential until well into the competitive season. The inability to perform at optimal levels early in the season may prove costly, both in success and potential serious injury. In addition, extreme cyclic variations in body composition and physiological condition may reduce the ath-

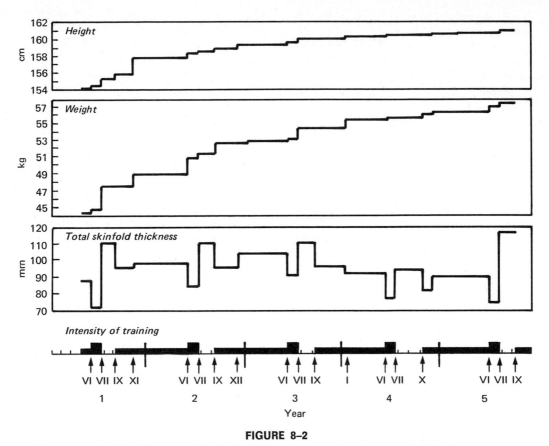

FIGURE 8–2

Changes in height, weight, and total skinfold thickness in young gymnasts as they progress from periods of limited, moderate and heavy activity. (From Parízková, Annals N. Y. Acad. Sci. 110: 666, 1963).

lete's longevity. Observations of a number of professional athletes suggest that those who maintain themselves in reasonable condition throughout the year are able to continue their sport longer and more successfully than those who go into hibernation during the off-season.

In the previous discussion, it was demonstrated that peak levels of conditioning can be maintained by training at frequencies considerably less than those required during the season. Strength can be maintained by one full workout every 10 to 14 days. Cardiovascular endurance, however, is maintained by training a minimum of three times per week. Therefore, an off-season program can be designed that requires no more than three days of activity per week. In addition, the workout periods need not exceed one to two hours in length. This totals only 3–6 hours of training per week, which is a minimum investment in time for the resulting benefits.

The athlete and coach must give considerable thought to the design of the off-season conditioning program. All too frequently this is left strictly to chance. One of the most important factors is that it must be fun and enjoyable for the athlete. The activities that are selected should differ somewhat from those used during the season to prevent boredom. Occasional or frequent competition is suggested, since this provides additional motivation to participate. Several professional football teams have organized formal competition in basketball for their athletes in the off-season as a part of the off-season training program. This activity is physically demanding, has components of training that are similar to those for football, and the stimulus of competition maintains interest and enthusiasm.

The period of training during the off-season also allows the athlete to concentrate on the development of areas in which he is weak. The swimmer who lacks upper body strength can use this time to concentrate on the development of his strength in this area in a way that will be applicable to his performance in the pool. The wrestler who lacks cardiovascular endurance can use this time to develop his endurance through running or bicycling. The off-season presents the athlete with a relatively free, unstructured period of time in which he can work on all aspects of his performance. As the athlete gets older, this off-season time becomes even more critical. He will notice that aging will gradually decrease his peak levels of performance, and he will find that it becomes increasingly more difficult to regain peak levels, if his condition is allowed to deteriorate with periods of inactivity.

With this in mind, it is important that off-season conditioning programs be designed for the individual, as much as possible. Every off-season program must also attend to the areas of strength, power, muscular endurance, flexibility, cardiovascular endurance, and body composition. An activity such as circuit training (refer to the section on circuit training in Chapter 5) meets almost every need in each of these areas. An hour of circuit training, three days per week, combined with two to three hours of vigorous, game-type activities each week, e.g., basketball, handball, squash, and badminton, should provide a balanced off-season program for most athletes. If the athlete has a particular weakness, he can devote an additional hour or two to developing this specific area. Another approach would be to combine running 3–5 mi per day, three days per week, with strength, power, and muscular endurance training exercises and selected flexibility exercises. Specific exercises should be selected on the basis of the needs of the individual and the demands of the sport.

Lastly, the athlete should receive sound nutritional counseling to assure him of a properly balanced diet which will provide the essential vitamins and minerals and assist in controlling his weight. This is an area of considerable ignorance, lack of knowledge, and many myths. Nutrition will be discussed in greater detail in Chapter 10, Ergogenic Aids.

In conclusion, it should be realized that the off-season training program is an extremely important aspect of the athlete's total training program, although it is frequently given little thought or attention and is left strictly to chance. The coach and athlete should work closely together to design a program that will meet the needs of the athlete and provide him some variation from his typical or traditional approach to training. The off-season provides an excellent opportunity to develop a basic foundation for each of the various components of physical training. For example, each program should devote at least some time to each of the following areas.

- Strength
- Power
- Muscular endurance
- Flexibility
- Speed
- Agility and neuromuscular coordination
- Cardiovascular endurance
- Body composition
- Nutrition

Ideally, the athlete would be provided with an individualized program to follow on his own, which would provide him with the opportunity to report at the beginning of the new season in peak physical condition.

GENERAL SUMMARY

Most athletes regard the conclusion of a long season of intense physical training and competition as the beginning of a welcomed period of rest and relaxation. While this rest and relaxation are certainly necessary and well-deserved, unfortunately, many interpret this as a time to go into physical hibernation. However, physical conditioning cannot simply be put into storage and recalled at will when needed. *If you don't use it, you lose it.* Research evidence abundantly demonstrates that periods of physical inactivity will lead to losses in strength, power, muscular endurance, flexibility, and cardiovascular endurance. While the losses in strength and power are somewhat gradual, the loss in cardiovascular endurance capacity occurs very rapidly. Body composition will also change with inactivity, particularly without concomitant changes in diet. These changes would include a loss in the lean body weight and an increase in fat weight, which would result in a substantial increase in relative fat.

To prevent or minimize the physiological changes that result from periods of physical inactivity, the athlete is strongly advised to participate in an off-season program of physical training. The off-season program should be varied so it includes activities that are enjoyable, but it should be sufficiently structured so each of the major components of physical training are stressed. The off-season program is also an opportune time to work on areas of weakness where supplemental training would be of considerable value. Circuit training provides one of the more versatile approaches to off-season conditioning, since it stresses each of the major components in a relatively brief workout. This type of activity performed three times per week and coupled with a vigorous game-type of activity several days each week would provide the athlete with an interesting, challenging, and physiologically rewarding program that would fully prepare him for the start of the new season.

REFERENCES

ÅSTRAND, P. O., and RODAHL, K. *Textbook of Work Physiology.* New York: McGraw-Hill Book Co., 1970.

BRYNTESON, P., and SINNING, W. E. "The Effects of Training Frequencies on the Retention of Cardiovascular Fitness." *Med. Sci. Sports* 5 (1973): 29–33.

CLARKE, D. H. "Adaptations in Strength and Muscular Endurance Resulting from Exercise." In *Exercise and Sport Sciences Reviews*, vol. 1, edited by J. H. Wilmore. New York: Academic Press, 1973.

DRINKWATER, B. L., and HORVATH, S. M. "Detraining Effects in Young Women." *Med. Sci. Sports* 4 (1972): 91–95.

JENSEN, C. R., and FISHER, A. G. *Scientific Basis of Athletic Conditioning.* Philadelphia: Lea & Febiger, 1972.

MICHAEL, E.; EVERT, J.; and JEFFERS, K. "Physiological Changes of Teenage Girls During Five Months of Detraining." *Med. Sci. Sports* 4 (1972): 214–18.

POLLOCK, M. L. "Quantification of Endurance Training Programs." *Exercise and Sport Sciences Reviews*, vol. 1, edited by J. H. Wilmore. New York: Academic Press, 1973.

SALTIN, B.; BLOMQVIST, G.; MITCHELL, J. H.; JOHNSON, JR., R. L.; WILDENTHAL, K.; and CHAPMAN, C. B. "Response to Submaximal and Maximal Exercise After Bed Rest and Training." *Circulation* 38 (Suppl. 7) (1968).

SIEGEL, W.; BLOMQVIST, G.; and MITCHELL, J. H. "Effects of a Quantified Physical Training Program on Middle-Aged Sedentary Men." *Circulation* 41 (1970): 19–29.

SECTION C

Special Considerations in Physical Training

Considerable variation exists both within and among athletes relative to their performance potential. This results from a number of factors, some of which are outside the control of either the coach or athlete, e.g., genetic constitution, but many can be either controlled, e.g., taking water to prevent dehydration, or adaptations can be made to reduce or enhance the potential influencing factor, e.g., acclimatization to altitude or thermal stress.

First, the various environmental factors that can influence athletic performance will be discussed in Chapter 9. How does the athlete contend with extreme variations in temperature, both hot and cold? How does humidity interact with temperature to influence the performance of the athlete? Can the athlete perform at moderate or, even, high altitudes without experiencing decrements in his performance potential? What performance limitations does the athlete experience when exercising under increased atmospheric pressures, as in underwater diving? Chapter 10 discusses how performance can be improved by the use of various ergogenic or work-producing aids and how other agents that are thought to be ergogenic in nature have a relative small influence on the athlete's performance. This will include a discussion of drugs, oxygen, diet, warmup, and social facilitation, among other topics. Chapters 11 and 12 will deal with the special problems of the female athlete and with the growing and aging athlete. In addition to the special considerations of the aging athlete, Chapter 13 will discuss the role of exercise in preventive medicine, with particular reference to coronary artery disease and obesity.

9

Environmental Factors and Athletic Performance

INTRODUCTION

Frequently, the athlete is expected to perform under less than optimal environmental conditions. The athlete who trains at sea level is forced to make rather extensive physiological adjustments to compete successfully at higher altitudes. Training in cool climates does little to prepare the athlete to compete under conditions of extreme heat and humidity. Similarly, sudden exposure to cold can have a dramative influence on athletes' performances if they have not had an opportunity to acclimatize to the colder environment.

The environment dictates to a large extent the quality of an athlete's performance. There are many things the athlete can do or adaptations he can make to better prepare him for variations in the environment, either expected or unexpected. The purpose of this chapter is to inform the athlete and coach about making these necessary preparations. This chapter will be of limited value for those sports that are performed in a controlled indoor environment, such as basketball, wrestling, and swimming, with the exception of competition at altitudes. However, for sports such as cross country, football, and soccer, the importance of preparing for radical changes in environmental conditions must be recognized. Football provides an excellent example. The football season usually starts in July or August, depending on the level, i.e., high school, college, or professional, and the region. In most regions of

the United States, this is the hottest season of the year. When the heat is combined with the high humidity in certain sections of the country, there is a potentially lethal situation. The padding and clothing worn by football players add another stress, since they create a closed microenvironment in which it is difficult to lose body heat. Even under normal conditions of temperature and humidity, this clothing creates potential problems of heat stress. During one three-year period, seven high school and five college football players died as a result of heat stress.[*] At the other extreme, while of considerably less consequence, football players are exposed to subfreezing temperatures in certain regions of the United States, as the season draws to a close. This, too, can create many problems, such as frost bite and an increased potential for serious injury.

VARIATIONS IN TEMPERATURE AND HUMIDITY

The topic of body temperature regulation reviewed in Chapter 2, Acute Responses to Exercise, is considerably important to an understanding of the problem of exercising in extremes in temperature. Since the body is

---

[*] From D. K. Mathews and E. L. Fox, *The Physiological Basis of Physical Education and Athletics* (Philadelphia: W. B. Saunders Co., 1971) p. 104.

substantially less than 100 percent efficient, it will produce a considerable amount of heat as it generates energy to perform various physical tasks. In cold environments, this metabolic heat production is necessary to assist in maintaining the body temperature. In hot environments, however, it is a liability, since it adds to the body's heat load. Chapter 2 describes how the body's temperature is regulated very precisely by the hypothalamus through four major processes: convection, radiation, conduction, and evaporation. At rest, temperature is closely regulated at approximately 98.6° F, but during exercise a much higher level is attained, sometimes exceeding 105° F. The body appears to select a new thermostatic "set-point" as the athlete goes from rest to strenuous exercise. This allows him to function more efficiently, since chemical reaction rates and oxygen availability are increased. When these regulatory mechanisms fail or when the environmental conditions are such that these four processes are inadequate to cope with the environmental stress, heat or cold, the athlete is placed in a potentially lethal situation. Therefore, a basic knowledge of how the body performs under various environmental temperatures and how to cope with environmental extremes is essential for both the coach and athlete.

Exercise in the Heat

The ability of the athlete to successfully perform in the heat depends on the degree of heat, the humidity, the air movement, intensity and duration of effort, and extent of his previous exposure to similar environmental conditions. The latter factor is referred to as acclimatization. Also of major importance is the athlete's fluid and mineral intake schedule both prior to, as well as during, competition. Each of these factors must be considered when preparing the athlete for competition in the heat.

Degree of heat.   The higher the ambient, or existing, temperature, the greater the stress placed on the athlete. At rest, with a "neutral"

temperature of 70–80° F, the average man gives off an excess of 80 Kcal of heat per hour as the by-product of producing metabolic energy. Of this, approximately 25 percent or 20 Kcal/hour are dissipated or removed from the body by evaporation and the remainder is lost by radiation, convection, and conduction. As the athlete exercises at different levels of intensity up to exhaustion, the metabolic needs of the body increase in a linear manner and up to 900 Kcal/hr or more can be produced as a by-product of metabolism. This presents the body with a considerably greater challenge in dissipating, or ridding itself of, this excess heat. When exercising in a cold environment, this heat load is actually beneficial, assisting in the maintenance of a normal body temperature. However, even when the exercise is conducted in a thermally neutral environment, i.e., 70–80° F, the metabolic heat load places a considerable burden on the cardiovascular system, since the heat must be transported from the central core of the body out to the periphery.

As the temperature of the surrounding environment increases, the gradient between the athlete and environment decreases, i.e., the temperature of the environment approaches, and can even exceed, the skin and core, or deep body, temperature. This results in an even greater reliance on evaporation as the major avenue of heat loss, since radiation, convection, and conduction lose effectiveness as the environmental temperature increases. Evaporation requires sweating, therefore, an increased dependency on evaporation means an increased demand for sweating. Since a high percentage of the fluid lost in sweat comes from the blood plasma, an even greater demand is imposed on the cardiovascular system. As the environmental temperature increases, more blood is needed to transport heat to the periphery, and an increasing sweat rate reduces the existing blood volume causing the total volume of blood that is available to supply the exercising muscles to be reduced in direct proportion to the intensity of the heat. This results in a reduction in overall performance potential, particularly for activities of an endurance nature.

In long-distance runners, sweat losses may approach 6 to 10 percent of the runner's body weight. Such severe dehydration limits subsequent sweating and makes the athlete susceptible to heat cramps, heat stroke, or heat exhaustion.

Radiation, conduction, and convection, while working to cool the athlete on cool days when there is a breeze and partial or total cloud cover, can actually contribute to the heat load of the body if the climatic conditions are right. The athlete exercising at 75° F on a crystal clear day with no measurable wind will notice considerably more heat stress than when exercising at the same temperature but with a cloud cover and slight breeze. At temperatures above 88–92° F, radiation, convection, and conduction will substantially add to the heat load rather than acting as an avenue of heat loss.

Clothing is an important consideration for the problem of heat stress. Obviously, the more clothing worn, the smaller the available area for evaporation to take place. The foolish practice of exercising in a rubberized suit to promote weight loss is an excellent illustration of how a microenvironment (environment inside the suit) can be created in which the temperature and humidity can reach a sufficiently high level to cause heat stroke or exhaustion if exercise is continued. A football uniform provides a similar microenvironment that is inherently dangerous in hot weather. It is strongly advocated by exercise scientists and sports physicians that the athlete wear as little clothing as possible. Where clothing is necessary or required, it should be of loose weave to allow the skin beneath to breathe.

Humidity. An additional factor that is of considerable importance with regard to exercise in the heat is the relative humidity, or the degree of moisture in the surrounding air. Sweating contributes to the loss of body heat *only* if the sweat evaporates from the skin. It is the process of evaporation that results in a heat loss, since the evaporation of 1 ml of water requires 0.58 Kcal; thus, the evaporation of a liter (approximately a quart) of water

would yield a heat loss of 580 Kcal. Man is capable of sweating up to 2 liters or more per hour. If the surrounding air is totally saturated with water vapor, i.e., 100 percent humidity, it is impossible for sweat to evaporate, since there is no dry or unsaturated air available to pick up the resulting water vapor. A perfect example of this is the contrast between the bodily sensations in the middle of the desert at a temperature of 100° F, and 10 percent relative humidity compared to those in Houston, Texas, at 80° F, and 95 percent relative humidity. In the former, the body sweats profusely, but evaporation occurs so rapidly that the individual is not conscious of the fact that he is sweating. In the latter situation, only a limited amount of sweat can evaporate, since 95 percent of the surrounding air is filled with water vapor. The result is a continuous bath of sweat, which never seems to stop.

This example points to the importance of humidity in athletic performance in the heat. In the previous section, it was stated that evaporation is the major method of regulating body temperature in the heat. If the air is saturated with water vapor, no evaporation can occur even at the lower environmental temperatures, and at the higher temperatures, the body has no way of losing heat, so the body temperature will rise until death results.

It is clear that temperature by itself is not an accurate index of the total physiological stress imposed on the athlete. Humidity, air velocity, and the degree of cloud cover (radiation), as well as temperature, all directly influence the degree of stress felt by the athlete. The proportional contribution to the total stress from each of these factors is not clearly understood, and it probably varies with changing environmental conditions. Efforts have been made to quantify these four factors into a single index. In the 1920's, the effective temperature index was developed, which was later altered to account for the effect of radiation. The latter index was called the corrected effective temperature. In the 1970's, a wet globe thermometer was devised to simultaneously account for conduction, convection, evaporation, and radiation, providing a single temperature reading to estimate the potential cooling capacity of the surrounding environment. Unfortunately, this instrument has not been widely used to monitor the environmental conditions for various athletic events.

Dehydration. One of the greatest problems associated with exercise in the heat, particularly under conditions of high humidity, is dehydration. Since sweating is the major avenue of heat loss when exercising in the heat, the total amount of fluid lost becomes very important as the duration of the activity is extended over time. Man is able to sweat at the rate of 2 liters per hour for short periods of time and is able to sustain sweating at the rate of 1 liter per hour, or more, for periods of 3 hours, or longer. Marathon runners commonly lose 5 to 7 lb as a result of the 26.2-mi race, even though they are drinking freely during the race. Along with water, salts and other critical electrolytes are also lost at a substantial rate.

Dehydration presents a serious threat to the athlete. It is estimated that the deep body temperature will rise from 0.3 to 0.5° F for every 1 percent loss in body weight. This rise is the result of several factors, one of which is the loss in blood volume, i.e., a large percentage of the water lost in sweating comes from the blood volume. This reduces not only the blood available to transport heat from the core to the periphery but also the effective blood volume available to supply the exercising muscles. The result is a decrease in performance capacity.

The problem of dehydration is not unique to those athletes competing under conditions of thermal stress. In 1967, a county medical society in Iowa recommended that high school wrestling be abolished as a sport. This group of physicians was concerned with the hazardous health practices used by high school wrestlers to "make weight" for a specific weight class. This recommendation created a major wave of hysteria that quickly spread to other states. In the athletic world, Iowa and wrestling are considered inseparable. To ban wrestling in Iowa would be comparable to banning skiing in Colorado, swimming in California, or football in Texas.

Why were these physicians concerned? A group of researchers from the University of Iowa (Tipton et al., 1975) set out to define the problem and recommend a solution. They found that the high school wrestlers were losing a considerable amount of body weight over a period of 17 days, some losing nearly 30 lb, or almost 2 lb per day! In addition, they found that most of the weight loss occurred in the last few days prior to certification and that the greatest weight loss occurred in the youngest boys and lightest weight classes. Simple calculations indicated that most of the weight that was lost came from dehydration, not from a loss of body fat. Analysis of the wrestler's urine samples confirmed the fact that substantial dehydration had occurred. It is a well-known fact that physical performance is impaired when fluid and electrolyte balances are upset by dehydration, and, as described above, it is apparent that the temperature regulatory mechanisms would also be compromised. In addition, possible signs of kidney damage were identified.

From this, it appears that voluntary dehydration, exemplified by the wrestler, is an undesirable practice and should be discouraged. This would apply to any athlete trying to make weight through a rapid loss of body fluids, e.g., football players, boxers, and even jockeys. The advantages gained are far outweighed by the disadvantages and the primary danger is the potential for serious medical complications. The athlete should focus on weight loss as a long-term process, losing no more than 1 to 2 lb per week. A 10 to 15-lb weight loss over a 7 to 14-day period is essentially a loss of body fluids, not fat. A fat loss should be the desired goal, since excess fat reduces the athlete's performance potential, while the body fluids are essential for optimal performance.

Fluid and Mineral Replacement. For many years, it was considered dangerous for athletes to stop and drink water or other fluids either during practice or competition. It was feared that the intake of fluids would cause cramping of the stomach and intestine; therefore, all fluids were generally withheld until after the practice or competition. Then, coaches started to realize that with copious sweating large quantities of salt were being lost, and salt losses were associated with muscle cramps. This led to the practice of requiring athletes to take salt tablets by the handfuls, yet fluids were still withheld!

From our present knowledge of dehydration and fluid ingestion during exercise, we now know how dangerous and foolish the above practices were. Ingestion of fluids during exercise is essential whenever dehydration is a potential problem. Fluid ingestion both before and during exercise in the heat has been shown to reduce the increase in rectal temperature, as exercise is prolonged up to two hours. For the same level of work and thermal stress, exercise with fluid ingestion results in a deep body temperature that is approximately 1.5° F lower compared to the same situation with no fluid ingestion. Most teams with sound medical leadership are now stopping, periodically, during practice for a fluid break. Either water or some other fluid fortified with minerals and electrolytes is distributed freely. The frequency of such breaks is dictated by the climatic conditions; the more severe the heat stress and subsequent dehydration, the more frequent the breaks. In the game situation, fluid should be made available at all times that the athlete is not in competition and he should be encouraged to drink as much as possible. Since research shows that man does not drink as much as he should to replace the fluid that is lost, athletes should be told to drink even more than their thirst tells them they need. Fluid intake prior to competition or practice should be encouraged.

Little is known about the most appropriate time and proportions of mineral and electrolyte intake. Under no circumstances should salt tablets be given and fluid withheld. This creates a situation where sweating is impaired and the body temperature will continue to rise. It is also known that fluids containing sugar reduce the speed by which the fluid is removed from the stomach.

Gisolfi (1975) has made several recommendations with regard to fluid replacement. In addition to ingesting fluid prior to exercise, he suggests drinking 200–300 ml (approximately one half of a pint) of a glucose-electrolyte solution every 15 to 20 min. Since it is essential to replace as much fluid as possible, the glucose content should be less than 2.5 gm/100 ml. Finally, the solution should be cool, slightly hypotonic, and palatable to the individual. Lastly, he states that the loss of salt in sweat is usually insignificant compared to the water lost and that a liberal salting of foods at meal time is the most effective method of replacing the lost salt.

Acclimatization.   Do repeated exposures to hot environments help the athlete to adapt better to thermal stress, thus improving his athletic performance? Many studies have investigated this problem and have concluded that repeated exposure to heat causes a gradual adjustment that enables the athlete to tolerate the associated stress better. Apparently, almost total acclimatization can occur within a 5- to 14-day period.

What changes take place as a result of acclimatization? First, the body has an increased ability to produce sweat, although at lower levels of heat stress less sweat is produced. The sweat that is produced is a more dilute sweat, thus conserving the body's mineral stores. There is a lowered skin and body temperature for the same level of work, and the heart rate response to a standardized, submaximal level of exercise is reduced. This latter response is the result of either or both an increased blood volume and a reduction in skin blood flow, both of which would increase the stroke volume. In addition, more work can be accomplished prior to reaching the point of fatigue or exhaustion.

The acclimatization process seems to require more than just exposure to a hot environment. While the research literature is not in total agreement on this point, it does appear that exercise in a hot environment is required in order to attain acclimatization that will carry over to exercise in the heat. For individuals or teams that are training in environments cooler than those in which they will be competing, it is important to achieve thermal acclimatization prior to the contest or event. This would improve the individual's performance, in addition to reducing the associated physiological stress. Normal workouts in the heat for 5 to 7 days should provide nearly total acclimatization, although the intensity of the workout should be reduced to 70–80 percent during the first few days to prevent heat stress.

Heat Disorders and Their Prevention. When the body is unable to successfully adapt to thermal stress, three forms of failure exist. Heat cramps, the least serious of the three heat disorders, is the result of dehydration and the salt loss accompanying high rates of sweating. It is characterized by severe cramping of the skeletal muscles, primarily those muscles used in the exercise. Heat exhaustion is the second type of heat disorder and is characterized by a body temperature of 101–104° F, extreme tiredness, breathlessness, dizziness, and tachycardia or rapid pulse. These symptoms appear to be the result of a reduced sweat production, thus limiting the body's major avenue of heat loss. Heat stroke is the most serious of the three disorders and is characterized by a body temperature of 105–106° F, or higher, cessation of sweating, and total confusion or unconsciousness. If left untreated, the victim of heat stroke is likely to die. While a few people under normal, nonexercising conditions in the heat experience either heat stroke or exhaustion, many athletes push themselves to the point where they are extremely vulnerable to a serious heat disorder. The football player who is wearing a full uniform and protective equipment is particularly vulnerable in a hot environment. The uniform restricts evaporative cooling. The layer of air between the skin and the uniform becomes saturated with water vapor, thus sweat pours off, but little evaporative cooling takes place. The obese player, or the player with a thick layer of subcutaneous fat, has the added problem of the fat providing a thermal barrier to heat dissipation which

makes a substantial contribution to his total heat stress.

To prevent heat disorders, several simple precautions should be taken. Competition and practice outdoors should not be held when the wet bulb temperature is over 78° F. Wet bulb temperature reflects the humidity as well as the absolute temperature, therefore, it is a more sensitive indication of the physiological stress. Scheduling practices and contests either in the early morning or at night is one way of overcoming the severe heat stress of midday. Fluids should be made readily available and the athlete required to drink as much as he can, stopping every 10 to 20 min in the higher temperatures for a "fluid break." Clothing should be as brief as possible, loose-weaved, and of a light color, since dark colors absorb heat while light colors reflect. The athlete should always "underdress" because the metabolic heat load will soon make extra clothing an unnecessary burden. Lastly, the athletes should be closely watched for the clinical signs mentioned above, sure warnings of impending danger.

The American College of Sports Medicine issued a position statement in 1975 which dealt specifically with heat injuries during distance running. The following statement, in part, applies to all sports where heat injuries might be a problem.

Prevention of Heat Injuries
During Distance Running*

Based on research findings and current rules governing distance running competition, it is the position of the American College of Sports Medicine that:

1. Distance races (> 16 km or 10 miles) should not be conducted when the wet bulb temperature—globe temperature** exceeds 28° C (82.4° F).
2. During periods of the year, when the daylight dry bulb temperature often exceeds

---

* Position statement of the American College of Sports Medicine which appeared in *Medicine and Science in Sports*, vol. 7, no. 1, 1975.

** Adapted from D. Minard, "Prevention of Heat Casualties in Marine Corps Recruits." *Milit. Med.* 126:261 (1961). WB-GT = 0.7 (WBT) + 0.2 (GT) + 0.1 (DBT).

TABLE 9–1. Wind-Chill-Factor Chart*

Estimated wind speed (mph)	Actual Thermometer Reading (°F)											
	50	40	30	20	10	0	−10	−20	−30	−40	−50	−60
	Equivalent Temperature (°F)											
calm	50	40	30	20	10	0	−10	−20	−30	−40	−50	−60
5	48	37	27	16	6	−5	−15	−26	−36	−47	−57	−68
10	40	28	16	4	−9	−24	−33	−46	−58	−70	−83	−95
15	36	22	9	−5	−18	−32	−45	−58	−72	−85	−99	−112
20	32	18	4	−10	−25	−39	−53	−67	−82	−96	−110	−124
25	30	16	0	−15	−29	−44	−59	−74	−88	−104	−118	−133
30	28	13	−2	−18	−33	−48	−63	−79	−94	−109	−125	−140
35	27	11	−4	−20	−35	−51	−67	−82	−98	−113	−129	−145
40	26	10	−6	−21	−37	−53	−69	−85	−100	−116	−132	−148
	Green				Yellow				Red			

(Wind speeds greater than 40 mph have little additional effect.)	LITTLE DANGER (for properly clothed person). Maximum danger of false sense of security.	INCREASING DANGER Danger from freezing of exposed flesh.	GREAT DANGER

Trenchfoot and immersion foot may occur at any point on this chart.

* Adapted from *Runner's World* 8: 28 (1973). Reproduced by permission of the publisher.

27° C (80° F), distance races should be conducted before 9:00 A.M. or after 4:00 P.M.

3. It is the responsibility of the race sponsors to provide fluids which contain small amounts of sugar (less than 2.5 g glucose per 100 ml of water) and electrolytes (less than 10 mEq sodium and 5 mEq potassium per liter of solution.)

4. Runners should be encouraged to frequently ingest fluids during competition and to consume 400–500 ml (13–17 oz.) of fluid 10–15 minutes before competition.

5. Rules prohibiting the administration of fluids during the first 10 kilometers (6.2 miles) of a marathon race should be amended to permit fluid ingestion at frequent intervals along the race course. In light of the high sweat rates and body temperatures during distance running in the heat, race sponsors should provide "water stations" at 3–4 kilometer (2–2.5 mile) intervals for all races of 16 kilometers (10 miles) or more.

6. Runners should be instructed in how to recognize the early warning symptoms that precede heat injury. Recognition of symptoms, cessation of running, and proper treatment can prevent heat injury. Early warning symptoms include the following: piloerection on chest and upper arms, chilling, throbing pressure in the head, unsteadiness, nausea, and dry skin.

7. Race sponsors should make prior arrangements with medical personnel for the care of cases of heat injury. Responsible and informed personnel should supervise each "feeding station." Organizational personnel should reserve the right to stop runners who exhibit clear signs of heat stroke or heat exhaustion.

It is the position of the American College of Sports Medicine that policies established by local, national, and international sponsors of distance running events should adhere to these guidelines. Failure to adhere to these guidelines may jeopardize the health of competitors through heat injury.

Exercise in the Cold

Exercise in the cold presents far fewer problems of a severe medical nature. Additional clothing can always be worn during the athletic contest to maintain the athlete in a warm and comfortable environment. The extremities, particularly the hands and feet, are most subject to discomfort and injury from exposure to cold.

As with heat, the temperature alone is not a valid index of the degree of stress felt by the individual. The wind creates a chill factor, and the more moist the surrounding air, the greater the physiological stress. A dry, still day at 10° F in the direct sun can be quite comfortable, yet on a moist, windy day with complete cloud cover at 40° F, the cold can be quite penetrating. Table 9–1 lists equivalent temperatures for various absolute, dry bulb temperatures and wind velocities.

The ability to acclimatize to cold is open to question. If acclimatization does occur as a result of repeated exposures, it is of relatively little value with regard to athletic performance. Of much greater significance are the protective measures taken by physicians, trainers, and coaches to assure the most favorable circumstances for the athlete. Proper protective clothing is important. Tightly woven garments will help maintain a small heat pocket between the skin and clothing. Gloves, hats or caps, and double pairs of stockings are also helpful. Thermal underwear is recommended for the arms, legs, and torso in extreme cold, but as the temperature rises and metabolic heat builds, a serious heat problem could develop. Once the athlete starts to warm up and starts to sweat, he should remove his excess clothing. Sweat-soaked, wet clothing can create problems in a dry environment where evaporation occurs naturally with its resultant cooling effect.

ALTITUDE

With the awarding of the 1968 Olympic Games to Mexico City came a number of questions and a great deal of confusion as to what influence competition at 7,340 ft would have on athletic performance. Physiologists had been interested in altitude as a physiological stressor for a number of years prior to this time, but with the reality of Olympic competition only a few years away, physiologists, athletes, and coaches alike began to realize that little was known about athletic competition at moderate and high altitudes. Would performance in all activities suffer, or would altitude influence only the endurance activities? Would performance in the long jump, high jump, pole vault, shot put, javelin, discus, and hammer be improved due to the lower density of the surrounding air? Would those who live at altitude have an advantage when competing at altitudes, and if so, could the sea level resident move to altitude for several weeks or a month and achieve acclimatization? These and many other questions stimulated a great deal of research between 1963 and 1968, research which has continued to the present time.

Oxygen Transport

The major problem associated with competition at altitude is the reduced availability of oxygen at the tissue level. The surrounding air has the same percentage of oxygen as that found at sea level (20.93 percent), but due to the lower total pressure, the partial pressure of oxygen is reduced in inverse proportion to the increase in altitude. At sea level, the partial pressure of oxygen is 159 mmHg (760 $\times$ 0.2093), while at 8,000 ft the total pressure drops from 760 to 564 mmHg, and the partial pressure of oxygen drops to 118 mmHg. This only reduces the saturation of hemoglobin from 97 percent at sea level to approximately 92 percent at 8,000 ft. It was once thought that it was this small drop in saturation that reduced $\dot{V}O_2$ max approximately 15 percent at this altitude. However, it is also important to remember that the partial pressure of oxygen in the arterial blood drops from about 94 mmHg at sea level to 60 mmHg at 8,000 ft. Assuming a tissue partial pressure of 20 mmHg, the pressure differential drops from

74 to 40 mmHg, or nearly a 50 percent reduction in the diffusion gradient. If the tissue partial pressure were to drop to 0 mmHg, which may be possible for small localized areas of tissue under conditions of exhaustive exercise, the respective gradients would be 94 and 60, or a 36 percent reduction in the diffusion gradient. Since the diffusion gradient is responsible for driving the oxygen from the blood into the tissue, this is an even greater consideration than the small 5 percent reduction in hemoglobin saturation.

From the above data, it appears that the oxygen delivery system is restricted in direct proportion to the decrease in total pressure or in inverse proportion to the altitude. Are similar decrements noted in performance and in the various physiological parameters assessed during exercise?

Physical Performance at Altitude. Sprint-type or anaerobic activities are generally not influenced to a great extent by altitude. These are activities that require only a matter of seconds for completion. Consequently, the demands on the oxygen transport system are minimal, which explains why performance is generally unaffected. It has been postulated that at the higher altitudes, 8,000 ft and above, sprint-type or throwing performances may even be enhanced due to the decreased air density which reduces the frictional resistance of air to running or to the objects being thrown. Limited experience tends to support this theory.

Activities requiring a longer duration, i.e., those with a higher aerobic component, are influenced by increases in altitude. It appears that the greater the aerobic component, the more the activity will be influenced by altitude, and the higher the altitude, the greater the decrement in performance. The decrement in performance is approximately proportional to the decrease in maximal oxygen uptake.

Physiological Function at Altitude. As was mentioned, there is a reduction in maximal oxygen uptake in inverse proportion to the increase in altitude. This is illustrated in Figure 9–1. Consequently, at submaximal levels

of work, the individual will be working at a higher percentage of his capacity. It also appears that the individual calls on his anaerobic metabolism, i.e., reaches anaerobic threshold, at a much lower absolute level of work but probably at approximately the same relative level.

The pulmonary ventilation is increased at higher altitudes, both at rest and during exercise. Since the air at higher altitudes is less dense, the increase in ventilation is a compensatory mechanism to bring the same number of molecules of oxygen into the lung as the individual would take in at sea level. Since the number of molecules of oxygen for a given volume of air is less at higher altitudes, an additional volume of air is necessary to supply the same total number of molecules of oxygen. This increased ventilation acts much the same as hyperventilation at sea level, in that the CO_2 in the alveoli is reduced, causing more CO_2 to diffuse from the blood, which results in an increase in pH of the blood. This is referred to as a respiratory alkalosis and is compensated for by the kidneys where the excess bicarbonate is removed to normalize the blood pH.

The cardiovascular system also undergoes substantial changes to compensate for the increase in altitude and decrease in partial pressure of oxygen. The heart rate at standardized submaximal levels of work is elevated in direct proportion to the decrease in oxygen partial pressure. The stroke volume appears to be uninfluenced by altitude, since studies have shown no change in stroke volume for the same absolute level of work when sea-level values are compared with values at different altitudes. However, this point is unresolved at the present time, since studies have also shown slight increases, as well as decreases, in stroke volume for the same level of work at higher altitudes compared to sea level. This apparent conflict is probably the result of the methodological problems of obtaining accurate estimates of stroke volume from determinations of cardiac output. However, since the change in stroke volume, if real, is small at best, the elevated heart rate at submaximal levels of work results in an increase in cardiac

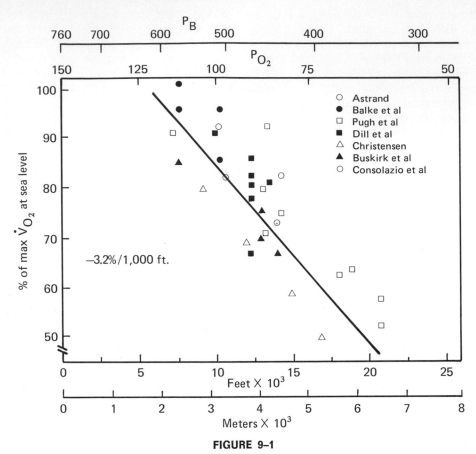

FIGURE 9–1

Reduction in maximal oxygen uptake in relation to increases in altitude, and a decrease in the barometric pressure (PB) and partial pressure of oxygen in the ambient air (pO₂). The symbols represent data of various authors. (From E. R. Buskirk et al., "The Effects of Altitude on Physical Performance, pp. 65–71, edited by R. F. Goddard. Chicago: Athletic Institute, 1967.

output. Thus, since the amount of oxygen available to the tissues from a certain volume of blood is limited due to the reduced partial pressure of oxygen and the subsequent drop in diffusion gradient, a greater volume of blood is delivered to the exercising tissues.

This discussion of cardiovascular alterations refers only to submaximal levels of work. At maximal or exhaustive levels, the maximal stroke volume does not appear to be influenced, but the peak or maximal heart rate is reduced at higher altitudes. This results in a decrease in the maximal cardiac output. With a decrease in the diffusion gradient to push oxygen across the membrane from the blood into the tissues along with this reduction in maximal cardiac output, it is not difficult to understand why both maximal oxygen uptake and performance in aerobic activities are affected by increases in altitude. The reason for the decrease in maximal heart rate is not known at the present time.

Acclimatization

As man extends his exposure to altitude for days and weeks, his body gradually acclimatizes. The body is able to partially adapt to the decreased partial pressure of oxygen found with increasing elevations. However, the athlete is never able to completely compensate for the increased elevation. While performance will improve with continued exposure, it will never reach the level that the athlete could attain at sea level, providing his general level of conditioning has not changed.

One of the first adaptations made at altitude is an increase in the number of circulating red blood cells. The actual amount of increase is not well understood, however, as there is also a substantial loss in plasma volume due to a generalized dehydration. This causes a concentration of the existing red cells, i.e., hemoconcentration. Further research using isotopically tagged, or labeled, red cells will enable a more accurate quantification of this response. Along with the increase in red cells there is an increase in hemoglobin. The net effect of both the red cell and hemoglobin increase is to increase the oxygen-carrying capacity of a fixed volume of blood.

The loss in plasma volume that occurs immediately upon arriving at a higher altitude is a transient response. After a week or more at this altitude, the plasma volume will start to increase back to sea-level values. Whether it fully returns to sea-level values is not clear on the basis of the existing research. Several studies have shown a complete recovery, others have shown only a partial recovery, while still others have shown an increase above sea-level values.

Maximal oxygen uptake is decreased upon first reaching higher altitudes, but the adaptative changes in blood volume, red cell mass, and hemoglobin will gradually increase the maximal oxygen uptake but not to the prealtitude, sea-level values. Performance in activities of a predominantly aerobic nature will show a similar improvement as the athlete becomes acclimatized, but the ultimate performance will still be below that observed at sea level.

Altitude Training

Researchers in several early studies on the influence of altitude on athletic performance, trained athletes at higher altitudes and found, on returning to sea level, that their performances had improved over their prealtitude sea-level performances. Athletes themselves have noted similar improvements following altitude training. Frederick (1974) states that altitude training has become a basic ingredient of success for many world-class distance runners. He further states that every gold medal winner in the 1972 Munich Olympic Games from the 1,500 meters through the marathon were altitude trained.

While the above practical examples are impressive, they are not totally supported by controlled research studies. Several studies have shown no improvement in sea-level performance following altitude training. In several studies where altitude training was found to have an influence on post-altitude, sea-level performance, the subjects were not well trained prior to going to altitude, so it is difficult to discern how much of their post-altitude improvement was due solely to training, independent of altitude.

While the research literature is in apparent conflict on this matter, it is possible to construct a strong theoretical argument for altitude training. First, altitude training evokes a substantial tissue hypoxia (reduced oxygen supply), which is felt to be essential for initiating the conditioning response. Secondly, the major adaptations of increased red blood cell mass and hemoglobin levels will provide a major advantage with regard to oxygen delivery on return to sea level. While evidence suggests these latter changes are transient, lasting only several days, this would still provide an advantage for the athlete. Maximum ventilation volume appears to be enhanced, as does maximum cardiac output, although the latter is not well documented. Putting all of these adaptations together would give the endurance athlete a distinct advantage upon returning to sea level.

What about the athlete who normally trains

at sea level and must compete at altitude? What can he do to prepare most effectively for his competition? While the research is not clear on all aspects of this question, it appears that the athlete should either compete within 24 hours of arrival at higher altitudes or train at higher altitudes for at least two weeks prior to competition. Even two weeks, however, is not sufficient for total acclimatization. That would require a minimum of 4 to 6 weeks. Competing within the initial 24 hours does not provide much in the way of acclimatization, but the exposure is brief enough where the classic systems of altitude sickness have not become totally manifest.

When training at higher altitudes, the coach or athlete should select an altitude between 5,000 and 10,000 feet, since the former is considered the lowest level at which an effect will be noticed, and the latter is the highest level for efficient conditioning. When first reaching higher altitudes, the magnitude of the work out should be reduced to approximately 60–70 percent of the intensity of the sea-level work out schedule, gradually working up to a full work out within 10 to 14 days. Symptoms of altitude sickness may persist for a few days, e.g., shortness of breath, headache, dizziness, nausea, and disturbed sleep, but they will gradually disappear.

DIVING

As man takes to water, an entirely different physical and physiological environment is encountered, which requires a full understanding on the part of the diver. As he dives below the surface of water, the diver is subjected to an increasing pressure, while at higher altitudes, the problem was one of a decreasing pressure. Fresh water weighs 62.4 lb per cubic foot while salt water, due to the salt content, weighs 64.0 lb per cubic foot. Descending to a level of 33 ft produces 14.7 lb *per square inch* (psi) pressure on the diver from the water alone. Since the atmosphere provides an additional 14.7 psi, the total pressure on the diver would

be 29.4 psi (water pressure + air pressure). As the diver descends to 66 ft, the water pressure doubles from 14.7 to 29.4 psi, which when added to the air pressure of 14.7 psi, makes a total pressure of 44.1 psi.

The data in the above discussion is critical to the diver for several important reasons. First, the air he breathes on the surface will be compressed to one half of its original volume in the lung at 33 ft below the water's surface. Conversely, the volume of air in his lung at a 33 ft depth will expand to twice its original volume by the time he reaches the surface. If breathing from a self-contained underwater breathing apparatus (SCUBA), it would be extremely dangerous for the diver to take in a deep breath at a depth of 33 ft and to hold this breath as he ascended to the surface. Overdistension of the lung would result, with rupturing of the alveoli and pulmonary hemorrhage. If air bubbles end up in the circulatory system as a result of this extensive damage, emboli develop and can block major vessels, leading to extensive tissue damage, if not death. Thus, it is important for the diver to always blow out or exhale as he ascends to the surface.

An additional factor that must be considered relative to the increased pressure with dives is the increased partial pressure of the individual gases. Breathing air at a depth of 33 ft doubles the partial pressure of each of the gases. At depths approaching 100 ft, the partial pressures are four times greater than on the surface. It is at 100 ft, when breathing air, that problems of nitrogen narcosis develop. Nitrogen narcosis is known as the "rapture of the deep." The diver develops symptoms similar to those of alcohol intoxication in which the effect is primarily on the central nervous system. Judgment is distorted, and foolish decisions frequently result in serious injury or death.

Another problem caused by the high partial pressures at the lower depths is oxygen poisoning. Breathing high concentrations of oxygen for long periods of time during deep dives drives a great deal of oxygen into solution. The oxygen in solution is used preferentially over that carried in combination with hemoglobin in the red blood cell. Consequently, oxygen is not released from the red cell and a carrier is not available to remove the CO_2 produced. An excess of both O_2 and CO_2 develops in the tissues, causing visual distortion, confusion, rapid and shallow breathing, and convulsions. The use of oxygen in diving is to be avoided whenever possible.

Lastly, the high partial pressures of nitrogen in diving will force nitrogen into the blood and tissues. If the diver attempts to ascend too rapidly, this additional nitrogen cannot be delivered to and released through the lungs quickly enough, and it becomes trapped as bubbles in the circulatory system and tissues, causing discomfort and pain. While the joints and ligaments are most often involved, occasionally, emboli can form in the circulatory system, causing more serious complications. This is referred to as decompression sickness, or the bends. Treatment involves placing the diver into a recompression chamber, where the pressure of nitrogen is increased again and then gradually returned to the ambient pressure. This period of recompression forces the nitrogen back into solution and the gradual decrease in pressure then allows the nitrogen to escape through the respiratory system. To prevent this condition, charts have been created which provide the necessary information relative to the time sequence for ascending from various depths. Strict adherence to the respective time table for the depth submerged will allow a safe ascent without the problem of decompression sickness.

One last word of caution. Annually, a number of deaths result from underwater swimming. Typically, the diver forcefully hyperventilates and then attempts to swim as far as possible on a single breath of air. Unfortunately, the individual may become unconscious and drown before realizing he is in trouble and needs to come to the surface for a breath of air. In hyperventilating, the CO_2 levels are greatly reduced. Since CO_2 is a potent stimulus for breathing, its reduction in the blood decreases the stimulus for breathing and the oxygen concentration drops below critical levels, resulting in a loss of consciousness.

While hyperventilation will allow new records to be set in underwater swimming, it is a practice that must be strongly discouraged due to this inherent danger.

GENERAL SUMMARY

Frequently, athletic competition is conducted under environmental conditions that are less than optimal. Heat, cold, humidity, and altitude each present unique problems for the athlete, which need not seriously handicap his performance if he understands the situation and plans in advance the proper preventive and precautionary procedures.

This chapter attempts to briefly summarize the nature of these various environmental stresses and to provide the coach and athlete with suggestions for coping with them more successfully. In hot environments, performance is compromised in proportion to the severity of the heat stress. Evaporation becomes the most important avenue of heat loss, but this presents potential problems of dehydration if the fluid loss is not rapidly replaced. As the humidity increases, the problem becomes considerably more serious. Practicing in the heat for a week or two will almost fully acclimatize the athlete to the heat stress. In addition, ingestion of fluids before practice and frequently during practice and competition will reduce the degree of heat stress and aid performance. In cold environments, acclimatization does not significantly contribute to the athlete's performance, but proper clothing can play a major role. It is important to dress warmly but not to overdress, for this can cause heat stress.

Altitude directly influences the oxygen transport system. As the altitude increases, the total atmospheric pressure decreases, and this results in a proportional decrease in the partial pressure of the respiratory gases. The partial pressure of oxygen decrease reduces slightly the degree of saturation of the arterial blood with oxygen, but more importantly, it decreases the partial pressure of oxygen in the arterial blood, thus substantially lowering the diffusion gradient. The result is a decreased maximal oxygen uptake and a decrement in performances of an aerobic nature. Acclimitization will reduce the magnitude of these performance decreases but will not totally overcome the influence of altitude, i.e., performance will not equal that at sea level.

Lastly, diving involves another unique environment for performance in which the major consideration is the increased pressure under the surface of the water. This increased pressure will have a substantial influence on the breathing pattern of the diver and will also affect the amounts of nitrogen and oxygen that are driven into solution in the tissues and blood. If these are too great, they can lead to problems of nitrogen narcosis, decompression sickness, and oxygen poisoning.

REFERENCES

ÅSTRAND, P. O., and RODAHL, K. *Textbook of Work Physiology.* New York: McGraw-Hill Book Co., 1970.

BALKE, B. "Variation in Altitude and its Effect on Exercise Performance." In *Exercise Physiology*, edited by H. B. Falls. New York: Academic Press, 1968.

BUSKIRK, E. R.; KOLLIAS, J.; PICONREATIQUE, E.; AKERS, R.; PROKOP, E.; and BAKER, P. In *The Effects of Altitude on Physical Performance*, pp. 65–71, edited by R. F. Goddard. Chicago: Athletic Institute, 1967.

COSTILL, D. L. "Hazards of the Heat." In *The Complete Runner.* Mountain View, Calif.: World Publications, 1974.

DEVRIES, H. A. *Physiology of Exercise for Physical Education and Athletics.* 2nd ed. Dubuque, Iowa: William C. Brown Co., 1974.

FREDERICK, E. C. "Training at Altitude." In *The Complete Runner.* Mountain View, Calif.: World Publications, 1974.

GISOLFI, C. V. "Exercise, Heat, and Dehydration Don't Mix." *Rx Sports and Travel*, May–June 1975, pp. 23–25.

KARPOVICH, P. V., and SINNING, W. E. *Physiology of Muscular Activity*, 7th ed. Philadelphia: W. B. Saunders Co., 1971.

MARGARIA, R., ed. *Exercise at Altitude.* Amsterdam: Excerpta Medica Foundation, 1967.

MATHEWS, D. K., and FOX, E. *The Physiological Basis of Physical Education and Athletics.* Philadelphia: W. B. Saunders Co., 1971.

TIPTON, C. M.; ZAMBRASKI, D. J.; and TCHENG, T. K. "Iowa Wrestling Study: Lessons for Physicians." *Rx Sports and Travel*, January–February 1974, pp. 19–22.

VAN HANDEL, P. "Drinks for the Road." *Runner's World*, 9, July 1974, pp. 29–31.

10
Ergogenic Aids*

INTRODUCTION

As the skill level of athletes in various sports improves from year to year and as athletic records reach new heights, the margin between success and failure in the world of sport becomes smaller. Consequently, coaches and athletes alike look for that slight edge that might assure victory and delay defeat. For some athletes, a special diet may be the deciding factor, others may rely on altering psychological states, while still others may try various hormones or pharmacological agents. Substances or phenomena that elevate or improve the performance of the individual above the expected level are referred to as *ergogenic aids* (Morgan, 1972a). Weight lifters have taken anabolic steroids in an attempt to increase muscle mass and strength. Distance runners have loaded up on carbohydrates two to three days prior to competition in an attempt to pack extra glycogen into the active muscles. Hypnosis has been tried on a number of athletes in various sports in an attempt to get them over specific "hang-ups." Even the cheers of the crowd supporting the home team may place the visiting team at a distinct disadvantage.

While a number of substances and phenomena have been labelled as ergogenic aids, it must be proven that they actually facilitate

the athlete's performance before they can be legitimately classified as ergogenic. The purpose of this chapter is to investigate the various substances and phenomena that have been used by athletes in order to determine their ergogenic potential. Simply because a professional all-star athlete consumes large quantities of a particular substance several hours prior to game time and attributes his success to this practice does not prove that this substance has mystical, power-inducing qualities that will assure other athletes of similar success. While science, with carefully controlled investigations, does not have all of the answers, this is an area where scientific studies are essential to differentiate between a truly ergogenic response and a pseudo-ergogenic response in which the performance is improved simply because the athlete expects it to improve.

DRUGS AND HORMONES

Numerous drugs and hormones have been suggested as having ergogenic properties. Golding (1972) has listed a number of these including:

Adrenaline	Coramine
Alcohol	Lecithin
Alkalies	Metrazol
Amphetamines	Noradrenaline
Caffeine	Steroids
Cocaine	Sulfa drugs

This section will be confined to a study of alcohol, amphetamines, and anabolic steroids,

---

* Sections of this chapter were adapted from William P. Morgan, ed., *Ergogenic Aids and Muscular Performance.* (New York: Academic Press, 1972.)

the three major drugs or hormones that have received the most widespread use and national attention.

Alcohol

Cooper (1972a) states that alcohol is the number one drug problem in the United States. While others classify alcohol as a food, Cooper feels that alcohol is correctly classified as a drug, due to its influence on the central nervous system. Unfortunately, little is known about the influence of varying amounts of alcohol on athletic performance. Obviously, alcohol intake to the point of intoxication would result in an erratic, unpredictable performance. The influence of small amounts of alcohol just prior to or during a contest is not clearly understood.

Several studies have been conducted in the laboratory to observe the effects of small and moderate doses of alcohol on strength, muscular endurance, and cardiovascular endurance. The results from these studies conflict somewhat since several found improved performance and several found decreased performance, but the majority found no difference in performance. It would appear safe to conclude that alcohol has little, if any, ergogenic properties, but that it could be detrimental to optimal performance if taken in sufficient quantity.

Amphetamines

Amphetamines are prescription drugs that stimulate the central nervous system. They have been used as appetite suppressants for individuals on weight-loss programs under close medical supervision. Unfortunately, they have found their way into the athletic arena as a stimulant with possible ergogenic properties. Amphetamines have been referred to as "pep pills," "uppers," "bennies," "greenies," and "dexies," just to name a few of the many words, or terms, popularly used to identify this particular drug. Athletes have found amphetamines readily available, even though they are

a prescription drug. Supposedly, amphetamine usage by an athlete will help him run faster, throw farther, jump higher, and prolong the time it takes to reach total fatigue, or exhaustion. Do controlled scientific research studies support these claims?

Physiologically, amphetamines are known to increase alertness; reduce sense of fatigue; increase vasoconstriction, blood pressure, and heart rate; elevate blood sugar; and increase muscle tension. It is generally regarded as a potent, central nervous system stimulant. Does this insure that the drug will aid physical performance?

A number of studies have been conducted to answer this question, but, unfortunately, as in other areas, the results are in direct conflict with one another.

Two of the most widely read and quoted studies were supported by the American Medical Association and published in 1959. Smith and Beecher (1959) observed the influence of 14–21 mg of amphetamine sulfate per 70 kg of body weight on running, swimming, and weight throwing performance. They found that 75 percent of the tests resulted in an improved performance of 1 to 4 percent with amphetamine administration. This was a double-blind study in which neither the experimenter nor the athlete knew which capsules were being administered, the amphetamine or a placebo, i.e., a capsule of identical size, shape, and color containing sugar, gelatin, or some similar ingredient that has no direct specific effect. Karpovich (1959) conducted a similar study, using 10–20 mg of amphetamine sulfate prior to track running, swimming, and treadmill running. Of the fifty-four subjects, the performance of three improved, the performance of one was poorer, and the remaining fifty showed no difference in performance as a result of the amphetamine administration.

Possibly the best designed and controlled study conducted in this area was reported by Golding and Barnard in 1963. They used a double-blind procedure in which either 15 mg of d-amphetamine sulfate or a placebo were administered, three times each. Approximately 2 to 3 hours after either the drug or the placebo was administered, the subject was given two treadmill tests to exhaustion, the second following the first by 12 min. The purpose of having two treadmill tests to exhaustion was to determine whether amphetamines would "pick up" the subject after one exhaustive bout and make him better able to tolerate the second bout. Amphetamines supposedly abolish or delay the onset of fatigue. Two groups of subjects were used, one that was considered to be conditioned and a second that was considered to be unconditioned. No differences were found between the placebo and amphetamine treatments for either the first or second treadmill runs for either the conditioned or the unconditioned groups.

Additional studies have produced essentially similar results, i.e., the amphetamines appear to have little or no effect on performance. This includes studies of oxygen uptake capacity, oxygen debt, and reaction and movement time, among others. In studies dealing directly with fatigue, or with the sensation or feeling of fatigue, administration of amphetamines may have a small, but significant, effect.

From the above results, it is difficult to draw conclusions about amphetamines as an ergogenic agent. While most studies suggest that amphetamines do little to facilitate performance, those few studies that have reported significant improvements in performance point to the need for additional studies of a highly controlled and more comprehensive nature. It is quite possible that the laboratory tests used in some studies do not accurately duplicate the conditions in the playing situation. Treadmill-running time, reaction time, and oxygen debt may be far removed from the actual stress encountered in the sport or event. Future studies must be sensitive to this point. If future studies show amphetamines to be potent ergogenic aids, the moral and ethical issue of whether they should be allowed in sport must be considered, in addition to the critical problem of the potential medical risks associated with acute and extended usage of amphetamines.

The use of amphetamines in athletics has become widespread over the past twenty years.

During the mid-1970's, many law suits were filed against team trainers and team physicians for administering amphetamines to injured athletes in an effort to get them back into action sooner. While these occurred primarily at the professional level, evidence is also plentiful indicating extensive use of amphetamines by athletes even at the high school level. Since these are prescription drugs, the amphetamines that are being used at each level of competition have to be prescribed by a physician. In no other way can they be legally obtained! The prevalent practice of having amphetamines readily available for individual athletes or athletic teams would suggest that a number of physicians have disregard for the standards of their profession.

Are amphetamines potentially harmful? Experience would tend to suggest that they are inherently dangerous. Deaths have been attributed to excessive amphetamine usage where the athlete pushed beyond his normal state of exhaustion. One of the claims made for amphetamines is that they delay the onset of fatigue. It is possible that, rather than delaying the onset, they delay the sensation of fatigue, enabling the individual to push dangerously beyond his normal limits to the point of circulatory failure. Amphetamines can be highly toxic, and they also can be physically addictive if taken regularly. Extreme nervousness, acute anxiety, aggressive behavior, and insomnia are also frequently mentioned side effects of regular usage.

When used in athletic contests, do amphetamines improve actual performance? Many physicians and scientists have observed that the player on amphetamines frequently feels he is having an outstanding performance, when in actuality his performance may be well below normal. The player's self image appears to be grossly distorted. Jim Bouton, a former major league pitcher, told in his book, *Ball Four*, of the pitcher who was visited on the mound by his manager. He told the manager that he was throwing as well as anyone and that he never felt better. It must have been quite a shock to that pitcher when the manager sent him to the showers for giving up three home runs on three consecutive pitches. Cooper (1972b) cites several examples of bicycle races where all of the participants were given a detailed urine analysis to determine amphetamine usage at the conclusion of the race. Interestingly, traces of amphetamines were found only in those who finished the race at the back of the pack. Thus, it should be concluded that the possible benefits of taking amphetamines, if any, are far outweighed by the potential risks.

Anabolic Steroids

It has been estimated that over 70 percent of world-class weight lifters, shot putters, discus throwers, and javelin throwers either have used anabolic steroids in the past or are presently using them. Androgenic-anabolic steroids are nearly identical to the male sex hormones. The androgenic properties of these hormones accentuate secondary, sexual characteristic development. The anabolic properties are responsible for acceleration of growth through accelerated bone maturation and increased development of muscle mass. The synthetic steroids have been altered to reduce the androgenic properties and increase the anabolic effects. Anabolic steroids have been given for years to youngsters with delayed growth patterns to normalize their growth curves. Theoretically, steroid administration will result in both increased weight, as well as increased strength. Consequently, the athlete who is dependent on size and strength would naturally be interested in steroids. Are anabolic steroids ergogenic in nature? Can they facilitate the actual performance of the athlete? Secondly, and of greater importance, are there inherent medical risks in taking steroids?

A number of studies have attempted to investigate the above questions in an organized and systematic fashion. Fowler and associates (1965) conducted a controlled study of anabolic steroid usage relative to physical performance in healthy young men. Ten of the subjects were athletes, five received the steroid

(20 mg of androstenolene per day) and five received a placebo. An additional thirty-seven untrained subjects were randomly assigned to one of four groups: placebo; steroid; placebo + exercise; steroid + exercise. No differences were noted between the placebo and steroid groups following 16 weeks of training, although the exercising subjects exhibited improved performances. Steroid usage did not result in either a strength or weight gain.

Johnson and O'Shea (1969) created quite a stir in athletic circles when they reported that a group that lifted weights and took anabolic steroids for a 3-week period of time had substantially greater increases in weight, strength, muscle girth, and maximal oxygen uptake than a matched group that only lifted weights. Protein powder was given to all of the subjects to supplement their diets during the training period. Weight gain in the steroid group averaged 2.5 kg, or 5.5 lb, while the nonsteroid group gained only 0.3 kg. The most amazing finding from this study was the increase of more than 15 percent in $\dot{V}O_2$ max with essentially no aerobic training. These changes also occurred over a period of only 3 weeks. Unfortunately, both investigators and subjects knew what supplements each subject was receiving. Subsequent studies have not found changes in $\dot{V}O_2$ max.

Recent studies have been evenly balanced between those that have found no statistically significant change in body size and physical performance attributable to taking steroids and those who have found steroids to have a considerable influence on weight and strength. How can this basic inconsistency be explained? It may be due to lack of proper controls; an inadequate number of subjects in the study; failure to use a protein supplement; different drugs, dosages, or methods of drug administration; or to any one or a combination of these causes; or it may be due to any of a number of other possibilities. The basic problem, however, is not the inconsistency of the findings in these studies but the inability to scientifically observe the effects of the drug dosages that are actually being used in the athletic world. It is estimated that some athletes are taking five to ten times the recommended daily dosage. For obvious reasons, it would be unethical to design a study that used a dosage that exceeded the recommended dosage.

Golding (1972) reported interviews by Dr. Fritz Hagerman with athletes competing in the World Pentathlon Games in 1966 and in the 1968 Olympic Games in Mexico City. Using just two examples, one shot-putter's weight increased from 225 to 280 lb over a two-year period with anabolic steroids, and the athlete achieved his lifetime best performance during this time. In the second example, a discus thrower's weight went from 220 to 268 lb in less than six months while taking steroids and his throws increased from the low 180's to 207 ft. In both examples, the dosage was from two to eight times the recommended dosage. This response does appear to be typical of the athlete who takes exceptionally high doses. Thus, if the dosage is high enough, the drug does appear to have a substantial effect on weight gains. Controlled research has failed to identify the source of these weight gains. Is it muscle, water, or fat? Likewise, it is not clear as to whether these weight gains translate into improved athletic performance. An additional 20 lb of fat or water would be detrimental for most athletes, and even if the 20-lb gain were muscle, there is no evidence that this would aid performance. Unfortunately, because of the inability to study these higher doses in a controlled study, most of these questions will never be properly answered.

Even if anabolic steroids are eventually shown to be beneficial for athletic performance, two questions must be resolved. First, is it morally and ethically right for the athlete to artificially induce changes in his performance potential? Most athletes feel it is wrong for their competitors to do anything that might artificially improve performance, yet many of these same athletes are "forced" into taking steroids in an effort to "keep up" with the other athletes in their sport or event who are chronic steroid users. Cooper (1972b) has quoted an estimate that 80 percent of all weight lifters, shot putters, discus throwers, and javelin throwers of national caliber are using anabolic steroids! It is difficult to be the only athlete in an event at a particular meet who has not been using steroids. Although the pressures on the athlete are great, are the potential gains worth the possible risks associated with steroid use?

This leads to the second question, what are the potential risks associated with the recommended doses of anabolic steroids? First, there is evidence that demonstrates that the use of steroids by individuals who are not fully mature will lead to an early closure of the epiphysis of the long bones. Since steroid use is also associated with an increase in the rate of growth of the long bones, it is difficult to determine whether the individual's final height will be less than, greater than, or the same as the height that would have been achieved without steroids. At least the potential for reducing height exists. Large doses of anabolic steroids suppress the natural secretion of gonadotropin and may cause atrophy of the tubules and interstitial tissue of the testes and possible atrophy of the testicles themselves. Enlargement or hypertrophy of the prostate is another possible side effect. Liver damage from a form of chemical hepatitis has also been identified. Lastly, and possibly of greatest concern, neither scientists nor physicians know the potential long-term effects of chronic steroid usage.

One alternative to steroids that has recently been proposed is cyproheptadine. Cyproheptadine is a prescription drug, i.e., a histamine and serotonin antagonist, which has been shown to induce weight gains in underweight adults, probably through appetite stimulation. This drug is being used with athletes, but no controlled studies have been conducted to determine the results of its use. Even with the underweight adults, the composition of the weight gain was not analyzed. Since cyproheptadine is basically an appetite stimulant, it is probable that the weight gain is largely the result of fat accumulation and fluid retention and not due to an increase in muscle mass. Such a weight gain would have little value in athletics.

NUTRITION

The possible influence of nutrition on athletic performance has not been researched in depth, and, as a result, only a limited amount of information is available on the subject. Unfortunately, many fine athletes have attributed their success to various nutritional rituals. One of baseball's leading home run hitters in the late 1960's and early 1970's was relatively small in stature and did not appear overly muscular. When asked how he was able to generate the power necessary to hit the ball over the fence, he attributed this skill to eating honey just prior to game time. Other athletes have advocated buffalo meat, dessicated liver, vitamins A, C, and E, to name just a few. Do these nutritional aids work? Is performance enhanced? Unfortunately, this is an area that has been contaminated with individual biases, traditional beliefs and practices, and superstition (Horstman, 1972).

Horstman (1972) states that the most common conclusion drawn by the various authors who have investigated the role of nutrition in athletics is that a well-balanced diet is all that is necessary to insure optimal performance. While much of the acclaim for certain foods or substances can be passed off or attributed to the psychological affect, i.e., a particular substance is expected to aid performance, evidence is accumulating that indicates that there are certain nutritional manipulations that can be made to improve the athlete's performance.

Protein

Is it necessary for the athlete who is in training for the purpose of increasing strength and muscle bulk to supplement his normal dietary intake of protein? Protein is essential for the growth and development of the various tissues of the body, since amino acids are the body's "building blocks." It was thought for many years that proteins had to be supplemented in rather large quantities. In fact, at one time it was thought that the muscle consumed itself as fuel for its own contractions, and that pro-

tein supplementation was essential to prevent the muscles from wasting away. It is now recognized that little protein is consumed as fuel for muscular work. If fats or carbohydrates are available, they are selected in preference to proteins as sources of energy.

Studies have shown that work performance is neither enhanced nor inhibited by protein supplementation or deprivation. Horstman (1972) summarizes the situation well when he states that the average diet in our Western culture provides adequately for the protein needs of the average Western man. With heavy physical training or work, the caloric intake may exceed 5,000 Kcal, which should provide adequate total protein if the proportion of protein from the total calories is maintained. One possible exception to this is the finding that substantial increases in muscle mass and strength, when under the influence of anabolic steroids, appear to be dependent on protein supplementation.

Fat and Carbohydrate

At one time, carbohydrate was regarded as the chief fuel for muscular contraction. It is now realized that fat is a major, if not the most important, source of fuel for light-to-moderate levels of exercise. This does not imply that the athlete should attempt to store more body fat, since he probably is already storing more than he needs. A pound or two of fat is sufficient to provide the total energy needed for a grueling 26.2 mi, 3-hour marathon run. A theory has been proposed that the higher levels of fat found in women provide them with an advantage in long-distance races, but this has yet to be proven. Thus, fat is not considered to have any special ergogenic properties.

The biggest breakthrough in athletic nutrition came in the 1960's when a group of Scandinavian researchers started experimental observations of carbohydrate storage and utilization with prolonged, endurance-type exercise. Earlier work had suggested that carbohydrate supplementation would facilitate endurance performance. This was confirmed by the finding that exhaustion was always accompanied by hypoglycemia or low blood sugar. Studies in the early 1960's confirmed the importance of carbohydrates when they demonstrated a depletion of the muscle glycogen stores concomitant with hypoglycemia and the attainment of the exhausted state. The use of the muscle biopsy, introduced in the 1960's, enabled scientists to discover these facts. Typically, studies have shown that as the work is prolonged, the glycogen stores in the muscles become progressively depleted. As the individual reaches the state of exhaustion, the glycogen stores are nearly or totally depleted. These studies all suggest that the initial glycogen content of the active muscle is important with respect to defining the endurance potential of the individual, i.e., the greater the glycogen content, the higher the endurance capacity.

From the above findings, it is evident that the endurance athlete could improve his performance considerably if he could increase the glycogen content of his muscles. Bergström et al. (1967) investigated this problem. Each of the subjects was given three different diets, each for a prescribed period of time. One diet was high in carbohydrate, one high in fat and protein, and one was a mixed diet; each contained the same number of calories. Prior to starting the diet, the subject depleted his muscle glycogen stores by riding a bicycle ergometer to exhaustion at approximately 75 percent of his maximal oxygen uptake. This was followed by three days on the prescribed diet and then a second ride to exhaustion. Prior to the second ride, a muscle biopsy was obtained to determine glycogen content. The total length of time the subject could ride before reaching exhaustion and the initial glycogen content were as follows:

Diet	Glycogen Content gm/100 gm of wet tissue	Riding Time to Exhaustion, min
Mixed	1.93	125.8
High fat and protein	0.69	58.8
High carbohydrate	3.70	189.3

These results support the conclusion that endurance performance can be significantly altered by manipulating the diet, in this case by loading up on carbohydrates prior to competition to enhance the glycogen stores.

A similar example of this phenomenon was shown in an experiment by Karlsson and Saltin (1971). Their subjects each participated in two 30–km races, one subject with a high carbohydrate diet following muscle glycogen depletion, and one with a normal, mixed diet. The average muscle glycogen content was elevated on the high carbohydrate diet to nearly double the level attained on the mixed diet. In addition, the times in the 30–km race were substantially faster following the high carbohydrate diet; the improvement coming primarily in the last half of the race!

With this information available, how does the athlete proceed to enhance his muscle glycogen stores? Londeree (1974) has summarized the steps necessary to optimize the glycogen loading phenomenon. First, he points to the fact that carbohydrates are normally stored in limited quantities and that only a limited quantity of carbohydrate can be absorbed from the intestine during the actual competition; thus, it is necessary to enlarge the glycogen stores. To increase glycogen storage, the individual must, first, totally deplete his glycogen stores. This can be accomplished by an exhaustive exercise bout of an extended duration, i.e., greater than 60–90 min. This should be done approximately 7 days prior to the competition. The greater the depletion, the greater the additional storage of glycogen. Once depleted, the glycogen stores are maintained in this depleted state by continued training and a low carbohydrate diet. A certain amount of carbohydrate is essential, so the diet should not be totally void of carbohydrate. Approximately 3 to 4 days prior to competition, the diet is changed to one that is predominantly carbohydrate. Additional fluids must also be ingested since 3–4 gm of water are stored with each gram of glycogen. While on the high-carbohydrate diet, activity should be tapered to low levels to maximize the additional storage of glycogen.

A warning must be given to those who advocate this type of dietary manipulation. Several physicians have become concerned about the possibility of medical risks associated with this kind of dietary practice. Angina-like symptoms (chest pain) have been noted in several athletes who have used this diet. In one case, this was associated with an abnormal electrocardiogram. It is not possible, at the present time, to establish a cause-effect relationship. It seems unlikely that carbohydrate loading would be dangerous to the young, healthy athlete. It might be wise for the older athlete to proceed with caution, however, until this phenomenon is better understood. Most endurance athletes are unknowingly practicing carbohydrate loading to a great extent just by the nature of their rigorous training programs. While they might not go through a 3–4 day, extensive reduction in carbohydrate intake following an exhaustive, glycogen-depleting workout, they do periodically deplete their glycogen stores and consume considerable quantities of carbohydrates.

Carbohydrate loading increases the total quantity of glycogen available in the muscle. How does this, in itself, improve performance? During prolonged endurance competition when the body depletes its carbohydrate stores, can't the body perform equally well by using fat as the main source of fuel? A number of studies have shown conclusively that while fat is a major source of fuel for low-intensity exercise —up to 70 percent—that, as the intensity of the exercise increases, the reliance on carbohydrates increases. Once the anaerobic threshold is reached and the oxygen supply is unable to meet the oxygen demands, the body shifts to a dependence on carbohydrate utilization. Horstman (1972), in his review of athletic nutrition, has provided an insight into why this shift occurs. In calculating the actual energy production from a given fuel, it is possible to calculate the efficiency of utilization. This is defined simply as the kilocalories of energy produced per minute from a specific fuel per liter of oxygen consumed, or the energy derived per liter of oxygen. Glucose yields 5.01 Kcal/liter of oxygen, and fat yields

only 4.65 Kcal/liter of oxygen. This provides a distinct advantage for carbohydrate utilization when the exercise intensity reaches the upper levels, since there is a greater energy yield for the same amount of oxygen that is consumed.

Vitamins and Minerals

Historically, massive doses of various vitamins and minerals have been taken by certain athletes with the hope of improving their athletic performance. The many problems and diseases associated with various vitamin deficiencies are well known, but do athletes generally have vitamin or mineral deficiencies? Even if deficiencies do not exist, will supplementation of any one vitamin or mineral above the recommended daily dose result in better performance by an athlete? While these questions have been researched extensively, debate still continues over the conflicting results.

B-complex vitamins are among those vitamins known to influence physical performance. They are involved in coenzyme activity with the metabolism of fats and carbohydrates. Deficiencies have been shown to decrease athletic performance. On the other hand, supplementation with B-complex vitamins, primarily thiamine (B_1), has been shown to both improve performance, as well as to have no influence on performance. Additional research is needed to provide a conclusive answer to the question of whether B-complex supplementation is of any value for the athlete.

Vitamin C also plays an important role in energy metabolism. Similar to a deficiency in the B vitamins, a deficiency in vitamin C will result in a decrease in physical performance. With regard to the question of supplementation, the research literature is equivocal. Early studies of vitamin C supplementation and physical performance showed no distinct advantage in levels of vitamin C in excess of the recommended daily dosage. More recent studies, however, have reopened interest in this area. A number of studies conducted since 1960 have shown vitamin C supplementation to result in prolonged endurance capacity. These more recent findings point to the need for additional studies to clarify the role of vitamin C in endurance performance relative to its mechanism of operation and to the optimal dosage.

Vitamin E must be considered the wonder vitamin of this century since it has been touted as the cure for almost every one of man's ills. As with the vitamins discussed previously, research literature relative to the influence of vitamin E on athletic performance conflicts. Using wheat germ oil, a rich source of alpha tocopherol and a most potent source of vitamin E, several studies have shown improvements in endurance performance, while several have shown little or no effect from the vitamin. Again, the evidence must be considered inconclusive at this time, indicating the need for further study of a highly controlled nature.

From the above studies, it would appear that the B-complex vitamins and vitamins C and E have ergogenic properties, but this conclusion is certainly open to debate. Additional studies are essential, since vitamin supplementation is expensive and can even be toxic as in the case of the fat soluble vitamins, i.e., A, D, E, and K, which are stored in the body. The water soluble vitamins are rapidly excreted in the urine; thus, supplementation with these vitamins, even if they have no measurable effect on performance, leaves the athlete with nothing more than expensive urine.

With minerals, it is well known that deficiencies can reduce the efficiency of the athlete, particularly when exercising in the heat. Sweating reduces the body's sodium and chloride stores. In addition, exercise can substantially alter the body's balance for potassium, calcium, magnesium, and phosphorus. Again, as in the case of vitamins, it is essential to replace those minerals that have been lost, but is supplementation above normal levels an aid to performance?

The use of salt tablets has been advocated for years to supplement the normal salt ingested in food when the athlete is exercising under conditions where there is excessive water and mineral loss through sweating. While replacement of sodium chloride lost in sweat is desirable, care must be taken not to ingest more salt than necessary. Excessive salt intake can lead to undesirable potassium loss and increased water retention. Generally, according to most review articles, a liberal salting of food or the ingestion of an electrolyte solution, such as Gatorade, Sportade, ERG, or other similar, readily available commercial beverages, is sufficient to maintain sodium and chloride levels, without having to ingest salt tablets.

Aspartates have been used as ergogenic aids for a number of years. Aspartates are potassium and magnesium salts of aspartic acid, which supposedly work in an intermediate position in the Krebs cycle to reduce the accumulation of blood ammonia. Increased levels of blood ammonia are thought to be one possible cause of fatigue; thus, aspartates are considered to have possible ergogenic effects by delaying the onset of fatigue. In Golding's review of aspartates (1972), it is again clear that the existing literature is not in agreement. Several studies of a well-designed and controlled nature demonstrated rather remarkable gains in endurance from aspartate administration, but several have shown aspartates to have no influence at all. Again, additional research is needed to clarify the actual role of aspartates in prolonging activities of an endurance nature.

Water

Seldom is water regarded as an ergogenic aid. It is consumed by everyone, has no caloric or nutritional benefits, but is essential to life. From the discussion of dehydration in Chapter 9 and from Costill's (1972) extensive review, it appears that water is an ergogenic aid. Ingesting fluids prior to endurance competition is an effective way to maintain the body temperature at a reduced level and limit the extent of dehydration. For a more detailed discussion of this, refer to the section on dehydration in Chapter 9, Environmental Factors and Athletic Performance.

Precontest Meal

For years, the athlete has been given the traditional steak dinner several hours prior to competition. Possibly, this practice originated from the early belief that the muscle consumed itself as fuel for muscular activity and that steak provided the necessary protein to counteract this loss. It is now recognized that this is probably the worst possible meal that the athlete could eat prior to competition. Steak contains a high percentage of fat which takes many hours to be fully digested. The digestive process competes for the available blood with the muscles that are used in the contest. Because of this, the precontest meal, no matter what its content, should be given no later than three hours prior to the contest. Another factor to consider is the emotional climate at the time of this meal. Extreme nervousness is frequently present, and even the choicest steak is not enjoyed. The steak would be psychologically more satisfying to the athlete the night before the contest.

Many athletes are starting to use a liquid pregame meal, since it is palatable, digests relatively easily, and is less likely to result in nervous indigestion, nausea, vomiting, and abdominal cramps. Those who have experimented with liquid precontest meals have found them to be highly satisfactory. At the present time, this would appear to be the best available choice as a pregame meal.

OXYGEN

During the professional football game of the week on television, it is not uncommon to see the premier running back break loose for a 35-yd touchdown run, struggle back to the bench, grab a face mask, and start breathing 100 percent oxygen. How much does he gain over a normal recovery breathing the surrounding air?

Initial attempts to scientifically investigate the ergogenic properties of oxygen began in the early 1900's, but it was not until the 1932 Olympic Games that oxygen was considered to be a potential ergogenic aid for athletic performance. At that time, the Japanese swimmers won great victories, and many attributed their success to the fact that they breathed pure oxygen prior to competition. Was this success due partly to their use of oxygen or was it solely due to the fact that they were better athletes at the time of competition?

Oxygen can be supplemented in one of three ways: increasing the partial pressure of oxygen in the inspired gas mixture; using the normal concentration of oxygen in air under compression; or using an increased partial pressure of oxygen in the inspired gas mixture that is under compression. Also, oxygen can be supplemented prior to competition, during competition, during recovery from competition, or during any combination of these three.

Oxygen breathing prior to exercise has a limited effect on that exercise. If the bout is of a short duration, the total amount of work performed or the rate of work can be increased by breathing oxygen, and submaximal work can be performed at a lower pulse rate. For exercise bouts in excess of 2 min, or when the interval between the oxygen breathing and actual performance exceeds 2 min, the influence of breathing oxygen is greatly diminished. This simply reflects the limits of the oxygen storage potential of the body.

When oxygen is administered during the exercise, definite improvements in performance are noted. The amount of work performed and the rate of work are substantially increased. Likewise, submaximal work is performed more economically, at a lower physiological cost to the individual. The ergogenic properties of oxygen are not as clearly defined during the recovery period. The few studies that have been conducted have shown little, if any, effect. However, the studies that have been conducted have not used maximal, exhaustive exercise, which may account for their inability to demonstrate a substantial effect.

From a practical standpoint, oxygen administration prior to exercise would have little value because of the time limitations in athletics mentioned above. Likewise, administration during exercise would have limited value, for obvious reasons. Oxygen breathing during the recovery period could have some limited value, although this needs to be confirmed by a well-controlled research study. The recovery period would appear to be the only practical time to administer oxygen, but only if it speeded up the recovery process, allowing the athlete to re-enter the contest or game in a more fully recovered state. Wilmore (1972) provides an extensive review of this entire area.

BLOOD DOPING

Ekblom et al. (1972) created quite a stir in the sports world in the early 1970's. Their research indicated that by withdrawing between 800 and 1,200 ml of blood from a subject and then reinfusing the red cells back into that subject some four weeks later, a considerable improvement in $\dot{V}O_2$ max and treadmill performance time could be demonstrated. The subjects in this study were divided into two groups: Group I had 800 ml of blood withdrawn in a single day, and Group II had 1,200 ml of blood withdrawn over an eight-day period. Immediately following the blood withdrawal, hemoglobin concentration dropped 13 and 18 percent and $\dot{V}O_2$ max decreased by 13 and 18 percent in groups I and II respectively, while both groups decreased 30 percent in treadmill performance. At the end of four weeks, the red cells were reinfused. Treadmill performance time increased 23 percent and $\dot{V}O_2$ max increased 9 percent over the values prior to the initial blood withdrawal.

These results suggest a remarkable ergogenic effect from infusing or reinfusing red blood cells. While this procedure is relative safe in the hands of competent physicians, it, nevertheless, has inherent dangers associated with it. Even though performance appears to be improved by laboratory standards, field tests must be given to test its true ergogenic potential. The potential risks of such a procedure seem to outweigh any potential benefits, above and beyond the ethical issue involved.

WARM-UP AND TEMPERATURE VARIATIONS

Most athletes warm up prior to competition. For some this may consist of simple stretching, while for others it may be a time for an intensive bout of work. Does this precompetition activity facilitate the athlete's performance during the competition, or is this merely a traditional formality that has been carried down through the years? Before this question can be answered, it is important to recognize the different forms of warm-up. Warm-up activities can be identical to those used in competition, or they can be directly related (free-throw shooting drill without the stress of actual competition) or indirectly related (calisthenics for some muscle groups) activities. Lastly, warm-up can be as passive as hot showers or a massage.

Attempting to determine the specific effects of warm-up is extremely difficult, since the effect appears to differ with the activity, as well as with the form of the warm-up. Franks (1972) has provided an outstanding summary of the research through the early 1970's. There is evidence to support both the beneficial and detrimental effects of the warm-up. Warm-up facilitates accuracy, movement time, range of motion, and strength in movements of selected parts of the body, but it does not appear to affect reaction time. Sprints and distance runs are improved with warm-up, but agility runs are not. Baseball throwing speed and softball distance throw are improved with warm-up but not the accuracy of the throw. Franks (1972) concludes that some forms of warm-up can be detrimental to jumping, agility, running, sprinting, baseball throw for accuracy, and cycle endurance and speed tasks.

While many coaches and athletes feel that the warm-up is essential to prevent injuries, there is little direct research evidence to support this contention. This lack of supporting evidence is true for burst-type activities, as well. However, until this critical aspect of warm-up can be explored more fully, it would seem wise to continue using the warm-up as a precautionary, preventive procedure.

It appears that the efficacy of the warm-up

depends on the type of warm-up, as well as on the sport. The coach or athlete who has questions about a particular sport should refer directly to the specific research studies dealing with that sport. Unfortunately, no general conclusions can be drawn at this time.

Passive hot and cold applications have also been proposed as potential ergogenic aids. Falls (1972) concludes that cold applications are more likely to provide an ergogenic effect than hot applications. The benefit of a cold application, e.g., a shower, lies in its effect on circulatory function. Cold causes a peripheral vasoconstriction and possibly a reflex vasodilation within the muscle, which makes more blood available for the active tissues. In addition, the cold application cools the body surface which enhances its ability to dissipate body heat. Heat applications have the opposite effect and tend to reduce efficiency in performances of an endurance nature. Heat applications that are used for warming and loosening a joint, e.g., shoulder of the pitcher in baseball, may have a substantial effect, but this depends largely on the individual.

SOCIAL AND PSYCHOLOGICAL FACTORS

when two teams, which are evenly matched, What advantage does the home team have struggle to the last second to determine who wins? Does the cheering crowd give the home team a distinct advantage in this situation and put the visiting team at a disadvantage? Does hypnosis and post-hypnotic suggestion influence the athlete's performance? These and other related questions will be discussed in this section. The social and psychological factors associated with athletic performance are difficult to assess with any degree of validity and reproducibility. This is unfortunate, since these factors may be much more significant in determining the final outcome of competition than the physiological factors discussed previously.

Social Facilitation

While the field of social facilitation encompasses a broad range of specific areas, this section will focus on the area of audience effect, i.e., how performance is influenced by the presence of others. Singer (1972) presents an extensive review of the entire field of social facilitation as an ergogenic aid for those who desire additional information.

When observing the effect of an audience on performance, the nature of the audience must be defined. How large is the audience? Are they hostile (visiting team) or supportive? Are they of the opposite sex compared to the performers? Is the audience active or passive? Singer (1972) noted the problems of conducting a controlled research study with an active audience. The principle problem in a controlled research setting is motivating the audience to be consistent in their active encouragement of the athlete or team. Thus, most studies have involved a passive audience that simply observes and gives no verbal encouragement.

Most of the available research supports the theory that a passive audience facilitates physical performance, although some experiments show the audience to have an inhibiting and disturbing effect on the individual. Where the audience has been shown to have a disturbing effect, it is not clear whether this is a function of the situation or the subject. Competition in front of a passive audience might be a stimulus to the skilled athlete but may threaten the unskilled, nonathlete. Some evidence exists that suggests that the more highly skilled the performer, the more positive the influence exerted by the audience.

Singer (1972) points out that task difficulty and anxiety level, as well as skill level, influence the effect of the audience on the subsequent performance. In an attempt to integrate these factors, he concludes that simple tasks demanding physical energy, repetition, power, strength, or endurance are probably enhanced by an audience. Motor skills requiring complex coordination, finely executed movements, and intense concentration may be impaired by the presence of observers until the skills are well learned. The more highly skilled athlete in any activity should be favorably influenced by an audience. Singer feels that the most highly skilled athletes are, in most instances, unaffected by the crowd's behavior, whether they are encouraged or "booed." Some athletes become too "psyched" playing in front of an audience and never attain the potential they exhibit in practice. Also, there is some evidence suggesting that performance can be impaired by a hostile audience.

Hypnosis

Morgan (1972b) conducted an extensive review of the existing research literature relative to hypnosis as an aid to athletic performance. Unfortunately, as mentioned in previous sections of this chapter, the literature is in conflict. While some investigators have reported absolutely no improvement in muscular strength and endurance with hypnosis, others have reported that simply being in a trance can either decrease or increase performance. Most people assume that superhuman feats of strength can be performed under the influence of hypnosis on the basis of the many popular accounts in the media. A critical look at the existing literature, however, does not totally support this assumption. In fact, the research studies are nearly evenly balanced between those that show improvement and those that show no difference between the hypnotic and the waking state. Controlled research in this particular area is extremely difficult to design and execute, due to various methodological problems and the variability of the subjects' response to hypnosis. Morgan (1972b) concludes by stating that while hypnotic suggestions of enhanced muscular strength and endurance are sometimes effective, they cannot be counted upon to consistently facilitate performance.

It appears that hypnosis is most effective when used to correct psychomotor problems, reduce pain, resolve aggression conflicts, and control anxiety states in the competitive athlete (Morgan, 1972b). Certainly, considerable additional research will be necessary before the coach and athlete, as well as the scientist, understand fully the potential of hypnosis in sport.

Mental Practice

When the athlete mentally rehearses his event or sport using the image of a perfectly executed, skilled performance, this is referred to as "mental practice." How effective is this imaginary practice? Will it facilitate the performance of the skilled athlete?

It appears from a recent review by Corbin (1972) that mental practice does facilitate the performance of a skilled performer. While some studies showed little or no improvement with mental practice, most of the studies reviewed showed a substantial influence. The degree of improvement, however, depends on several factors. The individual must have had some previous experience with the task, although it is not fully understood whether the skill level of the performer is a factor or not. The ability to conceptualize also appears to influence the athlete's success. Possibly one of the most important results of the athlete's use of mental practice is the improvement in the ability to concentrate on that specific task. Constant mental rehearsals in practice may allow the athlete to focus more fully on the task during the actual competition.

GENERAL SUMMARY

In his never-ending search for excellence and improved performance, the athlete has tried numerous drugs, hormones, and diets, as well as many other physical substances and phenomena such as hypnosis and mental practice. Often, the athlete has used these aids indiscriminately with complete disregard for his health and safety. Furthermore, if an athlete becomes successful after using one of these substances or phenomena, the word spreads quickly, and, soon, athletes in all parts of the world are using the substance or phenomena without waiting for evidence of its effectiveness or information about its side effects. Just as important are the moral and ethical considerations.

This chapter has reviewed the more widely used substances and phenomena thought to have ergogenic properties and has raised more questions than it has answered. With regard to drugs and hormones, it was concluded that alcohol had no apparent effect on athletic performance when consumed in small doses, but that it can have a substantial detrimental effect when given in large doses. Amphetamines have been shown to improve, as well as have no influence on, athletic performance, which suggests a need for further study of a more highly controlled nature. Anabolic steroids have been shown to cause great increases in weight and strength in individual athletes who have taken extremely high doses. However, controlled research studies using only the recommended daily dosage have shown both increases, as well as no change, in weight and strength. With both amphetamines and steroids, the potential medical risks must be given serious consideration.

One of the areas that receives great attention and interest from athletes who are concerned with improved performance is nutrition. Can you alter what you eat to improve performance? While it appears that the average athlete consumes a sufficient quantity of protein and that supplementation has little additional effect, there is evidence to indicate that carbohydrate loading is an effective nutritional manipulative technique, which can increase general muscular endurance by increasing the storage of muscle glycogen. The technique of carbohydrate loading is discussed in detail in this chapter. Various vitamins and minerals have been proposed as ergogenic aids. From the available research, it appears that vitamins B-1, C, and E may have ergogenic properties. While the evidence available is not conclusive, it indicates the need and value of additional studies in this area. Aspartates have also been proposed as ergogenic aids, but, again, the

research literature is equivocal about their effectiveness.

Oxygen is an ergogenic aid when given immediately before a short duration contest, i.e., less than two minutes in length, or when given during the contest or work bout. These ergogenic properties are not as certain when oxygen is administered during the period of recovery. The issue of blood doping has yet to be resolved.

Warm-up and hot and cold applications were also discussed as potential ergogenic aids. While warm-up appears to be beneficial for certain activities or contests, for others, it either has no effect or it can actually be detrimental. Cold applications, such as cold showers, do appear to improve the cardiovascular function of the individual during controlled bouts of exercise.

Lastly, the area of social and psychological factors was investigated. It appears that the influence of social facilitation and hypnosis are unpredictable and may depend entirely on the subject, the task, and the surrounding environment. Mental practice, however, does appear to facilitate the performance of even highly skilled athletes, possibly through improving their ability to concentrate.

REFERENCES

BERGSTRÖM, J.; HERMANSEN, L.; HULTMAN, E.; and SALTIN, B. "Diet, Muscle Glycogen, and Physical Performance." *Acta Physiol. Scand.* 71 (1967): 140–50.

COOPER, D. L. "Understanding the Drug Menace." *Bulletin Nat. Assoc. Secondary School Principles.* 56 (1972a): 53–60.

COOPER, D. L. "Drugs and the Athlete." *J. Amer. Med. Assoc.* 221 (1972b): 1007–11.

CORBIN, C. B. "Mental Practice." In *Ergogenic Aids and Muscular Performance*, ed. W. P. Morgan. New York: Academic Press, 1972.

COSTILL, D. L. "Water and Electrolytes." In *Ergogenic Aids and Muscular Performance*, edited by W. P. Morgan. New York: Academic Press, 1972.

EKBLOM, B.; GOLDBARG, A. N.; and GULL-BRING, B. "Response to Exercise After Blood Loss and Reinfusion." *J. Appl. Physiol.* 33 (1972): 175–80.

FALLS, H. B. "Heat and Cold Applications." In *Ergogenic Aids and Muscular Performance*, edited by W. P. Morgan. New York: Academic Press, 1972.

FOWLER, W. H.; GARDNER, G. W.; and EGSTROM, G. H. "Effect of Anabolic Steroid on Physical Performance in Young Men." *J. Appl. Physiol.* 20 (1965): 1038–40.

FRANKS, B. D. "Physical Warm-Up." In *Ergogenic Aids and Muscular Performance*, edited by W. P. Morgan. New York: Academic Press, 1972.

GOLDING, L. A. "Drugs and Hormones." In *Ergogenic Aids and Muscular Performance*, edited by W. P. Morgan. New York: Academic Press, 1972.

GOLDING, L. A., and BARNARD, R. J. "The Effect of d-amphetamine Sulfate on Physical Performance." *J. Sports Med. Phys. Fit.* 3 (1963): 221–24.

HORSTMAN, D. H. "Nutrition." In *Ergogenic Aids and Muscular Performance*, edited by W. P. Morgan. New York: Academic Press, 1972.

JOHNSON, L. C., and O'SHEA, J. P. "Anabolic Steroid: Effects on Strength Development." *Science* 164 (1969): 957–59.

KARLSSON, J., and SALTIN, B. "Diet, Muscle Glycogen, and Endurance Performance. *J. Appl. Physiol.* 31 (1971): 203–6.

KARPOVICH, P. V. "Effect of Amphetamine Sulfate on Athletic Performance." *J. Amer. Med. Assoc.* 170 (1959): 558–61.

LONDEREE, B. "Pre-event Diet Routine." *Runner's World.* 9 (1974): 26–29.

MORGAN, W. P. (ed.) *Ergogenic Aids and Muscular Performance.* New York: Academic Press, 1972a.

MORGAN, W. P. "Hypnosis and Muscular Performance." In *Ergogenic Aids and Muscular Performance*, edited by W. P. Morgan. New York: Academic Press, 1972.

SINGER, R. N. "Social Facilitation." In *Ergogenic Aids and Muscular Performance*, edited by W. P. Morgan. New York: Academic Press, 1972.

SMITH, G. M., and BEECHER, H. K. "Amphetamine Sulfate and Athletic Performance." *J. Amer. Med. Assoc.* 170 (1959): 542–57.

WILMORE, J. H. "Oxygen." In *Ergogenic Aids and Muscular Performance*, edited by W. P. Morgan. New York: Academic Press, 1972.

11
The Female Athlete

INTRODUCTION

While females have competed successfully in athletics for many years, the athletic arena has traditionally been the domain of the male. During the early 1970's, female athletics underwent a dramatic revolution. Demands were made for equality in budget, facilities, equipment, coaching, and competitive opportunities for a position in the world of athletics comparable to that enjoyed by the male. While the demand for equality of opportunity was generally met, with moderate to major reluctance, the demand by some females that traditionally all male sports be sexually integrated was met with heated discussion and debate. In this controversy the question arose, repeatedly, whether female athletes were genetically inferior to male athletes in physical and physiological characteristics. Were the sexes created equal in their potential athletic ability? These questions and their answers have important implications, not only for the athletic world, but, also, for many areas of employment in which physical performance characteristics are critical. Can females perform the duties of firefighting, police work, flying commercial airplanes, working on telephone lines, or similar positions that require unusual physical demands.

This chapter will focus on similarities and differences between males and females in those areas that directly influence athletic performance. Of primary concern will be the areas of body build and composition, strength, cardiovascular endurance capacity, and motor skill development and athletic ability. By looking at the record books, it is apparent that the female athlete performs at a substantially lower level than her male counterpart in almost all athletic events, or contests. On the basis of world records in the year 1974, the male was 11.1 percent faster in the 100-yd dash, jumped 19.9 percent higher in the high jump, ran 14.0 percent faster in the 1-mi run, and swam 7.3 percent faster in the 400-meter freestyle swim. Do these differences result from biological differences between the sexes or do they reflect the social and cultural restrictions that have been placed on the female during her pre-adolescent and adolescent development?

BODY BUILD AND COMPOSITION

The statement that the mature male and female differ in body build and composition does not require scientific validation. However, even in the mature adult, the differences that presently exist between the male and female are considerably greater than they need to be. At the time when full maturity is reached, the average female is 5 in. shorter than the average male, 30 to 40 lb lighter in total weight, 40 to 50 lb lighter in lean body weight, and considerably fatter, i.e., 25 versus 15 percent relative body fat. Up to the age of thirteen to fourteen years, however, the average female is either equal to, or greater than, the average male in both height and weight. This is undoubtedly due to the earlier maturation of the female. Once full maturity is reached, the male will have broader shoulders, narrower hips, and a greater chest girth relative to his total body size. In terms of absolute values, the male has a greater amount of subcutaneous fat in the abdominal and upper regions of the body, while the female carries substantially more fat in the hip and lower regions of the body. The female's hips are equal in width to the males even though the width of the other bones and areas are, on the average, 10 percent, or more, greater in the male. The two sexes are equal in girth measurements at the abdomen, hips, and thigh. Additionally, the average female, on the basis of somatotype, tends more toward endomorphy, or fatness, while the average male tends to be more linear (ectomorphy) and muscular (mesomorphy).

In terms of body composition, the 18- to 22-year-old female will average between 22 and 26 percent relative body fat, while the male of similar age will average between 12 and 16 percent. These differences are due to both a lower absolute lean weight and a higher absolute fat weight in the female. Whether these differences are primarily biological or genetic in nature, or whether environmental and cultural factors are of major importance is not clearly understood at the present time. However, evidence is now available that shows that each of these factors is important and that each of them makes a significant contribution to the total differences observed.

The higher levels of the androgen hormones in the male are undoubtedly responsible for his greater lean body weight. Similarly, the higher levels of the estrogen hormones in the female are at least partially responsible for her greater amount of fat weight. The mature female has higher amounts of essential fat due to the fat in breast and in other sex-specific tissues. The significant question that needs to be answered is how much additional fat the female should possess? At what point does this additional fat become nonessential and limit athletic performance?

It is difficult to design a research experiment to answer the above questions. However, insight into the problem is gained by observing the relative body fats of national and world-class athletes whose sport, event, or activity require speed, endurance, and mobility. Figure 7–12 illustrates the relative body fat values for a large number of track and field athletes. While the values are highly variable for the group as a whole, close inspection of the data reveals that the runners are considerably leaner than those competing in the field events. Of the 27 runners evaluated, 7 had relative fat values under 10 percent and 18 had values under those of the college-age male (approximately 15 percent). Costill and associates (1970) reported an average value of 7.5 percent fat for 114 male competitors at the 1968 United States Olympic marathon trial. Two of the women in Figure 7–12 had values of approximately 6 percent fat (determined by underwater weighing). One of these women had started running because she was considered obese and wanted to use exercise in addition to diet to reduce her weight to a more normal level. She became enthusiastic with her running program, expanded it, and became a world-record-holding, long-distance runner. While the low relative body fats for these runners may be largely the result of their inherited constitutions, this illustration suggests that the high intensity, endurance type of exercise engaged in by these female athletes is also a most significant factor. Training at distances of up to 100 mi, or more, per week requires extraordinarily high levels of caloric expenditure. Thus, it appears that the female athlete can approach the relative fat values observed in male athletes, although considerably more research will be necessary to confirm this conclusion. In addition, it would seem that the average values of relative fat for the fully mature female are considerably above the level that might be considered ideal. The sedentary life style acquired by the average female once she reaches puberty undoubtedly accounts for these comparatively high values. Likewise, it is difficult to justify the extraordinarily high values of the few female shot-putters illustrated in Figure 7–12. These values should not be interpreted as essential for success in this event. Refer to Chapter 7, Body Build and Composition, for further discussion of this topic.

STRENGTH

It is well recognized that the average male is considerably stronger than the average female. Composite strength scores from several different studies suggest that men are approximately 30 to 40 percent stronger than women. Even at ages of 7 through 17 years, while the values are relatively close, the female is not able to exhibit the same level of strength. These results are somewhat misleading, however, for when individual values are considered for specific areas of the body, it is found that leg strength is nearly identical in the two sexes. When expressed relative to body size, leg strength is identical, and when leg strength is expressed relative to lean body weight, to more accurately reflect muscle mass, the females are slightly stronger! With reference to upper-body strength, however, females are only 30 to 50 percent as strong as males.

Can females benefit from strength-training exercises? Several studies have confirmed that weight training in adolescent and college-age girls can produce significant gains in strength in each of the areas trained. Brown and Wilmore (1974) reported bench-press strengths of 115 to 187 lb and leg-press strengths of 125 to 175 lb in seven, nationally ranked, female, track-and-field throwing-event athletes, five of whom had just completed a six-month, intensive weight-training program. These values are considerably greater than those reported for normal, untrained males of similar ages but well below values reported for male weight lifters. A recent study (Wilmore, 1974) has demonstrated that the mean strength of young, nonathletic women can be improved by as much as 30 percent by a ten-week weight-training program. Some of the women in this study doubled their strength in selected areas during this relatively short training period. In comparison with a group of nonathletic young men on an identical program, these women exhibited greater gains in strength, although their initial values were lower.

From the above, it appears that the female has the potential to develop substantially high levels of strength which are considerably higher than those normally identified in the average, typically sedentary, female. Yet, while strength training does produce large increases in the female's total body strength, it does not appear to result in concomitant gains in muscle bulk. This is an important point, since most female athletes would like to increase their basic levels of strength but would be quite unwilling to strength train if they suspected that they would develop excessively large, bulky muscles. The inability of the average female to gain substantial amounts of muscle with strength training is undoubtedly due to her relatively low levels of testosterone compared to the average male. Some females will notice an increased bulkiness accompanying their strength training, but it is felt that they probably have naturally high testosterone levels.

Will the female ever be able to attain the same levels of strength as the male for all major regions of the body? From the similarity of the strength of the legs between the two sexes, it appears that the quality of muscle is the same, irrespective of sex. However, because of the higher levels of testosterone in the male, the male will continue to have a larger total muscle mass. If muscle mass is the major determinant of strength, then the male will always have a distinct advantage. If the levels of strength are independent of muscle mass, then the potential for absolute strength may be similar in both the sexes. Since the basic mechanisms allowing the expression of greater levels of strength have yet to be defined, it is impossible to draw any conclusions at the present time.

CARDIOVASCULAR ENDURANCE

In general, the female has a smaller stroke volume than the male for an equivalent, submaximal level of work. She is able to partially compensate for this by increasing her heart rate response to that level of work. This lower stroke volume is at least partially related to her smaller body size. Another factor of importance to the female, when compared to the male, is her lower hemoglobin concentration. Several studies have suggested that females may have values as much as 10 percent lower than males of the same age. Because of a lower maximal stroke volume and a similar maximal heart rate which reduce the maximal cardiac output, in addition to lower hemoglobin levels, the female's oxygen-carrying and oxygen-delivery capacity is apparently considerably less than the male's. This should result in a substantial difference in endurance capacity between the sexes, since the relationship between endurance capacity and $\dot{V}O_2$ max is very high. The values for males and females are quite similar up to ten to fifteen years of age. Beyond this age, however, the female's capacity decreases rather markedly, while the male's continues to improve. This was illustrated in Figure 2–12. For the college-age male and female, this difference is quite large with the female exhibiting a mean $\dot{V}O_2$ max between 30 and 44 ml/kg × min, while the mean value for males ranges between 45 and 53 ml/kg × min. These differences would tend to agree with and be partially explained by the physiological observations noted above relative to the female's reduced maximal cardiac output and reduced hemoglobin levels. The lack of an observed difference in $\dot{V}O_2$ max at the younger ages is probably due to similarities in maximal cardiac output and hemoglobin levels up to the age of puberty, at which point the differences start to appear.

While the above discussion appears to have resolved this entire area of cardiovascular endurance capacity, recent research indicates that the female's endurance capacity at ages beyond ten years does not necessarily have to be reduced or even substantially below that of the male of similar age. Hermanson and Andersen (1965) investigated the endurance capacity of both sedentary and athletic college-age populations and found the athletic men and women to have $\dot{V}O_2$ max values of 71 and 55 ml/kg × min, respectively, compared with values of 44 and 38 ml/kg × min, respectively, in the sedentary men and women. While the athletic men were noticeably superior, the athletic women had values twenty-five percent greater than the sedentary men.

Wilmore and Brown (1974) investigated cardiovascular endurance capacity in highly trained, female endurance athletes at various ages up to and including the fourth decade of life. Eleven subjects of national and international caliber were selected from a population of female distance runners. One of these women had won five consecutive United States and International Cross-country championships. Another held the best time in the world for females in the marathon, and a third held the best time in the world for females in the 50–mi run. The average $\dot{V}O_2$ max value for this group of women was 59.1 ml/kg × min, which is considerably higher than that for average women and men of similar age. National-caliber men long-distance runners studied by Costill and Winrow (1970) averaged 70.3 ml/kg × min, 15.9 percent higher than these women. However, the three best runners

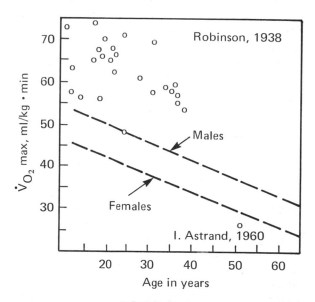

FIGURE 11–1

$\dot{V}O_2$ max values for female distance runners compared to normal untrained males and females. Normal male values obtained from S. Robinson, "Experimental Studies of Physical Fitness in Relation to Age." Arbeitsphysiol. 10 (1938): 251–323. Normal female values obtained from I. Åstrand, "Aerobic Work Capacity in Men and Women with Special Reference to Age." Acta Physiol. Scand. 49: Suppl. 169, 1960.

among the eleven women averaged 67.4 ml/kg × min, or only 4.1 percent lower than the average value for the ten, nationally ranked, men marathon runners of almost exactly the same age.

Figure 11–1 demonstrates the range of values for both young and older female distance runners compared to average values for the untrained male and female. It is obvious that females have the potential for levels of endurance that are far greater than they normally possess. When $\dot{V}O_2$ max is expressed relative to the athlete's lean body weight, rather than to total body weight, the female athlete is nearly identical to the male athlete in $\dot{V}O_2$ max. Davies (1971) found that when the $\dot{V}O_2$ max was expressed relative to the actual active muscle mass, the differences between the sexes disappeared entirely. While this may imply that men and women have the same endurance potential, Drinkwater (1973) makes the important observation that women must still carry their entire body weight as part of their total workload, which would undoubtedly hinder their actual performance. However, this would not be a factor in an activity such as bicycling, which provides a more equal opportunity for females to compete against males.

MOTOR SKILLS AND ATHLETIC ABILITY

With the exception of one activity, the softball throw for distance, boys and girls are quite similar in their performance of physical activities up to the age of ten to twelve years. Tests of specific motor skills or general athletic ability show few differences between the sexes during this period of development. Past the age of twelve, however, the male becomes considerably stronger, possesses greater muscular and cardiovascular endurance, and becomes more proficient in almost all motor skills. This phenomenon is illustrated in Figure 11–2 for selected motor skills.

From Figure 11–2 it is obvious that the female lags far behind the male at all ages in the softball throw, the female throwing only half of the distance of the male at any particular age. In an unpublished study, Grimditch and Sockolov investigated why females perform so poorly in the softball throw. Postulating this difference to be the result of insufficient practice and experience, they recruited over 200 males and females from three to twenty years of age to throw the softball for distance with both the dominant and nondominant arms. The results are illustrated in Figure 11–3. As they had theorized, there was absolutely no difference between the males and females for the nondominant arm, up to the age of ten to twelve years, just as with each of the other motor skill tasks shown in Figure 11–2. The results for the dominant arm were in agreement with what had been reported previously (Figure 11–2). Thus, the softball throw for distance using the dominant arm appears to be biased by the previous experience and practice of the males. When the influence of experience and practice was removed by using the nondominant arm, this motor skill task was identical to each of the others.

Athletic performance differences were briefly discussed in the introduction to this chapter. The female is outperformed by the male in almost all sports, events, or activities. This is quite obvious in such activities as the shotput in track and field, where high levels of upper body strength are critical to successful performance. The female uses a shot which is 55 percent lighter and yet the world record for the female is still some 1.5 ft shorter than the distance for the male. In the 400–meter freestyle, however, the winning time for the men in the 1924 Olympic games was 16 percent faster than for the women, but this difference decreased to 11.6 percent in the 1948 Olympics and to only 7.3 percent in the 1972 Olympics. The fastest female, 400-meter free style swimmer in the early 1970's swam faster than the world-record-holding male for the same distance in the mid-1950's. Therefore, in this particular event the gap between the sexes is narrowing, and there are indications that this is also true for other events and for other sports. Unfortunately, it is difficult to make valid comparisons, since the degree to which

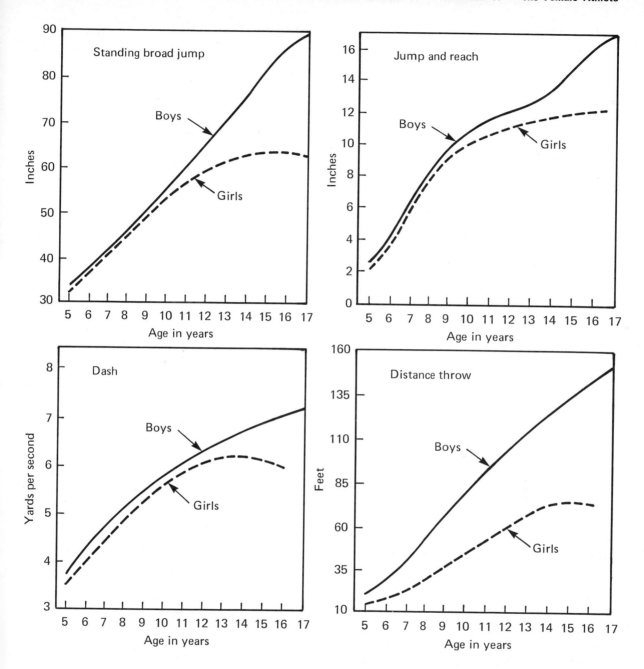

FIGURE 11–2

*Performance of selected motor-skill test items for young boys and girls. (From Anna Es-
penschade and Helen Eckert, "Motor Development,"* Science and Medicine of Exercise and
Sport, *2nd ed., pp. 326–30. Edited by Warren R. Johnson and E. R. Buskirk. Copyright © 1974
by Warren R. Johnson and Elsworth R. Buskirk. Copyright © 1960 by Warren R. Johnson.
Reprinted by permission of Harper and Row, Publishers, Inc.)*

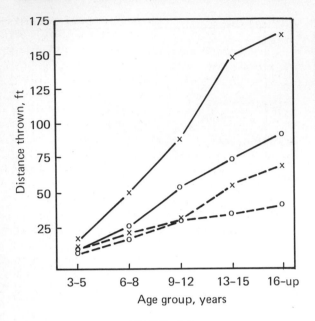

FIGURE 11–3

Softball throw for distance in males and females using the dominant and nondominant arms. (From G. Grimditch and R. Sockolov, unpublished observations. University of California, Davis, 1974.)

the sport, activity, or event has been emphasized is not constant, and factors such as coaching, facilities, and training techniques have differed considerably between the sexes over the years. While the performance gap appears to be closing, it is far too early to predict whether it will ever close completely for any or all sports.

MENSTRUAL AND GYNECOLOGICAL CONSIDERATIONS

One of the great concerns about female participation in athletics is in the area of gynecological considerations and menstruation. Do females run a high risk of damaging their reproductive organs as a result of vigorous running, jumping, or contact sports? Should females avoid exercise and competition during the flow phase of their menstrual cycle? These and many other questions were the subject of

an extensive review article by Ryan in 1975.

First, there appears to be a high degree of variability among females with regard to exercise and competition during the various phases of the menstrual cycle. Many females have few or no menstrual difficulties under any conditions, whether they are active or sedentary. On the other hand, a significant number of females have dysmenorrhea, or other menstrual difficulties, which apparently are neither helped nor aggravated by vigorous physical activity. Recently, there have been reports of a total absence of menstruation in females who train for long-distance running. This may be related to their exceptionally low, total body weight and reduced levels of body fat, since several studies have reported an absence of menstruation in chronically underweight females. These female distance runners frequently train 70 to 100 mi or more per week, and their relative body fat typically decreases to 10 percent or less (see Figure 7–12). Return of menstruation usually follows a reduction in training intensity.

Physical performance seems to be best in the immediate postmenstrual period, up to the fifteenth day of the cycle. The number of females who perform poorly during the flow phase of the cycle is about the same as the number who experience no difference. Some have even noted an improved performance during flow, establishing records and winning world-class competitions. Again, the individual variability is so great that no general rules of thumb can be given. Full participation in activities of all types should be allowed during the flow phase for those who experience no difficulties, and provisions should be made for those who do experience difficulties, so they are not forced into undesirable activities.

The potential for gynecological injuries has been a major concern in athletics for centuries. Females at one time were discouraged from participating in any activity where there was considerable running, jumping, or bodily contact. The uterus was considered to be highly vulnerable to major injuries, which could have serious consequences later in life. It is now recognized that injuries to the female reproductive organs are rare. Unlike the male, the female's organs are internal and in an extremely well-protected position. The breasts are in a more vulnerable position, but even here, serious injury is extremely rare, even in contact sports. Followup studies on former female athletes indicate that they have normal pregnancy and child birth, and, in fact, may have shorter delivery times and a faster return to normal activities.

GENERAL SUMMARY

From the preceding discussion, there appear to be substantial differences between the average female and the average male in almost all aspects of physical performance beyond the age of ten to twelves years. Prior to this time, there are few, if any, differences between the sexes. What happens to the female once she reaches puberty? Is she physically over the hill, reaching her peak at a relatively early age, or are there other factors or circumstances which might account for her reduced physical capabilities? Recent studies on highly trained, female athletes suggest that the female is not appreciably different from her highly trained, male counterpart, at ages beyond puberty. It appears that the average values used for comparative purposes beyond the age of puberty are for relatively active males and relatively sedentary females. Somewhere between the ages of ten to twelve years of age, the average female substitutes the piano for climbing trees, and sewing for chasing the boys down the street. In Chapter 8 it was pointed out that once one assumes a sedentary lifestyle, the basic physiological components of general fitness deteriorate. Strength, muscular endurance, and cardiovascular endurance are lost, and body fat tends to accumulate. Similar trends can be noted for the male by the time he reaches thirty to thirty-five years of age, an age which corresponds to a reduction in his activity patterns. So, what appear to be dramatic biological differences between the sexes, in fact, may be more related to the cultural and social restrictions of the female after puberty. Further research into this intriguing area is certainly needed.

With regard to the female athlete, there appears to be little difference between her and her male counterpart in terms of strength, endurance, and body composition. Strength of the lower extremities, when related to body weight and lean body weight, is similar between the sexes, although the male maintains a distinct superiority in upper-body strength. Strength training, formerly condemned as a mode of training for women because of its supposed masculinizing effects, is now recognized as extremely valuable in developing the strength component, which is usually the weakest link in the physiological profile of the female athlete.

Endurance capacity in the highly trained, female distance runner is approximately equal to the capacity of the highly trained, male distance runner, when the values are expressed relative to lean body weight. For the better female runners, these values are relatively close when expressed relative to body weight. Although the female is far below the male in lean body weight, the highly trained, female distance runner has a relative body fat similar to the male distance runner.

Because of these similarities, and because their needs arc basically the same, there is little reason to advocate different training or conditioning programs on the basis of sex.

REFERENCES

ÅSTRAND, P. O., and RODAHL, K. *Textbook of Work Physiology.* New York: McGraw-Hill Book Company, 1970.

BEHNKE, A. R., and WILMORE, J. H. *Evaluation and Regulation of Body Build and Composition.* Englewood Cliffs, N.J.: Prentice-Hall, 1974.

COSTILL, D. L.; BOWERS, R.; and KAMMER, W. F. "Skinfold Estimates of Body Fat Among Marathon Runners." *Med. Sci. Sports* 2 (1970): 93–95.

COSTILL, D. L., and WINROW, E. "Maximal Oxygen Intake Among Marathon Runners." *Arch. Phys. Med. Rehab.* 51 (1970): 317–20.

DAVIES, C. T. M. "Body Composition in Children: A Reference Standard for Maximum Aerobic Power Output on a Stationary Bicycle Ergometer." In *Proceedings of the III International Symposium on Pediatric Work Physiology. Acta Paediatr Scand.* Suppl. 217, 1971.

DRINKWATER, B. L. "Physiological Responses of Women to Exercise." In *Exercise and Sport Sciences Reviews*, vol. 1, edited by J. H. Wilmore. New York: Academic Press, 1973.

HERMANSON, L., and ANDERSEN, K. L. "Aerobic Work Capacity in Young Norwegian Men and Women." *J. Appl. Physiol.* 20 (1965): 425–31.

KLAFS, C. E., and LYON, M. J. *The Female Athlete: Conditioning, Competition, and Culture.* St. Louis: C. V. Mosby Co., 1973.

MAYHEW, J. L., and GROSS, P. M. "Body Composition Changes in Young Women with High Resistance Weight Training." *Res. Quart.* 45 (1974): 433–40.

PLOWMAN, S. "Physiological Characteristics of Female Athletes." *Res. Quart.* 45 (1974): 349–62.

RYAN, A. J. "The Female Athlete: Gynecological Considerations." *J. Health, Phys. Educ. Rec.* 46 (1975): 40–44.

WILMORE, J. H. "Alterations in Strength, Body Composition and Anthropometric Measurements Consequent to a 10-week Weight Training Program." *Med. Sci. Sport* 6 (1974): 133–38.

WILMORE, J. H. "Exploding the Myth of Female Inferiority." *Physician and Sportsmed.* 2 (1974): 54–58.

WILMORE, J. H., and BROWN, C. H. "Physiological Profiles of Women Distance Runners." *Med. Sci. Sport* 6 (1974): 178–81.

12

The Growth and Aging Process

INTRODUCTION

Age-group competition has grown considerably over the last decade and is now a major force in the world of sport. Little League baseball and Pop Warner football are examples of this type of sport or activity for boys as is Bobby Sox softball for girls and mini-bike racing, swimming, track and field, and long-distance running are for many other youngsters. Moreover, age-group competition no longer stops with youngsters in their early years but goes on into old age. The man or woman who turns forty can begin a new career in athletics if he or she has an interest and some talent in track and field events. Masters', or seniors', competition in track and field starts at age forty, and competition is broken into age groups by decades, e.g., forty to forty-nine years, fifty to fifty-nine years, sixty to sixty-nine years, and above. Men in their eighties have been observed in formal competitions, and many men in their seventies have completed the official, 26-mi, 385-yd marathon! Similar age-group competitive experiences are available in swimming.

With this tremendous interest in age-group competition, many questions have been raised. Is competition physically or psychologically harmful for the preadolescent? Should eight-year-olds be competing in long-distance running? Does pitching a baseball place traumatic stress on the elbow of the youngster's pitching arm? How does a sedentary, forty-five-year-old male prepare himself for formal competition, when, hearing about age-group competition, his urge to be an athlete is rekindled? These and many other questions of a similar nature will be answered in the following pages as we focus attention on both the growth and aging process.

DEVELOPMENT AND AGING OF THE TISSUES

Bone

Bone is the principal calcified tissue of man. The bone matrix is formed of collagen fibers in which small cells called osteocytes are embedded. The long bones of the body are preformed of cartilage. Even prior to birth, the cartilage is slowly converted to bone by the process of ossification, which involves the deposition of the bone minerals, calcium and phosphorus, into the bone matrix. Ossification occurs in an orderly process, allowing the bone to grow until ossification is completed. Figure 12–1 illustrates a typical long bone which has not yet reached full growth. The central portion of the bone, or the shaft, is referred to as the diaphysis. The ends of the bone are formed of cartilaginous epiphyseal centers. At birth, the entire shaft, or diaphysis, has been ossified and growth continues at both ends of the long bones. Between the diaphysis and the epiphyseal centers lies the growth plate, or the epiphyseal line. When growth is completed, the diaphysis and epiphysis are fused, and the growth plate disappears.

There is a wide variation in the average age

FIGURE 12–1

Growth of the long bones. (From R. L. Larson, "Physical Activity and the Growth and Development of Bone and Joint Structures." In Physical Activity: Human Growth, and Development, *edited by G. L. Rarick. New York: Academic Press, 1974. Reproduced by permission of the publisher.) Note: (1) medial epicondylar epiphysis of the humerus, (2) metaphysis of the humerus, (3) diaphysis of the humerus. Arrow refers to the growth plate of the proximal radial epiphysis.*

at which the different bones reach full growth or maturity, ranging from the preteens to the early twenties. On the average, girls achieve full maturity several years before boys. Exercise, generally, is regarded as being essential for proper bone growth. While exercise does not appear to influence the length of long bone growth, it does increase the width of the bone and gives the bone greater tensile strength.

In this chapter, we are interested in the process of bone growth, primarily, in order to understand the potential for injury. An injury to an immature bone could result in the premature cessation of growth. The greatest concern is with the potential injury of the epiphyses, since a fracture at the epiphyses and growth plate could disturb the blood supply and disrupt the growth process. Fortunately, such injuries are relatively few and seldom occur in sports. In one study of thirty-one epiphyseal injuries, only 23 percent were sports induced, the remainder resulting from falls and vehicular accidents (Larson, 1974).

One type of serious epiphyseal injury that occurs in athletics is called "traumatic epiphysitis." One form is "Little Leaguer's elbow," a condition resulting from repetitive strains to the medial epicondylar epiphysis of the humerus. According to Larson, studies have shown that twelve-year-old boys can throw a baseball up to seventy miles per hour, causing a sudden pull on the epiphysis, which anchors the tendons of the involved muscles, that may result in its separation (Figure 12–2), or the repetitive stress of throwing may produce an inflammatory response, i.e., traumatic epiphysitis. In a well-controlled study published in 1965, Adams found epiphysitis by X-ray examination in *all* 80 pitchers in a group of 162, young boys who were studied, while only a small percentage of the nonpitchers and the control group of nonplayers exhibited similar changes.

Larson and McMahan (1966) reviewed 1,338 consecutive, athletic injuries seen by a group of four orthopedists in one practice. They reported that 20 percent of these injuries were in the age range of fourteen years of age and younger. Only 6 percent of all injuries in fifteen-year olds and younger involved the epiphysis. They also stated that this type of injury does not always result in crippling, or

FIGURE 12–2

An example of a separation of the epiphysis. (From R. L. Larson, "Physical Activity and the Growth and Development of Bone and Joint Structures." In Physical Activity: Human Growth, and Development, *edited by G. L. Rarick. New York: Academic Press, 1974. Reproduced by permission of the publisher.)*

permanent, trauma and that early recognition is important.

Of all the sports, competitive baseball appears to be the most dangerous on the basis of its potential for serious injuries, which largely result from the pitching motion. Some leagues have replaced the pitcher with a pitching machine. This would seem to be the only sensible approach until the youngster reaches an age at which pitching is not a major source of injuries. Pop Warner football and the other competitive sports and activities have a relatively good record with regard to bone injury. While the potential for injury in football is generally considered high, apparently the small size of the player, the matching of boys by size, and good protective equipment provide a relatively safe environment for the young football player.

Older athletes, i.e., those over forty yrs, have a greater potential for bone injury than the younger athletes who have reached full maturity. While it varies considerably among individuals, the density of bone starts to decrease at about the age of forty. This is due to a decrease in the calcium and phosphorus content of the bone. The result is a more porous bone, which is more likely to break when placed under extreme stress. The more porous bone also takes longer to fully heal when it is broken. Recent evidence suggests that supplementation of calcium intake can reduce the extent of this bone mineral loss. Endurance activities also appear to limit mineral loss.

Muscle

The ultrastructure and growth characteristics of muscle tissue were discussed in detail in Chapter 1. From birth through adolescence there is a steady increase in the muscle mass of the body that parallels the youngster's gain in weight. With puberty, there is a peak acceleration in the development of muscle in boys, which corresponds to the sudden increase in testosterone production. Girls do not experience this period of rapid acceleration but their muscle mass does continue to increase. Once a girl reaches puberty, her estrogen levels increase, which promotes the deposition of body fat. While muscle is still capable of developing as a girl passes puberty, its rate of development, relative to the increase in body weight, decreases.

When the female reaches sixteen to eighteen years and the male eighteen to twenty-two, the muscle mass is at its peak, unless it is increased further through either diet and exercise, or both. The muscle mass will remain relatively stable from this age through the ages of thirty to forty years, if physical activity levels remain constant and do not decrease. With older age, there is a decrease in the total muscle mass, which may result from both atrophy of selected muscle fibers and a decrease in the number of muscle fibers. The decrease in fibers may be the result of nerve fiber degeneration.

One area of major controversy with regard to muscle development in youngsters is the use of weight training to develop muscular strength and endurance. For many years, young boys and girls were discouraged from using weights for fear that they might injure themselves and prematurely stop their growth processes. Studies on animals suggest that heavy-resistance exercise would lead to a stronger, broader, and more compact bone. However, since it is nearly impossible to load these animals to the same extent as youngsters, it has not been practical to design an experiment that accurately defines the risks associated with heavy-resistance exercise in youngsters. It would appear that the potential for injury and structural damage from heavy-resistance exercise is extremely low, but since the future of the youngster is at stake, it is appropriate to take a conservative approach until additional studies can be conducted. Thus, a program using low weights and high repetitions would be preferred to one using high weights and low repetitions. One of the safest techniques for strength training in youngsters would be to use the isokinetic concept, in which resistance is matched to the force applied, so that the youngster does not have to contend with actual weights, i.e., barbells and dumbbells. Refer to Chapter 4, Strength, Power, and Muscular Endurance, for a more detailed description of this technique.

Changes in strength with age parallel the increases and decreases in muscle mass. Peak strength is usually attained by the age of twenty years in females and between twenty and thirty years in males. Strength remains relatively stable until ages of thirty-five to forty-five years and then decreases gradually with increasing age. deVries (1974) has stated that by sixty years of age, the male has lost not more than 10 to 20 percent of his maximum strength. The loss of strength with aging in the female appears to proceed at a slightly faster rate. This loss of strength with age consists of two components: a decrease in ability to maintain maximum static force, and a decrease in ability to accelerate mass (deVries, 1974).

Fat

Fat cells form and fat starts to deposit in these cells early in the development of the fetus and continues indefinitely. While evidence suggests that the actual number of fat cells becomes constant sometime during the teens, each fat cell has the ability to increase in size at any age. If the number of fat cells is actually fixed early in life, it is important to keep the total fat content of the body low during this period of time. In this way, the total number of fat cells will be minimized, and the chances of extreme obesity as an adult will be greatly reduced.

The degree of fat accumulation with growth and aging will depend entirely on the dietary and exercise habits of the individual, in addition to his heredity. While heredity is unchangeable, diet and exercise can be manipulated to either increase or decrease the fat stores. At birth, the body weight is 10 to 12 percent fat, and by the time the individual reaches physical maturity, the fat content reaches 15 and 25 percent of the total body weight for males and females, respectively. Figure 12-3 illustrates the relationship between relative, or percent, body fat and age for males and females. Both relative and absolute fat increase with age once physical maturity is reached. This is probably due to an increase in dietary intake, in addition to a decrease in levels of physical activity, although there is a reduced ability to mobilize fat with age. Beyond the age of thirty, there is also a progressive decrease in the lean body weight, which is primarily the result of decreased muscle mass and reduced mineral content of the bones. Both of these decreases are, at least partially, the result of decreased levels of physical activity.

Nervous System

As the child grows, he or she develops better agility and coordination which is a direct

FIGURE 12–3

Changes in relative body fat with age for males and females. (From J. Parízková, "Body Composition and Exercise During Growth and Development." In Physical Activity: Human Growth and Development, *edited by G. L. Rarick. New York: Academic Press, 1974. Reproduced by permission of the publisher.)*

function of both the central and peripheral nervous systems. During the early stages of development, myelination of the nerve fibers must be completed before fast reactions and skilled movement can occur. Conduction velocity along a nerve fiber is considerably slower if myelination is absent or incomplete. Late in life, as the aging process progresses, conduction velocity along a nerve fiber may tend to slow. Speed of reaction and movement both slow down with age, and while this may be partially due to a decreased conduction velocity in the peripheral nervous system, both sensory and motor, several investigators feel that the main cause lies in the central nervous system. Some evidence suggests that the more active the individual nerve cells, the more likely they are to retain their optimal function and to resist the aging process. This would be a major benefit of remaining physically active throughout life.

GENERAL PHYSIOLOGICAL FUNCTION

In almost all of the physiological systems, function appears to improve until maturity, or shortly before, and then plateaus for a period of time, before starting to decline with old age. Unfortunately, it is difficult to define the role of aging apart from the sedentary life style of the average individual. Both lead to a decrease in general physiological function. Recent evidence suggests that the rate of decrease associated with aging can be reduced or slowed by increasing the level of physical activity.

Basal Metabolic Rate (BMR)

The BMR, or lowest metabolic rate that the individual attains during a twenty-four-hour day, decreases at a rate of approximately 3 percent per decade from the age of three through eighty, although longitudinal studies that have followed the same individuals over twenty-year periods, or longer, suggest a more conservative decrease of only 1 to 2 percent per decade. Up to the age of twenty to thirty, this decrease is assumed to reflect a more efficient metabolism. Beyond thirty years of age, this decrease could be a result of the decrease in lean body weight referred to earlier in this chapter. It would be interesting to determine if physically active individuals, particularly those performing heavy-resistance exercise on a regular basis, have this same decrease in BMR. Likewise, it would be interesting to determine whether increasing muscle mass through heavy-resistance weight training would increase the BMR in older people. An increased BMR might reduce the degree of fat accumulation that seems to accompany the aging process.

Pulmonary Function

A number of cross-sectional studies have demonstrated that lung function is markedly altered by age. During the period of growth, the static lung volumes, as well as the functional pulmonary tests, increase to the time of physical maturity. Shortly after reaching this peak, however, there is a gradual reduction with age. Vital capacity, $FEV_{1.0}$ (the greatest volume of air that can be exhaled in the first second of a forced vital capacity test) and forced, expiratory flow rate all exhibit a linear decrease with age, starting at twenty to thirty years of age. While these volumes and rates are decreasing, the residual lung volume increases and the total lung capacity remains unchanged; thus, the ratio of the residual volume to the total lung capacity (RV/TLC) increases. In the early twenties, 18 to 22 percent of the total lung capacity is represented by the residual volume, but this increases to 30 percent, and higher, as the individual reaches fifty years of age. Smoking appears to accelerate this process.

The changes in the above volumes and flow rates are matched by the changes in maximal ventilatory capacity during exhaustive exer-

cise. Maximal expiratory ventilation ($\dot{V}E$ max) will increase with age to the point of physical maturity, and then it will decrease with the aging process. From cross-sectional data for males, the $\dot{V}E$ max, for four- to six-year-old boys, will average about 40 liters/min, increase to 110–140 liters/min at full maturity, and decrease to 60 to 80 liters/ min for sixty- to seventy-year olds. Females follow the same general pattern, although their absolute values will be considerably lower for each age level, due, primarily, to their smaller stature.

The above changes are probably the result of a combination of factors, but the most important is the loss in elasticity of the lung tissue and chest wall, which increases the work or the effort involved in breathing. The decrease in mobility of the chest wall with age appears to be the major cause of reduction in the function of the lung.

Cardiovascular Function

A number of changes occur in cardiovascular function as the individual ages. Figure 12–4 illustrates the linear decrease in maximal heart rate with age. Children frequently exceed 200 beats/min, while the average sixty-year old has a maximal heart rate of approximately 160 beats/min. It has been estimated that the maximal heart rate decreases by slightly less than one beat per year as the individual ages. The average maximal heart rate for each age level can be estimated from the following equation:

$$HR_{max} = 220 - age$$

It should be recognized that this represents only an estimate of the mean or average value for the age. Individual values could deviate from this estimated value by $\pm$ 20 beats/min, or more.

Peak, or maximum, stroke volume and cardiac output values appear to decline with age, although the number of studies conducted and number of subjects used are quite limited. Peripheral blood flow capacity is reduced with aging, but the density of the capillaries does

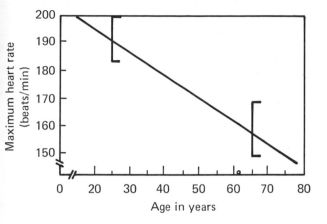

Relation between maximum rate and age*

FIGURE 12–4

Decrease in maximal heart rate with age. (From K. L. Andersen, R. J. Shephard, H. Denolin, E. Varnauskas, and R. Masironi, Fundamentals of Exercise Testing. *Geneva: World Health Organization, 1971. Reproduced by permission of the publisher.)*

not appear to change. It is difficult to determine whether the decreases in stroke volume, cardiac output, and peripheral blood flow are directly the result of the aging process or the result of an increasingly sedentary life style, which leads to cardiovascular deconditioning. Recent studies would tend to suggest that both are involved, but the relative contribution by each is not known.

Maximal Aerobic Capacity

The purpose of the basic pulmonary and cardiovascular adaptations that are made with varying levels of exercise is to accomodate the need of the exercising muscles for oxygen. Thus, the decreases in pulmonary and cardiovascular function with age suggest that aerobic capacity, or $\dot{V}O_2$ max, experiences a similar decline with age. Robinson, in 1938, demonstrated this phenomenon in a cross-sectional sample of boys and men ranging in age from six to ninety-one years. He found that $\dot{V}O_2$ max attained its peak value at seventeen to twenty years of age and then decreased as a linear

function of age (see Figures 6–5 and 11–1). Adams et al. (1972) found a similar relationship between $\dot{V}O_2$ max and age (Figure 12–5) in a large population of adult males. Studies of girls and women have shown essentially the same trend, although the female starts her decline at a much younger age (refer to Chapter 11), probably due to an earlier assumption of a sedentary lifestyle.

Again the questions must be asked: How much of the observed decrease is a result of biological aging? How important is the habitual level of physical activity in determining the rate of decline? Andersen and Hermansen (1965) gained insight into these questions when they compared the $\dot{V}O_2$ max values for a group of sixty-three, cross-country skiers, fifty to sixty-six years of age, with a group of office workers and a group of industrial workers of similar ages and with a group of twenty to thirty-year-old students. They found the following:

Group	Age Range (yr)	$\dot{V}O_2$ max (ml/kg × min)
Skiers	50–66	48
Office workers	50–60	36
Industrial workers	50–60	34
Students	20–30	44

These data support the contention that the decline in $\dot{V}O_2$ max with age, demonstrated in several studies, is not strictly a function of age, although the possibility that heredity might be an important factor in the high $\dot{V}O_2$ max values of the older skiers should not be discounted. Figure 6–5, in Chapter 6, illustrates the results of a similar type of study. A group of twenty-five of the best sprint and distance runners over forty years of age in the United States was brought into the laboratory for a comprehensive series of tests. While their $\dot{V}O_2$ max values were considerably higher than those of average men of the same age, the relative rate of decline with age closely paralleled the rate of decline illustrated by Robinson's (1938) data for normal men. Were these older athletes genetically superior, or can their comparatively high values be attributed to their training programs? The answer to these ques-

195

FIGURE 12–5

Decrease in V̇O₂ max with age. Symbols refer to the four age groups studied. (From W. C. Adams et al., "Multistage Treadmill Walking Performance and Associated Cardiorespiratory Responses of Middle-aged Men," Clin. Sci. 42, 1972. Reproduced by permission of the publisher.)

tions will have to await studies of a longitudinal nature.

It is of considerable interest to look at the extremes in age relative to endurance performance. One five-year-old boy has run a 7:51.1 mi and a 6-hr and 56-min marathon (26 mi, 385 yd). At the other extreme are individuals in their seventies running full marathon distances, and farther. The human body has a tremendous ability to adapt to physical stress. Is this magnitude of stress harmful in any way to the very young or to the very old athlete? The limited information presently available suggests that no measurable physiological damage results from such training. In most cases, these very young and relatively old endurance runners are some of the best physical specimens for their ages, as determined by routine physical examinations. Still, to be on the cautious side, periodic examination by the

family physician is recommended to identify any problems as early as possible. To date, few problems of a significant nature have materialized. Also, whether young or old, the potential athlete should approach his training program in a conservative manner, starting slowly and building up gradually. For the older individual, proper medical clearance, including an exercise electrocardiogram must precede both training and competition. This will be discussed in detail in the following chapter.

PSYCHOLOGICAL ASPECTS

Is formal, organized competition or participation in vigorous physical activity damaging to the emotional health and psychological development of the athlete? For the mature athlete, this presents no major problem, but many parents, educators, physicians, and psychologists have expressed concern over the potential for undesirable, emotional experiences in the developing young athlete. The question has been raised whether children who compete in formal, highly organized activities are likely to develop undesirable behavior patterns as a result of the pressures to win and be successful by adult standards. Does the eleven-year-old boy competing on the all-star, Little League team experience pressures and situations that would lead to immediate or future behavior or emotional problems?

Only limited research has been conducted in this area. Skubic (1954, 1955) studied both Little League and Middle League (thirteen to fifteen years of age) baseball athletes in a small community in California. Using parents' opinions and the Galvanic skin-resistance measurement, she found essentially no difference between the athletes in formal competition compared to those who participated informally in physical education softball. There were few athletes who had any serious emotional problems that could be related to the stress of competition. Generally, her results suggested that formal competition at this age level was not detrimental to the child, but actually facilitated social and emotional growth.

On the other hand, Sherif et al. (1961) conducted a fascinating study, which has been referred to as the "Lord of the Flies" or "Robber's Cave" experiment. In this study, a group of boys at a summer camp were divided into two subgroups. During the initial part of the study, the groups were separated during much of the day, but they had periods of interaction. No problems between the groups developed during this part of the study. For the second phase of the study, the groups were put into situations where they were always in competition with each other in camp life, as well as in sports and games, both for recognition and for tangible rewards. During this phase, members of the individual groups developed strong allegiances to their own group and extreme hostility toward the other group. Night raids,

cheating, and other forms of aggressive and undesirable behavior began to develop. This phase of the study was discontinued when several members of both groups started developing symptoms of serious psychological disturbances. During the third, and last, phase of the experiment, an attempt was made to bring the two groups back together in cooperative ventures, removing all forms of competition between the groups. It took considerable time to achieve the goal of working in a genuinely cooperative effort.

From these examples, it can only be concluded that competition can have both positive and negative influences on the emotional development of the youngster. Of major importance is the climate in which the competition takes place. If the climate is such that winning is the only goal and parents are allowed to say and do whatever they please without giving the child sound guidance in coping with the stress of the situation, the child will be likely to have a negative experience. In short, the nature of the child's experience will depend almost entirely on the local situation. If competition is organized with this in mind, and the goal is to satisfy the needs of the child and not the adult, the experience should be positive and facilitate sound emotional growth and psychological development.

TRAINING THE YOUNG AND THE OLDER ATHLETE

Must special consideration be given to the young or older athlete when developing individualized programs of training? Generally, both the youngster and the older athlete will adapt well to the same type of training routine designed for the mature athlete. Heavy-resistance exercises with weights should be avoided by the younger athletes and isometric exercises should be avoided by older athletes. The latter suggestion is made because the unusually high increase in blood pressure that is associated with isometric contractions could cause serious complications in the older athlete. Older ath-

FIGURE 12–6

Variation in physical dimensions and physiological function with age. (From I. Åstrand, "Aerobic Work Capacity; Its Relation to Age, Sex, and Other Factors." American Heart Association Monograph, *No. 15, 1967. By permission of the American Heart Association, Inc.)*

letes should progress slowly in the early stages of their training programs to reduce the considerable stiffness and soreness that are likely to occur. Particular attention should be given to stretching exercises to help alleviate the potential joint and muscle problems that seem to be more common in the older athlete.

GENERAL SUMMARY

This chapter has outlined those physiological and body composition alterations that accompany the aging process from birth to old age. Most of these changes are illustrated in Figure 12–6, which summarizes data from a large number of studies and was compiled by Åstrand (1967). In addition, potential physiological and psychological problems associated with competition in the young and older athlete were discussed. It appears that strenuous physical exercise and intense competition can be of considerable value to athletes of all ages providing that the athletes have proper medical clearance and guidance and that the goals of competition are adjusted to serve the needs of the athlete.

REFERENCES

ADAMS, J. E. "Injury to the Throwing Arm." *Calif. Med.* 102 (1965): 127–32.

ADAMS, W. C.; McHENRY, M. M.; and BERNAUER, E. M. "Multistage Treadmill Walking Performance and Associated Cardiorespiratory Responses of Middle-aged Men." *Clin. Sci.* 42 (1972): 355–70.

ANDERSEN, K., and HERMANSEN, L. "Aerobic Work Capacity in Middle-Aged Norwegian Men." *J. Appl. Physiol.* 20 (1965): 432–36.

ÅSTRAND, I. "Aerobic Work Capacity; Its Relation to Age, Sex, and Other Factors." *American Heart Association Monograph* No. 15. New York, 1967.

DE VRIES, H. A. *Physiology of Exercise for Physical Education and Athletics.* 2nd ed. Dubuque, Iowa: William C. Brown, 1974.

LARSON, R. L. "Physical Activity and the Growth and Development of Bone and Joint Structures." In *Physical Activity: Human Growth and Development*, edited by G. L. Rarick. New York: Academic Press, 1974.

LARSON, R. L., and McMAHAN, R. O. "The Epiphyses and the Childhood Athlete." *J. Amer. Med. Assoc.* 196 (1966): 607–12.

ROBINSON, S. "Experimental Studies of Physical Fitness in Relation to Age." *Arbeitsphysiol.* 10 (1970): 251–323.

SHERIF, M.; HARVEY, O. J.; WHITE, B. J.; HOOD, W. R.; SHERIF, C. W. *Intergroup Conflict and Cooperation. The Robber's Cave Experiment.* Norman, Oklahoma: University of Oklahoma Book Exchange, 1961.

SKUBIC, E. "Studies of Little League and Middle League Baseball." *Res. Quart.* 27 (1954): 97–110.

SKUBIC, E. "Emotional Responses of Boys to Little League and Middle League Competitive Baseball." *Res. Quart.* 26 (1955): 342–52.

13
Physical Activity for Health and Fitness*

INTRODUCTION

Throughout the previous chapters of this book, emphasis has been totally focused on the relationship of physical activity to various aspects of athletic performance. Discussion has centered on the male and the female athlete, the young and the old athlete, the basic elements of athletic performance, the influence of the environment on performance, and the role of selected ergogenic aids. This final chapter will look briefly at the health-related aspects of physical activity, a topic of considerable importance to the athlete and nonathlete alike. How important is physical activity to the health, fitness, and general well-being of the average individual in today's world with its emphasis on sedentary living? Can man, who was designed for strenuous activity, successfully adapt to this newly imposed sedentary lifestyle?

DISEASES OF MODERN LIVING

Chronic and degenerative diseases of the cardiovascular and pulmonary systems are the major causes of serious illness and death in the United States. Cardiovascular disease alone

---

* Parts of this chapter were prepared in collaboration with Dr. William L. Haskell, Stanford University School of Medicine, for use by the Preventive Medicine Center, Palo Alto, California.

affects more than twenty-seven million Americans each year, resulting in over one million deaths, and costs the individual, government, and private industry over 50-billion dollars annually. While infectious diseases, such as influenza, tuberculosis, and pneumonia, were the major causes of death in the early 1900's, diseases of our modern lifestyle, such as cancer, lung, and heart disease, have now attained the distinction of being the major causes of death. Cardiovascular disease, including heart disease and stroke, now kills more Americans each year than all other causes of death combined, including infant mortality and accidents!

Most individuals consider themselves to be healthy, until they experience some overt sign of illness. However, with chronic degenerative diseases, such as heart disease and cancer, the individual is generally unaware that the disease process is smoldering and slowly progressing from a minor affliction to one of major proportions. As one grows older, the frequency and rate of these undetected disease processes accelerate. Fortunately, early detection and proper treatment of the various chronic diseases can substantially reduce their intensity and the resulting number of deaths. Perhaps even more important, alteration of factors associated with an increased risk for a particular disease can either prevent the development of that disease or delay its onset for many years. This would include changing dietary habits, increasing habitual physical activity, abstaining from the use of tobacco, moderating alcohol intake, and improving the ability to handle psychological stress.

A discussion of each of the various chronic diseases would require considerably more space than is available. Consequently, discussion has been limited to those two areas where physical activity is known to play a predominant role, heart disease and obesity. Both are now considered to be of childhood origin; thus, the preventive aspects are very important.

Heart Disease

As man ages, his coronary arteries, i.e., those arteries that supply the heart muscle itself, become progressively narrower as a result of fat being deposited along the inner wall of the artery. This process of progressive narrowing is referred to as atherosclerosis. Kannel and Dawber (1972) have stated that atherosclerosis is not only a disease of the aged but that it is primarily a pediatric problem, since the pathologic changes that lead to atherosclerosis begin in infancy and progress during childhood. Fatty streaks, or lipid deposits, which are thought to be the probable precursors to atherosclerosis, are common in children by the age of 3 to 5 yr. Enos et al. (1953) demonstrated that over 70 percent of autopsied Korean War combat casualties, with an average age of 22.1 yr, already had at least moderately advanced coronary atherosclerosis. McNamera et al. (1971) found evidence of coronary atherosclerosis in 45 percent of Vietnam war casualties, with 5 percent exhibiting severe manifestations of the disease.

Between the years 1900 and 1970, heart disease tripled as a major cause of death. This three-fold increase is a relative increase, expressed in deaths per 100,000 population. Since the population of the United States has more than doubled over this seventy-year period, the absolute number of deaths from heart disease has risen even more dramatically. It is presently estimated that cardiovascular disease is identifiable in approximately 25 percent of the adult American population. Furthermore, heart disease has become the leading cause of death in men of ages 35 to 45 yr. Heart disease has become a national tragedy!

Risk Factors.   Over the years, scientists have attempted to determine the basic etiology, or cause, of the atherosclerotic process. Several studies have been conducted that have closely observed the members of entire communities for extensive periods of time. When a substantial number of deaths occur over a fifteen- to twenty-year period, it is possible to group those individuals who died from heart attacks to determine what risk factors they possessed in common. While this approach does not specifically define the actual causal mechanisms, it does provide the researcher with a valuable insight into the disease process.

The factors identified in these long-term, longitudinal, population studies are referred to as risk factors. The factors associated with an increased risk for the premature development of heart disease can be grouped into those over which the individual has no control and those that can be altered through basic changes in life style. Those that are beyond the individual's control include heredity, sex, age, and race. Those factors that can be altered include elevated blood fats (cholesterol and triglycerides), elevated blood pressure (hypertension), cigarette smoking, obesity, diabetes, abnormalities of the electrocardiogram, anxiety and tension (stress), and physical inactivity. Evidence is now available suggesting that these risk factors can be identified at an early age. Studies of college students indicate that coronary and stroke mortality rate can be predicted at this relatively young age. In a study of ninety-six boys, eight to twelve years of age (Wilmore and McNamara, 1974), 19.8 percent had cholesterol values in excess of the suggested, high-normal value of 200 mg/100 ml, 5.2 percent exhibited abnormal resting electrocardiograms, and 37.5 percent had in excess of 20 percent relative fat. Elevated blood pressure was not observed.

Role of Exercise.   A number of research studies have identified inadequate physical activity as a risk factor in heart disease. Naughton and

Bruhn (1970) have reported the incidence of heart attack in sedentary populations to be approximately twice that found in men who are physically active, either in their jobs or in their recreational pursuits. They suggest that the clinical manifestations of the disease should be preventable if suitable activity programs are instituted early in life. Fox et al. (1971) conclude that the existing evidence suggests, but falls short of actually proving, that an increase in habitual physical activity is beneficial in the prevention of heart disease. There are studies that also suggest that the patient who has survived his first heart attack will be less likely to have a second attack or die from a subsequent attack if he has been active in a physical-conditioning, rehabilitation program.

From the above data, it is impossible to state, unequivocally, that exercise will provide protection from a premature heart attack. The available evidence suggests that an increase in habitual physical activity is beneficial. Fox (1973) has concluded that the likely benefits of habitual physical activity will be more in the area of an improved quality of life than in life extension. Obviously, the identification of the preventive role of exercise in heart disease must await further study of a longitudinal nature. While this may take fifty years, or more, to resolve beyond a shadow of a doubt, it would be prudent to subscribe to the theory that physical activity is important until it is proven otherwise.

Obesity

Obesity and overweight constitute two of the most serious medical and health problems in the United States today. It is ironic that while millions of people are dying of starvation each year in all parts of the world, many Americans are dying as an indirect result of an overabundance of food. The prevalence of obesity and overweight in this country has increased dramatically over the past fifteen years. Presently, as many as 10-million teenagers are overweight, representing about 20 percent of the total U.S. teenage population. For the adult population over forty years of age, 30 percent of all men and 40 percent of all women are more than 20 percent above their ideal weight. It has also been demonstrated that the average individual in this country will gain approximately one pound of additional weight each year after the age of twenty-five. Such a seemingly small gain, however, results in 30 lb of excess weight by age fifty-five. Since the bone and muscle mass decreases by approximately ½ lb per year, this means a 45-lb gain in fat over this thirty-year period!

Overweight versus Obesity.   What is the distinction between the terms "overweight" and "obesity"? Also, what is meant by the term "ideal weight"? First, overweight is defined as any body weight that exceeds the normal or standard weight for a particular individual, based on his or her age, height, and frame size. These values are established solely on the basis of population averages. It is quite possible to be overweight according to these standards and yet have a body fat content lower than normal. Football players have frequently been found to be overweight, while actually being much leaner than individuals of the same age, height, and frame size who are of normal weight or even underweight. There are also individuals who are not overweight by the standard tables, but who are actually obese.

Obesity refers to the condition in which the total amount of body fat exceeds that considered optimal for a particular individual's body weight. This implies that the amount of body fat must be assessed much more accurately than can be guessed from the standard tables, which are based on height and frame size. The hydrostatic, or underwater, weighing technique is probably the most accurate of the clinical research techniques available for estimating body fat, but it is not practical for the assessment of the general population, due to the length of time and cost for each test. A much simpler technique, which is not as accurate as hydrostatic weighing but is much faster and inexpensive, involves measuring with calipers the thickness of two layers of skin plus the interposed layer of fat at several sites. Theoretically, the skinfold thickness will vary directly with the thickness of the underlying subcutaneous fat, which is related to the total body fat. The quantity of fat is normally expressed as a percentage of the individual's total body weight. Exact standards for allowable fat percentages have not been universally agreed on; however, men with over 25 percent body fat and women with over 35 percent should be considered obese.

The concept of ideal weight is closely related to these upper limits of body fat. It is felt that the average male should possess approximately 15 percent of his weight as fat and the average female aproximately 23 percent. This will vary somewhat between individuals, but it does provide a realistic target to aim for. As an example, assume that a 180-lb man had 20 percent of his body weight as fat. He would possess 36 lb of fat. The remaining weight, 144 lb, is referred to as the lean body weight, or mass, and consists essentially of bone and muscle components. In order for this man to reach a level of 15 percent fat, he would have to lose 11 lb, providing his lean body mass remained the same. (See calculations in Table 13–1). This would give him a target, or ideal, weight of 169 lb. Ideal weight is determined by dividing the lean body weight by the fraction of the total body weight that is desired to be lean. For 15 percent fat, the fraction would be .85, or 85 percent lean weight.

It should be clear that to identify those people with obesity problems, it is necessary to first determine the actual, or relative, fat content of the body. Simply referring to even the most sophisticated standard weight tables is not sufficient to identify a large percentage of the obese population. It is quite possible to be obese by the above criteria and still be within, or even below, the allowable limits established in these tables.

Etiology of Obesity.   At one time, obesity was thought to be the result of basic hormonal imbalances in the blood, resulting from a failure of one or more of the endocrine glands. Later, it was believed that only a small fraction of the total obese population could be accounted for in this manner, and that it was gluttony, rather than glandular malfunction, that caused the majority of obesity problems. Fortunately, the results of more recent medical and physiological research show that obesity can be the result of any one, or a combination of many, factors. Its etiology is not as simple or straightforward as was once believed.

A number of recent experimental studies on animals have linked obesity to hereditary, or genetic factors. Indirect studies suggest a similar link for man. According to several studies (Mayer, 1972), only 8 to 9 percent of children with parents of normal weight were found to be obese, whereas 40 percent and 80 percent were considered to be obese when either or both parents, respectively, were obese.

Obesity has also been experimentally and clinically linked with both physiological and psychological trauma. Hormonal imbalances, emotional trauma, and alterations in basic homeostatic mechanisms have all been shown to be either directly or indirectly related to the onset of obesity. Environmental factors, i.e., cultural habits, inadequate physical activity, and improper diets, have also been shown to contribute to obesity.

Thus, obesity is of complex origin, and the specific causes undoubtedly differ from one

TABLE 13–1.   Calculating Ideal or Target Weights

Weight 180 lb	Relative fat 20%
Total fat = 20% × 180 lb = 36 lb	
Lean body weight = 180 lb − 36 lb = 144 lb	
Ideal weight = X = 144 ÷ .85 = 169 lb	Ideal relative fat 15%
Target weight loss = 180 lb − 169 lb = 11 lb	

person to the next. Recognizing this fact is important both in the treatment of existing obesity and in the application of measures to prevent its onset. To attribute obesity solely to gluttony is most unfair and very damaging psychologically to obese individuals who are concerned and are attempting to correct their problem. Several studies have even shown that obese individuals actually eat less than normal individuals of similar sex and age, although they get far less physical activity.

Health Problems in Obesity. Obesity has been directly related to four different types of health problems: changes in various normal body functions; increased risk of developing certain diseases; detrimental effects on established diseases; and adverse psychological reactions.*

Just as the cause of obesity varies from one individual to another, so do the prevalence and extent of changes in body function. However, there are certain trends that are specifically linked to obesity. Respiratory problems are quite common among the obese. They have difficulty in normal breathing, a greater incidence of respiratory infections, and a lower exercise tolerance. Lethargy, associated with increased levels of carbon dioxide in the blood, and polycythemia (increased red blood cell production) due to lowered arterial blood oxygenation, are also common results from obesity. These can lead to blood clotting (thrombosis), enlargement of the heart, and congestive heart failure. Hypertension and atherosclerosis have also been linked to the obese individual, as have metabolic and endocrine disorders, such as impaired carbohydrate metabolism and diabetes. Obesity has also been associated with an increased risk of gallbladder disease, digestive diseases, and nephritis. More importantly, the mortality rate of the obese is substantially higher for each of these diseases than for people of normal weight.

The effect of obesity on existing diseases is not clearly understood at the present time.

Obesity can contribute to the further development of certain diseases, and weight reduction is usually prescribed as an integral part of the treatment of the disease. Conditions such as angina pectoris, hypertension, congestive heart failure, myocardial infarction, varicose veins, diabetes, and orthopedic problems would benefit from weight reduction.

It is possible that psychological problems actually cause obesity in a substantial percentage of the obese population. Further emotional or psychological problems can arise from the existence of the condition itself. There is definitely a social stigma to obesity in our society, which contributes substantially to the problems of those who are obese. Consequently, the obese individual may also need psychiatric assistance in his efforts to lose weight.

Treatment, Prevention, and Controls. On paper, weight control seems to be a very simple matter. The energy consumed by the body in the form of food must be equal to the energy expended by the body in physical activity. In both cases, the energy is expressed in calories. The body will normally maintain a balance between the caloric intake and the caloric expenditure. However, when this balance is upset, a loss or gain in weight will result. It appears that both weight losses and weight gains are basically dependent on only two factors, dietary and exercise habits.

The sole purpose of a weight-reduction diet is to create a caloric deficiency, i.e., the caloric intake is lowered so that the caloric expenditure exceeds the intake. It has been estimated that the loss of one pound of fat requires a caloric deficit of 3,500 calories. To lose one pound a week, the caloric deficit would have to average 500 calories/day, which is approximately the equivalent of five, scrambled eggs, three and one-half cans of beer (12-oz can), or a six-ounce sirloin steak. A reasonable, or sensible, weight loss would be one to two pounds per week. Losses any greater than this should not be attempted, unless under direct medical supervision. By losing just 1 lb of fat a week, an individual will lose 52 lb in only one year! Few people become obese that rapidly.

---

* U.S. Department of Health, Education, and Welfare, Public Health Service, *Obesity and Health* (Washington, D.C.: Government Printing Office, 1966).

Weight loss should be a long-term project. Research has demonstrated, and experience has proven, that rapid weight losses are usually short-lived and the original weight is quickly regained. Rapid weight losses are generally the result of large losses of body water. Since the body has built-in safety mechanisms to prevent an imbalance in body water levels, the water loss will, eventually, be replaced. Thus, the individual wishing to lose 20 lb of fat is advised to attempt to attain this goal in a six- to twelve-month period.

Many special diets have been popular in recent years, such as, the drinking man's diet, Dr. Stillman's diet, and Dr. Adkin's diet. Each claims to be the ultimate in terms of effectiveness and comfort in weight loss. Likewise, each diet has its loyal following of confirmed believers, who make a strong case for the superiority of their particular diet over the others. Is there a superior diet? Research tends to show that almost all of these diets are effective, but *no one single diet has been shown to be any more effective than any other*. Again, the important factor is the development of a caloric deficit, while maintaining a balanced diet that is complete in all respects with regard to vitamin and mineral requirements. The diet that meets these criteria and is best suited to the comfort and personality of each individual is the best diet.

Several agents, or aids, have been advocated for assisting an individual in reducing his caloric intake. Anorexigenic agents (agents used to decrease or suppress the appetite), such as amphetamines, have been prescribed with varying success, but they produce side effects such as insomnia, irritability, and tenseness. Thyroid hormone has also been used, but its effects are highly questionable and it produces side effects similar to the amphetamines.

Recently, human chorionic gonadotropin, a hormone derived from the urine of pregnant women, has been used to promote rapid weight loss. Daily injections of this hormone, in addition to a 500-calorie/day diet, supposedly produce a one-pound-per-day weight loss. Recent evidence, however, shows human chorionic gonadotropin to be no more effective than an injection of plain salt water. The weight that is lost appears to be strictly the result of the 500-calorie/day diet.

Diuretics have been suggested, but the resulting weight loss is almost entirely salt and water. Therefore, these should be used only for those patients who have problems of water retention or hyperhydration. Total fasting has been shown to be helpful in the initial stages of weight loss in highly obese individuals, but hospitalization and close supervision of the patient is required. It must be emphasized that, regardless of their effectiveness, none of the above mentioned agents, or aids, should be used except under the prescription and close supervision of a physician.

For many years, it has been a common belief that exercise is of little help in programs of weight reduction and control. The classic examples are the statements that to lose one pound of fat, a person must chop wood for seven hours, walk thirty-five miles, or climb a ten-foot staircase 1,000 times. These examples are intended to show the foolishness of trying to lose weight through exercise. It is also argued that the appetite increases as a result of exercise, and that this increase in caloric intake has the same, or greater, caloric value as the expenditure from the exercise itself.

Both of these concepts have been proven false. In fact, research has proven that exercise is probably the most efficient way to lose weight and that it also results in weight losses of a permanent nature.

Inactivity is a major cause of obesity in the United States. In fact, inactivity may be a far more significant factor in the development of obesity than overeating! Thus, exercise must be recognized as an essential component in any program of weight reduction or control.

When planning an exercise program, it is important to remember that one seldom obtains something for nothing. An effortless exercise program, of course, would be ideal but such a program would be unrealistic. With the popularity of exercise increasing, there are many gimmicks, gadgets, and fads on the market. While some of these are legitimate and effective, many are of no practical value for either exercise or weight loss. To exercise efficiently and make substantial progress requires work and sweat.

The physical activity level of any individual can be increased by concentrating on four basic areas. First, one should have a regular formal exercise schedule, consisting of a warm-up period, the formal exercise or exercises, and a cooling-off period. This formal exercise should be undertaken at least three

TABLE 13–2. Energy Expenditure by a 150-Pound Person in Various Activities*

Activity	Gross Energy Cost Calories per Hour
A. *Rest and Light Activity*	*50–200*
Lying down or sleeping	80
Sitting	100
Driving an automobile	120
Standing	140
Domestic work	180
B. *Moderate Activity*	*200–350*
Bicycling (5½ mph)	210
Walking (2½ mph)	210
Gardening	220
Canoeing (2½ mph)	230
Golf	250
Lawn mowing (power mower)	250
Bowling	270
Lawn mowing (hand mower)	270
Fencing	300
Rowing (2½ mph)	300
Swimming (¼ mph)	300
Walking (3¾ mph)	300
Badminton	350
Horseback riding (trotting)	350
Square dancing	350
Volleyball	350
Roller skating	350
C. *Vigorous Activity*	*Over 350*
Table tennis	360
Ditch digging (hand shovel)	400
Ice skating (10 mph)	400
Wood chopping or sawing	400
Tennis	420
Water skiing	480
Hill climbing (100 ft. per hr.)	490
Jogging (5½ mph)	600
Skiing (10 mph)	600
Squash and handball	600
Cycling (13 mph)	660
Scull rowing (race)	840
Running (10 mph)	900

* From *Exercise and Weight Control*, Committee on Exercise and Physical Fitness of the American Medical Association and the President's Council on Physical Fitness.

times a week and can consist of anything from walking to jogging or swimming. Table 13–2 illustrates the energy cost in calories/hour for various types of activities. For example, individuals who play tennis for one and one-half hours, twice a week, would lose a pound of fat in slightly under three weeks, as long as the caloric intake remained the same.

Second, one should have supplementary physical recreation in addition to formal exercise. Gardening, golf, bowling, sailing, and dancing are just a few of the many active recreational pursuits that will result in a far greater expenditure of energy than the more commonly practiced art of television watching. Third, the total daily caloric expenditure can be increased in the course of one's usual daily activities by walking several flights of steps instead of using the elevator, by parking an extra block or more from work or the store, and by performing many of the other routine daily activities in a more active manner. The object is to look for ways of increasing the amount of physical work the body can perform each day, during the daily routine, in spite of mechanization.

Last, the physical activity level associated with one's job can be increased. This can be done in much the same manner as outlined above. Since approximately a fourth to a third of one's life is spent on the job, this time can be used much more efficiently if the basic activity levels on the job are increased.

From the information above, it appears that the most efficient and sensible approach to weight loss is through a combination of diet and exercise. Since a caloric deficit is the key to weight loss, the caloric intake would only have to be reduced and physical activity increased half as much as necessary as if either one was used exclusively by itself for weight loss. Thus, routine exercise is effective in weight control and weight reduction. Likewise, sedentary habits tend to lead to problems of overweight and obesity. A word of caution, however. It is quite possible, and even probable, that one's weight on the bathroom scale will change very little, if any, following a month or two of vigorous exercise. While this is discouraging and might lead one to suspect that the exercise program is not helping to reduce body fat, this phenomenon is a natural occurrence. During the initial stages of an exercise program the individual develops muscle as well as looses fat, both of which are highly desirable. For the first month or two, the gains in muscle are nearly the same as the losses in fat. As a result, the bathroom scale does not give an accurate measurement of the actual changes in the body's composition.

THE PRESCRIPTION OF EXERCISE

From the above discussion, it is obvious that the sedentary nature of modern man has led to a number of health-related problems. Many of these problems can be either resolved or prevented by prescribing programs of routine physical activity for the young and old, alike. The sport and exercise sciences have now progressed to the point where individualized exercise programs can be prescribed and tailored to the likes, needs, and physical capacity of the individual participant. The era of a single group program to fit people of all ages and capacities has come and gone. The individualized prescription of exercise is now a reality and is being used successfully throughout the United States.

Medical Clearance

Prior to beginning any exercise program, it is important that all individuals over thirty years old have a complete physical examination by their private physicians. This should include a discussion of the proposed exercise program, in the event that there are medical complications that might make a particular activity or sport undesirable. As an example, patients who have elevated blood pressure should be cautioned to avoid activities that use isometric contractions. Isometric contractions tend to cause a considerable rise in blood pressure and usually result in a Valsalva maneuver in which the intraabdominal and intrathoracic pressure are increased to the point of restricting the vena cava, thus limiting venous return to the heart. Both responses can lead to serious medical complications. The physical examination should include a health and family history, a resting electrocardiogram and blood pressure assessment, and an exercise-stress electrocardiogram performed on either a bicycle ergometer or treadmill (Figure 13–1). The stress electrocardiogram is extremely important since between 8 and 14 percent of the normal, asymptomatic adult population with normal resting electrocardiograms will demonstrate abnormalities in their electrocardiograms during or following exercise, which is indicative of coronary atherosclerosis. This does not preclude the participation of these individuals in an exercise program, but it does place them in a special, high-risk category in which exercise should be performed under the supervision of a physician.

Factors in Prescribing Exercise

Once an individual is cleared by the family physician, an exercise program can be prescribed. The exercise prescription involves four basic factors: mode or type of exercise, frequency of participation, duration of each exercise period, and intensity of the exercise bout. Each of these will be discussed individually.

Mode of Exercise. The prescribed exercise program should include, as its focus, a cardiovascular-endurance activity. Traditionally, walking, jogging, running, hiking, and swimming have been the activities prescribed most frequently. Unfortunately, these activities do not appeal to everyone, so additional activities need to be identified that will promote similar cardiovascular endurance development. Recently, bicycling and tennis were shown to cause significant improvements in endurance capacity. Strenuous activities, like handball and racketball, probably have a significant endurance component, but this has not, as yet, been substantiated by research. For these types

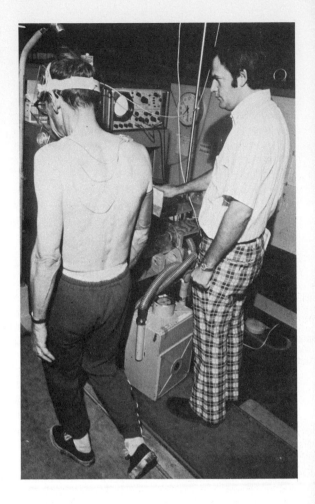

FIGURE 13–1

Illustrating an exercise stress test to exhaustion on a treadmill.

of activities, it is advisable to be preconditioned through one of the standard endurance activities, such as jogging, before undertaking serious competition. This introduces the concept of conditioning activities and maintenance activities. It is felt by some researchers, clinicians, and practitioners that in order to successfully compete in certain sports or activities, a basic preconditioning program is essential. Rather than using the sport or activity to get in shape, one would get in shape prior to participating in that sport or activity. If the activity required a moderate to high level of cardiovascular endurance, the individual would engage in a jogging, swimming, or bicycling program for several months, until he had increased his endurance capacity to the necessary level, at which time he would switch over to the sport. Conditioning activities would be used to bring the individual to the desired fitness level. The sport would then act as a maintenance activity to maintain the individual at that desired level of fitness.

When selecting activities, it is important to match individuals with activities that they will enjoy and be willing to continue throughout life. Exercise must be regarded as a lifetime pursuit, for the benefits are soon lost once participation stops. Motivation is probably the most important factor in a successful exercise program. Thus, selecting an activity that is fun, provides a challenge, and can provide the needed benefits is the most critical task in the exercise prescription process.

Exercise Frequency.   The frequency of participation is an important factor to consider, but it is probably less critical than either the exercise duration or intensity. Research studies conducted on this aspect have shown that 3 to 4 days per week is an optimal frequency (Pollock, 1973). This does not mean that 5, or more, days per week will not give additional benefits, but simply that, for health purposes, you are getting the best return for the amount of time invested. It is important that the individual limit himself to 3 to 4 days per week, initially, and build up to 5, or more, days per week, only if he enjoys what he is doing. All too often, an individual who starts out with great intentions and is highly motivated will exercise every day for the first few weeks, only to stop from utter fatigue. Obviously, additional days per week above the 3- to 4-day frequency are beneficial for weight loss purposes, but this level should not be encouraged until the exercise habit is firmly established.

Exercise Duration.   Several studies have demonstrated improvement in cardiovascular conditioning with endurance-exercise programs as brief as 5 to 10 min per day. Recent research (Pollock, 1973) has indicated that 20 to 30 min per day is an optimal amount. Again, optimal is used here in the context of greatest return for time invested, and the specified time refers to the time during which the individual is at his training heart rate (THR).

Exercise Intensity.   The intensity of the exercise bout is undoubtedly the most critical aspect of the three factors, frequency, duration, and intensity. How hard does one have to push himself? The ex-athlete immediately recalls the exhaustive workouts he endured to condition himself for his sport. Unfortunately, this concept gets carried over into the area of exercise for health. Evidence now suggests that a substantial training effect can be accomplished by training at between 60 and 80 percent of the individual's capacity (Pollock, 1973). There appears to be a training threshold above which a training response occurs. Some evidence suggests that training must be at a level that is at least 60 percent of one's capacity, and that training at levels below 60 percent results in little, if any cardiovascular benefit.

Exercise intensity is quantified by having the individual exercise at his own, individualized, training heart rate (THR). The THR is established by determining the individual's exercise capacity on a maximal exercise stress test. He is then assigned a heart rate that represents a set percentage of that capacity. A THR set at 75 percent of the individual's HRmax represents a level of only 60 to 65 percent of his $\dot{V}O_2$ max, but this will be sufficient to initiate a substantial training response. Some clinicians actually measure $\dot{V}O_2$ up to, and including, $\dot{V}O_2$ max. They establish the THR by using the heart rate equivalent to a set fraction of the $\dot{V}O_2$ max. As an example, when the individual is tested, heart rate and $\dot{V}O_2$ data for each minute are obtained and plotted against each other. If a training level of 75 percent of $\dot{V}O_2$ max is used, the $\dot{V}O_2$ at 75 percent is determined ($\dot{V}O_2$ max $\times$ 0.75) and the corresponding heart rate is selected as the THR.

The concept of THR is extremely valuable.

There is a high correlation between heart rate and the work done by the heart. Heart rate alone is a good index of myocardial oxygen consumption as well as coronary blood flow. If the THR concept is followed, the individual's heart will perform at the same level of work even though the metabolic costs of the work might vary considerably. When exercising at high altitudes or under extremes in temperature, the heart rate will be greatly elevated if the individual attempts to maintain the rate of work, e.g., run at a 6 min/mi pace. With the THR concept, the individual simply does less work under these extreme environmental conditions to maintain the same heart rate (THR). This is a much safer approach to the training program.

The THR concept automatically accounts for improvement. As the individual becomes better conditioned, his heart rate decreases for the same level of work, or conversely, the individual must actually perform more work in order to reach his THR.

THE EXERCISE PROGRAM

Once medical clearance has been obtained and the exercise prescription determined, it is necessary to integrate all of the information described above into a total exercise program. That is an integral part of the individual's overall health-improvement plan. The program should be designed, specifically, on the basis of the results of the medical evaluation, as well as on the basis of the individual's exercise capacity, interests, and personal needs. It should be designed to bring him to a reasonable level of fitness for his age, health status, occupation, and leisure-time interests. Once he has achieved this level, his program becomes one of fitness maintenance. At that time, the amount of physical activity required will become less, since the amount of activity needed to stay at the ideal level of fitness is less than it takes to get there. Also, once one reaches the ideal, or optimal, level of fitness, it is possible to safely and enjoyably participate in

a much greater variety of exercises and active sports or games.

The exercise program should include the following:

· A conditioning or physical fitness program
· A recreational activities guide
· A daily, living habits guide

The Conditioning Program

Exercise capacity varies widely among individuals, even when they are of similar ages and physical builds. That is why each program is based upon the individual's own, personal test results. The total time to perform the recommended program will vary between 30 and 45 min per session, depending on the individual's present level of fitness and his personal goals.

The recommended conditioning program consists of the following activities listed in the order in which they should be performed:

· A set of warm-up exercises
· A set of flexibility exercises
· An endurance conditioning period
· A set of strength exercises (optional)
· A cooling-down period

Warm-up Period.   The exercise session should begin with low-intensity, calisthenic and stretching exercises. Such a warm-up period will increase both heart rate and breathing to provide for the efficient and safe functioning of the heart, blood vessels, lungs, and muscles during the more vigorous exercise that follows. A good warm-up, also, will reduce the amount of muscle and joint soreness that may be experienced during the early stages of the exercise program.

Flexibility-Development Activities.   The flexibility exercises, such as those illustrated in Appendix B, are supplementary to those exercises performed during the warm-up period and are intended for those who have poor flexibility, as well as muscle and joint problems, such as low back pain. These exercises are to be performed slowly, as quick stretching

TABLE 13–3.   A Walking Program

Step	Peak O$_2$ Value	Workout Description	Time (min)	Miles
I	8.5	Walk 0.67 mi in 20 min	20	0.67
II	8.5	Walk 1 mi in 30 min	30	1.00
III	10.4	Walk 1.25 mi in 30 min	30	1.25
IV	12.0	Walk 1.50 mi in 30 min	30	1.50
V	14.0	Walk 1.75 mi in 30 min	30	1.75
VI	16.0	Walk 2.0 mi in 30 min	30	2.00

movements are potentially dangerous and can lead to muscle pulls or muscle spasms.

Endurance-Development Activities. Physical activities that develop endurance are the "heart" of the exercise program. They are designed to improve both the capacity and efficiency of the cardiovascular and respiratory systems. Also, they are the types of exercises that are most useful in helping to control or reduce body weight.

Activities such as walking, jogging, running, cycling, swimming, and hiking are good endurance activities. Sports such as handball, basketball, tennis, and badminton are also good, providing they are pursued vigorously. Activities such as golf, bowling, and softball are generally of little value from the standpoint of developing cardiorespiratory endurance, but they are fun and have definite recreational value. Tables 13–3 to 13–7 illustrate a progressive walk-jog-run type program.

Strength Exercises.   A series of strength-development exercises are illustrated in Appendix A, most of which require strength-training

TABLE 13–4.   A Walking-Jogging Program

Step	Peak O$_2$ Value	Work Description	Time (min)	Miles
I	17.2	Walk 2.25 mi in 30 min	30	2.25
II	24.5	Walk .25 mi in 3 min 45 sec Jog .25 mi in 3 min Repeat for 31 min	31	2.25
III	24.5	Walk .5 mi in 7 min 30 sec Jog .5 mi in 6 min Repeat for 34 min 30 sec	34.5	2.50
IV	24.5	Walk .25 mi in 3 min 45 sec Jog .75 mi in 9 min Walk .5 mi in 7 min 30 sec Repeat first two steps	33	2.50
V	24.5	Jog 1 mi in 12 min Walk .25 mi in 3 min 45 sec Repeat	31.5	2.50
VI	27.5	Walk .25 mi in 3 min 45 sec Jog 1 mi in 11 min Repeat for 33 min 15 sec	33.25	2.75

TABLE 13–5. A Jogging Program

Step	Peak O_2 Value	Workout Description	Time (min)	Miles
I	27.5	Jog 1 mi in 11 min Jog .5 mi in 6 min Repeat	34	3.00
II	27.5	Jog 3 mi in 33 min	33	3.00
III	30.5	Jog 1 mi in 10 min Jog 1 mi in 11 min Jog 1 mi in 10 min	31	3.00
IV	30.5	Jog 3 mi in 30 min	30	3.00
V	33.5	Jog 1 mi in 9 min 15 sec Jog 1 mi in 10 min Jog 1 mi in 9 min 15 sec	28.5	3.00
VI	33.5	Jog 3 mi at 9 min 15 sec/mi	28	3.00

equipment. Access to dumbbells, barbells, weight machines, or other strength-training devices is not essential, however, since one can gain a great deal from exercises that utilize body weight as the resistance.

If one participates in a weight-training pro- gram, it is advisable to start with a weight that is exactly one half of one's maximum strength. The individual should attempt to lift that weight ten consecutive times. If he can just barely do this, he is starting at the right weight. If he could have done more, he should go to

TABLE 13–6. A Jogging-Running Program

Step	Peak O_2 Value	Workout Description	Time (min)	Miles
I	33.5	Jog 3.25 mi at 9 min 15 sec/mi	30	3.25
II	36.5	Jog 3.375 mi at 8 min 30 sec/mi	29	3.38
III	36.5	Jog 3.5 mi at 8 min 30 sec/mi	30	3.50
IV	39.5	Jog-Run 3.5 mi at 8 min/mi	28	3.50
V	39.5	Jog-Run 3.75 mi at 8 min/mi	30	3.75
VI	39.5	Jog-Run 4.0 mi at 8 min/mi	32	4.00

TABLE 13–7. A Running Program

Step	Peak O_2 Value	Workout Description	Time (min)	Miles
I	42.5	Run 4 mi at 7 min 30 sec/mi	30	4.00
II	42.5	Run 4.25 mi at 7 min 30 sec/mi	32	4.25
III	42.5	Run 4.38 mi at 7 min 30 sec/mi	33	4.38
IV	45.5	Run 4.5 mi at 7 min/mi	31.5	4.50
V	45.5	Run 4.75 mi at 7 min/mi	33.25	4.75
VI	45.5	Run 5 mi at 7 min/mi	35	5.00

the next highest weight for his second set. If he did less than eight repetitions on his first set, he should reduce the weight lifted to the next lowest level for his second set. Once he has a weight that gets him to the point of fatigue by the eighth to tenth repetition, he has found his starting weight. Two or three sets of each lift should be performed per day, in which eight to ten repetitions count as a single set. As the individual increases his strength, he will be able to do more repetitions per set. Once he hits 15 repetitions, it is time to increase to the next highest weight. This training technique is referred to as progressive resistance exercise. For those lifts where the maximum strength has not been determined, the process of selecting an initial weight is largely one of trial and error.

Cooling Down Period.   Every exercise session should be concluded with a tapering down, or cooling-off, period. This is best accomplished by slowly reducing the intensity of the activity during the last several minutes of the workout. A slow, restful walk for several minutes keeps the blood from pooling in the extremities, and helps reduce the chances of developing muscle soreness. Stopping abruptly following an endurance bout of exercise causes blood to pool in the legs and may actually result in dizziness and fainting.

Recreational Activities

Recreational activities are an important part of any comprehensive, physical activity program. While these activities are engaged in, primarily, for enjoyment and relaxation, many of them also contribute to fitness development as well. Activities such as hiking, tennis, handball, squash, and certain team sports fall into this category. Guidelines to be used in the selection of these activities include the following: (a) Can they be learned or performed with at least a moderate degree of success? (b) Do they include opportunities for social development? and (c) Are they varied enough to maintain continued interest?

Many excellent opportunities exist for those individuals who have no recreational hobbies or activities but who would like to become involved. Local recreation centers or clubs, YMCA's, YWCA's, public schools, and community colleges offer instructional classes in a wide variety of activities for little, or no, cost. Often, the entire family can participate in these classes, an added bonus to a total health-improvement program.

Several words of caution are necessary. First, one should not be carried away by competitive activities. While the competitive spirit is natural and healthy, it does, occasionally, tend to overpower one's common sense. Second, contact-type sports or activities should be avoided, except for the exceptional individual who is in a highly trained and conditioned state. Also, it is important to keep in mind that these are, primarily, recreational activities, which are only one aspect of the total physical activity program. Once the individual has attained a reasonable state of fitness, however, these activities may be adequate to keep him there.

Life Pattern Alterations

Man has become a victim of his own technological progress. History has observed the transformation of homo sapiens into homo sedentarius. Fortunately, the trend toward a totally sedentary lifestyle is not irreversible. Simply by consciously altering a few basic habits, one can overcome much of this tendency toward sedentary living. The following suggestions are just a few of many changes that can be made in daily living habits to increase health and fitness levels.

1. Elevators and escalators are convenient but do little for health. Walk those stairways, starting with one or two flights and progessively increasing as the body becomes conditioned.
2. Park the car several blocks, or more, from your normal on-the-job parking place and briskly walk this extra distance.
3. Take a brisk walk during coffee or lunch breaks or before dinner.

4. Walk to the corner market or store for those short errands and give the car, the crowded roads, and the polluted air a well-deserved rest.
5. Wash your own car, mow your own lawn, and do your own handiwork. These can become hobbies, and the money saved can be applied toward a new bike.
6. Throw away the remote control for the television set and walk those few extra steps for channel changing or fine tuning. This might be just enough to break many of their TV habit.
7. Do not lie, when you can sit, and do not sit, when you can stand, and do not stand, when you can be moving.
8. Be innovative and see how much work you can save the machines.

GENERAL GUIDELINES FOR AN EXERCISE PROGRAM

When an inactive individual begins a physical activity program, there are several very basic and important factors that need to be considered.

Clothing

The choice of clothing will obviously depend upon the weather and the activity in which the individual plans to participate. However, clothing should always be comfortable, reasonably loose, and heavy or light enough to insure protection from heat, cold, and wind. Because of the heat generated with exercise, it is better to underdress rather than overdress. Women should avoid restrictive support garments or clothing that restrict either free movement or blood flow. In conditioning activities, such as jogging, men do not need to wear athletic supporters, since they frequently cause skin irritations.

One should not wear rubberized or plastic clothing while exercising. The increased sweat loss does not result in a permanent loss of body weight, and this practice can be very dangerous. The rubberized or plastic clothing does not allow the body sweat to evaporate, which is the principal mechanism for temperature regulation during exercise. The result can be a dramatic rise in body temperature, excessive dehydration and salt loss, and eventual heat stroke or heat exhaustion.

Shoes

The type and proper fit of shoe is important for any activity program. A good quality of tennis, basketball, or gym shoe is recommended for most types of activities. For programs of running, jogging, or walking, however, special shoes are recommended that have been designed specifically for these activities. These shoes should not fit tightly; the soles should be firm and the tops pliable; and they should have a good supporting heel. Ripple or crepe soles are excellent for use on hard surfaces. It is important to remember that good shoes and socks are the best prevention against blisters and against sore and aching feet, ankles, and knees.

Running Surfaces

For those individuals who include walking, running, or jogging in their activity programs, the matter of running surfaces should be given careful consideration. Beginners and individuals who are overweight or who have a history of foot, ankle, or knee problems should avoid hard surfaces, such as running tracks, cement, or asphalt. Grass or dirt paths usually provide good surfaces. Golf courses, parks, or rights-of-way along parkways can provide good variations in scenery and terrain. During bad weather, use the local YMCA, school, or church gymnasium or protected areas around shopping centers and around the home.

When to Exercise

Almost any time of the day is acceptable for exercising, except for an hour or two following a meal and during hot and humid weather. Since man seems to be a creature of habit, a specific time of day should be set aside for the activity program. Early morning before breakfast is often the best time for many people, since they have few conflicting commitments at that time of day.

Illness or Injury

The physical activity program should be modified or temporarily stopped during any illness, injury, or infection that might be aggravated by such a program. Use proper footwear and socks and take it easy at the beginning to avoid potential foot and leg problems. Also, switch to an activity that does not require one to support his weight while exercising, such as swimming or bicycling, to help eliminate foot or leg problems, without losing fitness. Any persistent illness or injury should be brought to the attention of the individual's personal physician.

Motivation

Physical activity programs are usually started with the best of intentions, but, all too often, the individual's enthusiasm tends to wane after a short period of time. Since the physical-activity program is intended to be a lifetime pursuit, it is important that the individual be properly motivated. Several helpful suggestions are listed below to help overcome the motivation problem.

- Either select activities you enjoy or learn to enjoy the activities in which you feel you must participate.
- Exercise at a regular time of the day and make this a part of your daily routine.
- Exercise with a partner or become a member of a formal group. However, do not get talked into competition.
- Take selected physiological and medical measurements and attempt to chart your improvement on each of these.
- Become educated in what you are doing. By reading, attending lectures or seminars, and by group discussion, attempt to understand the importance of a physical-activity program relative to your total health.

ENERGY EXPENDITURE AND PHYSICAL ACTIVITY

The amount of oxygen consumed is directly proportional to the energy expended in physical activity. At rest, man uses approximately 3.5 ml of oxygen per kilogram (2.2 lb) of body weight per minute (ml/kg $\times$ min). When walking slowly at 2 mph, one uses about 9.0 ml, and one uses 24 ml when walking rapidly at 5.0 mph. The amount of oxygen necessary to perform an activity is referred to as that activity's oxygen requirement. Thus, all physical activities can be classified according to their intensities as determined by their oxygen requirements.

A simplified system for classifying physical activities has been developed, using the concept of *metabolic equivalents*, or METS. One MET is equal to the resting oxygen uptake, approximately 3.5 ml/kg $\times$ min. An activity that is rated as two METS would, therefore, require two times the resting oxygen consumption, or 7 ml/kg $\times$ min, and an activity that is rated at 4 METS would require approximately 14 ml/kg $\times$ min (4 $\times$ 3.5 = 14).

A number of activities and their MET values are presented in Table 13–8. It should be noted that these values are only approximations, due to the variations in metabolic efficiency both within and between individuals. This table can also be used to select activities to supplement the endurance-training program.

GENERAL SUMMARY

Patterns of modern living have channeled the average American into an increasingly sedentary existence. Man, however, was designed and built for movement, and it appears that, physiologically, he has not adapted well to this reduced level of activity. Regular exercise is necessary to develop and maintain an optimal level of good health, performance, and appearance. It can increase an individual's physical working capacity by increasing muscle strength and endurance, enhancing the function of the

TABLE 13–8. Selected Activities and Their Respective MET Values

Self-Care Activities

Activity	METS
Rest, supine	1.0
Sitting	1.0
Standing, relaxed	1.0
Eating	1.0
Conversation	1.0
Dressing and undressing	2.0
Washing hands and face	2.0
Propulsion, wheelchair	2.0
Walking, 2.5 mph	3.0
Showering	3.5
Walking downstairs	4.5
Walking, 3.5 mph	5.5
Ambulation, braces and crutches	6.5

Housework Activities

Activity	METS
Handsewing	1.0
Sweeping floor	1.5
Machine sewing	1.5
Polishing furniture	2.0
Peeling potatoes	2.5
Scrubbing, standing	2.5
Washing small clothes	2.5
Kneading dough	2.5
Scrubbing floors	3.0
Cleaning windows	3.0
Making beds	3.0
Ironing, standing	3.5
Mopping	3.5
Wringing wash by hand	3.5
Hanging wash	3.5
Beating carpets	4.0

Occupational Activities

Activity	METS
Sitting at desk	1.5
Writing	1.5
Riding in automobile	1.5
Watch repairing	1.5
Typing	2.0
Welding	2.5
Radio assembly	2.5
Playing musical instrument	2.5
Parts assembly	3.0
Bricklaying and plastering	3.5
Heavy assembly work	4.0
Wheeling wheelbarrow 115 lb, 2.5 mph	4.0
Carpentry	5.5

Occupational Activities

Activity	METS
Mowing lawn by handmower	6.5
Chopping wood	6.5
Shoveling	7.0
Digging	7.5

Physical-Conditioning Activities

Activity	METS
Level walking, 2 mph (1 mi in 30 min)	2.5
Level cycling, 5.5 mph (1 mi in 10 min 54 sec)	3.0
Level cycling, 6 mph (1 mi in 10 min)	3.5
Level walking, 2.5 mph (1 mi in 24 min)	3.5
Level walking, 3 mph (1 mi in 20 min)	4.5
Calesthenics	4.5
Level cycling, 9.7 mph (1 mi in 6 min 18 sec)	5.0
Swimming, crawl, 1 ft/sec	5.0
Level walking, 3.5 mph (1 mi in 17 min)	5.5
Level walking, 4.0 mph (1 mi in 15 min)	6.5
Level jogging, 5.0 mph (1 mi in 12 min)	7.5
Level cycling, 13 mph (1 mi in 4 min 37 sec)	9.0
Level running, 7.5 mph (1 mi in 8 min)	9.0
Swimming, crawl, 2 ft/sec	10.0
Level running, 8.5 mph (1 mi in 7 min)	12.0
Level running, 10.0 mph (1 mi in 6 min)	15.0
Swimming crawl, 2.5 ft/sec	15.0
Swimming crawl, 3.0 ft/sec	20.0
Level running, 12 mph (1 mi in 5 min)	20.0
Level running, 15 mph (¼ mi in 1 min)	30.0
Swimming crawl, 3.5 ft/sec	30.0

Recreational Activities

Activity	METS
Painting, sitting	1.5
Playing piano	2.0
Driving car	2.0
Canoeing, 2.5 mph	2.5
Horseback riding, walk	2.5
Volleyball, 6-man recreational	3.0
Billiards	3.0
Bowling	3.5
Horseshoes	3.5
Golf	4.0
Cricket	4.0
Archery	4.5
Ballroom dancing	4.5

TABLE 13–8. Selected Activities and Their Respective MET Values—*Continued*

Recreational Activities

Activity	METS
Table tennis	4.5
Baseball	4.5
Tennis	6.0
Horseback riding, trot	6.5
Folk dancing	6.5
Skiing	8.0
Horseback riding, gallop	8.0
Squash rackets	8.5
Fencing	9.0
Basketball	9.0
Football	9.0
Gymnastics	10.0
Handball and paddleball	10.0

lungs, heart, and blood vessels; increasing the flexibility of joints, and improving the efficiency or skill of movement. For many adults with sedentary occupations, physical activity provides an outlet for job-related tensions or mental fatigue. It also aids in weight control or reduction, improves posture, contributes to a youthful appearance, and increases general vitality. Active individuals appear to have fewer heart attacks than their less active counterparts. Furthermore, if an active individual does suffer an attack, it probably will be less severe and his chances of survival are greater. Additionally, more than 50 percent of lower back pain or discomfort is due to poor muscle tone and flexibility of the lower back and to inadequate abdominal muscle tone. In many

TABLE 13–9. Physiological Changes Resulting from Endurance-Type Physical Conditioning

Heart
    Reduced resting heart rate
    Reduced heart rate for standardized, submaximal exercise
    Increased rate of heart rate recovery after standardized exercise
    Increased blood volume pumped per heart beat (stroke volume)
    Increased size of heart muscle (myocardial hypertrophy)
    Increased blood supply to heart muscle
    Increased strength of contraction (contractibility)

Blood Vessels and Blood Chemistry
    Reduced resting systolic and diastolic arterial blood pressure
    Reduced risk of hardening of the arteries (arteriosclerosis)
    Reduced serum lipids, i.e., cholesterol, triglycerides
    Increased blood supply to muscles
    Increased blood volume
    More efficient exchange of oxygen and carbon dioxide in muscles

Lungs
    Increased functional capacity during exercise
    Increased blood supply
    Increased diffusion of respiratory gases
    Reduced nonfunctional volume of lung (residual volume)

Neural, Endocrine, and Metabolic Function
    Increased glucose tolerance
    Increased enzymatic function in muscle cells
    Reduced body fat content (adiposity)
    Increased muscle mass (lean body mass)
    Reduced strain resulting from psychological stress
    Increased maximal oxygen uptake

instances, this disability could be prevented or corrected by proper exercise. And finally, much of the degeneration of bodily functions and structure associated with premature aging seems to be reduced by frequent participation in a program of proper exercise.

An individually prescribed exercise program to supplement the normal daily activities of most adults is essential for good health. There is a sound physiological basis for such a program. The physiological and medical benefits that generally occur as a result of an increased activity program are summarized in Table 13–9. The magnitude of change in each of these measurements is dependent on the types of activities pursued, their frequency and duration, and the degree of effort (intensity) put into the activity.

REFERENCES

ENOS, W. F.; HOLMES, R. H.; and BEYER, J. "Coronary Disease Among United States Soldiers Killed in Action in Korea." *J. Amer. Med. Assoc.* 152 (1953): 1090–93.

FOX, S. M. III. "Relationship of Activity Habits to Coronary Heart Disease." In *Exercise Testing and Exercise Training in Coronary Heart Disease*, edited by J. P. Naughton, and H. K. Hellerstein, New York: Academic Press, 1973.

FOX, S. M. III; NAUGHTON, J. P.; and HASKELL, W. L. "Physical Activity and the Prevention of Coronary Heart Disease." *Annals Clin. Res.* 3 (1971): 404–32.

KANNEL, W. B., and DAWBER, T. R. "Atherosclerosis as a Pediatric Problem." *J. Pediatrics.* 80 (1972): 544–54.

MAYER, J. *Human Nutrition: Its Physiological, Medical and Social Aspects*, p. 308. Springfield, Ill.: Charles C. Thomas, 1972.

MCNAMARA, J. J.; MOLOT, M. A.; STREMPLE, J. F.; and CUTTING, R. T. "Coronary Artery Disease in Combat Casualties in Vietnam." *J. Amer. Med. Assoc.* 216 (1971): 1185–87.

NAUGHTON, J. P., and BRUHN, J. "Emotional Stress, Physical Activity and Ischemic Heart Disease." *Disease-A-Month*, July 1970, pp. 3–34.

NAUGHTON, J. P., and HELLERSTEIN, H. K. eds. *Exercise Testing and Exercise Training in Coronary Heart Disease*. New York: Academic Press, 1973.

POLLOCK, M. L. "The Quantification of Endurance Training Programs." In *Exercise and Sport Sciences Reviews*, vol. 1, edited by J. H. Wilmore. New York: Academic Press, 1973.

WILMORE, J. H., and MCNAMARA, J. J. "Prevalence of Coronary Heart Disease Risk Factors in Boys 8 to 12 Years of Age." *J. Pediatrics* 84 (1974): 527–33.

Appendices

A
Strength Exercises

Neck Flexion and Extension ⬆
From a sitting position or a supine position on a bench, attach the appropriate weight to a head harness. Slowly curl or flex the head forward to the chest or extend the head backward as far as it will go.

Shoulder Shrug ▶
Holding the weight with an overhand or pronated grip, arms extended downward from a standing position, shrug the shoulders up and back, attempting to increase the range of joint movement with successive repetitions.

Military or Overhead Press ◀▲

Standing with the feet shoulder-width apart, bend the knees to a 45-degree angle and reach down and grab the bar with an overhand grip, hands spread shoulder-width apart. Lift the weight to the starting position by straightening the legs. As the bar approaches the hips, bend the knees slightly and snap the elbows under the bar. With the back straight, bar at chest level, lift the weight up and over head, locking the elbows out at full extension. Return the bar to the chest level.

Behind-the-Neck Press

Execute exactly as described for the military press, except return the bar behind the head to the back of the neck with each repetition.

Bent Rowing ▶

With the knees bent to a 45-degree angle, bend over at the waist, back parallel to the ground. Grasp the bar with an overhand grip, hands shoulder-width apart. Using the arms only, lift the bar to the chest, and return to the starting position.

Upright Rowing ◀▲

Grab the bar with the hands almost touching, using an overhand grip. Starting with the bar at waist or hip level, lift the bar to the height of the chin, elbows extended outward, and return to the starting position.

221

Lat Machine or Pull-Down
From a seated or kneeling position, grab the bar of the lat machine with an overhand grip, hands shoulder-width apart. Pull the bar down until it touches the base of the neck and shoulders, and return to the starting position.

Triceps Extension
From a standing position, hands close together in an overhand grip, bar of the lat machine at eye level, pull or press the bar downward through the full range of motion, and return to the starting position.

Lateral Arm Raise
With one dumbbell in each hand, arms hanging downward to the side of the body, raise both arms out to the side of the body to an overhead position, keeping the elbows locked in extension. Return to the starting position.

Bent-Arm Pull-Over ◀

Lying supine on the bench, with the barbell in an overhand grasp, hands shoulder-width apart, and with the barbell over head, lower it slowly over and behind the head, as far back as possible, and return to the starting position.

Biceps Curl ▶

Grasp the bar shoulder-width apart, using an underhand grip. Bring the bar to a position of rest against the thighs, elbows fully extended, and feet spread shoulder-width apart. Using only the arms, raise the bar to the chest and return to the starting position. Keep the back straight, and always return to a position with the elbows fully extended.

Dumbbell Curl ◀▲
Execute in exactly the same manner as the biceps curl, using a dumbbell instead of a barbell.

Bench Press ◀▲
From a supine position on a bench, take the weight with an overhand grip, hands shoulder-width apart, elbows fully extended. Lower the weight to the chest, and return to the starting position.

Incline Press
Execute in exactly the same manner as the bench press, except that the exercise is performed on a bench inclined to approximately a 45-degree angle.

Bar Dip
Starting with the weight supported by both arms extended on two bars, lower the body until the upper and lower arm form a 90-degree angle, and return to the starting position.

Back Hyperextension
Starting from the prone position, lying over the edge of a table, with a partner holding the legs, hold a weight behind the head and neck, and lower the head toward the floor. Raise the head, arching the back as much as possible, and return to the starting position.

Trunk Extension and Hip Flexion
With the feet spread shoulder-width apart, knees locked, and the barbell resting on the back of the neck, bend forward at the hips until the trunk is parallel to the floor, and return to the starting position.

Weighted Sit-Ups
From the supine position, with a weight behind the head and neck, knees bent to a 90-degree angle, curl the head and trunk forward to an upright sitting position, and return to the starting position. A somewhat similar exercise can be performed without a weight by using an inclined board.

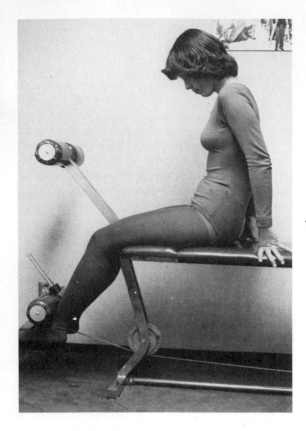

▶ Knee Extension
Sitting on the edge of the leg extension machine with the knee flexed to a 90-degree angle, extend the knee outward, until it locks out in full extension, then return to the starting position.

Knee Flexion ▶
Using a leg machine, assume a prone position, legs extended. Flex at the knee joint through the range of motion, and return to the starting position.

Stiff Leg Dead Lift

Start with the bar at waist height, overhand grip, hands and feet shoulder-width apart. Slowly bend forward at the hips, knees locked, until the trunk is parallel with the ground. Return to the starting position.

Squat

Standing erect, with the weight balanced comfortably across the top of the shoulders, using an overhand grip, hands spread shoulder-width apart, lower the weight by bending at the knees to a 90-degree angle, and return to the starting position. Keep the back straight.

Hack Squat

Follow the instructions for the squat, except hold the bar behind the legs, and elevate the heels on a block of wood.

Toe Raise

Standing erect, with the balls of the feet on a block of wood, assume the same position described for the squat. Rise up on the toes as far as possible, and return to a position where the heels are slightly lower than the block of wood.

B
Warm-up and Flexibility Exercises

Before beginning any training session, the muscles and joints of the body need to be loosened and stretched. The following illustrate simple, yet effective, exercises for accomplishing this purpose.

Head Rotation ▶
Standing up straight, with hands on hips and feet spread shoulder-width apart, slowly rotate the head clockwise in a full circle. Reverse to a counter-clockwise direction.

Chest and Shoulder Stretch ▼
Standing erect, arms bent in front of chest at shoulder height, with finger tips touching shoulders, pull the elbows back as far as possible, and return to the starting position. Then, swing the arms outward and sideward, and return them to the original position.

Trunk Rotation
Standing up straight, with feet placed shoulder-width apart and hands behind the head, rotate the trunk as far as possible to the right and return, then to the left and return. Move at a moderate pace, and try to gradually increase the range of movement.

Half-Knee Bend and Trunk Rotation
Standing up straight with feet together and hands on hips, bend the knees to a half-sit position, extend the arms out in front, and twist the trunk to the right. Return to the original position, and repeat this movement to the left.

Side Body Bend
Standing up straight, with feet placed shoulder-width apart and arms extended overhead, bend the trunk slowly to the left as far as it can go, and then return to the starting position. Repeat the same motion to the right. Again, try to increase the range of movement, gradually.

Side Leg Raise ◄

Lying on the floor on the right side with the head resting on the extended right arm, lift the leg upward to approximately a 45-degree angle. Hold in this position for 3–5 sec then return to the starting position. Repeat on the opposite side.

Modified Push-Up ►

With a limited upper-body strength, start with the modified push-up. Lie flat on the stomach, hands in a position to push the trunk upward, and the legs bent upward at the knees. Keeping the back straight and in line with the buttocks, raise the trunk until the arms are fully extended at the elbow. Lower the body to a position where the chest just touches the floor, and then push back up to the fully extended position. This exercise is to be done with the arms only, so immobilize the rest of the body.

Full Push-Up ◀
Once you have mastered thirty repetitions of the modified push-up, you have the strength to perform the full push-up. Perform this exercise exactly as you did the modified version, except now use the toes, and not the knees, as the point of support. This forces you to lift a greater percentage of your body weight.

Head and Shoulder Curl ▼
Lie on the back with the legs fully extended in front. Place the hands behind either the head or neck. Now, slowly curl the head and shoulders up to about a 45-degree angle as illustrated in the figure. Hold this position for about 5 sec, and then return to the starting position.

Full Sit-Up ◄◄

Start in the same position as the head and shoulder curl, lying on the back, but this time bend the knees to a 90-degree angle. With the hands behind the head, curl the head, shoulders, and trunk slowly upward to a full sitting position and touch one of the knees with the opposite elbow. Return slowly to the starting position and repeat. Start with ten repetitions and gradually build up to forty.

Trunk Lifter ◄◄

Lying on the stomach with the hands behind the head and a partner holding the feet, slowly extend the trunk upward as far as possible and hold in this position for 3–5 sec.

Leg Lifter ◄►
Lying on the stomach with a partner holding down the back, lift the right leg up as high as possible keeping the stomach and hips pressed flat against the floor. Hold in this position for 3–5 sec, and then return to the original position. Repeat with the left leg.

Hip-Flexor Stretch ◄►
Lying on the back, bring the right knee to the chest, grab the leg below the knee, and pull the knee slowly toward the chest. Hold this stretched position for 5 sec, and repeat with the opposite leg. Repeat for a total of five repetitions for each leg.

◀ **Lower-Back Stretch**
Lying on the back, bring both knees to the chest, grab each leg below the knee, and pull both knees slowly toward the shoulder. Hold this stretched position for 5 sec, and repeat for a total of five repetitions.

Upper-Trunk Stretcher ▼
Lying on the stomach, push the upper body off the mat to a position where the arms are fully extended. Concentrate on keeping the pelvis or hips flat on the floor. Hold in this stretched position for 5 sec, and repeat for a total of five repetitions.

◀ **Hamstring Stretcher**
Sitting on the floor with the legs extended out in front, force the knees flat against the floor, grab behind the knees, and slowly pull the head down toward the knees. Do not bounce or bob, but move slowly. Hold in this stretched position for 5 sec, and repeat for a total of five repetitions.

Lower-Leg and Heel Stretcher
Standing approximately 3 ft from a wall, extend the arms out, touching the wall, and gradually let the body lean forward toward the wall, keeping the feet planted firmly on the ground. You will feel the stretch in the lower leg and heel area. Hold in the stretched position for 5 sec, and repeat for a total of five repetitions.

Back Arch
Kneeling on the hands and knees, with the knees 3–4 in. apart directly under the hips, and the arms directly under the shoulders, drop the head forward, contract the stomach and buttocks muscles, and arch the lower back. Hold in this position for 3–5 sec, and then relax, repeating for a total of five repetitions.

Abdominal Stretch ◄

Starting in the kneeling position identical to that explained above for the back arch, swing the trunk forward over the shoulders, bend the elbows and lower the chest to the floor. Then, extend the arms forward, lower the head and raise the buttocks as high as possible by arching the back. Hold in this position for 5 sec, then relax, and repeat for a total of five repetitions.

Bar Hang ►

Locate a bar or some other suitable object that is just slightly taller than the extended reach. Use a stool or jump up and grab the bar, and then hang from the bar for 20–30 sec. Repeat for a total of two repetitions.

Back and Hip Stretcher ◆
Lying on the back with the arms extended to the sides, tilt the hips upward and bring the knees up and toward the head, keeping the arms and back pressed firmly against the floor. Hold in this stretched position for 5 sec, and then relax, repeating a total of three times.

Lower-Trunk Stretcher ◆
Lying flat on the stomach, reach back and grab the ankles, arch the back and pull the head up slowly as high as possible. Hold in this position for 5 sec, then relax, and repeat for a total of three repetitions.

Upper-Back Stretcher ◀▬

Lying flat on the back with the arms extended along the side of the body, raise the legs up and over the head and, keeping the knees locked in an extended position, attempt to touch the floor behind the head. Keep the back and arms flat on the floor. Hold in this position for 5 sec, then relax, and repeat for a total of three repetitions.

Kneeling Back Bend ▼▬

Kneeling with both knees and ankles on the floor, very slowly lean backward, attempting to touch the head to the floor. This should be attempted only after having developed above-average flexibility. Repeat for a total of three repetitions.

Sitting Groin Stretch
Sitting with the soles of the feet touching and the knees pointing outward, slowly push down on the knees, attempting to gradually, over time, push them to the floor. Hold in the stretched position for 5 sec, then relax, and repeat for a total of three repetitions.

Toe Pointer
Kneeling on the ankles and knees, slowly sit back on the heels with the ankles stretched backward. Gradually raise the knees from the floor. Hold in a stretched position for 5 sec, then relax, and repeat for a total of three repetitions.

C
Field Tests for Assessing Physical Fitness

INTRODUCTION

An extensive physical fitness assessment of athletes and the fitness-conscious public is available through elaborate testing facilities in human performance laboratories at most major universities and colleges, in some hospitals and research institutes, and even in several high schools. Unfortunately, however, these laboratory facilities can not meet the volume of tests requested by coaches, athletes, and the general population. As a result, field tests of the various components of physical fitness and athletic performance must be relied on. A field test is a simple test, which requires minimum equipment and facilities but which provides an accurate estimate of a particular component. This appendix includes one, or more, field tests for each of the basic components discussed in Section B, Fundamentals of Physical Training, of this book.

STRENGTH

Strength can be easily assessed by the one-repetition maximum test (1-RM). The basic muscle or muscle group to be tested is selected and the individual is given a series of trials to determine the greatest weight that he can lift just once for that particular lift. If the individual is an inexperienced weight lifter, this test is conducted largely through trial and error. Start with a weight that the individual can lift comfortably, then keep adding weight until he can lift the weight correctly just one time. If he can lift this weight more than once, more weight should be added until a true 1-RM is reached. While 1-RM's can be obtained for any basic weight-training exercise, test batteries usually select three or four exercises that represent the body's major muscle groups. Table C–1 gives a series of values for selected strength exercises for both males and females on the basis of body weight. While the strength requirements will differ for each sport or activity, and even by position within each sport, these values represent optimal values for the average athlete who is training mainly for general fitness. Specific standards for each sport have yet to be developed.

Additional strength tests are available using dynamometers, cable tensiometers, and elaborate force transducers and recorders. These tests, however, require expensive equipment and do not cause any substantial improvement in measurement accuracy. Refer to a recent text in measurement and evaluation [e.g., Baumgartner and Jackson, 1975] for additional information on these laboratory-types of tests.

POWER

Power is the application of strength through the dimension of time. Power can be assessed very accurately within the laboratory, using expensive force transducers and recorders.

TABLE C–1. Optimal Strength Values for Various Body Weights
(Based on the 1-RM test)

Body Weight lb	Bench Press Male	Bench Press Female	Standing Press Male	Standing Press Female	Curl Male	Curl Female	Leg Press Male	Leg Press Female
80	80	56	53	37	40	28	160	112
100	100	70	67	47	50	35	200	140
120	120	84	80	56	60	42	240	168
140	140	98	93	65	70	49	280	196
160	160	112	107	75	80	56	320	224
180	180	126	120	84	90	63	360	252
200	200	140	133	93	100	70	400	280
220	220	154	147	103	110	77	440	308
240	240	168	160	112	120	84	480	336

Several field tests have been proposed but lack objective validation. The sitting shotput and medicine ball throw have been used to estimate upper-body power, while the standing long jump and vertical jump have been used to estimate lower-body power. Unfortunately, standards for these tests have not been established.

The Margaria-Kalamen leg-power test (Mathews and Fox, 1971) represents a more objective measure of lower-body power. The subject begins by standing six meters in front of a series of steps. On command, he runs as quickly as possible up the stairs, stepping on every third step. A microswitch embedded in a rubber mat is placed on the third step and activates a timer when the subject hits this step. A second microswitch is placed on the ninth step, which stops the timer when hit (Figure C–1). The elapsed time represents the time required to move the body weight the vertical distance between the third and ninth steps. Power is then calculated by the formula,

$$\text{Power (kg} \times \text{meters/sec)} = \frac{\text{Body weight (kg)} \times \text{vertical distance (meters)}}{\text{elapsed time (sec)}}$$

Standards for power on the basis of the Margaria-Kalamen leg-power test have not yet been calculated. Costill et al. (1968) tested a group of college football players using the original version of this test.

MUSCULAR ENDURANCE

Muscular endurance has been measured in a number of different ways, including the greatest number of sit-ups that can be performed in a fixed period of time (usually 30 sec or 1 min) or the maximum number of push-ups, pull-ups, or bar dips that can be performed continuously in an indefinite time period. Many of these tests penalize the participant who has long legs, short arms, or a heavy body weight. To eliminate this bias, a concept has evolved that uses a fixed percentage of the individual's body weight as the resistance. The individual lifts this weight as many times as possible, until he reaches the point of fatigue or exhaustion. Firm guidelines have yet to be established for the percentages of the individual's body weight in relation to the muscle groups tested. In fact, it is debatable whether the weight used in the test should be a fixed percentage of the individual's body weight or a fixed percentage of the individual's 1-RM or absolute strength. For example, if the endurance test for the bench press movement were conducted using 50 percent of the individual's body weight as the resistance, a 180-lb man would be asked to lift 90 lb as many times as he could. A strong man of this body weight would be able to lift this 90-lb weight twenty, or more, times, while a relatively weak man who weighed 180 lb might not be able to lift the 90-lb weight even one time, i.e., the desig-

Switch mat
9th step

1.05 meters
vertical
distance (D)

6th step

Switch mat

3rd step

A ← 6 meters →

Clock 0.01 sec

FIGURE C–1

The Margaria-Kalamen leg-power test. (From D. K. Mathews and E. L. Fox, Physiological Basis of Physical Education and Athletics. *Philadelphia: W. C. Saunders Co., 1971. Reproduced by permission of the publisher.)*

nated weight exceeds his 1-RM. In this case, the test for muscular endurance would be highly dependent on strength. To isolate muscular endurance as a pure component, so that the test is not so dependent on the individual's strength, it is advocated that the test battery be established on the basis of the individual's strength and not his body weight.

In accordance with the above recommendation, it is suggested that a fixed percentage of 70 percent of the maximum strength be used to test muscle endurance. This percentage would be the same for all movements tested. Since this is a relatively new concept, norms or standards have yet to be established, but they could be easily established for each specific population to be tested. On the basis of limited test data, the recreational athlete or health-seeking exerciser should be able to perform twelve to fifteen repetitions, and the competitive athlete, twenty to twenty-five repetitions at 70 percent of his or her maximum strength for each of the movements tested.

SPEED

Speed can be estimated simply by measuring the time it takes to cover a set distance. This can be accomplished for the individual body segments, such as for the arm or leg, by using an elaborate system of microswitches and an electronic timer. The limb is placed on the first microswitch, and when the movement starts, the microswitch contact is broken, starting the timer. When the limb has travelled a set distance, the clock is stopped when the limb makes contact with a second microswitch. Total body speed can be measured by timing the athlete over a set distance from 20–100 yd. Again, norms or standards have not been established and would vary considerably by sex, age, body size, and sport. It is suggested that each sport or activity, and position within each sport, have its own standards for optimal performance. Many coaches have already done this for football (40-yd-dash time) and baseball (90-ft-dash or circle-the-bases time).

In order to differentiate speed into its two components, acceleration and peak velocity, the reader should refer to Chapter 5, where this was discussed at some length.

AGILITY

The concept of agility is difficult to precisely define operationally, even though there is general agreement among most coaches, athletes, and researchers as to what is meant by the term agility. Agility, typically, refers to the ability to move and change body position or directions rapidly, without losing balance or sacrificing speed. Agility is exemplified by the shifty halfback on a broken field run in football, or the supple gymnast, performing a complex, free-exercise routine. Unfortunately, there are no universally acccptcd tcsts of agility, although many test batteries exist, which use various shuttle run tests to estimate the agility component. While shuttle run tests have some merit, they are largely tests of speed and are far removed from assessing what is traditionally thought of in the athletic world as agility. This is an area where new tests or test batteries are needed. Refer to a standard measurement and evaluation text for examples of existing tests of agility [Baumgartner and Jackson, 1975].

FLEXIBILITY

Probably the most accurate tests of flexibility presently available, are those that assess the actual range of motion of the various joints. While this is easily accomplished by instruments such as the Leighton Flexometer and the electrogoniometer (illustrated in Chapter 5), these pieces of equipment are not readily available. Simple field tests include the sit-and-reach test (see Figure 5–2) and the back-hyperextension test (Figure C–2).

In the sit-and-reach test, the individual sits with his legs extended directly in front of him and the back of his knees pressed against the floor. The feet are placed against a stool to which a yard stick is attached, with the 14 in. mark placed at the point where the foot contacts the stool. The individual places the index fingers of both hands together and reaches forward slowly, as far as possible. The distance reached is noted on the yardstick and recorded. The knees must be kept in contact with the floor, and bouncing is to be discouraged. Standards for an athletic population are presented in Table C–2. Obviously, this test will be influenced by the length of the arms and legs of the individual, in addition to his or her flexibility.

The back hyperextension test is performed with the individual in the prone position, lying on the floor. With the individual's feet being held in place, the individual arches his back and lifts his chest and chin as far off the floor as possible (Figure C–2). The distance between the floor and the sternal notch is measured. Then, the individual sits on the floor with his back and buttocks against a wall, and the distance between the floor and sternal notch is measured again. The flexibility score is determined by the following equation:

$$\text{Back hyperextension} = \frac{\text{hyperextension height}}{\text{seated sternal height}} \times 100$$

Dividing the hyperextension height attained by the seated sternal hcight provides an estimate of the angle of flexibility, and partially negates the advantage of having a long trunk. Standards for the back hyperextension test are presented in Table C–2.

CARDIOVASCULAR ENDURANCE CAPACITY

Aerobic, or cardiovascular endurance capacity can be estimated on the basis of an endurance-run test. The Balke 1.5-mi run is suggested for general use by older adolescents and adults. For children and young adolescents, a shorter test of approximately 1.0 mi would be more appropriate. Running for a fixed distance has a distinct administrative advantage over a test

FIGURE C–2
Back hyperextension test.

that is based on the distance covered in a fixed time. With a fixed distance, each individual ends the test at the same place and scoring is accomplished simply by taking the time needed to complete that distance. Literally, hundreds of individuals can be tested simultaneously when a fixed distance is used. Table C–3 lists the various 1.5-mi run times and the estimated equivalent $\dot{V}O_2$ max. Previous studies have shown from moderate to high correlations, i.e., approximately r = 0.60 to r = 0.90, between running performance tests and $\dot{V}O_2$ max.

TABLE C–2. Standards for the Sit-and-Reach, and the Back-Hyperextension Flexibility Tests

	Sit-and-Reach	*Back Hyperextension*
Excellent	22 inches or greater	56 or greater
Good	20–21 inches	46–55
Average	14–18 inches	36–45
Fair	12–13 inches	26–35
Poor	11 inches or less	25 or less

From *Health Improvement Program*, National Athletic Health Institute, Inglewood, Calif. Reproduced by permission.

TABLE C–3. Estimated $\dot{V}O_2$ max for 1.5 Mile Endurance-Run Time* †

Time min:sec	Estimated $\dot{V}O_2$ max ml/kg × min
7:30 and under	75
7:31– 8:00	72
8:01– 8:30	67
8:31– 9:00	62
9:01– 9:30	58
9:31–10:00	55
10:01–10:30	52
10:31–11:00	49
11:01–11:30	46
11:31–12:00	44
12:01–12:30	41
12:31–13:00	39
13:01–13:30	37
13:31–14:00	36
14:01–14:30	34
14:31–15:00	33
15:01–15:30	31
15:31–16:00	30
16:01–16:30	28
16:31–17:00	27
17:01–17:30	26
17:31–18:00	25

* Adapted from K. H. Cooper, "A Means of Asessing Maximal Oxygen Intake," *J. Amer. Med. Assoc.* 203 (1968): 201–204.
† Refer to Table C–4 for a rating of the estimated $\dot{V}O_2$ max.

The 1.5-mi test can be run on either a track or on a 1.5 mi nonrepeating course. The latter may be preferred to assure that each individual covers a full 1.5 mi and does not stop a lap or two short. This test should be given only to those who are in condition or have been conditioned to run the distance. Pretraining is essential and will help resolve problems of pacing frequently encountered in endurance-running tests. Those over twenty-five to thirty years of age should not be encouraged to take this test until they have had a stress electrocardiogram (see Chapter 13) and been diagnosed as normal, in addition to having a routine physical examination.

BODY COMPOSITION

The individual's body composition can be most accurately estimated by the underwater weighing technique. While it is usually a laboratory technique, underwater weighing can be used as a field test also (see Figure 7–7). For the purposes of this book, it is assumed that the residual volume will not be assessable for measurement. It is possible in college-age individuals or younger to use an assumed constant residual volume without sacrificing too much accuracy. Estimated residual volumes by age and sex are listed in Table C-5.

TABLE C–4. Range of Maximal Oxygen Uptake Values with Age*

Age Group (yr)	Maximal Oxygen Uptake, ml/kg·min				
	Low	Fair	Average	Good	High
10–19	below 38	38–46	47–56	57–66	above 66
20–29	below 33	33–42	43–52	53–62	above 62
30–39	below 30	30–38	39–48	49–58	above 58
40–49	below 26	26–35	36–44	45–54	above 54
50–59	below 24	24–33	34–41	42–50	above 50
60–69	below 22	22–30	31–38	39–46	above 46
70–79	below 20	20–27	28–35	36–42	above 42

* Since females are generally 20 percent lower on the average compared to males, normal values for females can be obtained by shifting over one category to the right, e.g., the "fair" category for males would be considered "good" for females.

TABLE C–5. Estimated Residual Lung Volumes by Sex and Age

Age yr	Estimated Residual Volume (liters)
Females	
6–10	0.60
11–15	0.80
16–20	1.00
21–25	1.20
26–30	1.40
Males	
6–10	0.90
11–15	1.10
16–20	1.30
21–25	1.50
26–30	1.70

A scale is attached to the diving board or is hung from some other form of support, approximately 18–24 in. from the edge of the pool, at a point where the water is at least 3 ft deep. The scale should be accurately calibrated prior to use, by hanging known weights from it and noting the readings. Since the residual lung volume is measured in liters, weight must also be expressed in metric units, i.e., kilograms (weight in pounds divided by 2.205). The individual to be assessed sits on a chair, a weight, or some other type of seat suspended from the scale, or simply hangs from a rope or chain attached to the scale. The underwater weight of the individual is determined by having him totally submerge, exhaling as he goes under water. The highest weight attained at the conclusion of his maximal exhalation represents his gross underwater weight. A minimum of five to 10 trials should be given each individual, since it takes practice and experience before an accurate weight can be obtained. The average of the two or three heaviest trials is selected as the representative gross weight for that individual. The weight of the seat, chain, or other supporting material must then be subtracted from the gross weight in order to obtain the individual's actual, or net, weight underwater. Body density is then calculated as follows:

$$\text{Density} = \frac{\text{Body weight}}{\text{Body volume}}$$

Body Volume =

$$\frac{[\text{Weight (kg)} - \text{net underwater weight (kg)}]}{\text{density of water}}$$

$$- \text{estimated residual volume}$$

Since most pools are heated to approximately 76–78°F, a constant density of water of 0.997 will be used.

$$\text{Relative fat (\%)} = [(495/\text{density}) - 450]$$

$$\text{Fat weight} = \text{Weight} \times \text{Relative fat}/100$$

$$\text{Lean weight} = \text{Weight} - \text{Fat weight}$$

As an example of the above calculations, a male 18 years of age weighs 180 lb and has a net underwater weight of 8 lb. His estimated residual volume from Table C–5 would be 1.30 liters. His body composition would be calculated as follows:

$$\text{Weight} = 180 \text{ lb} = 81.6 \text{ kg}$$

$$\text{Net underwater weight} = 8 \text{ lb} = 3.6 \text{ kg}$$

Volume =

$$\frac{(81.6 - 3.6)}{0.997} - 1.3 = 78.2 - 1.3 = 76.9$$

$$\text{Density} = \frac{76.9}{81.6} = 1.061$$

Relative fat (%) =
$$[(495/1.061) - 450] = 466.5 - 450 = 16.5\%$$

$$\text{Fat weight} = 16.5\% \times 180 \text{ lb}/100 = 29.7 \text{ lb}$$

$$\text{Lean weight} = 180 \text{ lb} - 29.7 = 150.3 \text{ lb}$$

Anthropometric measurements can also be used to estimate the various components of body composition, i.e., body density, relative or absolute fat, and lean body weight. Skinfold thicknesses, body diameters or breadths, and body circumferences or girths have been used in the past with reasonable accuracy to estimate body composition. Table C–6 lists a series

TABLE C–6. Equations Based on Sex and Age for Determining Body Composition

Age (yr)	Equation	Study
Females		
9–12	Density = 1.079 − (0.043 × log of scapula skinfold*)	Parízková (1961)
13–16	Density = 1.102 − (0.058 × log of scapula skinfold*)	Parízková (1961)
17–35	Lean weight (kg) = 8.63 + [0.68 × weight (kg)] − [0.16 × scapula skinfold] − [0.10 × triceps skinfold] − [0.05 × thigh skinfold]	Wilmore and Behnke (1970)
Males		
9–12	Density = 1.094 − (0.054 × log of scapula skinfold*)	Parízková (1961)
13–16	Density = 1.131 − (0.083 × log of triceps skinfold*)	Parízková (1961)
17–35	Lean weight (kg) = 10.26 + [0.793 × weight (kg)] − [0.368 × abdominal skinfold]	Wilmore and Behnke (1969)
36–67	Lean weight (kg) = 6.14 + [0.84 × weight (kg)] − [0.63 × midaxillary skinfold]	Lewis et al. (1975)

* Take the log of the skinfold from a table of logarithms and multiply it by the designated constant.

of equations derived by various authors for different ages and both sexes. When estimating body composition, select an equation representative of the population to be tested.

The anatomical landmarks for the various sites are illustrated in Figures C–3 and C–4 and described as follows:

Scapula.   Inferior angle of the scapula with the fold running parallel to the axillary border.

Triceps.   Midway between the acromion and olecranon processes on the posterior aspect

FIGURE C–3

Skinfold measurement sites. (From Albert R. Behnke and Jack H. Wilmore, Evaluation and Regulation of Body Build and Composition, © 1974, p. 28. Reprinted by permission of Prentice-Hall, Inc., Englewood Cliffs, New Jersey.)

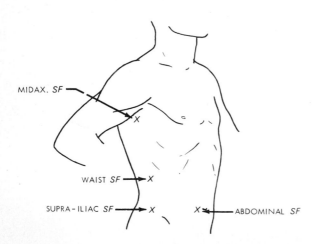

FIGURE C–4

Skinfold measurement sites. (From Albert R. Behnke and Jack H. Wilmore, Evaluation and Regulation of Body Build and Composition, © 1974, p. 28. Reprinted by permission of Prentice-Hall, Inc., Englewood Cliffs, New Jersey.)

FIGURE C–5

Technique for obtaining the triceps skinfold thickness. (From Albert R. Behnke and Jack H. Wilmore, Evaluation and Regulation of Body Build and Composition, © 1974, p. 28. Reprinted by permission of Prentice-Hall, Inc., Englewood Cliffs, New Jersey.)

of the arm, the arm held vertically, with the fold running parallel to the length of the arm.

Midaxillary. Vertical fold on the midaxillary line approximately at the level of the fifth rib.

Abdominal. Horizontal fold adjacent to the umbilicus.

Thigh. Vertical fold on the anterior aspect of the thigh midway between the hip and knee joints.

A special caliper* is used to assess the fat that lies directly beneath the skin. The skinfold is grasped firmly by the thumb and index finger, and the caliper is placed on the exact site ½ to 1 in. from the thumb and finger (Figure C–5).

Once one of the body composition parameters is assessed, the remaining parameters can be estimated by using the relationships defined earlier. As an example of this, if lean weight were estimated from selected measurements, fat weight would be the difference between the total body weight and lean weight, and relative fat would be calculated by the ratio of fat weight to total weight multiplied by 100 to convert from decimal to percentage.

---

* The Harpenden caliper (No. 3496) is recommended. Quinton Instruments, 2121 Terry Ave., Seattle, Wash. 98121.

REFERENCES

BAUMGARTNER, T. A., and JACKSON, A. S. *Measurement for Evaluation in Physical Education.* Boston: Houghton Mifflin Co., 1975.

BEHNKE, A. R., and WILMORE, J. H. *Evaluation and Regulation of Body Build and Composition.* Englewood Cliffs, N.J.: Prentice-Hall, 1974.

COSTILL, D. L.; HOFFMAN, W. M.; KEHOE, F.; MILLER, S. J.; and MEYERS, W. C. "Maximum Anaerobic Power Among College Football Players." *J. Sports Med. Physical Fitness* 8 (1968): 103–6.

LEWIS, S.; HASKELL, W. L.; KLEIN, H.; HALPERN, J.; and WOOD, P. O. "Prediction of Body Composition in Habitually Active Middle-aged Men." *J. Appl. Physiol.* 39 (1975): 221–5.

MATHEWS, D. K., and FOX, E. L. *The Physiological Basis of Physical Education and Athletics.* Philadelphia: W. B. Saunders Co., 1971.

PARÍZKOVÁ, J. "Total Body Fat and Skinfold Thickness in Children." *Metabolism* 10 (1961): 794–807.

WILMORE, J. H., and BEHNKE, A. R. "An Anthropometric Estimation of Body Density and Lean Body Weight in Young Men." *J. Appl. Physiol.* 27 (1969): 25–31.

WILMORE, J. H., and BEHNKE, A. R. "An Anthropometric Estimation of Body Density and Lean Body Weight in Young Women." *Amer. J. Clin. Nutr.* 23 (1970): 267–74.

Glossary of Terms

Acceleration: rate of change in velocity.

Acclimatization: adaptation to a particular environmental stress.

Acid-base balance: the proper balance of H and OH ions in the blood.

Acidosis: the situation in which the acid-base balance shifts to the acid side, due either to increased levels of unbuffered acids in the blood or to a reduction in the blood bicarbonates.

Actin: thin protein filament that acts with the protein filament myosin to allow muscle contraction.

Action potential: the change in the electrical potential across the cell or tissue membrane.

Acute: referring to something immediate or of short duration, e.g., a treadmill run to exhaustion would be an acute bout of exercise.

Adipose tissue: connective tissue in which fat is stored.

Adolescence: developmental period of time between the onset of puberty and the attainment of full physiological maturity.

ADP: adenosine diphosphate. A high energy phosphate compound from which ATP is synthesized.

Adrenal glands: endocrine glands located directly above each ·kidney, composed of the medulla (the hormones epinephrine and norepinephrine) and the cortex (cortical hormones).

Adrenaline: see epinephrine.

Adrenocorticotrophic hormone (ATCH): a pituitary hormone responsible for controlling the hormones released by the adrenal cortex.

Aerobic: in the presence of air or oxygen.

Aerobic power: synonomous with the terms maximal oxygen uptake, maximal oxygen consumption and cardiovascular endurance capacity.

Afferent nerve: sensory nerve that carries impulses from the sensory receptors, e.g., skin, eyes, ears, to the central nervous system.

Agility: the ability to change directions rapidly while maintaining total body balance and awareness of body position.

Aldosterone: hormone from the adrenal cortex responsible for sodium retention.

Alkaline reserve: the amount of bicarbonate in the blood available for buffering acids.

Alkalosis: the situation in which the acid-base balance shifts to the alkaline, or basic, side.

Alveolar air: that air present in the alveoli which is involved in the exchange of gases with the blood in the pulmonary capillaries.

Alveoli: small air sacs, located at the termination of the pulmonary tree, in which the exchange of respiratory gases takes place with the blood in the adjacent capillaries.

Amino acids: the basic building blocks of protein.

Amphetamine: prescription drug that stimulates the central nervous system.

Anabolic steroid: a prescription drug that has the anabolic or growth-stimulating characteristics of the male androgen, testosterone. Frequently taken by athletes to increase body size and muscle bulk.

Anabolism: the building up of body tissue.

Anaerobic: in the absence of oxygen.

Anaerobic threshold: that point where the metabolic demands of exercise cannot be met totally by available aerobic sources and at which an increase in anaerobic metabolism occurs, as reflected by an increase in the blood lactate.

Androgen: male sex hormone from the testis, and, in limited amounts, from the adrenal cortex.

Anemia: inadequate number of red blood cells, or low hemoglobin levels, limiting oxygen transport.

Angina pectoris: chest pain associated with a lack of blood to the heart.

Angstrom: unit of measure equal to 10^{-8} cm.

Anorexia: inadequate apetite, which, if chronic, e.g., anorexia nervousa, can lead to eventual death.

Anoxia: inadequate oxygen in the blood or tissues.

Anthropometry: the study of body measurements.

Antidiuretic hormone: hormone from the posterior pituitary gland, which promotes water retention through its action on the kidney.

Arteriole: a small artery that regulates the flow of blood from the arteries to the capillaries.

Arteriosclerosis: loss of elasticity of the arteries, or hardening of the arteries. The precursor to various diseases of the cardiovascular system, e.g., stroke and coronary artery disease.

Artery: a vessel which transports blood away from the heart.

Aspartates: potassium and magnesium salts of aspartic acid.

Athlete's heart: an enlarged heart, typically found in endurance athletes, due, primarily, to hypertrophy of the left ventricle. It is no longer considered to be a pathological or diseased condition, as it once was.

ATP: adenosine triphosphate. A high-energy compound from which the body derives its energy.

Atrium: one of the chambers of the heart. The right atrium receives blood from the systemic circulation, and the left atrium receives blood from the pulmonary circulation.

Atrophy: loss of size, or mass, of body tissue, e.g., muscle atrophy with disuse.

Autonomic nervous system: that portion of the nervous system that controls involuntary activity, e.g., smooth muscle and the myocardium, and includes both sympathetic and parasympathetic nerves.

Axis cylinder: the central core of the axon of the nerve fiber.

Axon: the fiber-like extension of the nerve cell, which transmits the nerve impulse away from the cell body.

Balance: the ability to have complete control of the body as it is moved through space.

Basal metabolic rate (BMR): the rate of body metabolism under the most optimal conditions of quiet, rest, and relaxation. The lowest rate of metabolism compatible with life.

Blood pressure: the force that blood exerts against the walls of the blood vessels or heart.

Body density: the density of the body is equal to the body weight divided by the body volume.

Bronchiole: small terminal branch of the bronchus.

Bronchus: the subdivision of the trachea, as it splits into two branches.

Buffer: a substance in the blood that combines with either acids or bases to maintain a constant acid-base, or pH, balance.

Calorie: a unit of heat energy defined as the amount of heat required to raise the temperature of one kilogram of water 1° C, from 15 to 16° C.

Calorimeter: a device for measuring the heat production of the body or of specific chemical reactions.

Capillaries: the smallest vessels in the vascular system which connect the arterioles and venules, where all exchanges of gases or materials between the circulatory system and the tissues or lungs take place.

Carbohydrate: a food substance that includes various sugars and starches and is found in the body in the form of glucose and glycogen.

Cardiac: relating to the heart, e.g., cardiac muscle and cardiac output.

Cardiac muscle: the myocardium, or muscle, of the heart.

Cardiac output: output, or volume, of blood pumped by the heart per minute. The product of heart rate and stroke volume.

Cardiovascular endurance capacity: the term used to define overall body endurance, or stamina. See aerobic power or maximal oxygen uptake.

Catabolism: the tearing down, or destruction, of body tissue.

Catalyst: a chemical substance that initiates or accelerates a chemical action without being altered as a result of the action.

Central nervous system: that division of the nervous system that includes the brain and spinal cord.

Cerebellum: the hindbrain, responsible for the smooth coordination of body movements.

Cerebral cortex: the portion of the brain that contains the primary and supplementary motor areas which control all movement patterns of a voluntary nature.

Cerebrum: the large forebrain.

Cholesterol: a lipid or fatty substance essential for life and found in various tissues and fluids. Elevated levels in the blood have been associated with an increased risk of cardiovascular disease.

Chronic: referring to something of an extended or long-term nature, e.g., physical training program of six-months duration.

Cinematography: the use of films to analyze movement.

Circuit training: selected exercises or activities performed in sequence, as rapidly as possible.

Collagen: a protein substance found in bones, cartilage, and white fibrous tissues.

Concentric contraction: a muscular contraction in which shortening of the muscle occurs.

Conditioned reflex: a nervous reflex pattern that is learned.

Conduction: transfer of heat or cold through direct contact with an object or medium.

Connective tissue: specialized tissue, such as ligaments and tendons, that connects various body structures.

Convection: the transfer of heat or cold from a body to a moving liquid or gas.

Coordination: the act of movement in an organized, controlled, and precise manner.

Coronary arteries: those arteries that supply the heart muscle or myocardium.

Cortex: refers to the outer layer, e.g., cerebral cortex is the outer layer of the brain.

Cortisol: a hormone from the adrenal cortex.

Creatine phosphate: an energy-rich compound, which plays a critical role in providing energy for muscular contraction.

Dead space: the volume of the various parts of the respiratory system in which no gas exchange occurs.

Dehydration: loss of body fluids.

Dendrite: the projection of the nerve cell that transmits impulses toward the cell body.

Diaphragm: the major muscle of respiration, which separates the thorax from the abdomen.

Diastole: the relaxation phase of each cardiac cycle, immediately following the contraction, or systole, of the heart.

Diastolic pressure: the lowest pressure of the arterial blood against the walls of the vessels or heart resulting from the diastole of the heart.

Diuretic: a substance that increases kidney function leading to a loss of body fluids through frequent urination.

Dynamometer: a device for measuring muscular strength.

Dyspnea: labored breathing.

Eccentric contraction: lengthening of the muscle under tension, as when lowering a heavy object.

Ectomorph: one of three categories of the somatotype in which the body is rated for the degree of linearity.

Edema: filled with fluid.

Effective blood volume: that volume of blood available to supply the exercising muscles.

Efferent nerve: also referred to as a motor nerve or motoneuron. Conducts impulses from the central nervous system to the various end organs, such as muscle.

Electrocardiogram (ECG): a recording of the electrical activity of the heart.

Electrocardograph: an instrument that picks up and produces a record of the electrical activity of the heart.

Electrogoniometer: an electronic device used to measure joint angles and changes in joint angles.

Electrolyte: any solution that conducts electricity by means of its ions.

Electromyogram (EMG): a recording of the electrical activity of a muscle or a group of muscles.

Endocrine gland: a ductless gland that produces and/or releases hormones directly into the blood stream.

Endomorphy: one of three categories of the somatotype in which the body is rated for corpulance or obesity.

Endurance: the ability to resist fatigue. Includes muscular endurance, which is a local or specific endurance, and cardiovascular endurance, which is a more general, total body endurance.

Enzyme: an organic catalyst that speeds the velocity of specific chemical reactions.

Epinephrine: one of the hormones of the adrenal medulla. Also referred to as adrenaline.

Epiphysis: that part of the long bone that ossifies separately before uniting with the main shaft, or diaphysis, of the bone.

Ergogenic aid: substance or phenomenon that elevates or improves physical performance.

Ergograph: an instrument or device used for recording muscular work.

Ergometer: a device for exercising the subject in a manner in which the physical work performed can be measured, e.g., bicycle ergometer.

Estrogen: female sex hormone.

Evaporation: the loss of heat through the conversion of the water in sweat to a vapor.

Exercise prescription: individualizing the exercise program on the basis of the duration, frequency, intensity, and mode of exercise.

External respiration: the process of bringing air into the lungs and the resulting exchange of gas between the alveoli and the capillary blood.

Fartlek training: speed play, where the athlete varies his pace at will from fast sprints to slow jogging; normally performed in the country, using hills.

Fascia: connective tissue surrounding and connecting muscle.

Fast twitch muscle fiber: one of several types of muscle fibers that have low oxidative capacity, high glycolytic capacity, and are associated with speed or power activities.

Fat: a food substance that is composed of gylcerol and fatty acids.

Fatigue: inability to continue work, due to any one or a combination of factors.

Fatty acid: along with glycerol, the product of the breakdown of fats.

Fat weight: absolute amount of body fat. Fat weight plus lean body weight equals total body weight.

Flexibility: the range of movement of a specific joint or a group of joints, influenced by the associated bones and boney structures, muscles, tendons, and ligaments.

Glucagon: a hormone from the pancreas that acts to increase blood glucose, or sugar, levels.

Glucose: a simple sugar which is transported in the blood and metabolized in the tissues.

Glycerol: a substance that combines with fatty acids to form fat.

Glycogen: the storage form of carbohydrates in the body, found predominantly in the muscles and liver.

Glycogen loading: manipulating exercise and diet to optimize the total amount of glycogen stored in the body.

Glycogenolysis: the metabolic breakdown of glycogen.

Glycolysis: breakdown of glycogen to lactic acid.

Golgi tendon organ: a proprioceptor located in series with muscle tendons.

Gonads: endocrine glands responsible for reproduction; the testes in males and ovaries in females.

Growth hormone (GH): a pituitary hormone responsible for controlling tissue growth. Also referred to as somatotrophic hormone.

Heat cramp: severe cramping of the skeletal muscles, due to excessive dehydration and the associated salt loss.

Heat exhaustion: a disorder due to an excessive heat load on the body, characterized by breathlessness, extreme tiredness, dizziness, and rapid pulse, and usually associated with a decrease in sweat production.

Heat stroke: the most serious heat disorder, characterized by a body temperature above 105° F, cessation of sweating, and total confusion or unconsciousness, which can lead to death.

Hematocrit: the relative contribution, or percentage, of the blood cells to the total blood sample.

Hemoconcentration: used in reference to an apparent increase in red blood cell number due to a plasma volume reduction, i.e., there is a relative, but not an absolute, increase.

Hemoglobin: iron pigment of the red blood cell that has a high affinity for oxygen.

Hormone: a chemical substance produced or released by one of the endocrine glands, which is transported by the blood to a specific target organ.

Hyperemia: an excessive amount of blood in a part of the body.

Hyperglycemia: elevated levels of glucose, or sugar, in the blood.

Hyperplasia: increase in size, due to an increase number of cells.

Hypertension: abnormally high blood pressure, usually defined in adults as a systolic pressure in excess of 140 mmHg and/or diastolic pressure in excess of 90 mmHg.

Hyperthermia: overheating.

Hypertrophy: increase in the size, or mass, of an organ or body tissue.

Hyperventilation: breathing rate and/or tidal volume increased above levels necessary for normal function.

Hypoglycemia: abnormally low blood glucose, or sugar, levels.

Hypotension: an abnormally low blood pressure.

Hypothalamus: that region of the brain involved in controlling or releasing many of the hormones of the pituitary gland.

Hypoxia: a lack of oxygen in the blood or tissues.

Inhibition: negative nervous control to restrict, or limit, the amount of force generated.

Innervation ratio: the ratio of the number of muscle fibers per motoneuron.

Insulin: a hormone produced by the pancreas that assists in the control of the blood sugar, or glucose, levels.

Internal respiration: the exchange of gases between the blood and tissues.

Interval training: training program that alternates bouts of heavy or very heavy work with periods of rest or light work.

In vitro: functioning outside of, or detached from, the body.

In vivo: functioning within the body.

Ion: an electrically charged atom or group of atoms.

Ischemia: a temporary deficiency of blood to a specific area of the body.

Isokinetic contraction: contraction in which the muscle generates force against a variable resistance.

Isometric contraction: contraction in which the muscle generates force, but there is no observable movement, e.g., pushing against a building.

Isotonic contraction: contraction in which the muscle generates force against a constant resistance and movement results, either shortening (concentric) or lengthening (eccentric).

Kinesthesis: a sense, or awareness, of body position.

Lactic acid: the end product of glycolysis, or anaerobic metabolism.

Latent period: period of time between the stimulus and the response to that stimulus.

Lean body weight: determined by subtracting the fat weight from the total body weight. That weight of the body which is not fat, e.g., bone, muscle, skin, organ weights, etc.

Ligament: connective tissue that binds bone to bone, to maintain the integrity of a joint.

Lipid: fat, or fat-like, substance.

Manometer: an instrument for measuring pressure.

Maximal oxygen consumption: see maximal oxygen uptake.

Maximal oxygen intake: see maximal oxygen uptake.

Maximal oxygen uptake (VO_2 max): the best physiological index of total body endurance. Also referred to as aerobic power, maximal oxygen intake, maximal oxygen consumption, and cardiovascular endurance capacity.

Menstruation: the periodic cycle in the uterus associated with preparation of the uterus to receive a fertilized egg.

Mental practice: mental rehearsal of the athletic event or sport.

Mesomorphy: one of three categories of the somatotype in which the body is rated for the degree of muscularity.

Metabolism: the sum total of the energy-producing and -absorbing processes in the body, i.e., the energy used by the body.

Micron: unit of measure equal to 0.001 mm.

Mitochondria: energy-producing bodies within the cell.

Motor area, or motor cortex: that area of the cerebral cortex which controls voluntary muscle movement.

Motor end plate: where the efferent or motor nerve attaches to the muscle fiber.

Motor nerve, or motoneuron: motor, or efferent, nerve which transmits impulses to muscles.

Motor unit: the motor nerve and the group of muscle fibers it supplies.

Muscle fiber: the structural unit of muscle. A single cell with multiple nuclei composed of a number of smaller units called myofibrils.

Muscle spindle: a sensory receptor located in the muscle itself, which senses changes in muscle tension.

Myelin sheath: the inner covering of the medullated nerve fiber.

Myocardium: the muscle of the heart.

Myofibril: the small elements which comprise the muscle fiber, composed of the proteins actin and myosin.

Myoneural junction: the junction between the muscle fiber and its nerve.

Myosin: a muscle protein that acts with actin, another muscle protein, to allow the muscle to contract.

Neurilemma: the outermost covering of a nerve fiber.

Neuron: the nerve cell; the basic structural unit of the nervous system. Conducts nervous impulses to and from various parts of the body.

Nitrogen narcosis: "rapture of the deep." A condition which is caused by breathing air underwater at depths where the partial pressure of nitrogen increases until it has a narcotic-like effect on the central nervous system, leading to distortions in judgment and sometimes to serious injury or death.

Norepinephrine: a hormone produced by the adrenal medulla and, also, a chemical transmitter substance at peripheral sympathetic nerve endings.

Obesity: an excessive amount of body fat. The state of being overfat.

One-repetition maximum (1-RM): the greatest amount of weight that can be lifted just one time.

Ossification: process of calcification or hardening of the bone during the growth process.

Overload: stressing the body or parts of the body to levels above that normally experienced.

Oxygen debt: the quantity of oxygen above normal resting levels used in the period of recovery from any specific exercise or muscular activity.

Oxygen poisoning: caused by breathing concentrations of oxygen for long periods of time during deep dives, resulting in visual distortion, confusion, rapid and shallow breathing, and convulsions.

Pacinian corpuscle: a proprioceptor located in muscle and tendon sheaths adjacent to joints.

Pancreas: an endocrine gland that produces both the hormones insulin and glucagon, which control blood glucose, or sugar, levels.

Parasympathetic nervous system: a major subdivision of the autonomic nervous system whose fibers arise from the midbrain, medulla, or sacral region of the spinal cord.

Parathormone: hormone produced by the parathyroid glands, which assists in controlling calcium and phosphorus levels.

Parathyroids: endocrine glands that are located on or embedded in the thyroid glands and that produce parathormone.

Pericardium: the fibrous sac that encapsulates the heart.

Periosteum: the fibrous membrane that surrounds bone.

Peripheral nervous system: that part of the nervous system that lies outside the central nervous system, i.e., spinal cord and brain.

pH: a system for expressing the degree of acidity or alkalinity of a solution, in which a value of 7.0 is neutral, greater than 7.0 alkaline, and less than 7.0, acidic.

Plasma: the liquid fraction of the whole blood.

Ponderal index: defined as height divided by the cube root of weight.

Power: the product of force and velocity. This is probably far more important than absolute strength alone.

Precapillary sphincter: small band of smooth muscle controlling the flow of blood to the true capillaries.

Progressive overload: gradually increasing the training stimulus in a systematic manner.

Progressive resistance exercise (PRE): the resistance used in training is progressively increased systematically as the body adapts to the training stimulus.

Proprioceptor: a sensory receptor sensitive to pressure, stretch, tension, pain, etc.

Protein: a food substance formed from amino acids.

Pulse: periodic expansion of the artery, resulting from the systole of the heart.

Pulse pressure: the mathematical difference between the systolic and diastolic pressures.

Radiation: the transfer of heat through electromagnetic waves.

Reaction time: the period of time between the presentation of a stimulus and the subsequent reaction to that stimulus.

Reciprocal inhibition: the inhibition of the antagonist muscles, which allows the agonists to move.

Reflex: an automatic, involuntary, unlearned response to a given stimulus.

Relative body fat: the ratio of fat weight to total body weight, expressed as a percentage.

Relative humidity: a ratio expressing the degree of moisture in the surrounding air.

Repetition running: similar to interval training but with long work intervals and long periods of recovery.

Residual volume: that volume of air remaining in the lung following a maximal expiration. Vital capacity plus residual volume equal total lung capacity.

Respiration: the exchange of gases at both the level of the lung and tissue.

Respiratory exchange ratio (R or RER): the ratio of carbon dioxide expired to oxygen consumed, at the level of the lungs.

Respiratory quotient (RQ): the ratio of the carbon dioxide produced in the tissues to the oxygen consumed by the tissues.

Ruffini receptor: a proprioceptor located in the joint capsule.

Sarcolemma: the membrane surrounding the muscle fiber.

Sarcomere: the functional contractile unit of muscle, which is a part of the myofibril.

Sarcoplasm: the fluid portion of the muscle fiber, or the muscle protoplasm.

Sarcoplasmic reticulum: network of tubules and vesicles within muscle fibers, which are necessary to allow excitation of the muscle fibers.

Sensory nerve: afferent or sensory nerves transmit impulses from the sensory organs to the central nervous system.

Skeletal muscle: muscle controlling skeletal movement that is normally under voluntary control.

Slow twitch muscle fiber: one of several types of muscle fibers that have high oxidative capacity, low glycolytic capacity, and are associated with endurance type activities.

Smooth muscle: involuntary muscle, such as that which lines blood vessels and the gastrointestinal tract.

Somatic nervous system: the voluntary nervous system, including both cranial and spinal nerves.

Somatogram: a chart on which somatotypes are plotted.

Somatotrophic hormone: a hormone released by the pituitary gland that influences growth. Also referred to as STH, or growth hormone (GH).

Somatotype: the characterization of the body physique in an objective and systematic manner.

Sphygmomanometer: an instrument used to measure arterial blood pressure.

Spirometer: an instrument used to measure the various lung volumes and dynamic lung function.

Strength: the ability of a muscle to exert force.

Stroke volume: the volume of blood pumped per contraction of the ventricle.

Sympathetic nervous system: a major division of the autonomic nervous system.

Synapse: the junction between two neurons.

Systole: the contraction phase of the cardiac cycle.

Systolic pressure: the greatest pressure in the vessels or heart during a cardiac cycle, resulting from the systole.

Tendon: connective tissue that attaches muscle to bone.

Testosterone: the predominant male androgen.

Thyroid gland: an endocrine gland located at the base of the neck, which produces several hormones regulating total body metabolism.

Thyroid-stimulating hormone: a pituitary hormone which controls the thyroid gland's release of thyroxin.

Thyroxin: a hormone produced by the thyroid gland, which assists in the control of total body metabolism.

Tidal volume: the amount of air inspired or expired during a normal breathing cycle.

Tonus: that quality of a muscle which gives it firmness in the absence of a voluntary contraction.

Total lung capacity: the sum of the vital capacity and the residual volume.

Valsalva maneuver: increased intraabdominal and intrathoracic pressure created by holding the breath and attemping to compress the contents of the abdominal and thoracic cavities.

Vasopressin hormone: a pituitary hormone which controls blood vessel diameter.

Vein: a vessel that transports blood back to the heart.

Velocity: speed, or the rate, of movement.

Ventilation: movement of air into and out of the lungs.

Ventricle: a chamber of the heart that expels, or pumps, blood into the lungs (right ventricle) or into the systemic circulation (left ventricle).

Venule: a small vein that provides the link between capillaries and veins.

Vestibular receptor: a proprioceptor located in the ear.

Viscosity: that quality of a fluid that describes its flow characteristics. Water has a low viscosity, while honey has a high viscosity.

Vital capacity: the greatest volume of air that can be expired following the deepest possible inspiration.

Work: the product of force and distance.

Index